Lecture Notes in Computer Science

Edited by G. Goos, J. Hartmanis, and

James A. Foster   Evelyne Lutton   Julian Miller
Conor Ryan   Andrea G.B. Tettamanzi (Eds.)

Genetic Programming

5th European Conference, EuroGP 2002
Kinsale, Ireland, April 3-5, 2002
Proceedings

 Springer

Volume Editors

James A. Foster
University of Idaho, Department of Computer Science
Moscow, ID 83844-1010, USA
E-mail: foster@cs.uidaho.edu

Evelyne Lutton
INRIA Rocquencourt
B.P. 105, 78153 Le Chesnay Cedex, France
E-mail: Evelyne.Lutton@inria.fr

Julian Miller
University of Birmingham, School of Computer Science
Birmingham B15 2TT, UK
E-mail: j.miller@cs.bham.ac.uk

Conor Ryan
University of Limerick, Department of Computer Science and Information Systems
Schuman Building, Limerick, Ireland
E-mail: conor.ryan@ul.ie

Andrea Tettamanzi
Università degli Studi di Milano, Dip. Tecnologie dell'Informazione
Via Bramante 65, 26013 Crema, Italy
E-mail: tettaman@dsi.unimi.it

The logo entitled "Evolving Human Figure Geometry" appearing on the cover is the work of Matthew Lewis (http://www.cgrg.ohio-state.edu/~mlewis/).

Cataloging-in-Publication Data applied for

Die Deutsche Bibliothek - CIP-Einheitsaufnahme

Genetic programming : 5th European conference ; proceedings / EuroGP 2002,
Kinsale, Ireland, April 3 - 5, 2002. James A. Foster ... (ed.). - Berlin ;
Heidelberg ; New York ; Barcelona ; Hong Kong ; London ; Milan ; Paris ;
Tokyo : Springer, 2002
    (Lecture notes in computer science ; Vol. 2278)
    ISBN 3-540-43378-3

CR Subject Classification (1998): D.1, F.1, F.2, I.5, I.2, J.3
ISSN 0302-9743
ISBN 3-540-43378-3 Springer-Verlag Berlin Heidelberg New York

Springer-Verlag Berlin Heidelberg New York
a member of BertelsmannSpringer Science+Business Media GmbH

http://www.springer.de

© Springer-Verlag Berlin Heidelberg 2002
Printed in Germany

Typesetting: Camera-ready by author, data conversion by PTP-Berlin, Stefan Sossna
Printed on acid-free paper   SPIN: 10846246   06/3142   5 4 3 2 1 0

Preface

This volume records the proceedings of the fifth European conference on Genetic Programming (EuroGP 2002) which took place in Kinsale, Ireland on April 3–5, 2002, continuing an established tradition of yearly meetings among the most prominent researchers on Genetic Programming in Europe and beyond; their proceedings have always been published in the LNCS series by Springer-Verlag.

EuroGP began life in Paris in 1998 as an international workshop (April 14–15, LNCS 1391); a second workshop took place in Göteborg in 1999 (May 26–27, LNCS 1598). Its first appearance as a conference was in the year 2000 in Edinburgh (April 15–16, LNCS 1802), followed by last year's conference held at Lake Como (April 18–19, LNCS 2038). Since the beginning, EuroGP has been co-located with a series of specialist workshops on applications of evolutionary algorithms (LNCS 1468, 1596, 1803, and 2037). In keeping with that tradition, the EvoWorkshops were also held in Kinsale this year at the same time (LNCS 2279).

Genetic Programming (GP) is a branch of Evolutionary Computation in which populations of computer programs are made to evolve and adapt to solving a particular problem or task by a process that draws its inspiration from Biology and Darwinian evolution. GP is a very versatile technique, which has been applied to a wide range of tasks, as a quick inspection of the 32 papers in these proceedings will easily reveal: economics, robotics, engineering, statistics, pharmacology, electronics, and finance are but some of the domains in which they have been employed. Although the rate of application of GP to problems is steadily growing, this conference is characterized by its concern with the theoretical foundations of GP: investigation of these issues is attaining an ever increasing depth and maturity.

A rigorous peer-review selection process was applied to the 42 submitted papers. This resulted in 18 plenary talks (little more than 40% of those submitted) and 14 research posters. Almost all submitted papers were reviewed by four members of the International Program Committee, the remaining ones receiving at least two reviews. The Program Committee was carefully selected for their knowledge and expertise, and, as far as possible, papers were matched with the reviewer's particular interests and special expertise. The results of this process are seen here in the high quality of papers published within this volume.

Of the 32 published papers, almost 75% have a European provenance, confirming the eminently European character of this conference, although the presence of Northern American researchers is significant, with almost 20%, whereas the rest of the world is sporadically represented by two papers.

The success of this conference is to be credited to the contribution of many people. In the first place, we would like to thank the members of the Program Committee for their diligence, patience, and commitment to the task of providing high quality reviews. We would also like to thank EvoNet, the Network of

Excellence in Evolutionary Computing, for their support, in particular, Jennifer Willies and Chris Osborne for their help with all organizational and logistical aspects. Finally, we would like to thank the members of EvoGP, the EvoNet working group on Genetic Programming.

April 2002

James A. Foster,
Evelyne Lutton,
Julian Miller,
Conor Ryan,
Andrea G.B. Tettamanzi

Organization

EuroGP 2002 was organized by EvoGP, the EvoNet Working Group on Genetic Programming.

Organizing Committee

Program co-chairs: James A. Foster (University of Idaho, USA)
                       Evelyne Lutton (INRIA, France)
Publicity chair: Julian Miller (University of Birmingham, UK)
Local chair: Conor Ryan (University of Limerick, Ireland)
Publication chair: Andrea G.B. Tettamanzi (University of Milan, Italy)

Program Committee

Wolfgang Banzhaf, University of Dortmund, Germany
Forrest Bennett III, FX Palo Alto Laboratory, USA
Shu-Heng Chen, National Chengchi University, Taiwan
Marco Dorigo, Free University of Brussels, Belgium
Terry Fogarty, South Bank University, UK
James A. Foster, University of Idaho, USA
Hitoshi Iba, University of Tokyo, Japan
Christian Jacob, University of Calgary, Canada
Maarten Keijzer, Danish Hydraulics Insitute, Denmark
Ibrahim Kuscu, University of Surrey, UK
William B. Langdon, University College London, UK
Sean Luke, University of Maryland, USA
Evelyne Lutton, INRIA, France
Nic McPhee, University of Minnesota, USA
Jean-Arcady Meyer, Université Pierre et Marie Curie, France
Julian Miller, University of Birmingham, UK
Peter Nordin, Chalmers University of Technology, Sweden
Simon Perkins, Los Alamos National Laboratories, USA
Riccardo Poli, University of Birmingham, UK
João C. F. Pujol, Centro de Desenvolvimento da Energia Nuclea, Brazil
Kazuhiro Saitou, University of Michigan, USA
Jonathan Rowe, University of Birmingham, UK
Peter Ross, Napier University, UK
Conor Ryan, University of Limerick, Ireland
Marc Schoenauer, Ecole Polytechnique, France
Moshe Sipper, Ben-Gurion University, Israel

Sponsoring Institutions

EvoNet: The Network of Excellence in Evolutionary Computing.

Table of Contents

Talks

Posters

Springer
Berlin
Heidelberg
New York
Barcelona
Hong Kong
London
Milan
Paris
Tokyo

A Pipelined Hardware Implementation of Genetic Programming Using FPGAs and Handel-C

Peter Martin

Department of Computer Science, University of Essex,
Wivenhoe Park, Colchester, CO4 3SQ, UK.

Abstract. A complete Genetic Programming (GP) system implemented in a single FPGA is described in this paper. The GP system is capable of solving problems that require large populations and by using parallel fitness evaluations can solve problems in a much shorter time that a conventional GP system in software. A high level language to hardware compilation system called Handel-C is used for implementation.

1 Introduction

The motivation for this work is that as problems get harder, the performance of traditional computers can be severely stretched despite the continuing increase in performance of modern CPUs. By implementing a GP system directly in hardware the aim is to increase the performance by a sufficiently large factor to be able to tackle harder problems and to make investigations into the operation of GP easier. This paper is an update to the work presented in [9] which describes how a GP system that includes initial population creation, fitness evaluation, selection, and breeding operators can be implemented in a Field Programmable Gate Array (FPGA) using a high level language to hardware compilation technique. Two major areas were singled out for further work in order to improve the performance: 1) extend the implementation to handle larger populations; 2) the use of pipelining to improve the parallelism of the hardware.

The changes needed and the results of implementing the changes are described in this paper. The paper begins with a brief survey of previous work using FPGAs for evolutionary techniques and a short summary of the Handel-C language and the target hardware. This is followed by a description of the revised design that stores the population in off-chip Static Random Access Memory (SRAM) and that also uses pipelining. The experimental setup is presented together with some results that illustrate the effect of the changes. The changes are then discussed and areas for further work are suggested.

2 Previous Work Using FPGAs in Evolutionary Computing

FPGAs have featured in the field of evolutionary computing under three distinct headings:

J.A. Foster et al. (Eds.): EuroGP 2002, LNCS 2278, pp. 1–12, 2002.

1) as a means of implementing the fitness functions of Genetic Algorithms or Genetic Programming [6,17];

2) as a platform for implementing a Genetic or Evolutionary Algorithm [3,4, 12,13,14];

3) in relation to evolving hardware by means of an evolutionary technique [2,8,15,16].

A more detailed review of this and other work can be found in [9].

3   Description of Handel-C and the Target Hardware

Handel-C is a high level language that is at the heart of a hardware compilation system known as Celoxica DK1 [1] which is designed to compile programs written in a C-like high level language into synchronous hardware. Since Handel-C targets hardware, there are some programming restrictions when compared to using ISO-C, and these need to be considered when designing code that can be compiled by Handel-C. Some of these restrictions particularly affect the building of a GP system. Firstly, there is no stack available, so recursive functions cannot be directly supported by the language. Secondly, there is a severe limit to the size of memory that can be implemented using standard logic cells on an FPGA because implementing memory is expensive in terms of silicon real estate. However, some FPGAs have internal RAM that can be used by Handel-C which is supported by the ram storage specifier.

The target hardware for this work is a Celoxica RC1000 FPGA development board fitted with a Xilinx XCV2000E Virtex-E FPGA having 43,200 logic cells and 655,360 bits of block ram, a PCI bridge that communicates between the RC1000 board and the host computer's PCI bus, and four banks of Static Random Access Memory (SRAM). Logic circuits isolate the FPGA from the SRAM, allowing both the host CPU and the FPGA to access the SRAM, though not concurrently.

4   System Architecture

The lack of a stack in Handel-C means that a standard tree based representation is difficult to implement because recursion cannot be handled by the language. Instead, a linear program representation is used [11], though other compact representations such as Cartesian Genetic Programming [10] in which programs are represented as graphs, are also worth considering. Using a linear representation, a program consists of a sequence of words which are interpreted by the problem specific fitness function. To ease the design, each program has a fixed maximum length that it can grow to. Crossover is performed by selecting crossover points at random in two individuals and swapping the nodes after the crossover points. If the length of a program would exceed the maximum, it is simply truncated to the maximum. Mutation is performed on an individual by replacing a word with a new randomly generated word which has the potential effect of changing both the functionality and the terminals of that node. The operators are chosen using an 8 bit random number and bit masks which eliminates less-than or greater-than comparisons which are inefficient in terms of logic. The probability of selecting each operator is 31/255 (12%) for mutation, 63/255 (24.5%) for copy and the remainder (63.5%) for crossover.

4.1 Extending the Population Size

Large populations are supported by storing the entire population in off-chip SRAM. The Celoxica RC1000 board has 8 MiB[1] of SRAM arranged as 4 banks of 2 MiB that can be directly addressed by the FPGA, and each bank is configured as 512 Ki 32bit words. In practice, one bank is reserved for storing the results of the run (fitness and lengths of each individual), leaving three banks available for the population. The total population size is determined by the program size chosen and the size of the program nodes. Table 1 illustrates the potential range that can be accommodated for a node size of 32 bits.

Table 1. Possible population sizes when using three 2 MiB memory banks and a word size of 32 bits for different program sizes.

Max. Program Length (words)	16	32	64	128	256	512	1024
Max. population size	98,304	49,152	24,576	12,288	6,144	3,072	1,536

External SRAM can only be written to or read from once per clock cycle, so care was taken in the design to ensure that parallel access to memory cannot occur. Similarly, the on-chip block select RAM must not be accessed more than once per clock cycle. Concurrent access to the block select RAMs is achieved by partitioning the rams into smaller blocks that can be accessed in parallel. Access to the SRAM is controlled by the pipeline.

4.2 Using Pipelines to Improve Performance

Implementing algorithmic parallelism or pipelining is a frequently used technique in hardware design that reduces the number of clock cycles needed to perform complex operations. Pipelines can be implemented at a number of levels and in this work pipelines have been used in several places; a high-level coarse grained control pipeline, and fine grained pipelines in the fitness evaluation function and functions that copy data to/from SRAM. The four major GP operations are divided among the stages of the pipeline: selection of individuals from the population for breeding, breeding new individuals, fitness evaluation of the individuals, and replacement of the new individuals in the population. Because of

---

[1] This paper uses the IEC recommended prefixes for binary multiples. MiB indicates 2^{20} bytes.

the need to control access to the main population in SRAM during the selection phase which reads individuals from SRAM into block ram, and writing modified programs back to SRAM, these two operations are combined into one stage. This leaves the breeding and fitness evaluation/replacement operations. Breeding is closely tied to selection and needs to occur before evaluation can take place so this is combined into the selection phase. Figure 1 illustrates the resultant architecture and the coarse-grained control pipeline. Stage1 is a pseudo random

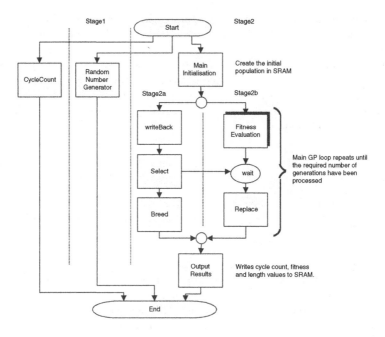

Fig. 1. Overall architecture of the pipelined GP system.

number generator based on a logical feedback shift register (LFSR), which runs continuously, generating a new random number every clock cycle. The random numbers are available to the rest of the machine with no overhead. Stage2 is the main GP machine and consists of two sub-stages. Communication between the WriteBack/Select/Breed sub-stage (stage 2a) and the Evaluate/Replace sub-stage (stage 2b) is via a two dimensional array of individuals in block ram, indexed by a global phase index which is toggled each time stages 2a and 2b complete. The WriteBack phase updates the main population in SRAM with the result of the preceding Evaluate/Replace phase. The Select phase selects a series of two parents using tournament selection and copies the selected individuals from SRAM to the on-chip working RAM and the Breed phase then creates a series of new individuals ready for stage 2b to use. Stage 2b performs parallel evaluations of the individuals and then determines which individuals should be replaced. Parallel evaluation is achieved by replicating the hardware for fitness evaluation. The individuals identified for replacement are in turn written back to the main population at the start of the next WriteBack/Select/Breed sub-stage. The wait between evaluation and replacement is needed because both selection and replacement require access to the global fitness vector. In practice this only comes into play when the evaluation phase takes less time than WriteBack and Selection, which only happens for very simple fitness functions.

A finer grained level of pipelining is implemented in the fitness evaluation function. FPGAs are synchronous devices, meaning that a clock is used to latch data into registers. In Handel-C all expressions are implemented using combinatorial logic, which if allowed to grow in depth can restrict the maximum frequency the FPGA can be clocked at. This is because of the delays introduced by the combinatorial paths. Therefore, to reduce logic depth, and hence improve on the clock frequency, it is often advantageous to split a complex expression into more but simpler expressions. This usually requires more clock cycles, but by pipelining the operations an effective single cycle throughput can be achieved. In this design, the function read, and decode is pipelined with the function evaluation, though the effectiveness of this is problem specific.

In conventional steady-state GP, once an individual has been evaluated it replaces the worst individual in the population. In a hardware implementation with parallel fitness evaluations this is expensive to implement since a global search is required. An alternative to this called survival-driven evolution, has been successfully used by Shackleford et al [14]. In this scheme only offspring that are fitter than the worst of their two parents will survive into the next generation by replacing one of the parents. This removes the need for any global search and this scheme was adapted to the current work by maintaining a record of the parents of each individual.

To compare the performance of different implementations a way of measuring the number of cycles used by the FPGA is needed. One possibility is to use the DK1 simulator, but in large designs with long running times this can take many hours of running which is often impractical. An alternative is to include a cycle counter in the design which can be read by external programs. The internal cycle counter runs in parallel with the rest of the hardware, incrementing a counter once per clock cycle. This approach could be extended to providing fine-grained measurement of the cycles required by the individual phases which would be valuable for evaluating the detailed performance of the design.

Once the GP machine has finished a run, the best program needs to be communicated to the outside world. The individual programs are already in SRAM, so they can be read directly by the host. The program fitness and lengths are written to SRAM when the GP machine has finished so they can also be read by the host. In addition, the cycle count(s), and other parameters are made available to the host via SRAM.

5   Experimental Setup

To evaluate the effect of the changes made, two experiments were performed. Firstly, a direct comparison with the previous design using the XOR problem was run. This was done to gauge the overall effect of storing the population in off-chip SRAM, and of implementing the pipelines. Next the Santa Fe Ant problem was implemented both as a demonstration of a hard problem and an example of where the function set is equivalent to that of a traditional CPU instruction set.

Each experiment was run using four different environments. Firstly, an ISO-C version of the algorithm was developed to prove the operation of the program because debugging tools for standard C are readily available, and the development time for C is considerably shorter than when using Handel-C and FPGA tools. Secondly, a PowerPC simulator was used to measure how many cycles the algorithm needed when run on a typical Reduced Instruction Set Computer (RISC) and thirdly, the design was implemented on an FPGA. Each problem was implemented with a range of parallel evaluations. Lastly to get a feel for the total effect of implementing a GP system in hardware when compared to using a popular software GP system, the problems were implemented using lilgp and a comparison made of the performance.

When the design is implemented on an FPGA, a host control program configures the FPGA, sets up the random number seed and other control parameters in SRAM, and initiates the GP run. Once the GP run has finished, the FPGA signals the host program and the host control program reads the fitness values from SRAM, decides which program(s) are suitable, reads the appropriate SRAM locations and outputs the program in a usable form. For the two experiments, host programs were also written to verify the programs, and in the case of the ant problem, display a simple graphical trace of the ant's behavior.

6   Experiment Descriptions and Results

6.1   Exclusive OR Problem

Description. The 2 bit XOR function $x = (a\bar{b}) + (\bar{a}b)$ uses the four basic two input logic primitives AND, OR, NOR and NAND which take two registers, R_a and R_b. The result is placed into R_a. These functions have been shown to be sufficient to solve the boolean XOR problem [5]. Execution is terminated when the last instruction in the program has been executed. The two inputs a and b were written to registers R_0 and R_1 before the fitness evaluation, and the result x read from register R_0 after the fitness evaluation. The full set of parameters is given in Table 2.

Comparing these results first with the results in [9] which achieved a $Speedup_{time}$ of 6 times for 4 parallel evaluations, it can be seen that splitting the algorithm into two sub-stages gives a useful increase in performance. However, the surprising result is that it takes longer to run the XOR problem when more evaluations are performed in parallel, in particular when 8 parallel

Table 2. Parameters for the XOR problem

Parameter	Value
Population Size	16
Functions	AND(R_a,R_b), OR(R_a,R_b), NOR(R_a,R_b), NAND(R_a,R_b)
Terminals	4 registers
Max Program Size	16
Generations	511
Fitness Cases	4 pairs of values of a and b
Raw Fitness	The number of fitness cases that failed to yield the expected result.

Table 3. Results of running the XOR problem. The results are the average of 10 runs for each configuration, each run using a different random seed.

Measurement	PowerPC		HandelC		
Parallel fitness evaluations	n/a	1	2	4	8
Cycles	13,723,187	74,819	73,232	72,184	81,767
Clock Frequency	200MHz	52MHz	48MHz	42MHz	37MHz
Number of Slices	n/a	1238	1247	1725	2801
$Speedup_{cycles}$	1	183	187	190	167
$Speedup_{time}$	1	47	44	39	31

evaluations are done. Detailed investigation showed that this was a side effect of the selection method. During selection the number of individuals selected from the main population is the number of parallel fitness evaluations wanted, and these are selected at random from the population, but only those individuals that are not currently being evaluated by the Evaluate/Replace sub-stage are valid candidates. When the number of individuals required is half the population size, many more attempts must be made by the selection phase to find valid individuals. This explains why when the number of parallel evaluations is 8, the run time is greater than when only two individuals are being selected.

The frequencies in table 3 for the Handel-C implementations is that reported by the place&route tools, and takes into account the delays introduced by the combinatorial logic and the delays introduced by the routing resources used on the FPGA. A lot of effort was spent to reduce the logic and routing delays in the design, with the result that this design runs substantially faster that the previous design which could only reach 18 MHz.

Running this problem with lilgp required approximately 165×10^9 cycles, or more than 12 times the number of cycles needed by the linear implementation.

6.2   Artificial Ant Problem

Description. The motivation for choosing this problem for a hardware implementation is two fold: Firstly it is a hard problem for GP to solve [7], and secondly it demonstrates that a custom hardware design can efficiently encode the function and terminal set as native 'instructions'. That is to say one of the attractions of using an FPGA is that custom instructions not normally found in production CPUs can easily be constructed. The full set of parameters is given in Table 4. The ANT problem was executed using the same environments as the XOR problem and the results are presented in Table 5.

Table 4. Parameters for the ANT problem

Parameter	Value
Population Size	512
Functions	IF_FOOD(T_a,T_b), PROGN(T_a, T_b)
Terminals	MOVE, LEFT, RIGHT, NOP
Max Program Size	32
Generations	511
Fitness Cases	One fitness case. The program was run until 1024 timesteps had elapsed or the ant had consumed all the food.
Raw Fitness	The number of pieces of food not eaten in the time available.

Table 5. Results of running the ANT problem

Measurement	PowerPC			HandelC		
Parallel fitness evaluations	n/a	2	4	8	16	32
Cycles	2.695e9	42.58e6	23.19e6	13.15e6	7.53e6	4.2e6
Clock Frequency	200MHz	40	38	36	33	31
Number of Slices	n/a	1,835	2,636	4,840	7,429	14,908
$Speedup_{cycles}$	1	69	116	204	358	642
$Speedup_{time}$	1	13	22	36	59	99

An example program from this problem found in one run is:

```
IF_FOOD(LEFT,RIGHT)
PROGN (NOP,RIGHT)
IF_FOOD (NOP,LEFT)
PROGN (MOVE,LEFT)
```

Figure 2 shows the speedup results for the Ant problem, and gives both the $Speedup_{cycles}$ and $Speedup_{time}$. These results show that for the Ant problem, increasing the number of parallel fitness evaluations increases the $Speedup_{cycles}$ factor linearly, but because the routing delay on the FPGA increases with larger designs, the maximum clock frequency decreases, offsetting some of the gains made by increasing the parallelism. The number of slices used for 32 parallel

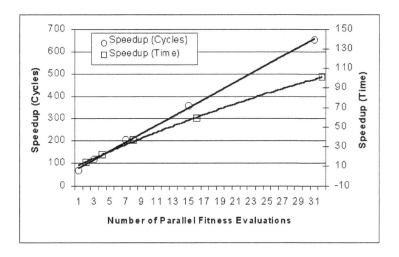

Fig. 2. The speedup factors for the number of cycles ($Speedup_{cycles}$) and the time ($Speedup_{time}$) for the Ant problem.

evaluations is nearly 80% of the total available on the chip. This is effectively the limit for the XCV2000E FPGA. It is worth remarking that a PC with 750 MiB of RAM was required to run the Handel-C compiler and the place&route tools before this design could be implemented, and a PC with a 1.4G Hz Athlon CPU required nearly four hours to complete the place&route. This is in contrast to a modest 500 MHz Pentium machine capable of compiling and running lilgp and other popular GP packages.

Running this problem using lilgp in the PPC simulator needed approximately 8.6×10^9 cycles, or over three times the number required by the linear implementation on a PPC processor, giving the FPGA using 32 parallel fitness evaluations a $Speedup_{cycles}$ of 2047 and a $Speedup_{time}$ of approximately 300 times over lilgp.

7 Discussion

7.1 Effect of Implementing Pipelines and Increasing Parallelism

A direct comparison between the work in [9] showed for the XOR problem that using a pipeline in the main control loop, and in the fitness function provides a useful speedup, but because the fitness evaluation is much shorter than the WriteBack/Select/Breed sub-stage, there is no benefit to increasing the number of parallel fitness evaluations. It was also clear that for small populations there is a limit to the number of parallel fitness evaluations that can be accommodated. However, the situation is reversed in the Ant problem because the time needed for fitness evaluation is much larger than the WriteBack/Select/Breed phase. Clearly for other problems where the fitness function takes a long time it would be worth devising efficient pipelines for the fitness evaluation functions.

7.2   Comparison to a Popular Software GP System

While this may appear to be an unfair comparison, a lot of work in GP is centered around exploring the detailed operation of GP, which often requires hundreds or thousands of runs with minor parameter changes, and performance is still likely to be an issue even with processors running at 2 GHz and beyond. This comparison was done to see if using a hardware implementation would be of benefit to researchers. The results show that where a fixed problem type needs to be run many times, a hardware implementation using many parallel fitness evaluations could reduce the time required for extended runs by over two orders of magnitude. While this looks promising, it must also be noted that changing parameters for a FPGA run requires a large investment in time and the hardware approach may not always be suitable.

7.3   Handel-C as an Implementation Language

Using Handel-C to implement this design has highlighted two major benefits: Firstly, the design of the system by someone trained as a software engineer with limited hardware experience was relatively straightforward. Secondly, it meant that the algorithm could be tested and debugged using traditional software tools. This is important when the time to compile a Handel-C design for the larger problems into a simulation on a 1.4 GHz PC is of the order of 25 minutes, and to place and route could take an hour or more. In contrast, compilation of the code using the GNU compiler took seconds.

An implication of using Handel-C is that to get the best throughput some familiar programming constructs must be abandoned and new techniques adopted. It is not possible to completely ignore the hardware aspects of a design, for example when interfacing to SRAM, and when trying to squeeze the last few nano seconds out of the design during the final place and route stages.

8   Further Work

The latest Virtex-II FPGAs from Xilinx are bigger and faster than the Virtex-E device used so far. These devices promise even better speedups, and initial studies using these devices have indicated that a further speedup of two to three times is possible. The Virtex-II devices also have larger gate counts and bigger on-chip block RAMs. The largest of these devices - the XC2V8000 could theoretically support up to 128 parallel fitness evaluations for the artificial ant problem. The initial indication is that by combining the faster clock frequency and more parallel fitness evaluations the ant problem could see a further 10 times speedup. Further work needs to be done to verify this.

Whilst the performance gains are substantial for one of the problems looked at, the costs associated with using this technology need to be evaluated with respect to software engineering effort, capital equipment costs and operational considerations, so that practitioners can make the appropriate choices when choosing a technology for implementing a GP system.

9 Conclusions

Moving the population storage to off-chip SRAM has allowed the design to solve problems requiring larger population sizes, an example of which is the Ant problem. Pipelining the breed, selection and evaluation phases gives a performance boost to problems that have short evaluation time requirements like the XOR problem. For problems like the Ant problem that require extended fitness evaluation times the benefits of using a pipeline are even greater, allowing the number of parallel fitness evaluations to be increased and the performance increasing in a nearly linear relationship.

References

1. Celoxica. Web site of Celoxica Ltd. www.celoxica.com, 2001. Vendors of Handel-C. Last visited 15/June/2001.
2. T. Fogarty, J. Miller, and P. Thompson. Evolving Digital Logic Circuits on Xilinx 6000 Family FPGAs. In P. Chawdhry, R. Roy, and R. Pant, editors, *Soft Computing in Engineering Design and Manufacturing*, pages 299–305. Springer-Verlag, 1998.
3. P. Graham and B. Nelson. Genetic Algorithms In Software and In hardware - A Performance Analysis Of Workstation and Custom Computing Machine Implementations. In K. Pocek and J. Arnold, editors, *Proceedings of the Fourth IEEE Symposium of FPGAs for Custom Computing Machines.*, pages 216–225, Napa Valley, Califormia, Apr. 1996. IEEE Computer Society Press.
4. M. Heywood and A. Zincir-Heywood. Register based genetic programming on FPGA computing platforms. In R. Poli, W. Banzhaf, W. Langdon, J. Miller, P. Nordin, and T. Fogarty, editors, *Genetic programming, proceedings of eurogp'2000*, volume 1802 of *LNCS*, pages 44–59, Edinburgh, 15-16 April 2000. Springer-Verlag.
5. J. Koza. *Genetic programming: on the programming of computers by means of natural selection.* MIT Press, Cambridge, MA, USA, 1992.
6. J. Koza, F. Bennett III, J. Hutchings, S. Bade, M. Keane, and D. Andre. Rapidly reconfigurable field-programmable gate arrays for accelerating fitness evaluation in genetic programming. In J. Koza, editor, *Late breaking papers at the 1997 genetic programming conference*, pages 121–131, Stanford University, CA, USA, 13–16 July 1997. Stanford Bookstore.
7. W. Langdon and R. Poli. Why ants are hard. In J. Koza, W. Banzhaf, K. Chellapilla, K. Deb, M. Dorigo, D. Fogel, M. Garzon, D. Goldberg, H. Iba, and R. Riolo, editors, *Genetic programming 1998: proceedings of the third annual conference*, pages 193–201, University of Wisconsin, Madison, Wisconsin, USA, 22-25 July 1998. Morgan Kaufmann.

8. D. Levi and S. Guccione. Genetic FPGA: Evolving Stable Circuits on Mainstream FPGA Devices. In A. Stoica, D. Keymeulen, and J. Lohn, editors, *Proc. of the First NASA/DoD Workshop on Evolvable Hardware*, pages 12–17. IEEE Computer Society, July 1999.

9. P. Martin. A Hardware Implementation of a Genetic Programming System using FPGAs and Handel-C. *Genetic Programming and Evolvable Machines*, 2(4):317–343, 2001.

10. J. Miller and P. Thomson. Cartesian genetic programming. In R. Poli, W. Banzhaf, W. Langdon, J. Miller, P. Nordin, and T. Fogarty, editors, *Genetic programming, proceedings of eurogp'2000*, volume 1802 of *LNCS*, pages 121–132, Edinburgh, 15-16 April 2000. Springer-Verlag.

11. P. Nordin and W. Banzhaf. Evolving turing-complete programs for a register machine with self-modifying code. In L. Eshelman, editor, *Genetic algorithms: proceedings of the sixth international conference (icga95)*, pages 318–325, Pittsburgh, PA, USA, 15-19 July 1995. Morgan Kaufmann.

12. S. Perkins, R. Porter, and N. Harvey. Everything on the chip: a hardware-based self-contained spatially-structured genetic algorithm for signal processing. In J. Miller, A. Thompson, P. Thomson, and T. Fogarty, editors, *Proc. Of the 3rd Int. Conf. on Evolvable Systems: From Biology to Hardware (ICES 2000)*, volume 1801 of *Lecture Notes in Computer Science*, pages 165–174, Edinburgh, UK, 2000. Springer-Verlag.

13. D. Scott, S. Seth, and A. Samal. A Hardware Engine for Genetic Algorithms. Technical Report UNL-CSE-97-001, University of Nebraska-Lincon, Dept Computer Science and Engineering, University of Nebraska-Lincon., 4 July 1997.

14. B. Shackleford, G. Snider, R. Carter, E. Okushi, M. Yasuda, K. Seo, and H. Yasuura. A High Performance, Pipelined, FPGA-Based Genetic Algorithm Machine. *Genetic Programming and Evolvable Machines*, 2(1):33–60, Mar. 2001.

15. A. Thompson. Silicon evolution. In J. Koza, D. Goldberg, D. Fogel, and R. Riolo, editors, *Genetic programming 1996: proceedings of the first annual conference*, pages 444–452, Stanford University, CA, USA, 28–31 July 1996. MIT Press.

16. G. Tufte and P. Haddow. Prototyping a GA pipeline for complete hardware evolution. In A. Stoica, D. Keymeulen, and J. Lohn, editors, *Proc. of the First NASA/DoD Workshop on Evolvable Hardware*, pages 18–25. IEEE Computer Society, July 1999.

17. Y. Yamaguchi, A. Miyashita, T. Marutama, and T. Hoshino. A Co-processor System with a Virtex FPGA for Evolutionary Computation. In R. Hartenstein and H. Grunbacher, editors, *10th International Conference on Field Programmable Logic and Applications (FPL2000)*, volume 1896 of *Lecture notes in Computer Science*, pages 240–249. Springer-Verlag, Aug. 2000.

Finding Needles in Haystacks Is Not Hard with Neutrality

Tina Yu[1] and Julian Miller[2]

[1]ChevronTexaco Information Technology Company, San Ramon CA 94583, U.S.A.
tiyu@chevrontexaco.com, http://www.improvise.ws

[2]School of Computer Science, University of Birmingham, Birmingham B15 2TT, U. K.
j.miller@cs.bham.ac.uk, http://www.cs.bham.ac.uk/~jfm

Abstract. We propose building neutral networks in needle-in-haystack fitness landscapes to assist an evolutionary algorithm to perform search. The experimental results on four different problems show that this approach improves the search success rates in most cases. In situations where neutral networks do not give performance improvement, no impairment occurs either. We also tested a hypothesis proposed in our previous work. The results support the hypothesis: when the ratio of adaptive/neutral mutations during neutral walk is close to the ratio of adaptive/neutral mutations at the fitness improvement step, the evolutionary search has a high success rate. Moreover, the ratio magnitudes indicate that more neutral mutations (than adaptive mutations) are required for the algorithms to find a solution in this type of search space.

1   Introduction

Many optimization problems can be defined as search problems: all possible solutions constitute the search space; the objective is to find the one that best solves the given problem. In many search problems, there is sufficient correlation between search points to allow heuristic search techniques to find good solutions faster than random search. However, there is one kind of search space, needle-in-haystack, which is difficult for heuristic search algorithms to outperform random search.

In a needle-in-haystack type of search space, a solution is either a needle or a piece of hay. In other words, a search algorithm either finds a perfect solution (the needle) or otherwise (the hay). No knowledge about the location of the needles can be obtained from examining the hays. In this kind of situation, a heuristic search algorithm works like a random search algorithm. When the number of solutions in the search space is small, finding a good solution is difficult, no matter what search algorithm one uses.

Evolutionary algorithms are heuristic search algorithms where the search process is directed by fitness: only solutions that have competitive fitness are considered in the solution population pool. An evolutionary algorithm selects solutions with good fitness and uses them to find solutions with better fitness.

What if the search space only has two possible fitness values (one for the needles and the other for the hays)? Evolutionary algorithms seem to become helpless in this kind of situation. In this study, we investigate building a network within the "hay" to provide a trail for the search process. In this way, the discovery of the "needle" solutions may become easier. Since the network connects solutions with the same

J.A. Foster et al. (Eds.): EuroGP 2002, LNCS 2278, pp. 13–25, 2002.

fitness (within the hays), it is called "neutral network". Moreover, an evolutionary algorithm utilizing such a network for search is said to support neutrality, a term borrowed from evolutionary biology.

Neutral theory [3] in evolutionary biology has inspired our work in incorporating neutrality in evolutionary algorithms (Section 2). Previously, we have devised a Genetic Programming (GP) system that utilizes neutrality to search for problem solutions [12]. When applied to a Boolean function problem, the solutions were found with a higher success rate. We analyzed the results and identified that high success rates are associated with a particular adaptive/neutral mutation ratio pattern. This work extends that finding by applying the system on four needles-in-haystack problems. Moreover, the relationship between neutrality and mutation rates is investigated.

The paper is organized as follows. Section 2 provides the background of this work. It first explains neutral theory in evolutionary biology and then gives a summary of our previous work on using neutrality for evolutionary search. Section 3 reviews related work. In Section 4, the GP system is described. Section 5 presents the four investigated needle-in-haystack problems. In Section 6, the experimental setup is given. The results are presented in Section 7. Section 8 discusses the experimental results and Section 9 gives our conclusions.

2 Background

The theory of natural evolution established by Darwin has had profound impact on biology. Most biologists are convinced that selection acting on advantageous mutations is the driving force of evolution. It was not until the late 1970s when molecular data became available, that the theory was challenged. In particular, Motoo Kimura found that the number of mutant substitutions in amino acid sequences of hemoglobin was too large to be explained by the theory of natural selection. Based on this discrepancy, he proposed the neutral theory, which states that most mutants at the molecular level in evolution are caused by random genetic drift rather than by natural selection [3]. In other words, the mutants involved are neither advantageous nor disadvantageous to the survival or reproduction of the individual. Around the same time, a similar theory was published by King and Jukes [4]. The two papers have provoked much controversy and are still subject to strong debate [6].

Darwinism has been the dominating principle behind the implementation of evolutionary algorithms: the evolved entities contain no *explicit* neutral mutants. In this way, a mutant is either advantageous or disadvantageous. Selection acts upon them to propagate those that are advantageous.

But can neutral mutations (those are neither advantageous nor disadvantageous) benefit evolutionary search? To investigate these questions, we have devised a methodology for systematic study of this subject [12]. In particular, we measure the number of neutral mutations that occur in the evolved entities during evolutionary search. In this way, the impact of neutrality on search performance can be analyzed quantitatively. Using this approach, we have studied a Boolean function problem. The results show that there is a positive relationship between neutral mutations and success rate: the larger the allowed neutral mutations quantity the greater is the possibility for the evolutionary search to find a solution.

The amount of neutral mutations is measured in the selection step, which evaluates both the fitness and the number of neutral mutations in the evolved entities. More precisely, an offspring solution is selected to replace the current winner only when it has a better fitness or it has the same fitness but its neutral mutants are within a specified range (the Hamming bound). On can envisage all solutions with the same fitness and satisfy the Hamming bound are connected in a network (neutral network). The search process selects solutions in the network one after another in the manner of a neutral walk. We found that such a walk can lead to a solution with a better fitness if it satisfies the fitness improvement criterion. The criterion is concerned with the ratio of adaptive and neutral mutations. The analysis indicated that when this ratio for the neutral walks was close to the ratio for the fitness improvement, a high probability of success occurred.

Adaptive and neutral mutations play different roles in the evolutionary search: adaptive mutations exploit the accumulated beneficial mutations while neutral mutations provide an exploratory power by maintaining genetic diversity. Under the dynamics of the evolutionary process, neutral mutants may contribute to the fitness later. For an evolutionary search to be successful, it requires a balance between exploitation and exploration. The ratio between adaptive and neutral mutations is therefore an appropriate fitness improvement criterion in evolutionary search.

3 Related Work

Tomoko Ohta studied the ratio of adaptive and neutral mutations in DNA sequence data to test her nearly neutral theory [10]. Unlike Kimura's neutral theory, which believes that a mutation is either selective or neutral, the nearly neutral theory believes that there is a class of mutations (very weakly selected mutations) whose behavior is influenced by both genetic drift and selection. Moreover, in small population genetic drift dominates while in large populations selection is more influential.

She tested this theory by comparing synonymous and nonsynonymous mutations of 49 mammalian genes. The results agree with the theory. Later, McDonald and Kreitman also studied the relative number of synonymous and nonsynonymous mutations within a species. The results, however, were contrary to the theory [8].

Claus Wilke and colleagues studied the evolution of digital organisms (as computer programs) using the Avida system [11]. They reported that under high mutation rates, an organism that has its neighbors (those accessible by one mutation step) with a similar fitness (not necessary the same fitness) had a higher reproduction rate. The reason is that such flat fitness landscape is more robust against mutations than a fitness landscape that has high and narrow peak. Although they didn't mention neutral networks (where the neighbors have the same fitness), one would expect the same findings.

This result is not surprising, as there have been various research reports about the buffer effect of neutral mutations against disruptive mutations [1]. The existence of neutral networks hence is beneficial to the organism's reproduction rate. We have reported a similar result on a Boolean function landscape in our previous work [12]. However, with needle-in-haystack landscapes, an opposite result is found: high mutation rates also give high reproduction rates. The details are given in Section 8.2.

Marc Ebner and colleagues also studied the relationship between neutral networks and evolvability [2]. Particularly, they investigated a search space with 2^{16} possible fitness values. Moreover, these fitness values were divided into 64 groups. Their selection criterion was similar to ours in that they allowed an individual with better or equal fitness to replace the current winner. They experimented with 3 different sizes of neutral network $(1, 2^{112}, 2^{320})$ using a single point mutation. They reported that the larger the network (more neutrality), the higher the average population fitness. This result is consistent with that in our previous paper where wider ranges of neutrality levels (6) and mutation rates (11) were investigated [12].

4 Cartesian Genetic Programming

Cartesian Genetic Programming (CGP) was first formally proposed in [9]. In CGP, a genotype is an integer string that encodes an indexed, feedforward, acyclic graph. Unlike the parse tree representation in the standard GP [5], a genotype-phenotype mapping is used to create the graph phenotype from the integer string genotype. Each node in the genotype contains a multiple number of genes; some of them are link values. The nodes that are not involved in the linked path between the inputs and outputs of the program are inactive in the phenotype. Such nodes have no effect on the behavior of the phenotype.

For example, Figure 1(a) is a genotype for even-5-parity function (described in Section 5) that is mapped into a phenotype in 1(b). The alleles in bold take value from the set $\{0,1\}$, which represent the Boolean function xor and eq respectively. The function inputs are denoted by labels 0 to 4 (and as x_0 to x_4 in the phenotype). The node outputs are labeled from 5 to 10. There are six nodes in the genotype; each has 3 genes (two input link values and one Boolean function value). The genotype is read from the last gene on the right (10) towards the left. The number 10 refers to the rightmost node (with genes 8 4 1) in the phenotype. It is an eq node with one input connected to the even-parity input number 4, and the other connected to the node with output link 8. The node with output link 9 is not involved in the phenotype because it is not refereed by any active nodes. The same applies to the node with output 7. These two inactive nodes are grayed in Figure 1(a). All other nodes outputs are referenced so are involved in the phenotype.

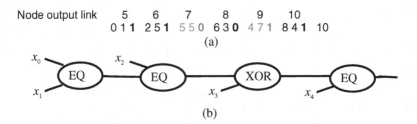

Node output link   5   6   7   8   9   10
         0 1 1   2 5 1   5 5 0   6 3 0   4 7 1   8 4 1   10
                                    (a)

                                    (b)

Fig. 1. A genotype (a) and its phenotype (b) for even-5-parity.

Mutations applied to inactive genes are neutral while on active genes can be adaptive or neutral (see Section 4.1). This genotype representation, in which some genes are active and others inactive, allows neutral mutations to be measured as Hamming distance. This is described in Section 4.1.

4.1 Neutrality Measured as Hamming Distance

When a mutation operation generates a different program with the same fitness, it involves a number of neutral mutations. Neutral mutations on active genes are the results of functional redundancy or introns, hence represent implicit neutrality. In contrast, neutral mutations on inactive genes represent explicit neutrality. Regardless the source of neutrality (implicit or explicit), the overall amount of neutral mutations between the parent-offspring genotypes pair can be measured according to their Hamming distance. For example, the following two genotypes have Hamming distance of 13. The number of active genes changes between the two genotypes is 12 (the node with output link number 6 contributes three active genes changes because it was inactive in Genotype 1 but becomes active in Genotype 2). The number of inactive genes changes is two (corresponding to the node with output link number 4).

Output link	2	3	4	5	6	7
Genotype 1	0 1 1	0 2 1	0 1 0	3 1 0	4 3 1	5 1 1
Genotype 2	0 0 1	2 1 0	1 3 0	3 0 1	2 5 1	6 5 0

Using Hamming distance to measure neutral mutations has two advantages:

- It provides a quantitative measurement of neutrality in evolutionary search.
- It provides a flexible way to implement neutrality in evolutionary algorithms.

5   Even-Parity Problems

Even-parity is a widely used benchmark problem in GP and Evolvable Hardware communities. The problem can be defined with a different number of Boolean inputs, e.g. even-3-parity, even-4-parity and so on. An even-parity function returns the value True if and only if an even number of inputs are True, otherwise it returns False.

Various research results show that the difficulty of the problem is highly dependent on the functions selected to construct the solution [14,7]. In particular, when only xor and/or eq functions are used, this problem has a needle-in-haystack property: there are only two possible fitness values. The search algorithm either finds a perfect solution or gets a solution that receives half of the mark. For example, with even-5-parity, the number of Boolean inputs is five. There are 2^5 different possible input combinations, hence 32 test cases. An even-5-parity constructed using xor and eq would either have fitness 16 or 32.

Table 1 shows the four such problems we investigate in this work. Note that the random search success rates were calculated by randomly generating 1,000,000 programs, except even-12 parity, where 4,000,000 trials were made (since it's a more difficult problem). No solution with fitness 4096 was found in this set of trials.

Table 1. Four needle-in-a-haystack even-parity problems.

Problem	even-5-parity	even-8-parity	even-10-parity	even-12-parity
Function Set	xor, eq	eq	eq	eq
Terminal Set	x_1 to x_5	x_1 to x_8	x_1 to x_{10}	x_1 to x_{12}
Possible fitness	16 and 32	128 and 256	512 and 1024	2048 and 4096
# of Test Cases	32	256	1024	4096
Random Search (success rate)	0.81%	0.063%	0.0054%	0%

6   Experimental Setup

6.1 Evolutionary Algorithm

The algorithm used for the experiments is a form of $1+\lambda$ evolutionary strategy, where $\lambda=4$, i.e. one parent with 4 offspring (population size 5). The algorithm is as follows:

1. Randomly generate an initial population of 5 genotypes with the lowest possible fitness and select one (randomly) as the winner.
2. Carry out point-wise mutation on the winning parent to generate 4 offspring;
3. Construct a new generation with the winner and its offspring;
4. Select a winner from the current population using the following rules:
   - If any offspring has a better fitness, it becomes the winner.
   - Otherwise, an offspring with the same fitness is randomly selected. If the parent-offspring pair has a Hamming distance within the permitted range (see Section 6.2), the offspring becomes the winner.
   - Otherwise, the parent remains as the winner.
5. Go to step 2 unless the maximum number of generations reached or a solution with needle fitness is found.

The mutation sites were selected randomly. A simple type checking is performed to make sure the new offspring is valid. If the gene site contains a function, it is changed to an alternative function. If the gene site is a connection link, it is replaced with another equally valid connection link.

6.2 Control Parameters

The genotype has 100 nodes; each has 3 genes (see Section 4). The total number of genes is therefore 300. Eleven different mutation rates and 7 neutrality levels were used in the experiments. Table 2 summarizes the parameters used for the experiments.

Table 2. Summary of control parameters.

Parameters	Values
Genotype Length	300
Mutation Rate (%) on genotype	1,2,4,6,8,10,12,14,16,18,20
Max Generation	10,000
Neutrality Level (Hamming distance range)	0,50,100,150,200,250,300
Population Size	5
Number of Runs	100

7 Results

We do not present the results of average population fitness because they do not give performance information in the needle-in-haystack type of problems (where only two fitness values are possible). For example, with even-5-parity, the average fitness in the initial population is 16. This value remains as the average fitness until a solution with fitness 32 is found. This average fitness pattern is the same for all neutrality level and mutation rate implementation, hence is not useful to identify the impact of neutrality on the search performance. Instead, we give the results of success rate.

For even-5-parity, all implementations (mutation rates and Hamming distances) have a 100% successful rate, i.e. all 100 runs find a solution (see Figure 2A). In contrast, even-8-parity (a harder problem) has lower success rates in some cases. In particular, the combination of low Hamming distance and low mutation rate has produced some unsuccessful runs (see Figure 2B).

When mutation rate is 1% or 2%, a small amount of neutrality (50) is able to improve success rates. However, when mutation rate is 4%, a neutrality level equal to Hamming distance 100 is required to improve the performance. For example, increasing mutation rate from 2% to 4% gives Hamming distance 0 a success rate jump from 82% to 94%. In comparison, increasing neutrality level from 0 to 50 on

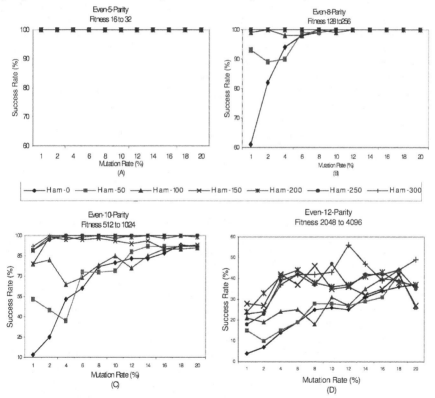

Fig. 2. Success rate results.

mutation rate 4% does not improve success rate. This suggests that raising mutation rate has a stronger impact than raising neutrality level on the evolutionary search. The relationship between neutrality and mutation rates will be discussed in more details in Section 8.2.

Regardless of mutation rates, increasing neutrality level beyond 150 does not improve or impair the performance; all of them have 100% success rate. This suggests that equilibrium between the benefits of exploitation and exploration is reached at this point. Indeed, the adaptive/neutral mutation analysis (see Section 8.1) shows that the exploitation/exploration ratios are very similar for all Hamming distance beyond 150 (see Figure 3B). Increasing neutrality or mutation rates do not affect this equilibrium.

Even-10-parity is harder than even-8-parity: there are more unsuccessful runs, especially when low Hamming distance values were used (see Figure 2C). Similar to even-8-parity, the success rate remains approximately the same after a certain Hamming distance value is reached (200 is the equilibrium point, see Figure 3C). Moreover, mutation rates are more influential in this problem: neutrality level 150 is required to give consistent improvement of success rates (in contrast to neutrality level 100 in even-8-parity).

Even-12-parity is the hardest among all; none of the implementations has 100% success rate (see Figure 2D). Although not as precise as other problems, even-12-parity reaches the equilibrium point around neutrality level 200. We also made 100 experimental runs using Hamming distance 0 and 100% mutation rate. Among them, 48 runs find a solution (48% success rate). This suggests that high neutrality and mutation rate are not sufficient for the search algorithm to find a solution to this problem. Modification of other parameters, such as gene length and the maximum number of generation, is required to improve performance.

The performance of the 7 different Hamming distances implementations can be roughly divided into two groups: the first group consists of neutrality level 0, 50, 100 while the second group consists of neutrality level 150, 200, 250 and 300. In the first group, increasing mutation rates increases success rates while in the second group little performance improvement is gained after mutation rate exceeds 4%. Nevertheless, the group with higher neutrality level also gives higher success rates.

8 Analysis and Discussion

The experimental results for applying neutrality on four needle-in-haystack problems give the following patterns:

- Neutrality does not have impact on success rates when the number of solutions in the search space is large (even-5-parity).
- However, when the difficulty level is slightly increased (even-8-parity), any amount of neutrality improves the success rates for 1% or 2% mutation rates.
- Increasing mutation rates also improves success rates. Yet, with a sufficient amount of neutrality, the success rates can be further increased. The required neutrality level is problem dependent; the harder the problem, the higher the required neutrality levels (100 for even-8-parity, 150 for even-10 & 12-parity).
- There is an equilibrium point, which gives the exploration/exploitation balance corresponding to the maximum possible performance. Increasing neutrality or mutation rates beyond this point has little effect on the performance.

- For more difficult problems (even-12-parity), high neutrality level and mutation rate is not sufficient for the evolutionary algorithm to find a solution.

These results indicate that for this type of needle-in-haystack fitness landscapes, the harder the problem is (in terms of the number of solution in the search space) the higher the neutrality level is required to give performance improvement. Moreover, it is important to note that neutrality does not impair search performance, in cases where it does not give performance improvement.

8.1 Adaptive/Neutral Mutations Analysis

We have also studied the adaptive/neutral mutation ratios for different Hamming distance and mutation rate implementations. Previously, we have proposed a hypothesis that when the adaptive/neutral mutation ratio during neutral walk is close to that of the fitness improvement step, the evolutionary search process is more likely to be successful (see Section 2). The four sets of experimental results are analyzed in the following subsections:

Even-5-Parity:

For even-5-parity, Hamming distance 150, 200, 250 and 300 implementations give the neutral walk adaptive/neutral mutation ratios (in dashed-lines) that are very close to those of fitness improvement step (in solid-lines). The difference between the two ratios is between 0.04 and 0.01 (see Figure 3A). Figure 2A indicates that these implementations have 100% success rates, which agrees with the hypothesis.

Hamming distance 50 and 100 implementations give the ratio differences that are larger than those given by other Hamming distance implementations do. However, they also have 100% success rates. As suggested in [12], we believe the magnitude of these ratios is also important to the success of evolutionary search.

The active/inactive gene change ratios for fitness improvements are all below 1 in this problem (regardless of neutrality level and mutation rates). This means that when a genotype of fitness 16 is transformed to a genotype of fitness 32, more inactive genes than active genes were changes (if the ratio is 1, an equal amount of active and inactive gene were changed). Such ratio pattern is also associated with 100% success rate. This indicates that for this problem, as long as more inactive genes (than active genes) were changed during the evolutionary process, the search will be successful.

Even-8-Parity:

With even-8-parity, Hamming distances 150, 200, 250 and 300 give similar active/inactive gene changes patterns as those in even-5-parity. The ratios for neutral walk and fitness improvement are close to each other; the range of the ratios is also between 0.6 and 0.4 (see Figure 3B). Similarly, they also have 100% success rates.

Hamming distance-100 also gives the two ratios that are not too far from each other (0.02 to 0.09). The three with the largest gap (mutation rates 4%, 6%, 10%) are associated with a slightly lower success rates. This is consistent with our hypothesis.

Hamming distance 50 implementation has a noticeable lower success rate when mutation rate is 1%, 2% or 4%. The active/inactive gene changes give the two ratios that are farther apart from each other. Moreover, the ratio for fitness improvement is higher than that in even-5-parity, i.e. more active gene changes were made. For example, mutation rate 1% has an active/inactive gene changes ratio of 1.07 (43/40). This ratio range (> 1) indicates that more adaptation (than genetic drift) was made for fitness improvement. Since this ratio is associated with a lower success rate, we believe that inactive gene change (exploration) is more important for this problem. Neutrality 50 with 1% mutation rate does not provide sufficient exploration, hence leads to a lower success rate.

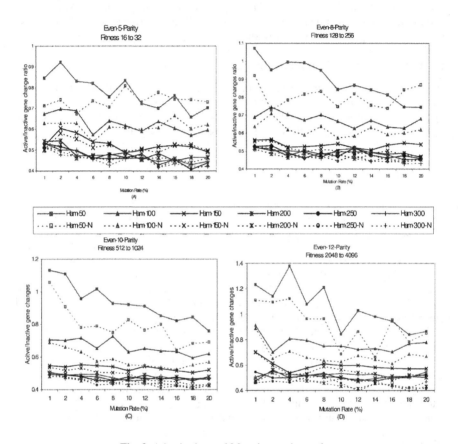

Fig. 3. Adaptive/neutral Mutations ratio results.

Mutation rate 2% and 4% give larger ratio gaps (0.22) than that of 1% mutation rate. Their success rates are also lower, which agrees with our hypothesis. Although the ratio difference for 6% mutation rate is similar to that of 1% mutation rate, it receives a higher success rate. We believe that this is because 6% mutation rate provides more exploration than 1% mutation rate (a lower ratio). In other words, high mutation rates complement neutrality level to provide exploration and achieve successful runs. We will discuss this more in Section 8.2.

Even-10-Parity:

The ratio pattern of even-10-parity is similar to even-8-parity in the following Hamming distance implementations: 200, 250 and 300. Figure 2C shows that they also have close to 100% success rates, just like those in even-8-parity. However, Hamming distance-150 implementation gives a different ratio pattern: the higher the mutation rates, the larger the ratio differences. For example, when mutation rate 1% is used, the active/inactive gene change ratio during neutral walk is 0.539 while the ratio for fitness improvement is 0.547 (a difference of 0.008). This distance increases as mutation rate increases. When mutation rate reaches 20%, the distance is 0.092. According to our hypothesis, high success rate is associated with low ratios distance. Indeed, Figure 2C shows that 20% mutation rate gives the lowest success rate; these success rates increase as mutation rates decrease.

The active/inactive gene change associated with 100% success rate is lower than the previous two problems (0.4 to 0.47). This suggests that more exploration is required for successful search in this problem. Neutrality level 50 and 100 implementations do not give enough inactive gene changes, hence are associated with lower success rates. Nevertheless, increasing mutation rate increases inactive gene changes (a lower ratio) and improves success rates.

Even-12-Parity:

The ratio pattern of even-12-parity has higher active gene changes than those in the other problems (see Figure 3D). They are also associated with lower success rates (see Figure 2D). This suggests that the algorithm does not provide sufficient inactive gene change (exploration) for the search to find a solution. Moreover, each time problem difficulty is increased (from even-5 to even-8 to even-10 to even-12), more inactive gene changes were required for the evolutionary search to be successful. This suggests exploration is more important than exploitation for search in needle-in-haystack type of space.

8.2 Relationship between Neutrality and Mutation Rates

The four needle-in-haystack problems show that both neutrality and mutation rates have a negative impact on the active/inactive gene change ratio: the higher they are, the lower the ratios. In other words, increasing neutrality or mutation rates increases *inactive* gene changes (more neutral mutations). Such increase of exploration also improves success rates.

However, this relationship does not apply to search space that has more than two possible fitness values. In [12], the problem we investigated has 8 possible fitness values. The study indicates that higher mutation rates give higher *active* gene changes (more adaptive mutations). Such increase of exploitation is beneficial when population average fitness is low but detrimental when the population has become fit. Moreover, increasing neutrality level does not always increase exploration. Nevertheless, higher neutrality level always gives higher success rates.

Yet, what is the relationship between neutrality and mutation rates? Can they replace each other? In the four problems we investigated, they both increase inactive gene changes. Thus, they complement each other in this type of needle-in-haystack problems to improve success rates. However, the following have to be noted:

- There is no quantitative measurement on which neutrality level gives the same performance as a certain mutation rate does. For example, 50 neutral mutations are about 16% of the total number of 300 genes. Yet, neutrality level 50 with 1% mutation rate does not give the same performance as neutrality level 0 with 16% mutation rate (see Figure 1).
- Once equilibrium point is reached, success rate is approximately the same regardless of neutrality level and mutation rate, i. e. the relationship between neutrality and mutation rate is irrelevant to the search performance.

9 Conclusions

Needle-in-haystack problems are hardly studied in the evolutionary computing community, possibly due to the difficulty of devising an evolutionary algorithm that outperforms random search. We investigated a set of four such problems and demonstrated that neutrality helps evolutionary algorithms to discover solutions in most cases. In situations where neutrality does not improve performance, it does not impair the search performance. This is an important message as it opens a new way to tackle the needle-in-haystack type of problems using an evolutionary approach.

The analysis of adaptive/neutral mutations ratios supports the hypothesis proposed in our previous work: when the ratio given by neutral walk is close to that of fitness improvement, the evolutionary search has a high success rate. Moreover, we have extended our study on ratio magnitude and deduced that a ratio of <1 (more exploration than exploitation) is required for the evolutionary search to be successful in needle-in-haystack type of search space.

Different levels of neutrality attain equilibrium of exploration and exploitation for the 4 different problems; increasing neutrality beyond such level gives insignificant advantage/disadvantage to the search performance. Moreover, the harder the problem, the higher neutrality level for its equilibrium.

Both neutrality and mutation rates have a positive impact on exploration in the needle-in-haystack type of problems. Consequently, they can supplement each other to improve success rates. However, this is not true for other type of problems. For example, our previous work on a Boolean function landscape gives a different result. We are currently investigating other types of problems to understand better the relationship between neutrality and mutation rates.

References

[1] Altenberg, L.: The evolution of evolvability in genetic programming. In: *Advances in Genetic Programming*, K. E. Kinner Jr., ed. MIT Press, (1994) 47-74.
[2] Ebner, M., Langguth, P., Albert, J., Shackleton, M. and Shipman, R.: On neutral networks and evolvability. In: *Proceedings of the 2001 Congress on Evolutionary Computation*, IEEE Press (2001) 1-8.
[3] Kimura, M.: *The Neutral Theory of Molecular Evolution*. Cambridge Univ. Press (1983).
[4] King, J. L. and Jukes, T. H.: Non-Darwinian evolution. *Science* Vol. 164 (1969) 788-798.
[5] Koza, J. R.: *Genetic Programming: On the Programming of Computers by Means of Natural Selection*. MIT Press (1992).
[6] Kreitman, M.: The neutral theory is dead. Long live the neutral theory. *BioEssays*, Vol. 18 (1996) 678-682.
[7] Langdon, W. B. and Poli, R.: Why "building blocks" don't work on parity problems. Technical report number CSRP-98-17. The University of Birmingham, July 13, 1998.

[8] McDonald, J. H. and Kreitman, M.: Adaptive protein evolution at the Adh locus in Drosophila. *Nature* Vol. 351 (1991) 652-654.

[9] Miller, J. F. and Thomson, P. Cartesian genetic programming. In: *Proceedings of the Third European Conference on Genetic Programming. LNCS*, Vol. 1802 (2000) 121-132.

[10] Ohta, T.: The nearly neutral theory of molecular evolution. In: *Annual Reviews Ecology & Systematic*, Vol. 23 (1992) 263-286.

[11] Wilke, C. O., Wang, J. L., Ofria, C., Lenski, R. E. and Adami, C.: Evolution of digital organisms at high mutation rate leads to survival of the flattest. *Nature,* Vol. 412 (2001) 331-333.

[12] Yu, T. and Miller, J.: Neutrality and the evolvability of Boolean function landscape. In: *Proceedings of the Fourth European Conference on Genetic Programming.* Springer-Verlag (2001) 204-217.

[13] Yu, T.: Structure abstraction and genetic programming. In*: Proceedings of the 1999 Congress on Evolutionary Computation.* IEEE Press (1999) 652-659.

Routine Duplication of Post-2000 Patented Inventions by Means of Genetic Programming

Matthew J. Streeter[1], Martin A. Keane[2], and John R. Koza[3]

[1]Genetic Programming Inc., Mountain View, California
mjs@tmolp.com

[2]Econometrics Inc., Chicago, Illinois
makeane@ix.netcom.com

[3]Stanford University, Stanford, California
koza@stanford.edu

Abstract. Previous work has demonstrated that genetic programming can automatically create analog electrical circuits, controllers, and other devices that duplicate the functionality and, in some cases, partially or completely duplicate the exact structure of inventions that were patented between 1917 and 1962. This paper reports on a project in which we browsed patents of analog circuits issued after January 1, 2000 on the premise that recently issued patents represent current research that is considered to be of practical and scientific importance. The paper describes how we used genetic programming to automatically create circuits that duplicate the functionality or structure of five post-2000 patented inventions. This work employed four new techniques (motivated by the theory of genetic algorithms and genetic programming) that we believe increased the efficiency of the runs. When an automated method duplicates a previously patented human-designed invention, it can be argued that the automated method satisfies a Patent-Office-based variation of the Turing test.

1   Introduction

Genetic programming can automatically create both the topology and sizing (numerical component values) for a wide variety of analog electrical circuits, controllers, and other devices such as sorting networks merely by specifying the device's high-level behavior [1-3].   Seven of the analog circuits and two of the controllers that have been automatically created by genetic programming infringe patents on that were issued between 1917 and 1962 (i.e., exactly duplicate the structure of the patented invention). Other genetically evolved results duplicate the functionality of 20th Century patented inventions in a novel way. One genetically evolved device (a sorting network) was an improvement over the invention described in the patent.

   This paper reports on a project in which we browsed patents of analog circuits issued after January 1, 2000 on the premise that recently issued patents represent current research that is considered to be of practical and scientific importance. The

J.A. Foster et al. (Eds.): EuroGP 2002, LNCS 2278, pp. 26-36, 2002.

paper describes how we used genetic programming to automatically create circuits that infringe, partially infringe, or duplicate the functionality of five post-2000 inventions that were patented by major commercial and university research institutions. Table 1 shows 14 patented inventions that have been duplicated by genetic programming, including the five inventions described in this paper.

Table 1. Fourteen patented inventions duplicated by genetic programming

Invention	Date	Inventor	Place
PID (proportional, integrative, and derivative) controller	1939	Albert Callender and Allan Stevenson	Imperial Chemical Limited
Second-derivative controller	1942	Harry Jones	Brown Instrument Company
Darlington emitter-follower section	1953	Sidney Darlington	Bell Telephone Laboratories
Ladder filter	1917	George Campbell	American Telephone and Telegraph
Crossover filter	1925	Otto Julius Zobel	American Telephone and Telegraph
"M-derived half section" filter	1925	Otto Julius Zobel	American Telephone and Telegraph
Elliptic filter	1934 - 36	Wilhelm Cauer	Gottingen, Germany
Philbrick circuit	1956	George Philbrick	George A. Philbrick Researches
Sorting network	1962	Daniel G. O'Connor and Raymond J. Nelson	General Precision, Inc.
Mixed analog-digital integrated circuit for producing variable capacitance	2000	Turgut Sefket Aytur	Lucent Technologies Inc.
Voltage-current converter	2000	Akira Ikeuchi and Naoshi Tokuda	Mitsumi Electric Co., Ltd.
Cubic function generator	2000	Stefano Cipriani and Anthony A. Takeshian	Conexant Systems, Inc.
Low-voltage high-current transistor circuit for testing a voltage source	2001	Timothy Daun-Lindberg and Michael Miller	International Business Machines Corporation
Low-voltage balun circuit	2001	Sang Gug Lee	Information and Communications University

2   Overall Method

We used genetic programming to breed a population of circuit-constructing program trees. Each constructing program tree is converted into a circuit by means of a developmental process that starts with a simple embryo. The functions in the circuit-constructing program trees include (1) component-creating functions that insert components (i.e., resistors, capacitors, and transistors) into a developing circuit, (2) topology-modifying functions (e.g., series division, parallel division, via between nodes, via to ground, via to power) that alter the topology of a developing circuit, (3) development-controlling functions (e.g., end, safe cut) that control development.

With the exceptions described in section 4 herein, we used the methods described in [1].

The embryo used on all five problems herein consisted of a single modifiable wire.

We used the same embryo, program architecture, function set, terminal set, control parameters, termination criteria, and computing machinery for all five problems. All runs were made on a home-built Beowulf-style [4] parallel cluster computer system consisting of 1,000 350 MHz Pentium II processors (each with 64 megabytes of RAM).

The only two differences between the runs of genetic programming for the five problems were that we used

(1) different (appropriate) types (models) of transistors for each problem, and

(2) a different fitness measure (and test fixture) for each problem.

3   Fitness Measures for Five Problems

The fitness measure specifies what time-domain or frequency-domain output values are desired, given various inputs. For each specific problem, a test fixture consisting of certain fixed components (such as a source resistor, a load resistor) is connected to the desired input port(s) and the desired output port(s) to measure the output.

3.1   Voltage-Current Conversion Circuit

The purpose of the voltage-current conversion circuit patented by Ikeuchi and Tokuda (U. S. patent 6,166,529) is to take two voltages as input and to produce as output a stable current whose magnitude is proportional to the difference of the voltages [5]. As a fitness measure for this problem, we employed four time-domain input signals (fitness cases). We included a time-varying voltage source beneath the output probe point to ensure that the output current produced by the circuit was stable with respect to any subsequent circuitry to which the output of the circuit might be attached. The weight of each fitness case was defined as the reciprocal of the patented circuit's error for that fitness case, so that the patent circuit was defined to have a fitness of 1.0.

3.2   Balun Circuit

The purpose of a "balun" (balance/unbalance) circuit, such as that described in U. S. patent 6,265,908, is to divide an input signal into two half-amplitude signals which are 180 degrees out of phase from each other [6]. Additionally, the circuit described in the patent is noteworthy in that it operates using a power supply of only 1 Volt. Our fitness measure for this problem consisted of a (1) frequency sweep analysis designed to ensure the correct magnitude and phase at the two outputs of the circuit and (2) a Fourier analysis designed to penalize harmonic distortion.

3.3   Cubic Signal Generator

U. S. patent 6,160,427 covers a "Compact cubic function generator" [7]. This is a computational circuit designed to produce as output the cube of an input signal. The patented circuit is "compact" in the sense that it requires a voltage drop across no more than two transistors at any point in the circuit. Our fitness measure for this problem consisted of four time-domain fitness cases using various input signals and time scales. The compactness constraint was enforced by allowing the evolutionary process access to only a 2-Volt power supply.

3.4   Register-Controlled Variable Capacitor

U. S. patent 6,013,958 covers a circuit whose behavior is equivalent to that of a capacitor whose capacitance is controlled by the value stored in a digital register [8]. For this problem, we used 16 time-domain fitness cases. The 16 fitness cases ranged over all eight possible values of a 3-bit digital register for two different input signals.

3.5   High-Current Load Circuit

U. S. patent 6,211,726 covers a circuit designed to sink a time-varying amount of current in response to a control signal. Toward this end, Daun-Lindberg and Miller of IBM employed a number of FET transistors arranged in a parallel structure, each of which sinks a small amount of the desired current [9]. Our fitness measure for this problem consisted of two time-domain simulations, each representing a different control signal. Each fitness case was weighted by the reciprocal of the patented circuit's error on that fitness case, so that the patent circuit was defined to have a fitness of 1.0.

4   Four New Techniques Employed in This Work

Broadly speaking, we used the methods for the automatic synthesis of circuits described in [1]. However, we employed four new techniques in these runs. Two of the new techniques were designed to increase the degree to which local substructures are preserved during the developmental process.

4.1   New Function for Connecting Distant Points

Most electrical circuits cannot be laid out in a plane. Instead, practical circuits require connections between distant points. The connections typically cannot be achieved in a totally planar circuit. Our previous work with the automatic synthesis of electrical circuits employed functions such as VIA and PAIR_CONNECT (described in [1]) to connect distant points in a developing circuit.

The premise of the crossover operation in genetic algorithms and genetic programming is that individuals that have comparatively high fitness are likely to have useful substructures. The VIA and PAIR_CONNECT functions have the disadvantage that when a subtree of one circuit-constructing program tree is swapped with a subtree of another circuit-constructing program tree, the connectivity of points within both the crossover fragment and the remainder is, almost always, very dramatically altered in a rather arbitrary and unpredictable way. That is, crossover usually significantly disrupts preexisting connections within a local area of the developing circuit (thereby disrupting the very local structures that probably contributed to the individual's comparatively high fitness and to the individual's selection to participate in the genetic operation in the first place).

To the extent that crossover dramatically alters the characteristics of the swapped genetic material, it acquires the characteristics of the mutation operation and its effectiveness in solving the problem approaches that of blind random search.

We addressed this problem concerning the VIA and PAIR_CONNECT functions in the runs described herein by employing a new two-argument function. The new NODE function replaces one modifiable wire (or component) with a series composition consisting of one modifiable wire, a port that can potentially be connected to other point(s) in the circuit, and a second modifiable wire. Prior to the execution of the developmental process, the circuit-constructing program tree is examined to identify the set of NODE functions that are not ancestors of any NODE function higher in the program tree. The NODE functions in this set are called "top-most NODE functions." For each such top-most NODE function, all the ports (if any) associated with NODE functions that are ancestors of the top-most NODE function are connected together. When the crossover operation moves any subtree within the subtree rooted by a particular top-most NODE function into another circuit-constructing program tree, all the ports of the moved subtree remain connected together. Moreover, all the ports in the unmoved remainder of the original remain connected together. We believe that this new approach based on local information encourages the preservation of building blocks and thereby increases the efficiency of the crossover operation.

4.2   New Symmetry-Breaking Procedure Using Geometric Coordinates

Parts in conventional schematic diagrams of electronic circuits carry unique (and consecutive) parts numbers. In earlier work, we used the unique part number (created when a component is first inserted into the developing circuit during the developmental process) to break symmetries and thereby determine the behavior of certain circuit-constructing functions. For example, the way in which the PARALLEL_0 and PARALLEL_1 topology-modifying functions carry out the parallel division was determined by referring to the unique parts numbers of neighboring components. Similarly, when a transistor was inserted into a developing circuit, its base, collector, and emitter were permuted by referring to the parts numbers of neighboring components.

The overall circuit-constructing program tree, of course, changes throughout the run of genetic programming. Thus, when neighboring parts change, the behavior of various circuit-constructing functions is dramatically altered in a rather arbitrary and unpredictable way (thereby disrupting the very local structures that probably contributed to the individual's comparatively high fitness and to the individual's selection to participate in the genetic operation in the first place).

To the extent that the genetic operations do not preserve locality, they acquire the characteristics of the mutation operation and their effectiveness in solving the problem begins to approach that of blind random search.

We addressed this problem in the runs described herein by breaking symmetry using the geometric coordinates of each node in the developing circuit (instead of the unique consecutive parts number). Specifically, the positive end of the single embryonic modifiable wire is defined to be at coordinate location (0,0), and its negative end is defined to be at coordinate location (1,0). The coordinate locations of new nodes that are created by functions that entail symmetry breaking (and those created by all other functions) are defined in terms of the coordinate locations of the existing nodes by recursively dividing the pre-existing modifiable wires into smaller and smaller new wires. In this way, the behavior of the functions that previously relied on the unique consecutive parts number can be defined in terms of information that is local to the region of the circuit where the symmetry-breaking is performed (instead of in terms of the circuit-wide information represented by component numbers). Again, we believe that this new approach based on local information encourages the preservation of building blocks and thereby increases the efficiency of the crossover operation.

4.3   New Function for Inserting Two-Leaded Components

The three-argument TWO_LEAD function replaces one modifiable wire (or component) with a series composition consisting of one modifiable wire, a two-leaded component (capacitor or resistor here), and a second modifiable wire. The third argument of the TWO_LEAD function consists of a subtree that contains a one-argument capacitor-inserting function or a one-argument resistor-creating function (both of which possess a single numerical parameter indicating the component value). The possibilities for the third argument are under control of a constrained syntactic structure which limits the choice to a resistor or capacitor. The remaining two arguments are the construction-continuing subtrees for each of the two modifiable wires created by this function.

4.4   New Transistor-Inserting Function

The six-argument Q function inserts a transistor into a developing circuit, with both the model and orientation of the transistor specified as parameters to the function. The first argument to the function specifies which transistor model is to be used. The set of available transistor models is specific to the problem at hand. The second argument establishes which end (polarity) of the preexisting modifiable wire will be bifurcated (if necessary) in inserting the transistor. It can take on the values BIFURCATE_POSITIVE or BIFURCATE_NEGATIVE. The third argument specifies which of six possible permutations of the transistor's three leads (base, collector, and emitter) are to be used. It can take on the values B_C_E, B_E_C, . . . E_C_B. That is, together, there are 12 possible ways of inserting a transistor. The remaining three arguments are the construction-continuing subtrees for each of the three modifiable wires created by this function.

5   Results

5.1   Voltage-Current Conversion Circuit

A circuit (Figure 1) emerged on generation 109 of our run of this problem with a fitness of 0.619. That is, the evolved circuit has roughly 62% of the average (weighted) error of the patented circuit. The evolved circuit was subsequently tested on unseen fitness cases which were not part of the fitness measure, and outperformed the patented circuit on these new fitness cases.

5.2   Balun Circuit

The best-of-run evolved circuit (Figure 2) was produced in generation 84 and has a fitness of 0.429. The patent circuit had a total fitness of 1.72. That is, the evolved circuit achieves roughly a fourfold improvement over the patented circuit in terms of our fitness measure. The evolved circuit is superior to the patented circuit both in terms of its frequency response and its harmonic distortion.

5.3   Cubic Signal Generator

The best-of-run evolved circuit (Figure 3) was produced generation 182 and has an average error of 4.02 mV. The patented circuit had an average error of 6.76 mV. That, the evolved circuit has approximately 59% of the error of the patented circuit over our four fitness cases.

5.4   Register-Controlled Variable Capacitor

Over our 16 fitness cases, the patented circuit had an average error of 0.803 mV. In generation 95, a circuit emerged with average error of 0.808 mV, or approximately 100.6% of the average error of the patented circuit. During the course of this run, we harvested the smallest individuals produced on each processing node (deme) which were compliant with a certain maximum level of error. Examination of these harvested individuals revealed a circuit created in generation 98 which matched the topology of the patented circuit. This circuit is presented in Figure 4.

5.5   High-Current Load Circuit

Our run for this problem eventually reached a plateau and produced a circuit that sunk the desired current into one of the negative power supplies (rather than to ground). This "cheating" circuit was not in the spirit of the patented invention. However, on generation 114 of this run (before the cheating solution appeared), a circuit emerged that duplicated Daun-Lindberg and Miller's parallel FET transistor structure. This circuit had a fitness (weighted error) of 1.82, or 182% of the weighted error for the patented circuit. This circuit is presented in Figure 5.

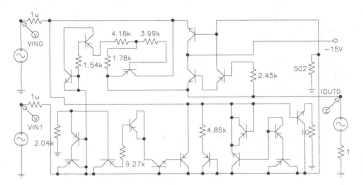

Fig. 1. Best-of-run voltage-current-conversion circuit from generation 109

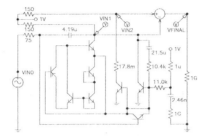

Fig. 2. Best evolved balun circuit from generation 84

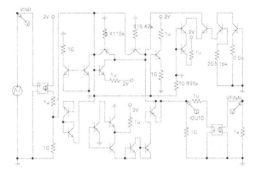

Fig. 3. Best-of-run cubic signal generation circuit from generation 182

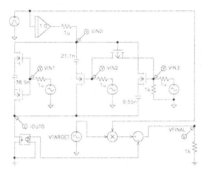

Fig. 4. Smallest compliant register-controlled capacitor circuit from generation 98

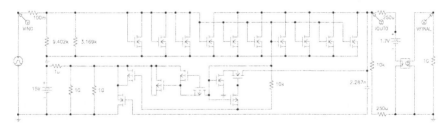

Fig. 5. Best-of-run high current load circuit from generation 114

6 Genetic Programming's High-Yield and Routineness

Methods for getting computers to solve problems automatically can be ranked by their "AI ratio." The *AI ratio* is the ratio of that which is delivered by the *artificial* system to the amount of *intelligence* that is supplied by the humans employing the method. The aim, of course, is to get computers to solve problems automatically with a high A-to-I ratio.

The defeat of the then-reigning human world chess champion by the Deep Blue system is an outstanding human-competitive result in the field of machine intelligence. However, there was a enormous of "I" provided by a team that worked on developing Deep Blue's software and hardware for many years in relation to the relatively small amount of "A" delivered by the system. Thus, Deep Blue has a very low A-to-I ratio. Most results produced in the fields of artificial intelligence, machine learning, and automated reasoning also have low AI ratios (regardless of whether the results are human-competitive).

Similarly, methods for getting computers to solve problems automatically can be ranked by their routineness. The word "routine" includes the connotation of "general purpose." However, "routine" is more demanding. When we use the term "routine" to describe a method for getting computers to solve problems automatically, we mean that there is a relatively effortless transition required to get the method to successfully handle additional problems within a particular domain and additional problems from a different domain.

Would the transition required to apply Deep Blue's methods to bridge be routine? Would the transition required to apply Deep Blue's methods to the problem of getting a robot to mop the floor of an obstacle-laden room be routine? What fraction of Deep Blue's methods could be brought to bear on programming a cellular automaton to perform a specific calculation? Classifying protein sequences? Designing an amplifier circuit? Devising a algorithm to solve a mathematical problem?

As can be seen in this paper, there was a relatively effortless transition required to get genetic programming to successfully handle additional problems within a particular domain. As we moved from problem to problem, we changed the specification of "what needs to be done" based on the inventor's statement of desired performance as stated in each patent.

As is apparent from much previous work in the field of genetic programming, a relatively effortless transition is required to get genetic programming to successfully handle additional problems from entirely different domains. Thus, we think it is fair to say that genetic programming is now capable of routinely delivering high-yield human-competitive machine intelligence.

7 Patent-Office-Based Variation of the Turing Test

In 1950, Turing proposed a three-person "imitation game" that might be used to determine whether machine intelligence had been achieved [10]. In the "imitation game," a judge tries to decide whether typewritten replies to questions came from a man or a woman. Turing's original test has been paraphrased in various ways over the years. One popular restatement of Turing's original test for machine intelligence is a two-person game in which a judge receives messages "over a wall" and tries to decide whether the messages came from a human or a machine.

Patent Offices in various countries have been in the business of performing a similar kind of "over the wall" test for over 200 years. For example, the U. S. Patent Office receives written descriptions of human-designed inventions and judges whether they satisfy the statutory requirement of being "[un]obvious ... to a person having ordinary skill in the art to which said subject matter pertains."

The Patent Office operates at arms-length and does not know who (or what) actually conceived the proposed invention when it passes judgment on a patent application. The inventor could be an exceptionally creative human or it could be something else (e.g., an automated process). If an automated method were able to duplicate a previously patented human-created invention, the fact that the original human-designed version satisfied the Patent Office's criteria of patent-worthiness means that the automatically created duplicate would also have satisifed the Patent Office's criteria. Thus, whenever an automated method duplicates a previously patented human-designed invention, the automated method can be viewed as satisfying a Patent-Office-based variation of the Turing test.

The original Turing test (and many of the popular restatements of it) deal with inconsequential chit chat. When an institution or individual allocates time and money to invent something and then also embarks on the time-consuming and expensive process of obtaining a patent, it has made a judgment that the work is of some practical or scientific importance. Moreover, the Patent Office also applies a statutory test of utility as a precondition to issuing a patent. Thus, the above Patent-Office-based variation of the Turing test differs from the original Turing test in that patented inventions represent non-trivial work by exceptionally creative humans.

8   Conclusions

Genetic programming was used to automatically create analog circuits that infringe, partially infringe, or duplicate the functionality of five post-2000 patented inventions. This work employed several new techniques (motivated by the theory of genetic algorithms and genetic programming). The paper also argued that when an automated method duplicates a previously patented human-designed invention, the automated method can be viewed as satisfying a Patent-Office-based variation of the Turing test.

References

1. Koza, John R., Bennett III, Forrest H, Andre, David, and Keane, Martin A. 1999. *Genetic Programming III: Darwinian Invention and Problem Solving*. San Francisco, CA: Morgan Kaufmann.
2. Koza, John R., Bennett III, Forrest H, Andre, David, Keane, Martin A., and Brave Scott. 1999. *Genetic Programming III Videotape: Human-Competitive Machine Intelligence*. San Francisco, CA: Morgan Kaufmann.
3. Koza, John R., Keane, Martin A., Yu, Jessen, Bennett, Forrest H III, and Mydlowec, William. 2000. Automatic creation of human-competitive programs and controllers by means of genetic programming. *Genetic Programming and Evolvable Machines*. (1) 121 - 164.

4.   Sterling, Thomas L., Salmon, John, Becker, Donald J., and Savarese, Daniel F. 1999. *How to Build a Beowulf: A Guide to Implementation and Application of PC Clusters.* Cambridge, MA: MIT Press.
5.   Ikeuchi, Akira and Tokuda, Naoshi. 2000. *Voltage-Current Conversion Circuit.* U. S. patent 6,166,529. Filed February 24, 2000 in U. S.. Issued December 26, 2000 in U. S.. Filed March 10, 1999 in Japan.
6.   Lee, Sang Gug. 2001. *Low Voltage Balun Circuit.* U. S. patent 6,265,908. Filed December 15, 1999. Issued July 24, 2001.
7.   Cipriani, Stefano and Takeshian, Anthony A. 2000. *Compact cubic function generator.* U. S. patent 6,160,427. Filed September 4, 1998. Issued December 12, 2000.
8.   Aytur; Turgut Sefket. 2000. *Integrated Circuit with Variable Capacitor.* U. S. patent 6,013,958. Filed July 23, 1998. Issued January 11, 2000.
9.   Daun-Lindberg, Timothy Charles and Miller; Michael Lee. 2001. *Low Voltage High-Current Electronic Load.* U. S. patent 6,211,726. Filed June 28, 1999. Issued April 3, 2001.
10. Turing, Alan M. 1950. Computing machinery and intelligence. *Mind.* 59(236) 433 – 460. Reprinted in Ince, D. C. (editor). 1992. *Mechanical Intelligence: Collected Works of A. M. Turing.* Amsterdam: North Holland. Pages 133 – 160.

Explicit Control of Diversity and Effective Variation Distance in Linear Genetic Programming

Markus Brameier and Wolfgang Banzhaf

Department of Computer Science, University of Dortmund,
44221 Dortmund, Germany
brameier,banzhaf@LS11.informatik.uni-dortmund.de

Abstract. We have investigated structural distance metrics for linear genetic programs. Causal connections between changes of the genotype and changes of the phenotype form a necessary condition for analyzing structural differences between genetic programs and for the two objectives of this paper: (i) Distance information between individuals is used to control structural diversity of population individuals actively by a two-level tournament selection. (ii) Variation distance is controlled on the effective code for different genetic operators – including a mutation operator that works closely with the applied distance metric. Numerous experiments have been performed for three benchmark problems.

1 Introduction

In contrast to other evolutionary search algorithms, like evolution strategies (ES), genetic programming (GP) may fulfill the principle of *strong causality*, i.e., small variations in genotype space imply small variations in phenotype space [12], only weakly [14]. Obviously, changing just a small program component may lead to almost arbitrary changes in program behavior. However, it seems to be intuitive that the more instructions are modified, the higher is the probability of a large fitness change.

The *edit distance*, sometimes referred to as *Levenshtein distance*, [6] between varying length character strings has been proposed as a metric for representations in genetic programming [9,13]. Such a metric not only permits to analyze genotype diversity within the population but offers a possibility to investigate the effect (*step size*) of variation operators. In [7] correlation between edit distance and fitness change of tree programs has been demonstrated for different variation operators and test problems.

This work applies the edit distance metric to operate selectively on *representative substructures* of the program representation used in linear GP (LGP). Correlation between structural and semantic distance as well as distribution of distances are documented for two different types of variation. One type uses recombination while the other one is based on (macro) mutations only.

J.A. Foster et al. (Eds.): EuroGP 2002, LNCS 2278, pp. 37–49, 2002.

The major objective of this contribution is to control structural diversity, i.e., the average program distance, in LGP populations *explicitly*. Therefore, we introduce a two-level tournament that selects for fitness on the first level and for diversity on the second level. In the course of these experiments development of both diversity and prediction performance are analyzed. We will see that prediction improves significantly if the diversity level of a population is increased.

The simplest form of diversity control might be to seed randomly created individuals regularly into the population during runtime. In [9] a more explicit maintenance of diversity is proposed by creating and seeding individuals that fill "gaps" of under-represented areas in genotype space. However, experimental evidence is not given for this rather complicated and computationally expensive approach. Until now, explicit diversity control is a rarely investigated technique in genetic programming. Recently, de Jong *et al.* [8] could improve parsimony pressure through Pareto-selection of fitness and tree size by adding a (third) diversity objective. A more *implicit control* of genetic diversity, by comparison, offer semi-isolated sub-population, called *demes*, that are widely used in the area of evolutionary computation (see e.g. [16]).

The second objective of this paper refers to the structural distance between a parent program and its offspring, i.e., the variation distance. The change induced by a variation operator on the effective, i.e., fitness-relevant, code may differ significantly from the amount of absolute change. By monitoring the *effective* variation distance, structural step sizes may be controlled more precisely in relation to the effect on program semantics. We will see that even strong restrictions of the maximum allowed mutation distance do not necessarily restrict freedom of variation.

2   Basics on Linear GP

Programs in tree-based genetic programming (TGP) denote expressions from a functional programming language like LISP [10]. In linear genetic programming (LGP) [1], instead, the program representation consists of variable-length sequences of instructions from an imperative programming language like machine code [11] or C [3]. *Operations* manipulate variables (*registers*) and constants and assign the result to a destination register, e.g., $r_i := r_j + 1$. Single operations may be skipped by preceding *conditional branches*, e.g., $if(r_j > r_k)$.

The imperative program code is divided into *effective* and *non-effective* instructions where only the effective code may influence program behavior (see program example printed in Section 5). The non-effective instructions are referred to as *introns*. This separation of instructions results from the linear program *structure* – not from program execution – and can be computed efficiently during runtime [3].

We distinguish two different variants of linear GP in this work. While the standard approach applies recombination by crossover to vary program length the other approach works with mutations exclusively. The *linear crossover* operator exchanges two arbitrarily long sub-sequences of instructions between two individuals. If the operation cannot be executed because one offspring would exceed the maximum length crossover is performed with equally long sub-sequences. *Macro mutations* include deletions or insertions of single (full) instructions here and represent an alternative growth operator to crossover. *Micro mutations* change the smallest program components that comprise a single operator, a register or a constant.

In [4] we report on *effective mutations* which guarantee explicitly that the effective code is altered. This reduces the probability that a mutation stays neutral in term of a fitness change. If an instruction is inserted its destination register is chosen in such a way that the instruction is effective at the corresponding program position.

3   Distance Metrics for LGP Programs

The *string edit distance* [6] operates on arbitrarily sequences of characters. It measures the distance between two strings by counting the number of basic operations – including insertion and exchange of single elements – that are necessary to transform one string into another. The string edit distance is calculated in time $O(n^2)$ [6] with n denotes the maximum number of components that are compared between two individual programs.

We apply the edit distance metric to measure the structural distance between the effective part of programs (*effective distance*) because a difference in effective code may be more directly related to a difference in program behavior (semantic distance). In contrast to a distance metric regarding the full program code (*absolute distance*) this includes some information on program semantics. It is important to realize that effective distance is not part of the absolute distance. Actually, two programs may have a small absolute distance while their effective distance is comparatively large (see Section 5).

Additionally, we regard the sequence of operators (from the effective instructions) only. The sequence corresponding to the example program in Section 5 is $(-, +, /, +, *, -, -, /)$ when starting with the last effective instruction. The distance of effective operator symbols has proven to be sufficiently precise to differentiate between program structures provided that the used operator set is not too small. On the one hand, this is due to the observation that in most cases the modification of an effective instruction changes the effectivity status of at least one instruction. The absolute operator sequence, instead, would not be altered by the exchange of single registers. On the other hand, this metric has been found to guarantee a sufficient correlation with fitness distance (see Section 7.1).

In general, a registration of absolutely every structural difference should not be necessary if we take into account that the correlation between semantic and structural distance is probabilistic. Obviously, less different genotypes are distinguished by our *selective* distance metric that represent the same phenotype (fitness).

Another important motivation for restricting the number of components compared in programs is that the time of distance calculation reduces significantly. Depending on the percentage of non-effective instructions there are k times more elements to compare if one regards the full sequence of operators in programs. Extending the distance measure to registers and constants of instructions, again, results in a factor of 4 maximum. In conclusion, computational cost of the edit distance would increase by a total factor of $(4k)^2$ up to $O(16k^2 \cdot n^2)$.

By using effective mutations we concentrate variation on effective instructions. In this way, step sizes become more closely related to the effective distance metric.

4   Control of Diversity

The effective edit distance between programs is applied for an active control of *genotype diversity*, that is the average *structural* distance between two randomly selected individuals in population. In order to control this distance we introduce the two-level tournament selection shown in Figure 1. On the first level, individuals are selected by fitness. On the second level, the two individuals with *maximum* distance are chosen among *three fitter* individuals, i.e., tournament winners of the first round. While an absolute measure like fitness may be compared between two individuals selection by a relative measure like distance or diversity necessarily requires a minimum of three individuals. In general, two out of n individuals are selected that show the largest sum of distances to the $n-1$ other individuals. While selection pressure on the first level depends on the *size* of fitness tournaments the pressure of diversity selection on the second level is controlled by the *number* of these tournaments. Additionally, a probability parameter controls how often diversity selection takes place.

The number of fitness calculations does not increase with the number of (first-level) tournaments if fitness of all individuals is saved and is updated only after variation. Only diversity selection itself becomes more computationally expensive the more individuals participate in it. Because n selected individuals require $\binom{n}{2}$ distance calculations an efficient distance metric is important here.

The multi-objective selection method prefers individuals that are fit *and* diverse in relation to others. In the two-level selection process fitness selection keeps a higher priority than diversity selection. Selecting individuals only by diversity for a certain probability, instead, does not result in more different directions among *better* solutions in the population. Dittrich *et al.* [5] report on a spontaneous formation of groups when selecting the most distant of three individuals that are represented by single real numbers.

In general, an explicit control of structural diversity increases the average distance of individuals. Graphically, the population spreads wider over the fitness landscape. Thus, there is a lower probability that the evolutionary process gets stuck in a local minimum and more different search directions may be explored in parallel.

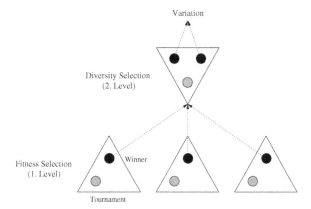

Fig. 1. Two-level tournament selection.

Controlling *phenotype diversity* by a selection for maximum *fitness* distance of individuals has been found less suitable here. Note that program fitness is related to an absolute optimum. Increasing relative fitness distance necessarily increases the diversity of fitness values in population which promotes worse solutions. Moreover, selection by fitness distance has almost no effect on problems that implicate a rather narrow and discrete fitness distribution.

5   Control of Variation Distance

One property of program representations in GP is that already smallest variations on the structural level may affect program behavior heavily. In linear GP these variations especially include the exchange of single registers. Several instructions that precede a varied instruction in a program may become effective or non-effective respectively. In this way, such micro mutations may not only affect the fitness but the flow of data in linear genetic programs. Even if bigger variations of program behavior are less likely with smaller structural variation steps, this effect is rather undesirable.

An *implicit control* of structural variation distance may be realized by imposing respective restrictions on the variation operators [4]. Unfortunately, a variation operator – even if it is operating on the effective code exclusively – can only guarantee for the *absolute* program structure that a certain maximum step size is not exceeded. Variation steps on the *effective* code may still be much bigger though bigger steps appear with a lower probability.

The concern of this contribution is an *explicit control* of the *effective* variation distance. Therefore, the structural distance between parent and offspring is measured explicitly by using the effective distance metric. The variation of a parent program is repeated until its effective distance to the offspring falls below a *maximum threshold.*

In the following extract of a linear program commented instructions are non-effective if we assume that the output is held in register r[0] at the end of execution. The program status on the right represents the result of applying a micro mutation to instruction number 8 (from the top). The first operand register r[3] is exchanged by register r[2]. As a consequence, five preceding (formerly non-effective) instructions become effective which corresponds to an effective mutation distance of five.

```
void gp(r)                              void gp(r)
  double r[5];                            double r[5];
{                                       {
  ...                                     ...

// r[4] = r[2] * r[4];                  // r[4] = r[2] * r[4];
   r[4] = r[2] / r[0];                     r[4] = r[2] / r[0];
// r[0] = r[3] - 1;                        r[0] = r[3] - 1;
// r[1] = r[2] * r[4];                     r[1] = r[2] * r[4];
// r[1] = r[0] + r[1];                     r[1] = r[0] + r[1];
// r[0] = r[3] - 5;                        r[0] = r[3] - 5;
// r[2] = pow(r[1], r[0]);                 r[2] = pow(r[1], r[0]);
   r[2] = r[3] - r[4];                     r[2] = r[2] - r[4];      <- mutation point
   r[4] = r[2] - 1;                        r[4] = r[2] - 1;
   r[0] = r[4] * r[3];                     r[0] = r[4] * r[3];
// r[4] = pow(r[0], 2);                 // r[4] = pow(r[0], 2);
// r[1] = r[0] / r[3];                  // r[1] = r[0] / r[3];
   r[3] = r[2] + r[3];                     r[3] = r[2] + r[3];
   r[4] = r[2] / 7;                        r[4] = r[2] / 7;
// r[2] = r[2] * r[4];                  // r[2] = r[2] * r[4];
   r[0] = r[0] + r[4];                     r[0] = r[0] + r[4];
   r[0] = r[0] - r[3];                     r[0] = r[0] - r[3];
}                                       }
```

An alternative metric to the edit distance between effective operator sequences is applicable for controlling step sizes of effective mutations. It simply calculates how many instructions have changed their effectivity status from the mutation point to the beginning of a program. This is exactly the *Hamming distance* between the status flags which needs calculation time $O(n)$ only (with n is the maximum program length here). Even if both metrics calculate similar distances we stick to the edit distance here for consistency reason.

Using an explicit control of the *fitness* distance between parent and offspring, instead, requires an additional fitness calculation after each iterated variation and can become computationally expensive, especially if a larger number of fitness cases is involved. By comparison, a structural distance like edit distance has to be re-calculated only once after each iteration while its computational costs do not directly depend on the number of fitness cases. It is also difficult to find appropriate maximum thresholds for fitness distance because those are usually problem-specific. Finally, it is not sensible to restrict *positive* fitness changes (fitness improvement) at all.

6   Experimental Setup

All techniques discussed above have been tested with three benchmark problems including an approximation, a classification, and a Boolean problem. Table 1 summarizes problem attributes and problem-specific parameter adjustments of our LGP system.

Table 1. Problem-specific parameter settings.

Problem ID	sinpoly	iris	8-parity
Problem type	Approximation	Classification	Boolean function
Problem function	$sin(x) \times x + 5$	real-world data set	even-N-parity (N=8)
Input range	$[-5, 5]$	$[0, 8)$	$\{0, 1\}$
Output range	$[0, 7)$	$\{0, 1, 2\}$	$\{0, 1\}$
Number of inputs	1	4	8
Number of outputs	1	1	1
Number of registers	1+4	4+2	8+0
Number of examples	100	150	256
Fitness function	SSE	CE	SE
Number of generations	500	500	250
Instruction set	$\{+, -, \times, /, x^y\}$	$\{+, -, \times, /, if >, if \leq\}$	$\{$AND, OR, NOT, $if\}$
Set of constants	$\{1, .., 9\}$	$\{1, .., 9\}$	$\{0, 1\}$

The first problem is referred to as *sinpoly* in the following and denotes an approximation of the sinus polynomial $sin(x) \times x + 5$ by non-trigonomical functions. Besides the input register – that is identical to the output register here – there are four additional calculation registers used with this problem. This additional program memory becomes important in linear GP, especially if the number of inputs is low by problem definition. Program fitness is the *sum of square errors* (SSE) between the predicted outputs and the example outputs.

The second problem *iris* is a popular classification data set that originates from the *UCI Machine Learning Repository* [2]. The real-world data contains 3 classes of 50 instances each, where each class refers to a type of iris plant. Fitness equals the *classification error* (CE), i.e., the number of wrongly classified inputs. A program output $p(i_k)$ is considered as correct for an input vector i_k if the distance to the desired class identifier $o_k \in \{0, 1, 2\}$ is smaller than 0.1, i.e., $|p(i_k) - o_k| < 0.1$.

Finally, we have tested a parity function of dimension eight (*even-8-parity*). This function outputs one if the number of set input bits is even, otherwise the output is zero. Note that the Boolean branch in the instruction set is essential for a high number of successful runs with this problem.

Table 2. General parameter settings.

Parameter	Setting
Population size	2000
Fitness tournament size	4
Maximum program length	200
Initial program length	2–20
Reproduction	100%
Micro mutation	25%
Macro mutation	75%
Instruction deletion	33%
Instruction insertion	67%
Crossover	75%

More general configurations of our linear GP system are given in Table 2. Exactly one genetic operator is selected at a time to vary an individual program. Moreover, either crossover or macro mutations are used as macro (growth) operator, but not in the same run. Macro mutations include two times more insertions than deletions here. This explicit growth tendency of the operator guarantees a sufficient growth of programs. Program length is meassured in number of instructions.

7   Results

7.1   Causality

First of all, we demonstrate experimentally that there is a causal connection between the structural distance and the semantic distance (fitness distance) of linear genetic programs when applying the edit distance metric on sequences of effective instruction operators as defined in Section 3.

The effective variation distance is meassured with both crossover and effective mutations. In both cases, Figure 2 demonstrates a clear positive correlation between program distance and fitness distance, i.e., shorter variation distances on code level induce shorter variation distances on fitness level. The respective distribution of variation distances in Figure 2 confirms this to be true for the vast majority of occurring distances. While, in general, shorter variation distances occur more frequently than longer distances, distribution of crossover distances is wider than the distribution of distances induced by (effective) mutations.

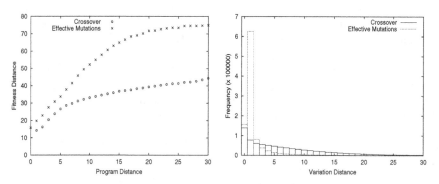

Fig. 2. Relation between program distance and fitness distance (left) and distribution of variation distances (right) for *iris* problem (similar for *sinpoly* and *8-parity*). Average figures over 100 runs.

Furthermore, distance distributions show that almost two thirds of all effective mutations result in distance one. Interestingly, even though macro mutations that insert or delete *full* effective instructions are applied in the majority of cases the effectivity of other (preceding) instructions changes for less than one third only. Obviously, evolution develops effective program structures which are less fragile against stronger variation. We found that the effectivity of an instruction is very often guaranteed by more than one (succeeding) instruction. When crossover is used the proportion of non-effective instructions in a program acts as another implicit mechanism that reduces variation strength.

7.2   Structural Diversity Selection

Table 3 shows average error rates obtained with and without selecting for structural diversity for the three test problems introduced in Section 6. Different selection pressures, i.e., selection probabilities, have been tested with three fitness tournaments. Higher selection pressures are induced by increasing the number of tournaments up to four or eight.

Table 3. Second-level selection for structural diversity with different selection pressures. Selection pressure controlled by selection probability and number of fitness tournaments (T). Average error over 200 runs. Statistical standard error in parenthesis. Percental difference from baseline results.

Variation	Selection		sinpoly		iris		8-parity	
	%	#T	mean (std)	Δ (%)	mean (std)	Δ (%)	mean (std)	Δ (%)
Crossover	0	2	3.01 (0.35)	0	2.11 (0.10)	0	58 (3.4)	0
	50	3	2.89 (0.34)	4	1.42 (0.08)	33	35 (2.4)	40
	100	3	2.77 (0.34)	8	1.17 (0.07)	44	27 (2.2)	53
	100	4	1.96 (0.22)	35	1.09 (0.07)	48	19 (1.8)	67
	100	8	0.69 (0.06)	77	—	—	—	—
Effective	0	2	0.45 (0.04)	0	0.84 (0.06)	0	15 (1.2)	0
Mutations	50	3	0.43 (0.03)	4	0.63 (0.05)	25	12 (1.0)	20
	100	3	0.30 (0.02)	33	0.60 (0.05)	29	10 (1.1)	33
	100	4	0.23 (0.02)	49	0.33 (0.04)	61	7 (0.8)	53
	100	8	0.17 (0.01)	62	—	—	—	—

It is conspicuous that in all three test cases linear GP works significantly better by using (effective) macro mutations instead of crossover. In [4] we have already demonstrated that the linear program representation, in particular, is much more suitable for being developed by mutations, especially if those are directed towards effective instructions. Nonetheless, the experiments with linear crossover show here that diversity selection is not depending on a special type of variation. Moreover, the application of this technique is demonstrated with a population-dependent operator. For each problem and both variation operators performance increases continuously with the influence of diversity selection in Table 3. The highest selection pressure tested for a problem results in a twofold or higher improvement of prediction error. To achieve this, problem *sinpoly* requires a stronger pressure with crossover than the two discrete problems.

Figure 3 illustrates the development of structural diversity during run for different selection pressures. The higher the selection pressure is adjusted the higher is the diversity. Interestingly, the average (effective) program distance does not drop even if diversity selection is not applied. Instead of a premature loss of diversity we observe an inherent increase of structural diversity with our linear GP approach. While diversity increases with crossover until a certain level and stays rather constant then, increase with effective mutations is more linear.

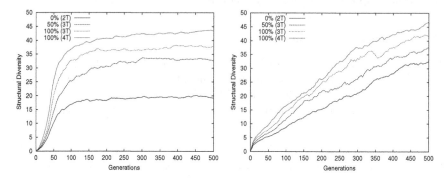

Fig. 3. Diversity levels after diversity selection with different selection pressures. Selection pressure controlled by selection probability and number of fitness tournaments (T). Macro variation by crossover (left) or effective mutations (right) for *iris* problem (similar for *sinpoly* and *8-parity*). Average figures over 100 runs.

Two major reasons can be found to explain this behavior: First, genetic programming is working with a variable-length representation. The longer effective programs develop during a run the bigger effective distances may become. The growth of effective code is more restricted with crossover than with effective mutations because a much higher proportion of non-effective code emerges with this operator – approximately 50–60% in the experiments conducted here. Nevertheless, by the influence of distance selection the average (effective) program length has been found to increase only slightly compared to the average program distance.

Second, both forms of variation, linear crossover and effective mutation, maintain program diversity over a run already implicitly, i.e., without an explicit distance control. For linear crossover the reason might lie in its high variation strength and in the higher amount of non-effective code that contributes to a preservation of (effective) code diversity, too.

When using mutations exclusively a high degree of innovation is introduced continuously into the population. This leads to a higher diversity than it occurs with crossover. The stronger it is selected for diversity, however, the more diversity is gaining ground in crossover runs. Compared to mutations the success of recombination depends more strongly on the composition of the genetic material in the population. The more different the recombined solutions are the higher is the expected innovativity of their offsprings.

7.3   Control of Effective Mutation Distance

As motivated in Section 5 we are interested in controlling the *effective* distance between parent and offspring. We restrict ourselves to the mutation-based approach here. In particular, we want to find out whether solution quality may be further improved by an explicit reduction of effective mutation distances. Therefore, a program is mutated repeatedly until its distance to the offspring falls below a maximum threshold. Each time a mutation is not accepted its effect on the program is reversed while the choice of the mutation point is free in every iteration.

The applied effective distance metric regards operators as smallest distance units (see Section 3). This corresponds to (effective) macro mutations which operate on instruction level (*macro level*), even if the effective distance may also be altered by micro mutations that operate *below* instruction level (*micro level*). In order to guarantee a sufficient code growth, macro mutations are applied more frequently than micro mutations here. As a result, most steps by effective mutations are larger than zero (about 80% in Figure 2) and measuring the distance between *full* effective programs does not promise a much higher precision. This is another reason, besides the arguments given in Section 3, why (effective) operator sequences represent a sufficient basis for distance calculation between linear genetic programs.

Table 4. Maximum restriction of effective mutation distance. Average error over 200 runs. Statistical standard error in parenthesis. Percental difference from baseline results.

Variation	Maximum Distance	sinpoly		iris		8-parity	
		mean (std)	Δ (%)	mean (std)	Δ (%)	mean (std)	Δ (%)
Effective	—	0.46 (0.06)	0	0.90 (0.06)	0	16 (1.2)	0
Mutations	10	0.35 (0.04)	24	0.72 (0.06)	20	13 (1.2)	19
	5	0.33 (0.04)	28	0.74 (0.06)	18	12 (1.2)	25
	2	0.28 (0.03)	39	0.68 (0.05)	24	11 (1.1)	31
	1	0.26 (0.03)	42	0.54 (0.05)	40	9 (0.9)	44

Table 4 compares average prediction errors for different maximum limits of mutation distance. The maximum possible distance equals the maximum program length and imposes no restrictions. For all three benchmark problems best results are obtained with the smallest maximum distance (1). This is all the more interesting if we consider that a restriction of variation distance always implies a restriction in variation freedom.

As we can see in Table 5 the average number of iterations during run increases only slightly if the maximum threshold is lowered. Not even one and a half iterations are necessary, on average, for the smallest distance and the maximum number of iterations (10 here) has hardly ever been exceeded. Both aspects together with the results from Table 4 emphasize that freedom of variation is not restricted significantly and that computational costs of this distance control are not expensive.

The results found here further correspond to the distribution of mutation distances in Figure 2 where only about 20–30% of all measured step sizes are larger than one. Obviously, larger disruptions of effective code as demonstrated with

Table 5. Average number of iterations until a maximum mutation distance is met.

Variation	Maximum	Iterations		
	Distance	sinpoly	iris	8-parity
Effective	—	1.00	1.00	1.00
Mutations	10	1.02	1.02	1.02
	5	1.06	1.05	1.05
	2	1.18	1.12	1.12
	1	1.37	1.18	1.20

the example program in Section 5 occur less likely. Effective parts of programs rather emerge to be quite robust against bigger effective mutations steps.

8   Future Work and Conclusion

A two-level tournament selection may also be used for implementing a complexity control. Compared to a weighted complexity term in the fitness function (*parsimony pressure*) [10], fitness selection is less influenced by a *complexity selection* on the second level and finding an appropriate weighting of objectives is not required. Moreover, the separation of linear genetic programs in effective and non-effective code offers the possibility for a *selective* complexity selection. That means it may be selected for smallest effective length or smallest non-effective length specifically.

We introduced an active control of diversity in form of a two-level selection process. By increasing the structural distance between programs, performance improved significantly for three different benchmark problems. Measuring structural differences specifically between effective subcomponents of linear genetic programs was found sufficiently precise to demonstrate causality.

We also restricted the mutation distance on level of effective code. This turned out to be most successful with the smallest maximum step size while the number of necessary repetitions of a mutation was small. In general, mutation distances on effective linear programs were found much smaller than it might be expected.

Acknowledgements.   This   research   was   supported   by   the   Deutsche Forschungsgemeinschaft (DFG), collaborative research center SFB 531, project B2.

References

1. W. Banzhaf, P. Nordin, R. Keller and F. Francone, *Genetic Programming – An Introduction. On the Automatic Evolution of Computer Programs and its Application.* dpunkt/Morgan Kaufmann, Heidelberg/San Francisco, 1998.
2. C.L. Blake and C.J. Merz, *UCI Repository of Machine Learning Databases* [http://www.ics.uci.edu/~mlearn/MLRepository.html]. University of California, Department of Information and Computer Science.

3. M. Brameier and W. Banzhaf, *A Comparison of Linear Genetic Programming and Neural Networks in Medical Data Mining*. IEEE Transactions on Evolutionary Computation, vol. 5(1), pp. 17–26, 2001.
4. M. Brameier and W. Banzhaf, *Effective Linear Program Induction*. Collaborative Research Center SFB 531, Computational Intelligence, Technical Report No. CI-108/01, University of Dortmund, 2001.
5. P. Dittrich, F. Liljeros, A. Soulier, and W. Banzhaf, *Spontaneous Group Formation in the Seceder Model*. Physical Review Letters, vol. 84, pp. 3205–3208, 2000.
6. D. Gusfield, *Algorithms on Strings, Trees and Sequences*. Cambridge University Press, 1997.
7. C. Igel and K. Chellapilla, *Investigating the Influence of Depth and Degree of Genotypic Change on Fitness in Genetic Programming*. In W. Banzhaf et al. (eds.), *Proceedings of the Genetic and Evolutionary Computation Conference*, pp. 1061–1068, MIT Press, Cambridge, 1999.
8. E.D. de Jong, R.A. Watson, and J.B. Pollack, *Reducing Bloat and Promoting Diversity using Multi-Objective Methods*. In L. Spector et al. (eds.), *Proceedings of the Genetic and Evolutionary Computation Conference*, pp. 11–18, MIT Press, Cambridge, 2001.
9. R. Keller and W. Banzhaf, *Explicit Maintenance of Genetic Diversity on Genospaces*, Internal Report, University of Dortmund, 1995.
10. J.R. Koza, *Genetic Programming*. MIT Press, Cambridge, MA, 1992.
11. P. Nordin, *A Compiling Genetic Programming System that Directly Manipulates the Machine-Code*. In K.E. Kinnear (ed.) *Advances in Genetic Programming*, 311–331, MIT Press, Cambridge, MA, 1994.
12. I. Rechenberg, *Evolutionsstrategie '94*. Frommann-Holzboog, 1994.
13. U.-M. O'Reilly, *Using a Distance Metric on Genetic Programs to Understand Genetic Operators*. In J.R. Koza (ed.), *Late Breaking Papers at the Genetic Programming '97 Conference*, Standford University, 1997.
14. J.P. Rosca and D.H. Ballard, *Causality in Genetic Programming*. In L.J. Eshelmann (ed.), *Proceedings of the Sixth International Conference on Genetic Algorithms*, pp. 256–263, Morgan Kaufmann, San Francisco, 1995
15. D. Sankoff and J.B. Kruskal (eds.), *Time Warps, String Edits, and Macromolecules: The Theory and Practice of Sequence Comparison*, Addison-Wesley, 1983.
16. R. Tanese, *Distributed Genetic Algorithms*. In J.D. Schaffer (ed.) *Proceedings of the Third International Conference on Genetic Algorithms*, 434–439, Morgan Kaufmann, San Mateo, CA, 1989.

Discovery of the Boolean Functions to the Best Density-Classification Rules Using Gene Expression Programming

Cândida Ferreira

Gepsoft, 37 The Ridings,
Bristol BS13 8NU, UK
candidaf@gepsoft.com
http://www.gepsoft.com

Abstract. Cellular automata are idealized versions of massively parallel, decentralized computing systems capable of emergent behaviors. These complex behaviors result from the simultaneous execution of simple rules at multiple local sites. A widely studied behavior consists of correctly determining the density of an initial configuration, and both human and computer-written rules have been found that perform with high efficiency at this task. However, the two best rules for the density-classification task, Coevolution$_1$ and Coevolution$_2$, were discovered using a coevolutionary algorithm in which a genetic algorithm evolved the rules and, therefore, only the output bits of the rules are known. However, to understand why these and other rules perform so well and how the information is transmitted throughout the cellular automata, the Boolean expressions that orchestrate this behavior must be known. The results presented in this work are a contribution in that direction.

1 Introduction

Genetic programming (GP) evolves computer programs by genetically modifying nonlinear entities with different sizes and shapes [1]. These nonlinear entities can be represented as diagrams or trees. Gene expression programming (GEP) is an extension to GP that also evolves computer programs of different sizes and shapes, but these programs are encoded in a linear chromosome of fixed length [2]. One strength of the GEP approach is that the creation of genetic diversity is extremely simplified as genetic operators work at the chromosome level. Indeed, due to the structural organization of GEP chromosomes any modification made in the genome results always in valid programs. Another strength of GEP consists of its unique, multigenic nature which allows the evolution of more complex programs composed of several sub-programs.

Cellular automata (CA) have been studied widely as they are idealized versions of massively parallel, decentralized computing systems capable of emergent behaviors (for overviews of CA theory and applications see, e.g., [3, 4]). These complex behaviors result from the simultaneous execution of simple rules at multiple local sites. In the density-classification task, a simple rule involving a small neighborhood and operating simultaneously in all the cells of a one-dimensional cellular automaton, should be capable of making the CA converge into a state of all 1's if the initial

J.A. Foster et al. (Eds.): EuroGP 2002, LNCS 2278, pp. 50-59, 2002.

configuration (IC) has a higher density of 1's, or into a state of all 0's if the IC has a higher density of 0's.

The challenging problem of density-classification started with the Gacs-Kurdyumov-Levin rule (GKL rule) [5], designed in 1978 by hand to study reliable computation and phase transitions in one-dimensional spatially extended systems. Although not especially designed for the density-classification task, the GKL rule was for some time the rule with best performance on this task [6]. In 1993, Lawrence Davis obtained a new rule modifying the GKL rule [7]. This new rule, Davis rule, achieved an accuracy slightly better than the GKL rule. Similarly, Rajarshi Das cleverly modified rules discovered by genetic algorithms (GAs), obtaining a new rule (Das rule) that performed slightly better than the GKL rule and the Davis rule [7]. Genetic programming discovered a new rule (GP rule) slightly better than the previous rules [7]. Gene expression programming discovered two new rules (GEP$_1$ and GEP$_2$ rules) better than all the previous rules [2]. And finally, Juillé and Pollack [8], using coevolutionary learning, discovered two new rules (Coevolution$_1$ and Coevolution$_2$) significantly better than all the previous rules.

However, the two best rules, Coevolution$_1$ and Coevolution$_2$, were discovered using a coevolutionary approach in which a GA evolved the rules and, therefore, only the output bits of the rules are known. However, if we want to understand why these rules perform so well and how the information is transmitted throughout the CA, it is mandatory to know the Boolean expressions that orchestrate the behavior of the CA. In this work, GEP is successfully applied to find the Boolean expressions behind the two best density-classification rules, providing a useful resource for future research on emergent behavior.

2 Genetic Algorithms

Gene expression programming belongs to a wider group of genetic algorithms as it uses populations of individuals, selects individuals according to fitness, and introduces genetic variation using one or more genetic operators [2, 6].

2.1 Fundamental Classes of Genetic Algorithms

Structurally, genetic algorithms can be subdivided in three fundamental groups: i) Genetic algorithms with individuals consisting of linear chromosomes of fixed length devoid of complex expression. In these systems, replicators (chromosomes) survive by virtue of their own properties. The algorithm invented by Holland [9] belongs to this group, and is known as genetic algorithm or GA; ii) Genetic algorithms with individuals consisting of ramified structures of different sizes and shapes and, therefore, capable of assuming a richer number of functionalities. In these systems, replicators (ramified structures) also survive by virtue of their own properties. The algorithm invented by Cramer [10] and later developed by Koza [1] belongs to this group and is known as genetic programming or GP; iii) Genetic algorithms with individuals encoded as linear chromosomes of fixed length which are afterwards expressed as ramified structures of different sizes and shapes. In these systems, replicators (chromosomes) survive by virtue of causal effects on the phenotype (ramified structures). The algorithm invented by myself [2] belongs to this group and is known as gene expression programming or GEP.

The fact that GEP shares with GP the same kind of ramified structure, shows that GEP can be used, for one thing, to retrace easily the steps undertaken by GP and, for another, to explore easily new frontiers opened up by the crossing of the phenotype threshold. Next follows a brief introduction to gene expression programming.

2.2 Gene Expression Programming

The phenotype of GEP individuals consists of the same kind of diagram representations used by GP. However, these complex entities are encoded in simpler, linear structures of fixed length - the chromosomes. Thus, the main players in GEP are two entities: the chromosomes and the ramified structures or expression trees (ETs), being the latter the expression of the genetic information encoded in the former. The process of information decoding (from the chromosomes to the ETs) is called translation. And this translation implies obviously a kind of code and a set of rules. The genetic code is very simple: a one-to-one relationship between the symbols of the chromosome and the functions or terminals they represent. The rules are also very simple: they determine the spatial organization of the functions and terminals in the ETs and the type of interaction between sub-ETs in multigenic systems.

In GEP there are therefore two languages: the language of the genes and the language of ETs and, in this simple replicator/phenotype system, knowing the sequence or structure of one, is knowing the other. In nature, although the inference of the sequence of proteins given the sequence of genes and *vice versa* is possible, practically nothing is known about the rules that determine the three-dimensional structure of proteins. But in GEP, thanks to the simple rules that determine the structure of ETs and their interactions, it is possible to infer exactly the phenotype given the sequence of a gene, and *vice versa*. This bilingual and unequivocal system is called *Karva* language. The details of this language are given below.

Open Reading Frames and Genes. In GEP, the genome or chromosome consists of a linear, symbolic string of fixed length composed of one or more genes. Despite their fixed length, GEP chromosomes code for ETs with different sizes and shapes, as will next be shown.

The structural organization of GEP genes is better understood in terms of open reading frames (ORFs). In biology, an ORF or coding sequence of a gene begins with the "start" codon, continues with the amino acid codons, and ends at a termination codon. However, a gene is more than the respective ORF, with sequences upstream of the start codon and sequences downstream of the stop codon. Although in GEP the start site is always the first position of a gene, the termination point not always coincides with the last position of a gene. It is common for GEP genes to have non-coding regions downstream of the termination point. (For now these non-coding regions will not be considered because they do not interfere with the product of expression.)

Consider, for example, the algebraic expression:

$$\frac{a \cdot b}{c} + \sqrt{d - e} \tag{1}$$

It can also be represented as a diagram:

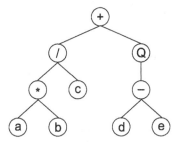

where "Q" represents the square root function.

This kind of diagram representation is in fact the phenotype of GEP chromosomes, being the genotype easily inferred from the phenotype as follows:

```
0123456789
+/Q*c-abde
```
(2)

which is the straightforward reading of the ET from left to right and from top to bottom (exactly as we read a page of text). The expression (2) is an ORF, starting at "+" (position 0) and terminating at "e" (position 9). These ORFs are called K-expressions (from Karva notation).

Consider another ORF, the following K-expression:

```
012345678901
*-/Qb+b+aaab
```
(3)

Its expression as an ET is also very simple and straightforward. To express correctly the ORF, the rules governing the spatial distribution of functions and terminals must be followed. The start position (position 0) in the ORF corresponds to the root of the ET. Then, below each function are attached as many branches as there are arguments to that function. The assemblage is complete when a baseline composed only of terminals (the variables or constants used in a problem) is formed. So, for the K-expression (3) above, the following ET is formed:

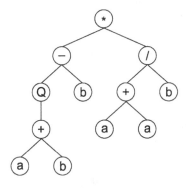

Looking at the structure of GEP ORFs only, it is difficult or even impossible to see the advantages of such a representation, except perhaps for its simplicity and elegance. However, when ORFs are analyzed in the context of a gene, the advantages of this representation become obvious. As stated previously, GEP chromosomes have fixed length, and they are composed of one or more genes of equal length. Therefore the length of a gene is also fixed. Thus, in GEP, what varies is not the length of genes but the length of the ORFs. Indeed, the length of an ORF may be equal to or less than the length of the gene. In the first case, the termination point coincides with the end of the gene and, in the last case, the termination point is somewhere upstream of the end of the gene.

As will next be shown, the non-coding sequences of GEP genes are extremely important for they allow the modification of the genome using any genetic operator without restrictions, producing always syntactically correct programs. The section proceeds with the study of the structural organization of GEP genes in order to show how these genes invariably code for syntactically correct programs and why they allow the unconstrained application of numerous genetic operators.

Structural Organization of Genes. GEP genes are composed of a head and a tail. The head contains symbols that represent both functions and terminals, whereas the tail contains only terminals. For each problem, the length of the head h is chosen, whereas the length of the tail t is a function of h and maximum arity n, and is evaluated by the equation:

$$t = h \cdot (n - 1) + 1 \tag{4}$$

Consider a gene for which the set of functions consists of $F = \{Q, *, /, -, +\}$ and the set of terminals $T = \{a, b\}$. In this case, $n = 2$; and if an $h = 15$ is chosen, then $t = 16$. Thus, the length of the gene g is 15+16=31. One such gene is shown below (the tail is shown in bold):

```
0123456789012345678901234567890
/aQ/b*ab/Qa*b*-ababaababbabbbba
```
(5)

It codes for an ET with eight nodes. Note that, in this case, the ORF ends at position 7 whereas the gene ends at position 30.

Suppose now a mutation occurred at position 2, changing the "Q" into "+". Then the following gene is obtained:

```
0123456789012345678901234567890
/a+/b*ab/Qa*b*-ababaababbabbbba
```
(6)

In this case, its expression gives a new ET with 18 nodes. Note that the termination point shifts 10 positions to the right (position 17).

Obviously the opposite might also happen, and the ORF can be shortened. For example, consider again gene (5) above, and suppose a mutation occurred at position 5, changing the "*" into "b", obtaining:

```
0123456789012345678901234567890
/aQ/bbab/Qa*b*-ababaababbabbbba
```
(7)

Its expression results in a new ET with six nodes. Note that the ORF ends at position 5, shortening the parental ET in two nodes.

So, despite their fixed length, GEP genes have the potential to code for ETs of different sizes and shapes, being the simplest composed of only one node (when the first element of a gene is a terminal) and the biggest composed of as many nodes as the length of the gene (when all head elements are functions with maximum arity).

It is evident from the examples above, that any modification made in the genome, no matter how profound, results always in a structurally correct ET as long as the structural organization of genes is maintained. Indeed, the implementation of high-performing genetic operators in GEP is a child's play, and Ferreira [2] describes seven: point mutation, RIS and IS transposition, two- and one-point recombination, gene transposition and gene recombination.

Multigenic Chromosomes. GEP chromosomes are usually composed of more than one gene of equal length. For each problem or run, the number of genes, as well as the length of the head, are *a priori* chosen. Each gene codes for a sub-ET and the sub-ETs interact with one another forming a more complex multi-subunit ET.

Consider the following chromosome with length 45, composed of three genes:

```
012345678901234012345678901234012345678901234
Q/*b+Qababaabaa-abQ/*+bababbab**-*bb/babaaaab          (8)
```

It has three ORFs, and each ORF codes for a sub-ET. Position 0 marks the start of each gene. The end of each ORF, though, is only evident upon construction of the respective sub-ET. In this case, the first ORF ends at position 8; the second ORF ends at position 2; and the last ORF ends at position 10. Thus, GEP chromosomes are composed of one or more ORFs, each ORF coding for a structurally and functionally unique sub-ET. Depending on the problem at hand, the sub-ETs encoded by each gene may be selected individually according to their respective fitness (for example, in problems with multiple outputs), or they may form a more complex, multi-subunit ET where individual sub-ETs interact with one another by a particular kind of posttranslational interaction or linking. For instance, algebraic sub-ETs are usually linked by addition or multiplication whereas Boolean sub-ETs are usually linked by OR, AND, or IF.

3 The Density-Classification Task

The simplest CA is a wrap-around array of N binary-state cells, where each cell is connected to r neighbors from both sides. The state of each cell is updated by a defined rule. The rule is applied simultaneously in all the cells, and the process is iterated for t time steps. In the most frequently studied version of the density-classification task, $N = 149$ and $r = 3$. The central cell is represented by "u"; the three cells to the left are represented by "c", "b", and "a"; and the three cells to the right are represented by "1", "2", and "3".

The task of density-classification consists of correctly determining whether ICs contain a majority of 1's or a majority of 0's, by making the system converge, respectively, to an all 1's state, or to a state of all 0's. As the density of an IC is a function of N arguments, the actions of local cells with limited information and communication must be coordinated with one another in order to classify correctly the ICs. Indeed, to find by hand, in a search space of 2^{128} transition rules, CA rules that perform well is an almost impossible task and, therefore, several evolutionary algorithms were used to evolve better rules than the GKL rule [2, 7, 8, 11, 12, 13]. The best rules with performances of 86.0% (Coevolution$_2$) and 85.1% (Coevolution$_1$) were discovered using a coevolutionary approach between ICs and rules evolved by a GA [8]. The Boolean expressions of these rules are not known and little or no knowledge can be extracted from the output bits of their rule tables. In the next section, GEP is used to find the solutions to these rules.

4 Discovering the Boolean Functions to the Best Rules for the Density-Classification Task

The space of possible rules for Boolean functions of seven arguments is the huge space of $2^{2^7} = 2^{128}$ rules, and the size of the space of possible computer programs that can be composed using the elements of the function and terminal sets is greater still. Therefore, the discovery of the Boolean functions to the Coevolution$_1$, and Coevolution$_2$ rules is no trivial task and, in fact, their discovery by GEP involved several optimization runs where the best solution of a run was used as seed to evolve better programs. This kind of strategy is inevitable while trying to solve real-world problems of great complexity. Good intermediate solutions are some times hard to find, and start everything anew is no guarantee that a perfect solution or even a better intermediate solution will be found. Therefore, it is advantageous to use a good intermediate solution as seed to start a new evolutionary cycle, with the advantage that the seed or the evolutionary conditions can be slightly changed before an optimization. For instance, we can increase the gene length, introduce or remove a neutral gene, introduce or remove new functions in the function set, linearize a multigenic solution, change the fitness function or the selection environment, change the population size, change the genetic operators or their rates, and so forth. The particular evolutionary strategy followed in each case is given below.

4.1 Experimental Setup

The total $2^7 = 128$ transition states of each rule consists of the fitness cases used to evaluate fitness. In all cases, the set of functions F = { N, A, O, X, D, R, I, M} (representing, respectively, NOT, AND, OR, XOR, NAND, NOR, IF, and Majority, where the first is a function of one argument, the second through fifth are functions of two arguments, and the last two are functions of three arguments), and the set of terminals T = {c, b, a, u, 1, 2, 3}. The fitness f_i of a program i is evaluated by the equation:

$$\text{If } n \geq \frac{1}{2} C_t, \text{ then } f_i = n; \text{else } f_i = 1 \tag{9}$$

where n is the number of fitness cases correctly evaluated, and C_t is the total number of fitness cases. Thus, for the entire set of fitness cases, $f_{max} = 128$.

4.2 Coevolution$_1$ Rule

The Coevolution$_1$ rule has a performance of 85.1% and was discovered using a coevolutionary approach between GA-evolved rules and ICs [8].

Gene expression programming found the solution to the Coevolution$_1$ rule in four phases. Firstly, chromosomes composed of nine genes of length 22 each were used. The sub-ETs were linked by IF, forming a huge multi-subunit ET. An intermediate solution with fitness 121 was found after 47093 generations of a small initial population of 30 individuals. Then, this intermediate solution was used as seed, and after 11785 generations a better solution with fitness 123 was found. Then, the genes of this intermediate solution were increased from 22 to 34 and populations of 50 individuals were left to evolve for 50000 generations. On generation 37362 an intermediate solution with fitness 127 was discovered. Finally, this program was used as seed to create another population, this time with 50 individuals. After 15189 generations the following perfect solution to the Coevolution$_1$ rule was found:

```
MAD21RMDuOa1ab1ucb31bbu1acc31bu1c1
XXM1ROM3Rubaaa3322c2ba13abcu3c1uc1
NOaANMbXIXbb3buc33bc2bba3b21u11uc1
XRRID1ADbDA2cb1bcuu1cbu133u1aaaa3c
AOaOIAcONuDbcca33auauba3332b11b2bb
MXIODuRXOA31122b3cb3a3bau1cbbbb312
MuIADIOXINMa1cua1uu1bu2cab1cuccc2a
NNIMOODR1ODuu31u132u12babc1bu2aub2
IuIIRDOXIMb2cu312ua23a2c3222ba2ab3
```

where the sub-ETs are linked 3-by-3 with IF, forming three big clusters that are, in their turn, linked also 3-by-3 with IF.

4.3 Coevolution$_2$ Rule

The Coevolution$_2$ rule has a performance of 86.0% and was also discovered using a coevolutionary approach between GA-evolved rules and ICs [8].

The solution to the Coevolution$_2$ rule was easier to find than the solution to the previous rule. For this problem, populations of 50 individuals with chromosomes composed of 9 genes of length 22 each were used. The sub-ETs were linked also by the IF function.

In one run, an intermediate solution with fitness 126 was found by generation 18660. This program was used as seed to initialize another evolutionary epoch. After 23807 generations the following solution was found:

```
X3ONOD2acaa1332baa3211
R1XuION1ua33aa3321cbc2
RMaDAM3u1bb13cuuc2bubu
RRRA22X23b31a3a3122aab
M3D33NM2b21u22aa31bc2b
AOAII3ac2a3c2ua2u21u33
DXO1DXI1ab23u11ba1bba1
IMXcDMR1ub1bcua231cuu1
MDIMAMO2ubac212c22ccac
```

which is a perfect solution to the Coevolution$_2$ rule. The sub-ETs encoded by each gene are linked 3-by-3 with IF, forming three big clusters that are, in their turn, linked also 3-by-3 with IF.

5 Conclusions

Gene expression programming is the most recent development on artificial evolutionary systems and one that brings about a considerable increase in performance due to the crossing of the phenotype threshold [14]. The crossing of the phenotype threshold allows the unconstrained exploration of the search space. Thus, in GEP, the implementation of high-performing search operators such as point mutation, transposition and recombination, is a child's play as any modification made in the genome results always in valid phenotypes or programs.

In this work, the recently invented algorithm was successfully applied to discover Boolean functions on seven-dimensional parameter spaces. The Boolean functions discovered by GEP consist of the solutions to the best known rules at coordinating the behavior of cellular automata in the density-classification task. The understanding of such complex behaviors is only possible if the programs behind the output bits of a CA rule are known. However, for the two rules analyzed here (Coevolution$_1$ and Coevolution$_2$), only the output bits were known. Therefore, the intelligible solutions to the most efficient CA rules at the density-classification task discovered in this work are most valuable for future research in complex emergent behavior.

References

1. Koza, J. R., *Genetic Programming: On the Programming of Computers by Means of Natural Selection*. Cambridge, MA, MIT Press, 1992.
2. Ferreira, C., 2001. Gene Expression Programming: A New Adaptive Algorithm for Solving Problems. *Complex Systems*, 13 (2): 87-129.
3. Wolfram, S., *Theory and Applications of Cellular Automata*. World Scientific, 1986.
4. Toffoli, T. and N. Margolus, *Cellular Automata Machines: A New Environment for Modeling*. MIT Press, 1987.
5. Gacs, P., G. L. Kurdyumov, and L. A. Levin, 1978. One-dimensional Uniform Arrays that Wash out Finite Islands. *Problemy Peredachi Informatsii* 14, 92-98 (in Russian).
6. Mitchell, M., *An Introduction to Genetic Algorithms*. MIT Press, 1996.
7. Koza, J. R., F. H. Bennett III, D. Andre, and M. A. Keane, *Genetic Programming III: Darwinian Invention and Problem Solving*. Morgan Kaufmann, San Francisco, 1999.
8. Juillé, H. and J. B. Pollack. Coevolving the "Ideal" Trainer: Application to the Discovery of Cellular Automata Rules. In J. R. Koza, W. Banzhaf, K. Chellapilla, M. Dorigo, D. B. Fogel, M. H. Garzon, D. E. Goldberg, H. Iba, and R. L. Riolo, eds., *Genetic Programming 1998: Proceedings of the Third Annual Conference,* Morgan Kaufmann, San Francisco, 1998.
9. Holland, J. H., *Adaptation in Natural and Artificial Systems: An Introductory Analysis with Applications to Biology, Control, and Artificial Intelligence*. University of Michigan Press, 1975 (second edition: MIT Press, 1992).

10. Cramer, N. L., A Representation for the Adaptive Generation of Simple Sequential Programs. In J. J. Grefenstette, ed., *Proceedings of the First International Conference on Genetic Algorithms and Their Applications*, Erlbaum, 1985.
11. Mitchell, M., J. P. Crutchfield, and P. T. Hraber, 1994. Evolving Cellular Automata to Perform Computations: Mechanisms and Impediments. *Physica D* 75, 361-391.
12. Mitchell, M., P. T. Hraber, and J. P. Crutchfield, 1993. Revisiting the Edge of Chaos: Evolving Cellular Automata to Perform Computations. *Complex Systems* 7, 89-130.
13. Das, R., M. Mitchell, and J. P. Crutchfield, A Genetic Algorithm Discovers Particle-based Computation in Cellular Automata. In Y. Davidor, H.-P. Schwefel, and R. Männer, eds., *Parallel Problem Solving from Nature - PPSN III,* Springer-Verlag, 1994.
14. Dawkins, R., *River out of Eden.* Weidenfeld and Nicolson, 1995.

Combining Decision Trees and Neural Networks for Drug Discovery

William B. Langdon[1], S.J. Barrett[2], and B.F. Buxton[1]

[1] Computer Science, University College, Gower Street, London, WC1E 6BT, UK
{W.Langdon,B.Buxton}@cs.ucl.ac.uk
http://www.cs.ucl.ac.uk/staff/W.Langdon,/staff/B.Buxton
Tel: +44 (0) 20 7679 4436, Fax: +44 (0) 20 7387 1397
[2] GlaxoSmithKline Research and Development, Harlow, Essex, UK

Abstract. Genetic programming (GP) offers a generic method of automatically fusing together classifiers using their receiver operating characteristics (ROC) to yield superior ensembles. We combine decision trees (C4.5) and artificial neural networks (ANN) on a difficult pharmaceutical data mining (KDD) drug discovery application. Specifically predicting inhibition of a P450 enzyme. Training data came from high throughput screening (HTS) runs. The evolved model may be used to predict behaviour of virtual (i.e. yet to be manufactured) chemicals. Measures to reduce over fitting are also described.

1 Introduction

Computers are very good at collecting and storing huge volumes of data (such as in data warehouses) but they have been less successful at extracting useful information from it. Machine Learning techniques have been used to extract or discover knowledge (KDD). However the exponential explosion of possible patterns defeats simple searches and so there is increasing interest in using heuristic methods, such as evolutionary computation, in data mining [Freitas, 1999]. Additionally in many cases Machine Learning techniques based on a single paradigm have not been sufficient and so people have investigated mechanisms for combining them [Kittler and Roli, 2001; Gunatilaka and Baertlein, 2001]. There are many possible interpretations of data fusion [Kelly, 1999], however existing classifier fusion techniques, such as committees of experts [Jacobs et al., 1991], bagging [Breiman, 1996] and boosting [Freund and Schapire, 1996], typically combine experts of the same type using a fixed way of combining their predictions. E.g. all the experts might be feed forward neural networks whose outputs are: simply summed, a weighted sum might be calculated, or a majority vote taken, to give the collective view of the classifier ensemble. That is, the fusion technique optimises the individual experts (e.g. using back propagation) while keeping the combination rule fixed. An interesting alternative is to pretrain the experts and optimise the combination rule. With a small number of experts [Sirlantzis et al., 2001] and a simple voting rule it might be feasible to try all possible combinations of experts. However there are 2^n (where n =

J.A. Foster et al. (Eds.): EuroGP 2002, LNCS 2278, pp. 60–70, 2002.
© Springer-Verlag Berlin Heidelberg 2002

number of experts) possible combinations in such a voting scheme. Binary GAs have been used to find good committees of experts [Opitz and Shavlik, 1996; Kupinski and Anastasio, 1999; Kupinski et al., 2000]. However genetic programming gives us the ability not only of deciding which experts to use in the ensemble but also how their predictions are to be combined. Because the individual experts are pretrained the GP does not need to know how they were trained and so has the ability to form superior ensembles of heterogeneous classifiers [Langdon and Buxton, 2001b].

Here we are particularly interested in data rich cheminformatics applications where we wish to be able to predict how chemicals, particularly potential drugs, will behave. Note that although we use training data given by high throughput screening (HTS) tests of real chemicals, the classifiers we evolve are able to classify not only existing chemicals but also to generalise to related areas of chemical space in particular (we hope) to virtual chemicals. I.e. chemicals that do not yet exist but which could be manufactured if predictions indicate they might be useful drugs.

Intelligent classification techniques, such as artificial neural networks (ANN), have had limited success at predicting potential drug activity. However we have shown genetic programming is able to fuse different neural networks to obtain better predictions [Langdon et al., 2001]. We shall show our system can also be used with C4.5 decision trees and indeed can combine C4.5 and ANN on this pharmaceutical classification task, predicting inhibition of a P450 enzyme. (GP achieves ensembles with the same performance as the with the ANN but using poorer initial classifiers.)

The system and problem have already been described in [Langdon and Buxton, 2001c] and [Langdon et al., 2001] so only summaries of Receiver Operating Characteristics (ROC) and the application are given in Sects. 2 and 3. Section 4 describes how the base classifiers were trained, while Sect. 5 summarises the evolutionary system. The results (Sect. 6) are followed by a discussion, including over fitting, (Sect. 7) and conclusions (Sect. 8).

2 Receiver Operating Characteristics

Any classifier makes a trade off between catching positive examples and raising false alarms. Where the costs of these are not known, difficult to determine or subject to change, it may be useful to be able to tune the classifier to favour one over the other. The Receiver Operating Characteristics (ROC) of a classifier provides a helpful way of illustrating this trade off [Swets et al., 2000].

Briefly any binary classifier can be characterised by two scalars. Its "true positive" rate (TP) and its "false positive" rate (FP). I.e. the fraction of positive examples it correctly classifies and the fraction of negative examples it gets wrong (false alarms). When plotted against each other TP v. FP lie inside a unit square. An ideal classifier has TP = 1 and FP = 0. I.e. the upper left corner of the square (see Fig. 3). Many classifiers have an adjustable threshold parameter. This allows the user to trade off TP (sensitivity) against FP (1 - specificity). By varying the threshold the FP,TP point traces a curve. A good classifier will have a curve which lies as close to (0,1) as possible. A very poor classifier's ROC will lie near the diagonal (0,0) – (1,1). It is common to use the area under the ROC as a measure of the classifier's performance.

[Scott et al., 1998] suggests the "Maximum Realisable Receiver Operating Characteristics" for a combination of classifiers is the convex hull of their individual ROCs, cf. also [Provost and Fawcett, 2001]. ("Lotteries" in game theory [Binmore, 1990] are somewhat similar.) However we have already shown GP can in some cases do better, including on Scott's own benchmarks [Langdon and Buxton, 2001a] and this pharmaceutical classification task (fusing ANN) [Langdon et al., 2001].

3   The Pharmaceutical Data

Details of the preparation of pharmaceutical data are given in [Langdon et al., 2001]. Briefly many thousands of chemicals have been tested to see if they inhibit one of the P450 enzymes involved in metabolism. This is an important screen in early drug discovery since P450 inhibition could be expected to lead to an adverse drug reaction were any of those molecules to make it to the clinical drug development stage (when a compound is first evaluated in humans).

The chemicals are a very diverse set, covering the most common types of drug or drug-like compounds, such as would be found in the big pharmaceutical company compound banks. Hence they probably have a range of inhibition mechanisms. Some 'primary' enzyme inhibition mechanisms are likely to be much more frequent within the tested set of compounds than others. This is precisely the kind of situation which can defeat individual classifiers.

Chemicals which gave inconsistent screening results were discarded. The remainder were separated into "active" (inhibitory) and "inactive". These were separately clustered (based on primary chemical structure) into 445 active clusters and 1811 inactive clusters. The chemical at the centre of each of these 2256 clusters was chosen to represent its cluster. Using a collection of in-house and publicly available software, a total of 699 numeric chemical features were computed for each centroid molecule. 1500 compounds (300 inhibitory, 1200 inactives) were selected for use as the training set, whilst the remaining 756 were retained as a separate "holdout" set. The 699 features were divided into 15 groups of about 50 each.

4   Training the Neural Networks and Decision Trees

Details how Clementine was used to train 4 feed forward neural networks on each of the 15 groups of features were given in [Langdon et al., 2001]. The training of the C4.5 decision trees was deliberately kept similar.

An imbalance between positive and negatives is common in many data mining tasks. However many machine learning techniques work best when trained on

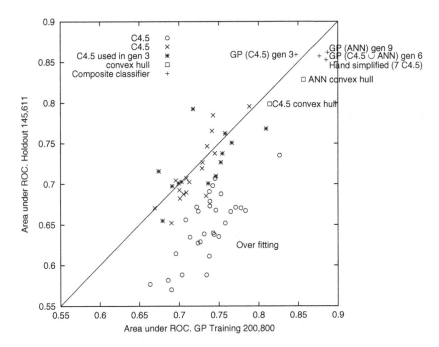

Fig. 1. Area under ROC (AUROC) curve of P450 decision trees (C4.5). Points below the diagonal indicate possible over training. 30 decision trees ⊙ which do not generalise were not used by GP. The convex hulls of the remaining 30 and the 60 neural networks are plotted as □. The AUROC of evolved classifiers is plotted with +.

"balanced data sets", i.e. data sets containing an equal mix of inhibitory and inactive examples. The 1500 compounds were used to create four data sets. Each contained the same 300 inhibitory chemicals and 300 different inactive chemicals. That is, each data set was balanced. As with the ANN, each decision tree was trained on one of the 15 groups of attributes selected from one of the four balanced data sets. Making a total of 60 classifiers.

The C4.5 decision trees were generated by Clementine (5.01) using "Build rule". Following problems with over fitting we used the following expert options: windowing (5% increment 1%), persistence 10, stop when reach accuracy of 70% and pruning (min unpruned 40%, tightness of fit 10%). Unfortunately many of the models still had poor generalisation (Clementine 6.0 is improved in this respect). The performance of each decision tree was measured on both the training and holdout sets, see Fig. 1. Those which performed significantly worse on the hold out data were not used by the GP (one sided test [Hanley and McNeil, 1983] p=0.1 and r=0). This left 30 decision trees. These were made available to genetic programming as functions.

5   Genetic Programming Configuration

The genetic programming data fusion system is deliberately identical (except for the choice of random constants) to that described in [Langdon and Buxton, 2001c], cf. Table 1.

5.1   Function and Terminal Sets

In order to use the decision trees (and neural networks) within GP they were exported from Clementine as C code and packaged up and presented to GP as 30 (60) problem specific functions. The GP is run separately from Clementine using 30, 60 or 90 files (depending if fusing C4.5 trees, ANN or both). There is one file for each decision tree or ANN. Each contains the classification given by the corresponding decision tree (or ANN) for the current chemical. Clementine decision trees not only return a predicted class but also their confidence. Prior to running the GP, the class and confidence were combined into a single floating point value between zero and one. For both classes, if the decision tree has zero confidence a value of 0.5 is used. If the chemical is predicted to have an inhibitory effect; as the confidence increases to 1.0 the value increases linearly to 1.0 (and decreases to 0 if inactive). This becomes the value returned by the function inside the GP system (with a neutral adjustable threshold bias).

Normally the output of a neural network is converted into a binary classification (i.e. the chemical is inhibitory or is inactive) by testing to see if the value is greater or less than 0.5. This gives a single point in the ROC square. I.e. one trade off between catching all positives but raising too many false alarms. However, for neural networks, decision trees or other classifiers, we can change this trade off. So that instead of getting a single point, we get a complete curve in the ROC square. This is achieved by replacing the fixed value of 0.5 by a tunable threshold. By continuously varying the threshold from 0 to 1, the output of any of the classifiers is biased from saying every chemical is inactive, through the usable range, to catching all positive examples but being 100% wrong on the negative examples (by saying all chemicals are inhibitory). In fact we leave the choice of suitable operating point to the GP, by making it the argument of the function. These arguments are treated like any other by the GP and so can be any valid arithmetic operation, including the base classifiers themselves.

The terminals or leaves of the trees being evolved by the GP are either constants or the adjustable threshold "T" (see Table 1).

5.2   Representation and Genetic Operators

Following earlier work [Jacobs et al., 1991; Soule, 1999; Langdon, 1998] each GP individual is composed of five trees. Each of which is capable of acting as a classifier. The use of signed real numbers makes it natural to combine classifiers by adding them. I.e. the classification of the "ensemble" is the sum of the answers given by the five trees. Should a single classifier be very confident about its answer this allows it to "out vote" all the others. Note that although this is like

Table 1. GP P450 Data Fusion Parameters

Objective:	Evolve a combination of decision trees and/or neural networks with maximum ROC convex hull area on P450 inhibition prediction
Function set:	INT FRAC Max Min MaxA MinA MUL ADD DIV SUB IFLTE 30 C4.5 (60 ANN) trained on P450 data
Terminal set:	T 0 0.5 1 plus 100 unique random constants -1..1
Fitness:	Area under convex hull of 11 ROC points (plus 0,0 and 1,1)
Selection:	generational (non elitist), tournament size 7
Wrapper:	$\geq 0 \Rightarrow$ inhibitory, inactive otherwise
Pop Size:	500
No size or depth limits	
Initial pop:	Each individual comprises five trees each created by ramped half-and-half (5:8) (half terminals are constants, each initial tree limited to 300)
Parameters:	50% size fair crossover [Langdon, 2000], crossover fragments $\leq$ 30 50% mutation (point 22.5%, constants 22.5%, shrink 2.5% sub-tree 2.5%)
Termination:	generation 50

some neural network "ensembles", the GP can combine the supplied classifiers in an almost totally arbitrary, non-linear way. It is not constrained to a weighted linear sum of all or even a subset of them.

Following [Angeline, 1998] and others, we use a high mutation rate and a mixture of different mutation operators. To avoid bloat, we also use size fair crossover [Langdon, 2000], see Table 1.

5.3   GP Training Data and Fitness Function

The 1500 examples used to train the decision trees were randomly split into 1000 to be used to train the GP and 500 (containing 100 inhibitory chemicals) kept back as a verification set. NB performance was finally evaluated on the 756 compounds which had not been used either by the GP or by Clementine.

Fitness of each individual is calculated on the training set. The adjustable threshold "T" is set to values 0.1 apart, starting at 0 and increasing to 1. For each setting, the evolved program is used to predict the activity of each chemical in the training set. These predictions are compared with measured activity. The proportions of inhibitory chemicals correctly predicted (TP) and the proportion of inactive ones incorrectly predicted (FP) are calculated. Each TP,FP pair gives a point on an ROC curve. The fitness of the classifier is the area under the convex hull of these (plus the fixed points 0,0 and 1,1).

6   Results

Figure 2 plots (for populations using 30 C4.5 decision trees, 60 ANN and both) the evolution of fitness of the best individual (on the training set) in the population. For the best in the population, the area under ROC on the verification set was also measured (lines with crosses in Fig. 2). The gap in performance on the training and verification sets is large and grows. This indicates GP is responsible for some over training. Analysis of these and other runs suggests the degree of over fitting is not well correlated to program size but instead length of training seems to be a better indicator. Accordingly, when we chose individual programs to represent the whole run, we took the best of each population from near the beginning of the run where the performance on the verification set was high. (These are shown with vertical lines in Fig. 2 at generations 3, 6 and 9.) Only then was their performance assessed on the holdout set. In the runs where the population contained ANN there was a marked drop in performance predicted by the verification set, indicating the ANN were themselves responsible for some over fitting. The drop in the C4.5 only population was smaller.

The performance of these three programs are not significantly different (plotted in Fig. 1 with +). However they are significantly better than, not only each classifier in their function set, but also the convex hull of these base classifiers (two □ in Fig. 1). An evolved program was simplified by hand to yield a simple addition rule of similar performance (also plotted in Fig. 1 with +). Even if we had been prepared to restrict the ensemble to this particular type of combination rule, the search problem is still far from trivial (2^{30}, 2^{60} and 2^{90}).

Figure 3 shows the ROC of the evolved classifiers, measured on the holdout set. Figure 3 also shows, for comparison, the ROC of the classifier produced by taking the convex hull of the 30 C4.5 decision trees and 60 ANNs (generated on the training data). Of course it is convex on the training data, but need not be on the hold out data. Note the convex hull of the ANN contains that of the C4.5, so it is also the convex hull of the ANN and C4.5 together.

7 Over Fitting

Over fitting is to some extent endemic in Machine Learning and it is no surprise to see it in GP. In fact it goes further than that. There is a case that natural evolution itself tends to over fit. When Darwin says finches have adapted to a particular type of food, an alternative view is they have become over fitted to their current environmental niche (i.e. their training data). Taken out of the niche and exposed to a new environment they may fare less well. Alternatively if the niche itself changes they may have to re-adapt or become extinct.

GP's environment is the fitness cases. Where these are small and static we must fear GP will over fit. If large volumes of data are available for training then it should all be used. Sampling [Gathercole and Ross, 1997; Gathercole, 1998; Teller and Andre, 1997] and/or caching [Handley, 1994; Langdon, 1998] techniques can be used to reduce run time.

The use of size fair crossover [Langdon, 2000] and mutation means we do not see explosive increase in program size (bloat [Langdon et al., 1999]) and preliminary experiments suggest over fitting is more closely related to number of generations over which the population has been exposed to the same environment than to the size of the programs. This supports [Schmiedle et al., 2001]'s

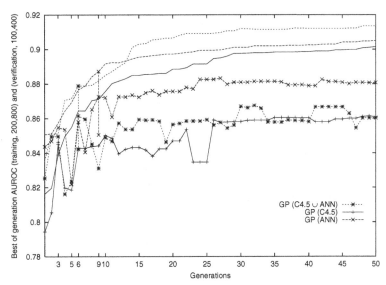

Fig. 2. Evolution of fitness for P450 inhibition prediction GP runs using decision trees, neural networks and both. Plot shows performance on training set (no crosses) and verification set (crosses) for best of each generation. Vertical lines show generation (3, 6 and 9) selected as output of each run (lower point is performance on holdout set).

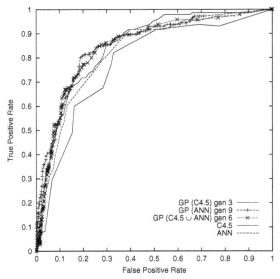

Fig. 3. Receiver Operating Characteristics of evolved composite classifiers (holdout data). In all 3 cases the evolved classifier lies outside the the convex hull of their base classifiers (lines without crosses). Note the convex hull classifiers are determined on the training set and so need no longer be convex when used to classify the holdout data. Also note the hull of the decision trees lies almost entirely within than of the ANN.

suggestion for pragmatic limits on run time, as an alternative to parsimony pressures (i.e. fitness rewards for smaller programs).

In traditional neural networks etc., over fitting may tackled by "regularization" parameters, which bias the learning system to produce simple or smooth functions. [Davidson et al., 2000] shows regularization can be incorporated into GP, provided we are prepared to restrict the nature of models we will allow to evolve or if we have some reason for preferring smooth or simple functions.

While [Sollich and Krogh, 1996] suggests it might be good to allow individual base classifiers to over fit we have seen little to support this. In preliminary experiments, over fit base classifiers dragged the population in the same direction as themselves, leading to the evolution of similarly over fit ensembles. This may be due to using the same data to train both the base classifiers and the GP, but initial experiments using different training data for the base and evolved classifiers were not encouraging (possibly due to insufficient training data).

8   Conclusions

In [Langdon and Buxton, 2001a] we showed, using [Scott et al., 1998]'s own bench marks, that genetic programming can do better than the receiver operating characteristics (ROC) convex hull both in theory and practice. Nevertheless we cannot guarantee GP will always do better and so it is important to demonstrate it on interesting applications. Here we have shown (cf. Figs. 1 and 3) that GP can be used in a large classification application (related to drug discovery) to automatically create ensembles of decision trees, neural networks and indeed both. Even though GP starts with poorer classifiers (all the C4.5 ROCs lie within the convex hull of the previously used neural network classifiers), ensembles of similar performance have been automatically evolved. While GP allows arbitrary combination rules, it can also be used to aid finding simple rules.

References

[Angeline, 1998] P.J. Angeline. Multiple interacting programs: A representation for evolving complex behaviors. *Cybernetics and Systems*, 29(8):779–806.

[Binmore, 1990] K. Binmore. *Fun and Games*. D. C. Heath, Lexington, MA, USA.

[Breiman, 1996] L. Breiman. Bagging predictors. *Machine Learning*, 24:123–140.

[Davidson et al., 2000] J.W. Davidson, D.A. Savic, and G.A. Walters. Rainfall runoff modeling using a new polynomial regression method. In *Proc. 4th Int. Conf. on Hydroinformatics*, Iowa City.

[Freitas, 1999] A.A. Freitas. Data mining with evolutionary algorithms: Research directions. Technical Report WS-99-06, AAAI, Orlando.

[Freund and Schapire, 1996] Y. Freund and R.E. Schapire. Experiments with a new boosting algorithm. In *Proc. 13th ICML*, pp148–156. Morgan Kaufmann.

[Gathercole and Ross, 1997] C. Gathercole and P. Ross. Tackling the boolean even N parity problem with genetic programming and limited-error fitness. In J.R. Koza et al., eds., *Proc. GP'97*, pp119–127, Stanford University. Morgan Kaufmann.

[Gathercole, 1998] C. Gathercole. *An Investigation of Supervised Learning in Genetic Programming*. PhD thesis, University of Edinburgh, 1998.

[Gunatilaka and Baertlein, 2001] A.H. Gunatilaka and B.A. Baertlein. Feature-level and decision level fusion of noncoincidently sampled sensors for land mine detection. *IEEE Transactions on Pattern Analysis and Machine Intelligence*, 23(6):577–589.

[Handley, 1994] S. Handley. On the use of a directed acyclic graph to represent a population of computer programs. In *Proc. WCCI'94*, pp154–159, Orlando. IEEE.

[Hanley and McNeil, 1983] J.A. Hanley and B.J. McNeil. A method of comparing the areas under ROC curves derived from the same cases. *Radiology*, 148:839–843.

[Jacobs et al., 1991] R.A. Jacobs, M.I. Jordon, S.J. Nowlan, and G.E. Hinton. Adaptive mixtures of local experts. *Neural Computation*, 3:79–87.

[Kelly, 1999], G. Kelly. Data fusion: from primary metrology to process measurement. In V. Piuri and M. Savino, eds., *Proc. 16th Instrumentation and Measurement Technology Conference. IMTC/99.*, vol 3, pp1325–1329, Venice, Italy. IEEE.

[Kittler and Roli, 2001] J. Kittler and F. Roli, eds.. *Second International Conference on Multiple Classifier Systems*, vol 2096 of *LNCS*, Cambridge. Springer Verlag.

[Kupinski and Anastasio, 1999] M. A. Kupinski and M. A. Anastasio. Multiobjective genetic optimization of diagnostic classifiers with implications for generating ROC curves. *IEEE Transactions on Medical Imaging*, 18(8):675–685.

[Kupinski et al., 2000] M.A. Kupinski, M.A. Anastasio, and M.L. Giger. Multiobjective genetic optimization of diagnostic classifiers used in the computerized detection of mass lesions in mammography. In K.M. Hanson, ed., *SPIE Medical Imaging Conference*, vol 3979, San Diego.

[Langdon and Buxton, 2001a] W.B. Langdon and B.F. Buxton. Genetic programming for combining classifiers. In L. Spector *et al.*, eds., *GECCO-2001*, pp66–73, San Francisco. Morgan Kaufmann.

[Langdon and Buxton, 2001b] W.B. Langdon and B.F. Buxton. Genetic programming for improved receiver operating characteristics. In J. Kittler and F. Roli, eds., *Second International Conference on Multiple Classifier System*, pp68–77.

[Langdon and Buxton, 2001c] W.B. Langdon and B.F. Buxton. Evolving receiver operating characteristics for data fusion. In J.F. Miller *at al.*, eds., *EuroGP'2001*, vol 2038 of *LNCS*, pp87–96, Lake Como, Italy. Springer.

[Langdon et al., 1999] W.B. Langdon, T. Soule, R. Poli, and J.A. Foster. The evolution of size and shape. In L. Spector *at al.*, eds., *Advances in Genetic Programming 3*, ch 8, pp163–190. MIT Press.

[Langdon et al., 2001] W.B. Langdon, S.J. Barrett, and B.F. Buxton. Genetic programming for combining neural networks for drug discovery. In *WSC6, 6th World Conference on Soft Computing in Industrial Applications*, Springer-Verlag. Forthcoming.

[Langdon, 1998] W.B. Langdon. *Genetic Programming and Data Structures*. Kluwer.

[Langdon, 2000] W.B. Langdon. Size fair and homologous tree genetic programming crossovers. *Genetic Programming and Evolvable Machines*, 1(1/2):95–119.

[Opitz and Shavlik, 1996] D.W. Opitz and J.W. Shavlik. Actively searching for an effective neural-network ensemble. *Connection Science*, 8(3-4):337–353.

[Provost and Fawcett, 2001] F. Provost and T. Fawcett. Robust classification for imprecise environments. *Machine Learning*, 42(3):203–231.

[Schmiedle et al., 2001] F. Schmiedle, D. Grosse, R. Drechsler, and B. Becker. Too much knowledge hurts: Acceleration of genetic programs for learning heuristics. In B. Reusch, ed., *Computational Intelligence : Theory and Applications*, vol 2206 of *LNCS*, pp479–491, Dortmund, Germany. 7th Fuzzy Days, Springer.

[Scott et al., 1998] M.J.J. Scott, M. Niranjan, and R.W. Prager. Realisable classifiers: Improving operating performance on variable cost problems. In P.H. Lewis and M.S. Nixon, eds., Proc. 9th British Machine Vision Conference, vol 1, pp304–315, University of Southampton, UK.

[Sirlantzis et al., 2001] K. Sirlantzis, M.C. Fairhurst, and M.S. Hoque. Genetic algorithms for multi-classifier system configuration: A case study in character recognition. In J. Kittler and F. Roli, eds., Second International Conference on Multiple Classifier System, pp99–108.

[Sollich and Krogh, 1996] P. Sollich and A. Krogh. Learning with ensembles: How over-fitting can be useful. In D.S. Touretzky et al., eds., Advances in Neural Information Processing Systems, vol 8, pp190–196. MIT Press.

[Soule, 1999] T. Soule. Voting teams: A cooperative approach to non-typical problems using genetic programming. In W. Banzhaf et al., eds., GECCO-1999, vol 1, pp916–922, Orlando. Morgan Kaufmann.

[Swets et al., 2000] J.A. Swets, R.M. Dawes, and J. Monahan. Better decisions through science. Scientific American, pp70–75, October.

[Teller and Andre, 1997] A. Teller and D. Andre. Automatically choosing the number of fitness cases: The rational allocation of trials. In J.R. Koza et al., eds., GP'97.

Evolving Fuzzy Decision Trees with Genetic Programming and Clustering

Jeroen Eggermont

Leiden Institute of Advanced Computer Science,
Universiteit Leiden,
P.O. Box 9512, 2300 RA Leiden,
The Netherlands
{jeggermo}@liacs.nl

Abstract. In this paper we present a new fuzzy decision tree representation for data classification using genetic programming. The new fuzzy representation utilizes fuzzy clusters for handling continuous attributes. To make optimal use of the fuzzy classifications of this representation an extra fitness measure is used. The new fuzzy representation will be compared, using several machine learning data sets, to a similar non-fuzzy representation as well as to some other evolutionary and non-evolutionary algorithms from literature.

1 Introduction

In recent years data mining problems have attracted the attention of the evolutionary computation community (especially since the rise of genetic programming (GP) [9,1]). In this paper we focus our attention on one of the application areas of data mining: classification (also known as categorical prediction).

In data classification the goal is to build or find a model in order to predict the category of categorical data based on some predictor variables. The model is usually built using heuristics (e.g., entropy) or some kind of supervised learning algorithm. Probably the most natural form for a classification model is the decision tree.

In this paper we will present a new tree-based genetic programming representation for classification using fuzzy logic. Fuzzy logic is a variation of traditional Boolean logic and is based on fuzzy set theory. In a Boolean view of the world everything is either true or false, black or white. This does not conform to the real world in which many shades of grey exist. In the traditional set theory an element is either a member of a set (and has all the corresponding characteristics) or not. In fuzzy set theory an element can be a partial member of a fuzzy set. The extent to which an element is member of a fuzzy set is measured in a membership value. The membership value of an element for a set is determined by the *membership function* μ_F of a fuzzy set F. This membership function is unique for every set and tells for each element to what extent it is a member of that set.

J.A. Foster et al. (Eds.): EuroGP 2002, LNCS 2278, pp. 71–82, 2002.

The first aim of our new *fuzzy* GP classifier is to evolve fuzzy decision trees which should be more intuitive as they can represent the vagueness of the real world. The second aim of our *fuzzy* GP is to offer classification accuracy that is similar or better than that of other (evolutionary) decision tree algorithms. The fuzzy decision tree representation we designed fuzzifies the continuous attributes so they can be handled in a natural and intuitive manner. Additionally each fuzzy tree found by our GP algorithm determines a fuzzy membership function for each class. We can use the information in the newly discovered fuzzy membership functions to get a better insight in the categories that were classified.

Related work on discovering fuzzy decision trees using tree-based genetic programming was performed by Mendes, Voznika, Freitas and Nievola [11]. They used an innovative co-evolutionary approach with strongly typed genetic programming [12,6] and evolution strategies. Strongly typed genetic programming is used to evolve a population of fuzzy decision trees for binary classification while a $(1 + 5)$-evolution strategy is applied to evolve the fuzzy membership functions for the continuous attributes. The results of their *Co-Evolutionary Fuzzy Rule Miner* (CEFR-MINER) system are very promising and we will compare the results of our own approach to theirs.

The contents of this paper is organized as follows: In Section 2 we describe our fuzzy decision tree representation for genetic programming and introduce a new fitness measure. Then in Section 3 we describe the experimental setup. The results of the experiments are discussed in Section 4. Conclusions and thoughts on future research are reported in Section 5.

2   A GP Representation for Fuzzy Decision Trees

In this section we will describe how we transform a standard decision tree representation into a fuzzy representation and we introduce a new fitness measure.

2.1   The Basis: A Full Atomic Representation

The basis for our *fuzzy* GP representation is a — what we will call *full atomic* — representation which is similar to the standard decision tree representation used by algorithms like C4.5 [14]. The function set (internal nodes) of a *full atomic* tree consists of atoms. Each atom is syntactically a predicate of the form (*variable$_i$ operator value*), where *operator* is a comparing operator (e.g., $\leq$ and $>$ for continuous attributes, $=$ for nominal or Boolean attributes). In the leaf nodes we have a *class assignment* of the form (*class := C*), where C is a category selected from the domain of the variable to be predicted. A small example tree can be seen in Figure 1. A *full atomic* tree classifies an instance I by traversing the tree from root to leaf node. In each non-leaf node an atom is evaluated. If the result is true the right branch is traversed, else the left branch is taken. This is done for all internal nodes until a leaf node containing a *class assignment* node is reached resulting in the classification of the instance.

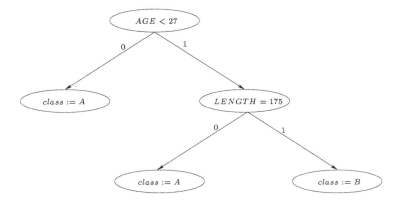

Fig. 1. An example of a *full atomic* tree

In our fuzzy representation the continuous attributes are fuzzified using fuzzy clusters. This means that we no longer need the "crisp" comparison operators ($\leq$, $>$) used by a *full atomic* representation. Instead we only have a function set using atoms of the form ($variable_i = value$), where *value* is nominal valued if $variable_i$ is nominal valued or *value* is a fuzzy term (e.g., *Low, Medium, High, Cold, Warm*) if $variable_i$ is continuous. In order to fuzzify the continuous attributes we first have to cluster them into a finite number of clusters.

2.2 Clustering and Fuzzification

We have chosen to use the same method of clustering and fuzzification as was used for fuzzy association rule mining in [5,15]. This means that we will use a simple K-means clustering algorithm for clustering the continuous predictor variables followed by fuzzification of the clusters. Although we could have used an evolutionary algorithm for clustering we decided on a K-means clustering algorithm since it is fast, easy to implement, deterministic and offers satisfying results.

In our approach all numerical predictor variables with a domain size greater than k are clustered, where k is one of the parameters of the algorithm. The performance of the K-means clustering algorithm is greatly dependent on the choice of the initial cluster centroids as well as instance order. We have therefore chosen to use the *Partition Around Medioids* initialization as proposed by Kaufman [7]. This initialization was (empirically) found to be the best of four classical initialization methods when looking at effectiveness, robustness and convergence speed [13].

For each clustered continuous predictor variable we have now k clusters and their mediods. We can now *fuzzify* the clusters by defining membership functions for each fuzzy cluster. We will use three different types of membership functions as defined in Definition 1.

Definition 1. *Let $F = \{F_1, \ldots, F_k\}$ be the set of fuzzy clusters for a particular quantitative attribute and let $M = \{m_1, \ldots, m_k\}$ be the set of its corresponding Medioids, then we define the following fuzzy membership functions:*

$$\mu_{F_1}(x) = \begin{cases} 1 & \text{if } x \leq m_1 \text{ ,} \\ \frac{m_2 - x}{m_2 - m_1} & \text{if } m_1 < x < m_2 \text{ ,} \\ 0 & \text{if } x \geq m_2 \text{ ;} \end{cases} \tag{1}$$

$$\mu_{F_i}(x) = \begin{cases} 0 & \text{if } x \leq m_{i-1} \text{ ,} \\ \frac{m_{i-1} - x}{m_{i-1} - m_i} & \text{if } m_{i-1} < x < m_i \text{ ,} \\ 1 & \text{if } x = m_i \text{ ,} \\ \frac{m_{i+1} - x}{m_{i+1} - m_i} & \text{if } m_i < x < m_{i+1} \text{ ,} \\ 0 & \text{if } x \geq m_{i+1} \text{ ;} \end{cases} \tag{2}$$

$$\mu_{F_k}(x) = \begin{cases} 0 & \text{if } x \leq m_{k-1} \text{ ,} \\ \frac{m_{k-1} - x}{m_{k-1} - m_k} & \text{if } m_{k-1} < x < m_k \text{ ,} \\ 1 & \text{if } x \geq m_k \text{ .} \end{cases} \tag{3}$$

where $i = 2, 3, \ldots, k - 1$.

A graphical representation of the fuzzy membership functions as defined in Definition 1 are shown in Figure 2. Note that the distances between the different Medioids m_i are not necessarily equal. By using simple triangular membership functions instead of the often used trapezium shaped functions we avoid the need for extra parameters.

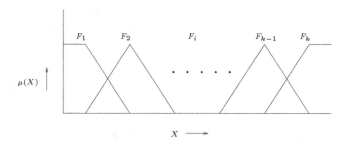

Fig. 2. The k fuzzy membership functions $F_1, \ldots, F_k$ for a continuous attribute

A small example tree of the *fuzzy* representation can be seen in Figure 3. When we classify an instance I using a *full atomic* tree the result is a single class. When we use a *fuzzy* tree the result is a set of class membership values $P = \{\rho(c)\}$ for each possible class c. Each membership value $\rho(c)$ indicates the extend to which an instance is classified as a member of a class c. In each non-leaf node N with left branch child L and right branch child R the fuzzy atom is evaluated resulting in a fuzzy membership value $\mu_N(I)$. We can now recursively calculate the set of class membership values P_N for this node by using

$$\rho_N(c) = (1 - \mu_N(I)) * \rho_L(c) + \mu_N(I) * \rho_R(c) \tag{4}$$

for each class c. When a leaf node containing a class assignment $(class := c_i)$ is reached this node returns a class membership value of one for class c_i and zero for every other class. Thus the class membership function for class A in the tree in Figure 3 is:

$$\rho(A) = (1 - \mu_{Young}(AGE)) + (\mu_{Young}(AGE) * (1 - \mu_{Medium}(LENGTH))) \tag{5}$$

and the class membership function for class B is:

$$\rho(B) = \mu_{Young}(AGE) * \mu_{Medium}(LENGTH). \tag{6}$$

We have chosen addition $(+)$ as a fuzzy OR to join the results of two subtrees and multiplication $(*)$ as a fuzzy AND operator. This way the sum of class membership values for an instance equals one. In fact, for each class the fuzzy tree determines a fuzzy membership function. Finally the class for an instance can be determined by the class with the highest membership value.

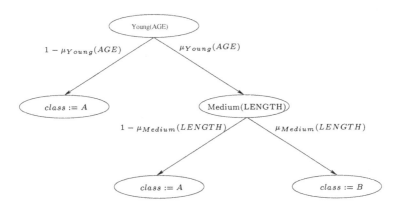

Fig. 3. An example of a *fuzzy* tree

Example 1. Observe the fuzzy tree in Figure 3. Suppose the want to classify an instance I with attributes I_{AGE} and I_{LENGTH} and the fuzzy membership function $\mu_{Young}(I_{AGE})$ returns 0.9 and $\mu_{Medium}(I_{LENGTH})$ return 0.3. We can then calculate the class member ship values $\rho(A)$ and $\rho(B)$ using the fuzzy membership functions in Equations 5 and 6. This gives us:

$$\rho(A) = (1 - 0.9) + (0.9 * (1 - 0.3)) = 0.73$$

and

$$\rho(B) = 0.9 * 0.3 = 0.27$$

Thus in this case we could say that the tree in Figure 3 predicts the class of instance I to be A (since $0.73 > 0.27$).

2.3   A New Fitness Measure

The goal of most algorithms used for data classification is to minimize the number of misclassifications (or maximize the number of correct classifications). For evolutionary algorithms this can be done by using a fitness function similar to:

$$fitness_{standard}(x) = \sum_{r \in trainingset} \chi(x, r), \qquad (7)$$

where $\chi(x, r)$ is defined as:

$$\chi(x, r) = \begin{cases} 1 & \text{if } x \text{ classifies record } r \text{ incorrectly;} \\ 0 & \text{otherwise.} \end{cases} \qquad (8)$$

However in the case of our fuzzy representation each individual returns a set of class membership values for each record to be classified. We can use these membership values in order to try to compute a more precise fitness value:

$$fitness_{precision}(x) = \sum_{r \in trainingset} (1 - \rho_x(r)), \qquad (9)$$

where $\rho_x(r)$ is the membership value for the target class of record r returned by individual x. Note that this *precision* fitness equals the standard fitness for non-fuzzy representations.

We used a structured/hierarchical fitness consisting of three fitness measures for selection in our *fuzzy* GP algorithm. The primary fitness value is the computed *precision fitness*, the secondary fitness value is the *standard fitness* and the last fitness value is the number of tree nodes in our decision tree. When the fitness of two individuals is to be compared we first look at the *precision fitness*. If the two individuals happen to have the same *precision fitness* we look at the secondary fitness value which is the number of misclassifications (*standard fitness*). If two individuals have the same *precision fitness* and *standard fitness* we compare the number of nodes in each individual. We only used the *precision fitness* measure during the evolutionary process. For selecting the best individual of an evolutionary run we first look at the *standard fitness* and if necessary the number of tree nodes (as a secondary fitness measure).

3   Experiments

We will compare our *fuzzy* GP representation to some other evolutionary and machine learning algorithms using several data sets from the UCI machine learning data set repository[1]. An overview of the different data sets can be seen in Table 1.

Table 1. An overview of the data sets used in the experiments

data set	records	attributes	classes	nr. of folds
Australian (statlog)	690	14	2	10
Pima indians diabetes	768	8	2	10
Ionosphere	351	34	2	10
Heart (statlog)	270	13	2	10
Iris	150	4	3	10

Apart from evaluating our GP system using the fuzzy membership functions described in Section 2.2 we can also use the discovered clusters in the traditional "Boolean" way. This variant of our GP system using a classical cluster approach will be called *cluster* GP.

In all experiments $k = 3$ was used for clustering. This allows for easy to read rules (e.g., we can use *Low, Medium, High* as fuzzy values). The settings used for our GP system are displayed in Table 2. Most surprising is probably the high mutation rate (0.9) we used. The reason for choosing this high mutation rate is to explore a larger part of the search space. Early experiments using smaller mutation rates (e.g., 0.1, 0.3, 0.5, 0.7) showed that only a small number of the evaluated individuals was unique (sometimes only 15%). In our GP system we use the standard GP recombination operators for trees. The mutation operator replaces a subtree with a randomly created subtree and the crossover operator exchanges/replaces subtrees between two individuals. The population was initialized using the ramped half-and-half initialization method to create a combination of full and non-full trees with a maximum tree depth of six. We used a generational model (comma strategy) with population size of 100 and a offspring size of 200. Parents were chosen by using tournament selection. We did not use elitism as the best individual was stored outside the population. Each newly created individual, whether through initialization or recombination, was automatically pruned to a maximum number of 63 nodes.

A single GP implementation was used for both *fuzzy* and *cluster* representation. It was programmed using the *Evolving Objects* library (EOlib) [8]. EOlib is an Open Source C++ library for all forms of evolutionary computation and is available from `http://eodev.sourceforge.net`.

---

[1] `http://www.ics.uci.edu/~{}mlearn/MLRepository.html`

Table 2. The main GP parameters

Parameter	Value
Population Size	100
Initialization	ramped half-and-half
Initial maximum tree depth	6
Maximum number of nodes	63
Parent Selection	Tournament Selection
Tournament Size	5
Evolutionary model	(μ, λ)
Offspring Size	200
Crossover Rate	0.9
Crossover Type	swap subtree
Mutation Rate	0.9
Mutation Type	branch mutation
Stop condition	99 generations

4   Results

Each algorithm is evaluated using n-fold cross-validation and the performance is the average misclassification error over n folds. In n-fold cross-validation the total data set is divided into n parts. Each part is chosen once as the testset while the other $n-1$ parts form the trainingset. In order to compare our results to other evolutionary techniques we will also mention the results of two other evolutionary classification systems: CEFR-MINER [11] and ESIA [10] as reported in these respective papers. CEFR-MINER is also a GP system for finding fuzzy decision trees and ESIA builds crisp decision trees using a genetic algorithm. We will also mention the results of C4.5 and its bagged and boosted versions as reported by Freund and Shapire [4] in order to compare our results to a non-evolutionary decision tree algorithm.

We performed 10 independent runs for our two GP algorithms to obtain the results (presented in Tables 3, 4, 5, 6 and 7). When available from the literature the results of CEFR-MINER, ESIA and C4.5 are reported. For two data sets (Australian and Heart) no results were reported forC4.5 and its bagged and boosted versions. In those two instances, marked with a *, we applied the data set to C4.5 ourselves. The best result for each data set is presented in bold.

If we look at the results on the Australian credit data set in Table 3 we see that both our algorithms outperform C4.5 and ESIA. In fact the worst result achieved by our *fuzzy* GP is still better than the result obtained by C4.5.

When we look at the results for the Pima indians diabetes data set in Table 4 we see that the bagged version of C4.5 is clearly the best. Our *fuzzy* GP algorithm takes second place as it is slightly better than the boosted C4.5. Again both *fuzzy* GP and *cluster* GP outperform the standard C4.5 algorithm and ESIA.

Table 3. Average misclassification rates (in %) with standard deviations, minimum and maximum using 10-fold cross-validation for the Australian credit data set

algorithm	average	s.d.	min	max
fuzzy GP	**14.5**	0.5	13.5	15.4
cluster GP	14.8	0.7	13.8	16.1
C4.5 *	15.9			
Bagged C4.5	N/A			
Boosted C4.5	N/A			
CEFR-MINER	N/A			
ESIA	19.4	0.1		

Table 4. Average misclassification rates (in %) with standard deviations, minimum and maximum using 12-fold cross-validation for the Pima indians diabetes data set

algorithm	average	s.d.	min	max
fuzzy GP	25.6	0.7	25.0	27.3
cluster GP	26.9	0.6	25.4	27.6
C4.5	28.4			
Bagged C4.5	**24.4**			
Boosted C4.5	25.7			
CEFR-MINER	N/A			
ESIA	29.8	0.2		

Table 5. Average misclassification rates (in %) with standard deviations, minimum and maximum using 10-fold cross-validation for the ionosphere data set

algorithm	average	s.d.	min	max
fuzzy GP	10.8	1.1	9.4	13.4
cluster GP	11.5	1.1	9.4	13.1
C4.5	8.9			
Bagged C4.5	6.2			
Boosted C4.5	**5.8**			
CEFR-MINER	11.4	6.0		
ESIA	N/A			

On the ionosphere data set (Table 5) the C4.5 based algorithms are clearly the best. Our *fuzzy* GP performs slightly better than CEFR-MINER and *cluster* GP.

When we look at the results on the heart disease data set in Table 6 we see that CEFR-MINER is clearly the best although it has a high standard deviation. Once again *fuzzy* GP is better than ESIA, C4.5 and *cluster* GP.

The results on the Iris data set in Table 7 were surprising to us as *cluster* GP clearly outperforms all other algorithms. When we look at the other algorithms we see that *fuzzy* GP is slightly better than the other (evolutionary) algorithms

Table 6. Average misclassification rates (in %) with standard deviations, minimum and maximum using 10-fold cross-validation for the heart data set

algorithm	average	s.d.	min	max
fuzzy GP	20.0	1.5	17.8	22.6
cluster GP	21.3	1.3	19.6	23.0
C4.5 *	22.2			
Bagged C4.5				
Boosted C4.5				
CEFR-MINER	**17.8**	7.1		
ESIA	25.6	0.3		

Table 7. Average misclassification rates (in %) with standard deviations, minimum and maximum using 10-fold cross-validation for the Iris data set

algorithm	average	s.d.	min	max
fuzzy GP	4.6	0.7	4.0	6.0
cluster GP	**2.1**	0.2	2.0	2.7
C4.5	5.9			
Bagged C4.5	5.0			
Boosted C4.5	5.0			
CEFR-MINER	4.7	7.1		
ESIA	4.7	0.0		

but not significantly. All evolutionary algorithms perform better than the C4.5 based algorithms which is surprising as well.

5   Conclusions and Future Research

In this paper we have introduced a new representation using clustering and fuzzification for classification problems with genetic programming. By using a *fuzzy* representation we offer a method for dealing with continuous attributes in a natural and intuitive way. This should help in the comprehensibility of the fuzzy decision trees discovered by our algorithm. Additionally the fuzzy membership functions found for the target classes can give additional information about the relations, if any, between those classes.

Looking at the results we notice the good performance of our two GP classifiers. Except for the Ionosphere data set both *fuzzy* GP and *cluster* GP offer performance that is better than or comparable to C4.5 and ESIA. Although *fuzzy* GP also beats the boosted version of C4.5 on two data sets it is clear that both bagging [2] and boosting [4] significantly improve C4.5. When we compare our *fuzzy* GP representation to another GP system using a fuzzy decision tree representation (CEFR-MINER) we see they both offer similar performance. Our *fuzzy* GP representation beats the *cluster* GP representation in all but one data set. However the difference in classification performance is quite small (except for the

Iris data set where *cluster* GP is best). When we look at the computation times *cluster* GP seems to be the better option as *fuzzy* GP takes up to three times as long. This difference in computation time is probably caused by the fact that *fuzzy* GP often has to traverse an entire fuzzy decision tree while *cluster* GP only has to traverse a single path in its crisp decision trees. It is surprising to see the excellent performance of the *cluster* GP algorithm on the Iris data set. On this data set it is significantly better than all the other algorithms which is probably due to "lucky" clustering.

Future research is divided into two parts. The first part is concerned with n-category classification. In this paper we have focussed most of our attention on solving binary classification problems as each n-category classification problem can be transformed into n binary classification problems. Our *fuzzy* GP representation should be able to perform n-category classification without such a transformation (as was done on the Iris data set).

The second part of our future research has to do with methods for improving classification performance. In [3] a fitness adaptation method called *precision* SAW is used to improve the performance of GP on symbolic regression. We think that the same method might be applicable to classification with our *fuzzy* representation. It would also be interesting to see if bagging and boosting can improve the classification performance of our *fuzzy* GP.

References

1. W. Banzhaf, P. Nordin, R.E. Keller, and F.D. Francone. *Genetic Programming – An Introduction; On the Automatic Evolution of Computer Programs and its Applications.* Morgan Kaufmann, 1998.
2. L. Breiman. Bagging predictors. *Machine Learning*, 26(2):123–140, 1996.
3. J. Eggermont and J. I. van Hemert. Adaptive genetic programming applied to new and existing simple regression problems. In J. Miller, M. Tomassini, P.L. Lanzi, C. Ryan, A.G.B. Tetamanzi, and W.B. Langdon, editors, *Proceedings on the Fourth European Conference on Genetic Programming (EuroGP'01)*, volume 2038 of *LNCS*, pages 23–35. Springer-Verlag, 2001.
4. Y. Freund and R.E. Schapire. Experiments with a new boosting algorithm. In *Proc. 13th International Conference on Machine Learning*, pages 148–146. Morgan Kaufmann, 1996.
5. J.M. de Graaf, W.A. Kosters, and J.J.W. Witteman. Interesting fuzzy association rules in quantitative databases. In L. de Raedt and A. Siebes, editors, *5th European Conference on Principles and Practice of Knowledge Discovery in Databases (PKDD'01)*, volume 2168 of *LNAI*, pages 140–151. Springer Verlag, 2001.
6. Th.D. Haynes, D.A. Schoenefeld, and R. L. Wainwright. Type inheritance in strongly typed genetic programming. In P.J. Angeline and K.E. Kinnear, Jr., editors, *Advances in Genetic Programming 2*, chapter 18, pages 359–376. MIT Press, Cambridge, MA, USA, 1996.
7. L. Kaufman. Finding groups in data: An introduction to cluster analysis. In *Finding Groups in Data: An Introduction to Cluster Analysis*. Wiley, New York, 1990.

8. M. Keijzer, J. J. Merelo, G. Romero, and M. Schoenauer. Evolving objects: A general purpose evolutionary computation library. In P. Collet et al., editor, *Proceedings of Evolution Artificielle'01*, LNCS. Springer Verlag, 2001. To appear.

9. J.R. Koza. *Genetic Programming*. MIT Press, 1992.

10. J.J. Liu and J.T. Kwok. An extended genetic rule induction algorithm. In *Proc. of the 2000 Congress on Evolutionary Computation*, pages 458–463, Piscataway, NJ, 2000. IEEE Service Center.

11. R.R.F. Mendes, F.B. Voznika, A.A. Freitas, and J.C. Nievola. Discovering fuzzy classification rules with genetic programming and co-evolution. In L. de Raedt and A.Siebes, editors, *5th European Conference on Principles and Practice of Knowledge Discovery in Databases (PKDD'01)*, volume 2168 of *LNAI*, pages 314–325. Springer Verlag, 2001.

12. D.J. Montana. Strongly typed genetic programming. *Evolutionary Computation*, 3(2):199–230, 1995.

13. J. Peña, J. Lozano, and P. Larrañaga. An empirical comparison of four initialization methods for the k-means algorithm. *Pattern Recognition Letters*, 20:1027–1040, 1999.

14. J.R. Quinlan. *C4.5: Programs for machine learning*. Morgan Kaufmann, 1993.

15. D. Palomo van Es. Fuzzy association rules and promotional sales data. Master's thesis, Leiden University, 2001.

Linear-Graph GP – A New GP Structure

Wolfgang Kantschik[1] and Wolfgang Banzhaf[1,2]

[1] Dept. of Computer Science, University of Dortmund, Dortmund, Germany
[2] Informatik Centrum Dortmund (ICD), Dortmund, Germany

Abstract. In recent years different genetic programming (GP) structures have emerged. Today, the basic forms of representation for genetic programs are tree, linear and graph structures. In this contribution we introduce a new kind of GP structure which we call linear-graph. This is a further development to the linear-tree structure that we developed earlier. We describe the linear-graph structure, as well as crossover and mutation for this new GP structure in detail. We compare linear-graph programs with linear and tree programs by analyzing their structure and results on different test problems.

1 Introduction of Linear-Graph GP

This paper introduces a new representation for GP programs. This new representation, named linear-graph, has been developed with the goal of giving a program the flexibility to choose different execution paths for different inputs. The hope is to create programs of higher complexity, so that we can evolve programs that can compete with the complexity and possibilities of hand-written programs.

Linear-graph is the logical next step after the introduction of linear-tree structure. We have shown the power of the linear-tree structure in [7], but trees are not really the structure of a complex hand written program. Graphs come one step nearer to the control flow of a hand written program, though there is still a long way until we can evolve programs of the complexity of hand-written. Our efforts are devoted is to create a GP-structure able to solve tasks, which cannot be completed with current structures. It is possible for the current structures like,

- (1) tree-based GP [8,9],
- (2) linear-based GP [10,3], or
- (3) graph-based GP[12,2,11],

to create more complex programs and hence solve more complex problems. However we think, that this structures need more time and resources to evolve such programs.

Let us look how the program flow of a hand-coded program could look like. Many programs contain decisions where another part of the program code will be called. After different program parts have been executed they flow together again. If one draws the possible program flows normally it will become a graph.

J.A. Foster et al. (Eds.): EuroGP 2002, LNCS 2278, pp. 83–92, 2002.

Linear-Graph structure

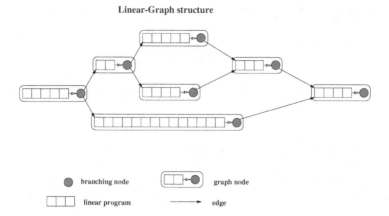

Fig. 1. Individual structure of a linear-graph representation.

So program flow of a linear-graph program is more natural than linear or tree GP-programs and similar to program flow of hand written programs.

In *linear-graph* GP each program $\mathcal{P}$ is represented as a graph. Each node in the graph has two parts, a *linear program* and a *branching node* (see Figure 1). The *linear program* will be executed when the node is reached during the interpretation of the program. After the linear program of a node is executed, a child node is selected according to the branching function of this node. If the node has only one child, this child will be executed. If the node has no child at all execution of the program stops. During the interpretation only the nodes of one path through the graph, from the root node to a leaf will be executed.

The implementation of linear substructures in our uses a variable length list of C instructions that operate on (indexed) variables or constants (see [5]). In linear GP all operations, e.g. a = b + 1.2, implicitly include an assignment of a variable. After a program has been executed its output values are stored in designated variables. The *branching function* is also a C instruction that operates on the same variables as the linear program, but this function only reads these variables. Table 1 contains a collection of all branching functions we used in our runs. Figure 2 shows an example of a short linear program and a branching function for one node in a linear-graph.

1.1 Recombination of Linear-Graph Programs

A crossover operation combines the genetic material from two parent programs by swapping certain program parts. The crossover for a linear-graph program can be realized in two ways. The first possibility is to perform the crossover similar to crossover in tree-based GP by exchanging subtrees (see [1]). Here we would exchange subgraphs instead of subtrees, Figure 3 illustrates the recombination method by exchanging a subgraph. In each parent individual the

Structure of a Linear-Graph node

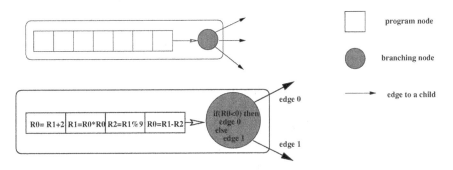

Fig. 2. The structure of a node in a linear-graph GP program (top) and an example node (bottom).

Table 1. All the branching operators used in the runs described here. The data register holds the input data of an individual and is only readable. The result register is the register which is used as output.

branching operator	description of the operator
result register < 0	If result register is less than zero the left child is chosen else the right child.
result register > 0	If result register is greater than zero the left child is chosen else the right child.
result register $<$ operand	If result register is less than the value of an operand the left child is chosen else the right child.
result register $>$ operand	If result register is greater than the value of an operand the left child else the right child.
data register < 0	If data register is less than zero the left child is chosen else the right child.
data register > 0	If data register is greater than zero the left child is chosen else the right child.
data register $<$ operand	If data register is less than the value of an operand the left child is chosen else the right child.
data register $>$ operand	If data register is greater than the value of an operand the left child else the right child.

crossover operator chooses a set of contiguous nodes randomly and exchanges the two subgraphs.

The second possibility is to perform linear crossover. Figure 4 illustrates the linear recombination method. A segment of random position and length is selected in each of the two parents for exchange. If one of the children exceeds the maximum length, crossover with equally sized segments will be performed. The linear crossover is performed for a given percentage of nodes of the graph, we performed this crossover for 10% of the graph nodes.

For linear-graph programs we use both methods but only one at a time. The following algorithm for the recombination of linear-graph programs is applied:

1. Choose the crossover points p_1, p_2 in both individuals.
2. Choose with a given probability $prob_{gx}$ the graph-based crossover method (go to step 3), and with the probability $1 - prob_{gx}$ the linear-based crossover method (go to step 4).
3. If the depth of one of the children does not exceed the maximum depth perform crossover, else go to step 4.
4. Perform linear-based crossover.

In our tests the parameter $prob_{gx}$, which defines the probability whether the graph-based or linear crossover method is used, was set to the 20 %.

1.2   Mutation

The difference between crossover and mutation is that mutation operates on a single program only. After applying recombination to the population a program is chosen with a given probability for mutation. The random mutation operator selects a subset of nodes randomly and changes either a node of a linear program, a branching function, or the number of outgoing edges. In other words, the mutation operator does not generate new linear sequences. The altered program is then placed back into the population.

2   Test Problems

As test problems we use two symbolic regression problems, a sine wave and the Rastrigin function and a classification problem the two chains, see below. The linear-graph structure is compared to a linear GP structure. In Section 3 the results for the regression and classifications problems are presented.

The fitness measure for the regression problem with program p is defined as mean squared error between all given outputs y (here one of the given functions $f(x)$) and the predicted outputs $p(x)$:

$$\text{fitness}(p) = \frac{\sum_{i=1}^{n}(p(x_i) - f(x_i))^2}{n}.$$

We chose 20 fitness cases for the sine function in the range from $[0, 2\pi]$ uniformly and including both endpoints and the Rastrigin function in the range of $[-2, 2]$, with 40 fitness cases.

For classification we used the chain problem [4], Figure 5 visualizes the two classes this problem. Fitness measured is the number of misclassifications. The task of the GP program is to find a relation that connects a given input x to its correct class, here $c \in \{0, 1\}$, so fitness cases can be written as input-output tuples (x, c). The quality of a program depends on its ability to find a generalized mapping deduced from the input-output pairs (x, c) of n fitness cases.

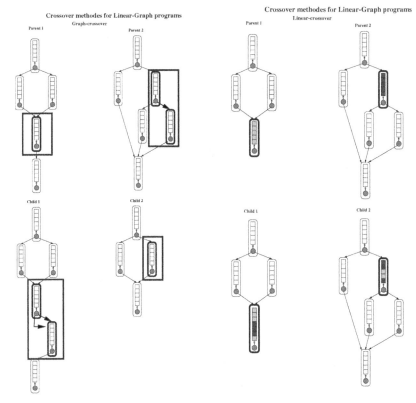

Fig. 3. Crossover-operation of two linear-graph programs using the graph-based crossover method. This crossover method exchanges two subgraphs of the programs.

Fig. 4. Crossover-operation of two linear-graph programs using the linear-based crossover method. This crossover method is a two-point crossover, which exchanges a part of the linear-code between the nodes.

All variants of GP have been configured with population size of 100 individuals, a maximum crossover and mutation rate of 100 %, and without ADF's. This means that in one generation each individual is selected for a crossover and after the crossover each individual will be mutated by the mutation operator. All variants use the arithmetic operations $(+, -, *, /)$. For the chain problem we use arithmetic operations $(\sin, \cos)$ additionally. For all test problems we allow jumps and an if-then-else function.

3   Experimental Results

In this section we describe the performance of the different GP structures with different population sizes on the three test problems from Section 2. All plots

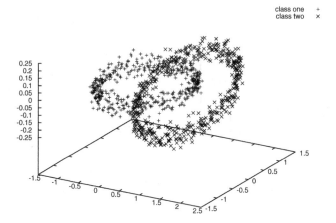

Fig. 5. This figure shows both links of a chain these represent the two classes of the chain problem [4]

show the average fitness of the best individual in different runs. The average is calculated over 50 runs with the same parameter set. In all runs we used tournament selection with a tournament size of 2. We have done two sets of runs, one with a population size of 10 and one with a population size of 100. In all runs we compare on the basis of number of nodes evaluated. So the difference in results cannot be interpreted by the fact that one structure has more or less resources to develop a good solution.

Figure 6 shows development of fitness values using the linear and linear-graph structure for the sine problem. We can see that for a population size of 100 individuals the linear-graph structure reaches a better fitness than the linear structure and the improvement of the fitness value for the linear-graph structure is faster than for the linear-structure. After 20.000 fitness evaluations the linear-graph structure reaches a fitness value which the linear structure reaches after 200.000 fitness evaluations. Even at this point we can see that the new structure supports the evolutionary process. Another very interesting result is the behavior of the linear-graph individuals during an evolution with small populations. Figure 6 also shows the development of fitness values for a population size of 10 individuals. With linear structures we observe the expected result, the performance is inferior to the result with 100 individuals. Even with the same number of fitness evaluations we can not reach the same result on average. The error bars also show the large variance in runs with a population size of 10. The linear-graph structure on the other hand, obtains the same fitness values as with 100 individuals, and error bars shows that these runs have a small variance.

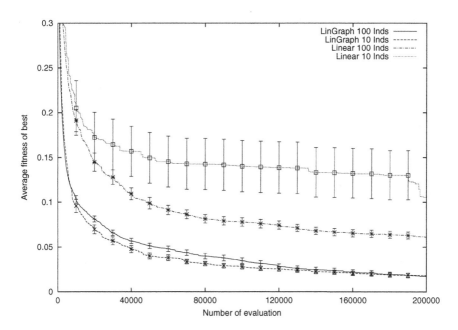

Fig. 6. The curves show the average fitness values for the sine regression problem with data form 0 to 2π. Each curve is an average of 50 runs. Zero is the best fitness for a individual.

Figure 7 shows the development of fitness values using the linear and linear-graph structure for the classification problem. The linear-graph structure reaches a better fitness than the linear structure with a population size of 100 individuals. Even the fitness development during the first 40.000 fitness evaluations is faster for the linear-graph structure. About 20.000 fitness evaluations the linear-graph structure reaches a fitness value which the linear structure reaches after 200.000 fitness evaluations. The behavior of linear-graph individuals during the evolution with small populations is similar to their behavior for the sine problem. The result for 10 individuals is not as good as with 100 individuals for the linear-graph structure, but it still outperforms the linear structure. The interesting result here is the performance of the linear-structure with a population size of 10 for this problem. We expected a similar result as for the sine problem. The error bars shows that there was a high variance for the different runs, however on average runs reach the same fitness as with 100 individuals.

The result for the Rastrigin function is shown in figure 8. The development of fitness values is similar to the case of the sine problem. Linear-graph structures outperform the linear structures with both population sizes. This result shows also the large error bars.The plot also shows that there is almost no difference between runs with population size of 10 or 100 for the linear-graph structure. The runs with the linear-graph structures are the only runs for the Rastrigin problem

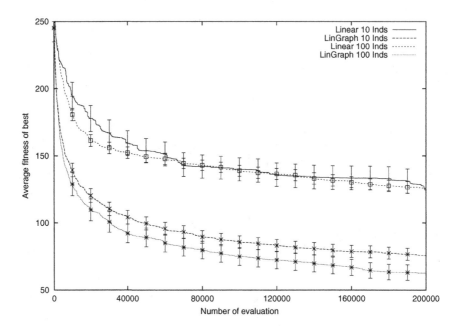

Fig. 7. The curves show the average fitness value of the chain problem. Each curve is an average over 50 runs. Zero is the best fitness for a individual. The x axis is the number of fitness evaluations and the y axis is the number of miss classifications. The chain problem contain 1000 data points, so that 100 means a classification error of 10 %.

where an individual could reach a fitness smaller than 0.2. For the linear structure best fitness is 2.9. This shows that behavior of the linear-graph structure is not only improving average behavior but also improving overall behavior.

4   Summary and Outlook

In conclusion we have observed that linear-graph structures outperform a linear structure significantly. We have also seen that even with a population size of 10 individuals only evolution reaches fitness values which are better than the fitness values of linear structures with 100 individuals. This allows GP to evolve individuals for problems with high cost in fitness evolution.

We have observed that the structure of a GP individual makes a significant difference in the evolutionary process and the expressiveness of code. Good performance of a structure may be caused by the effect of building blocks [6], which could be identified with the nodes in our linear-graph structure. In order to clarify whether this good performance of the linear-graph structure is a general phenomenon more experiments need to be run on a variety of test problems, but the results achieved so far are strong evidence that the new structure may lead

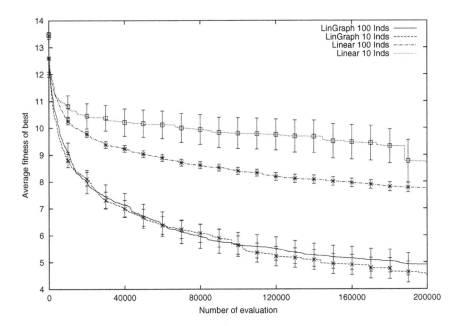

Fig. 8. The curves show the average fitness value of the Rastrigin problem. Each curve is an average over 50 runs. Zero is the best fitness for a individual. The x axis is the number of fitness evaluations.

to better result for a range of problems. But the astonishingly result was the behavior of the linear-graph structure during the evolution with small populations. A careful analysis is now needed to find out what reasons determine the improvements in performance of these new GP structures.

Acknowledgement. Support has been provided by the DFG (Deutsche Forschungsgemeinschaft), under grant Ba 1042/5-2.

References

1. P.J. Angeline. Subtree crossover: Building block engine or macromutation? In *Genetic Programming 1997: Proceedings of the Second Annual Conference*, pages 9–17, San Francisco, CA, 1997. Morgan Kaufmann.
2. P.J. Angeline. Multiple interacting programs: A representation for evolving complex behaviors. *Cybernetics and Systems (in press)*, 1998.
3. W. Banzhaf, P. Nordin, R. E. Keller, and F. D. Francone. *Genetic Programming – An Introduction On the Automatic Evolution of Computer Programs and its Applications*. Morgan Kaufmann, San Francisco und dpunkt verlag, Heidelberg, 1998.
4. M. Brameier and W. Banzhaf. Evolving teams of mutiple predictors with Genetic Programming. *Genetic Programming and Evolvable Maschines*, 2(4):381–407, 2001.

5. M. Brameier, P. Dittrich, W. Kantschik, and W. Banzhaf. SYSGP - A C++ library of different GP variants. Technical Report Internal Report of SFB 531,ISSN 1433-3325, Fachbereich Informatik, Universität Dortmund, 1998.
6. J. Holland. *Adaption in Natural and Artifical Systems*. MI: The University of Michigan Press, 1975.
7. W. Kantschik and W. Banzhaf. Linear-tree GP and its comparison with other GP structures. In J. F. Miller, M. Tomassini, P. Luca Lanzi, C. Ryan, A. G. B. Tettamanzi, and W. B. Langdon, editors, *Genetic Programming, Proceedings of EuroGP'2001*, volume 2038 of *LNCS*, pages 302–312, Lake Como, Italy, 18-20 April 2001. Springer-Verlag.
8. J. Koza. *Genetic Programming*. MIT Press, Cambridge, MA, 1992.
9. J. Koza. *Genetic Programming II*. MIT Press, Cambridge, MA, 1994.
10. J. P. Nordin. *A Compiling Genetic Programming System that Directly Manipulates the Machine code*. MIT Press, Cambridge, 1994.
11. Riccardo Poli. Evolution of graph-like programs with parallel distributed genetic programming. In Thomas Back, editor, *Genetic Algorithms: Proceedings of the Seventh International Conference*, pages 346–353, Michigan State University, East Lansing, MI, USA, 19-23 July 1997. Morgan Kaufmann.
12. A. Teller and M. Veloso. Pado: A new learning architecture for object recognition. In *Symbolic Visual Learning*, pages 81 –116. Oxford University Press, 1996.

Parallel Surface Reconstruction

Klaus Weinert, Tobias Surmann, and Jörn Mehnen

Dept. of Machining Technology,
University of Dortmund, Germany
{weinert, surmann, mehnen}@isf.mb.uni-dortmund.de
www.isf.de

Abstract. The task of surface reconstruction is to find a mathematical representation of a surface which is given only by a set of discrete sampling points. The mathematical description in the computer allows to save or transfer the geometric data via internet, to manipulate (e.g. for aerodynamic or design specific reasons) or to optimize the machining of the work pieces. The reconstruction of the shape of an object is a difficult mathematical and computational problem. For this reason a GP/ES-hybrid algorithm has been used. Due to the high complexity of the problem and in order to speed up the reconstruction process, the algorithm has been enhanced to work as a multipopulation GP/ES that runs in parallel on a network of standard PCs.

1   Introduction

Discrete approximation and pattern recognition are fundamental problems in mathematics and computer science. Mechanical engineering, medical science and object design have an urgent need for realistic and computer compatible descriptions of surfaces of real physical objects. In order to reproduce the shape of an object in a computer, the object surfaces are sampled using either optical or contact scanning techniques. Depending on the scanning system, thousands ranging to millions of discrete points with either regular or irregular distributions are generated. The task of surface reconstruction is to identify the properties of the original surface from the discrete sampling points and to generate a mathematical surface description that can be used for further processing in CAD systems. In CAD, two typical modeling techniques can be distinguished: NonUniform Rational B-Splines [1], which are commonly used to describe free-formed surfaces, and Constructive Solid Geometry (CSG), which uses elementary geometric objects (e. g. spheres, boxes, cylinders, etc.). Both models have their own specific advantages and disadvantages regarding their constructional and computational expense and CAD systems are often designed to support only one construction technique. However, technical demands as well as the natural appearance of real objects make it necessary to combine both approaches in one hybrid surface model. See Figure 1.

Both, discrete surface approximation and pattern recognition can be interpreted as optimization problems. Evolutionary algorithms belong to a class of probabilistic optimization strategies that have already proven to be robust and capable

J.A. Foster et al. (Eds.): EuroGP 2002, LNCS 2278, pp. 93–102, 2002.

Fig. 1. Turbine blade

of finding surprisingly good solutions even when applied to complex multimodal, multidimensional and multiobjective problems [2]. For example, evolution strategies (ES) [3,4] performed well in NURBS surface approximation [5,6], and genetic programming (GP) [7] has been successfully applied to design optimization [8] and surface reconstruction [9,10]. Howewver, common problems regarding the use of GP still remain (e. g. long calculation time, loss of diversity in a single population etc.). To address these issues, a parallel multi-population algorithm was implemented. Instead of expensive parallel processor computers a system which takes advantage of LAN-connected low-price standard PCs was used (these networks provide a high virtual calculation power that is often not used).

2   Surface Reconstruction by GP

2.1   Constructive Solid Geometry (CSG)

Mechanical machine components are typically composed using basic components such as boxes, spheres, cylinders, etc. Guo, Menon showed, that it is possible to build arbitrarily complex bodies using elementary elements and half spaces [11]. Each complex construction can be composed using simpler CSG objects that interact geometrically depending on the binary relations join ($\cup$), intersect ($\cap$) and subtract ($-$). Typically, a binary tree forms the basic data stucture used in CSG-CAD-systems. The primitive geometric forms (quadrics, boxes, tori, NURBS-solids, etc.) are used to form the terminal nodes of the binary tree. Correspondingly, the binary relations are used as inner nodes of the CSG tree. Due to its recursive structure, a CSG tree can be interpreted as a word from a context free language. Standard interfaces like STEP or IGES make use of this property. Figure 2 illustrates the composition of the CSG structure displayed at the top of the graph. Note, that for each CSG object, there is an infinite number of representing CSG trees, which means the CSG object representation is not unique. Following the demands of a designer, a surface reconstruction algorithm has to find the simplest constructive setup, i. e. the CSG tree with a minimum

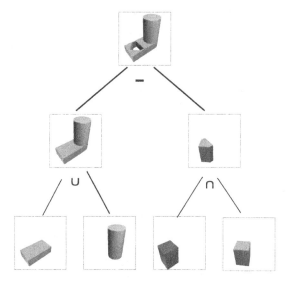

Fig. 2. Composition of a CSG structure

number of elements that resembles the digitized objects as realistically and exactly as possible.

For the reconstruction of objects that have their origin in CAD it is always possible to find a (not unique) finite reconstruction. Objects modelled manually can be approximated arbitrarily precise using NURBS surfaces. Thus, the search space is finite but with *a priori* unknown dimension. The reconstruction algorithm has to find the CSG construction that fits best into a given point set. Thus, an approximation and combinatorial problem have to be solved in parallel. The search space consists of a combination of real-valued vectors (position and orientation of each CSG element in R^3) and a variable dimensional graph structure (CSG tree).

2.2 GP/ES-Hybrid

Concerning its structure a CSG tree is well suited to represent the genome of an individual. For surface reconstruction there are two major problems to be solved:

- Determination of the construction logic. I. e. the algorithm has to find the correct structure of the CSG tree regarding the number, position and type of nodes.
- Fitting the terminals into the sampling points by adjusting their parameters (position, size, and tilt angles). For *NURBS* surfaces the control vertices also have to be adjusted.

These two problems lead to a GP/ES-hybrid algorith. The objective of the GP is to find the structure of the genome. Once the construction logic is found, the ES part adjusts the parameters of the primitive geometric objects. Therefore, the following genetic operators were applied to the CSG tree:

- Variation of the primitive's properties.
- Variation of the inner node functions.
- Removal and insertion of nodes.
- Replacement of a terminal by another one.
- Recombination by exchanging subtrees.

2.3   Fitness Function

The fitness function is confronted with the problem of mapping the genome to its phenotypic representation and to compare this representation with the given sampling points. Since the reconstructions are restricted to objects without undercuts, the fitness function can be simplified to a comparison of each scanning point with its projection on the CSG object parallel to the z-axis. Therefore, it is necessary to implement a function that calculates an intersection between a ray and the CSG object. Figure 3 shows two CSG elements (terminals) and a ray.

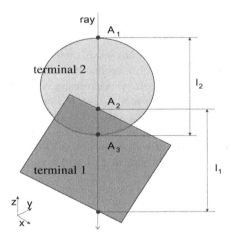

Fig. 3. Calculation of intersections of a ray and a CSG object

The intersections of the ray with each terminal defines the intervals I_1 and I_2. In order to model the surface of the resulting CSG structure, the corresponding intersection point A can be calculated from the intersection of the two intervals depending on the corresponding boolean operation in the CSG tree [12]. In the example A equals A_1, A_2 or A_3 if terminal 1 and terminal 2 are joined, intersected or subtracted. In order to evaluate the quality of a reconstruction, a comparison between the digitized points and the corresponding points on the CSG object surface has to be performed. Evolutionary algorithms excel for multi-objective optimization [13]. Here, an aggregation approach with the following criteria functions is used to form the multi-objective fitness function:

Δ_p describes the distance between a sampling point p and its corresponding point A on the surface of the individual.

ABN_p (angle between normals) represents the deviation of the normal vector of the sampling point p from the normal vector on the surface of the CSG object at the corresponding position. This value is calculated by the dot product of the two vectors. The result is normalized to an interval of $[0,1]$ (1 denotes best fit).

CT_p (curvature type) is a criterion that helps the algorithm to find the optimal terminal types to construct a CSG object. This function compares the curvature type of point p with the corresponding one on the individual's surface. The curvature type – like the values of the normal vectors – have been stored in the preprocessed sampling data. Thus, the evaluation time can be reduced drastically. CT_p yields 1 for an optimal match and 0 otherwise.

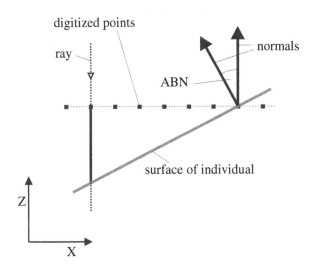

Fig. 4. Δ and ABN criteria

There is also a fitness criterion that does not refer to the points on the CSG object but to the individual's structure itself. This is the number of nodes N in the CSG tree. A good reconstruction excels not only by minimal Δ and maximal ABN and CT values, but also by its simplicity. Thus the number of elements of a genome has to be introduced into the fitness function. These four criteria can be weighted individually for each reconstruction to obtain results which focus on the desired quality of the reconstruction. The formula for calculating the fitness F_p of the individual at point p is as follows:

$$F_p = w_\Delta \frac{1}{1 + \Delta_p} + w_{ABN}\, ABN_p + w_{CT}\, CT_p - \frac{N}{c}$$

The parameters w_x are the weights of the criteria and c is a constant, which controls the influence of the number of nodes inserted into the individual. If the value of c is high, the influence of the number of nodes will be small, thus, an individual may be constructed from many terminals. The overall fitness $\overline{F}$ is the average over all F_p. The lower bound of the fitness is $-\frac{N}{c}$ indicating the worst case, while $w_\Delta + w_{ABN} + w_{CT} - \frac{N}{c}$ indicates an optimal reconstruction.

3   Parallel Processing

Since surface reconstruction is a very complex problem, there are many local optima in the search space. These local optima often consist of correctly found substructures. These suboptimal solutions begin to overrun the population in a panmictic population model. It has been shown that the algorithm found different substructures on every restart. The idea is to let the algorithm run for a while and to recombine the entire population with one of a different run in order to combine subsolutions to a better one [14]. So, a blackboard communication model has been applied to generate a nature analogous behavior of the

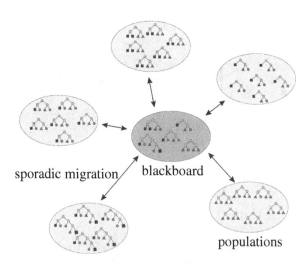

Fig. 5. Parallel GP with a blackboard model

reconstruction process. The aim is to feature many populations with their own environment (i. e. each population gets its own fitness parameters) and a sporadic exchange of genomes with other populations to produce individuals which have a high fitness regarding all environments.

3.1   Blackboard Communication Model

Each instance of a population posts and receives a certain number n of individuals to the blackboard every g generations. The received individulas become removed from the blackboard, so that the size of the blackboard stays constant during the enrire reconstruction process. The parameters n and g are specific for each population. So the migration rate can be adapted to the speed of the computer that carries the population (i. e. the migration may appear in similar time intervals on each computer).

The migration in this system is supposed to happen on each 5th to 1000th generation. This very sporadic transfer of data is the base for a very simple parallelization mechanism: The blackboard is formed by a shared folder in a Windows network. Each running surface reconstruction saves and loads individuals to and from this folder. This allows a decentralized and asynchronous parallelization in LANs. Each computer in the network can take part in the reconstruction by simply starting the algorithm.

Note that there are two modes for starting a reconstruction. On the initial start the blackboard has to be filled up with some individuals. Each algorithm which is started in this mode posts an amount of n individuals of its initial population. When adding a computer to a reconstruction process there may be no need to add further individuals to the blackboard. So the algorithm can be started without increasing the size of the gene pool.

4   Experiments

To show the usability of this parallelization approach, experiments were made. The intention of these experiments was to show that the structure of the object to be reconstructed is found faster by a multi-population model.

4.1   Experimental Environment

The object to be reconstructed during these tests has to consist of different substructures and types of terminals. In this case a cross-like object with rounded ends has been selected. Earlier experiments with a panmictic population model have shown that the algorithm sometimes did not find one or two spheres or one of the cylinders. Once the structure (here four spheres and two crossed cylinders) is found, the algorithm works like a standard ES to adjust the parameters of the single terminals. So, these experiments only run for 2000 generations to examine the behavior during calculation of the structure of the CSG tree. Figure 6 shows the target of the reconstruction on the left and a good result after 1500

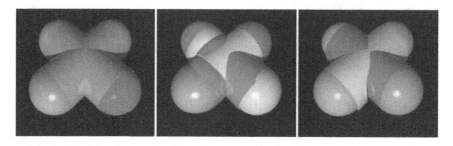

Fig. 6. Reconstruction target (left), result after 1500 (middle), and 4000 (right) generations

generations in the middle. Having recognized the structure correctly, the algorithm is able to find a mostly perfect reconstruction of the target. This result is illustrated by the right picture of figure 6.

The tests ran on a network of eight computers of equal performance. Each population size was 300. During each migration 10% of the individuals were randomly selected and sent to the blackboard.

In order to examine the influence of migration within a multi-population environment, the frequency ν of migration was varied during these tests from $\nu = \frac{1}{5}$ (i. e. every 5th generation) to $\nu = \frac{1}{1000}$ (i. e. every 1000th generation).

4.2   Results

The average results over 10 experiments for each migration frequency of $\frac{1}{1000}$, $\frac{1}{100}, \frac{1}{50}, \frac{1}{20}$ and $\frac{1}{5}$ are shown in Figure 7. The graphs show the values of $1 - \overline{F}$. Hence, smaller values represent better individuals. For the migration frequency of $\frac{1}{1000}$ the graph falls very slowly. This means the algorithm did not find the correct structure until the 2000th generation. This low migration frequency corresponds to a panmictic population model. Here each computer worked on its own till the 1000th generation. A frequency of $\frac{1}{20}$ leads to the best result. With higher frequencies the results get worse as the graph for $\frac{1}{5}$ shows. There are no significant differences between $\nu = 50$ and $\nu = 100$. The upper graph in figure 7 compares the fitness values of each run after 500 with the corresponding value after 1000 generations. There is a great speed-up not only by using a multi-population model but also by applying a correct choice of the migration parameters. Note that the computational power up of this parallelization is strong enough to leave the weight w_{CT} of the fitness function set to 0 during the tests.

5   Conclusion

Algorithms for high dimensional structure optimization problems do not only need high computational power, but also need special mechanisms to solve their

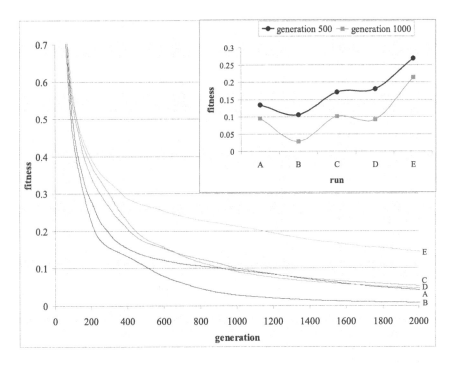

Fig. 7. Fitness evolution for $\nu = $ (from A to E) $\frac{1}{5}, \frac{1}{20}, \frac{1}{50}, \frac{1}{100}, \frac{1}{5}, \frac{1}{1000}$

tasks. In the case of surface reconstruction, parallelization features three advantages: High computational power, the possibility of performing and combining subsolutions and high speed-up concerning the number of participating computers.

The mechanism of exchanging data should be either of less overhead or of low frequency. Here, a blackboard approach has been applied that features a variable frequency of data exchange with little overhead.

Important for the field of structure optimization such as surface reconstruction is that the parallelization converges to a panmictic population model either for high and for low frequencies of migration. So this frequency has to be chosen correctly dependently on the given problem.

Acknowledgement. This research was supported by the Deutsche Forschungsgesellschaft as part of the Collaborative Research Center "Computational Intelligence" (SFB 531).

References

1. Piegel, L., Tiller, W.: The NURBS book. Springer-Verlag, Berlin (1997)
2. Sarker, R., Newton, Ch., Liang, K.H.: A Multiobjective Evolutionary Algorithm. In International ICSC 2000 Congress, ISA2000 Intelligent Systems and Applications, pages 125-131. ICSC Academic Press, Canada, 11.-15.- Oct. 2000

3. Schwefel, H.-P.: Evolution and Optimum Seeking. Whiley-Interscience, NY, USA (1995)
4. Bäck, Th.: Evolutionary Algorithms in Theory and Practice. Oxford University Press, NY, USA (1996)
5. Weinert, K., Mehnen, J.: Comparison of Selection Schemes for Discrete Point Data for Evolutionary Optimized Triangulations and NURBS Surface Reconstructions. In International ICSC 2000 Congress, ISA2000 Intelligent Systems and Applications, pages 104-110. ICSC Academic Press, Canada, 11.-15. Oct. 2000.
6. Weinert, K., Mehnen, J.: NURBS Surface Approximation of Discrete 3d-Point Data by Means of Evolutionary Algorithms. In Teti, R. (editor), ICME 2000, pages 263-268, Capri, Italy (2000). ISBN 88-87030-21-9.
7. Koza, J. R.: Genetic Programming: On the Programming of Computers by Means of Natural Selection. MIT Press, Cambridge, MA (1992)
8. Bentley, P. J.: evolutionary Design by Computers. Morgan Kaufmann Publishers, San Moreno, CA, USA (1999)
9. Keller, R. E., Mehnen, J.,Banzhaf, W.,Weinert, K.: Surface Reconstruction from 3D point data with a genetic programming / evolution strategy hybrid, volume 3 of Advances in Genetic Programming, chapter 2, pages 41-65. MIT Press, MA, USA (1999)
10. Mehnen, J.: Evolutionäre Flächenrekonstruktion. Phd thesis, Department of Mechanical Engineering, University of Dortmund, Germany (2001)
11. Guo, b., Menon, J.: Local shape control for free-form solids in exact CSG representations. Computer-Aided Design, 28(6/7):483-493 (1996)
12. Foley, J. D.,van Dam, A., Feiner, S. K., Hughes, J. F.: Computer Graphics – Principles and Practice. Addison-Wesley Publishing Company, Inc. (1990)
13. Deb, K.: Multi-Objective Optimization using Evolutionary Algorithms, Whiley, New York (2001)
14. Cantu-Paz, E.: Topologies, Migration Rates, and Multi-Population Parallel Genetic Algorithms, in Proceedings of the Genetic and Evolutionary Computation Conference, Vol. 1, pages 91-98, Morgan Kaufmann Publishers (1999)

Evolving Classifiers to Model the Relationship between Strategy and Corporate Performance Using Grammatical Evolution

Anthony Brabazon[1], Michael O'Neill[2], Conor Ryan[2], and Robin Matthews[3]

[1] Dept. Of Accountancy, University College Dublin, Ireland.
Anthony.Brabazon@ucd.ie
[2] Dept. Of Computer Science And Information Systems,
University of Limerick, Ireland.
{Michael.ONeill|Conor.Ryan}@ul.ie
[3] Centre for International Business Policy
Kingston Business School, London.

Abstract. This study examines the potential of grammatical evolution to construct a linear classifier to predict whether a firm's corporate strategy will increase or decrease shareholder wealth. Shareholder wealth is measured using a relative fitness criterion, the change in a firm's market-value-added ranking in the Stern-Stewart Performance 1000 list, over a four year period, 1992-1996. Model inputs and structure are selected by means of grammatical evolution. The best classifier correctly categorised the direction of performance ranking change in 66.38% of the firms in the training set and 65% in the out-of-sample validation set providing support for a hypothesis that changes in corporate strategy are linked to changes in corporate performance.

1 Introduction

At a macro-economic level, one of the crucial questions faced is how best to combine scarce resources in order to maximise the welfare or utility of a society. At a micro-economic level, managers face similar resource allocation decisions such as, how the tangible and intangible resources of an organisation should be allocated between present and potential activities, how these resources should be linked and how the allocations should change over time. Many of the most heavily researched areas in organisational theory and related fields revolve around these questions [13], [19], [9], [10]. The strategy of an organisation can be considered as the organisation of activities, the apparent raison d'être of management being to create an 'optimal' collection and linkage of activities given resource constraints and the co-evolutionary environment in which the organisation operates [18].

In a preliminary study, this paper addresses two primary research objectives. A basic and as yet unanswered question in strategic management is whether corporate strategy, decisions regarding firm scope and resource allocation, affect firm performance [21]. Research evidence drawn from studies of the performance

J.A. Foster et al. (Eds.): EuroGP 2002, LNCS 2278, pp. 103–112, 2002.
© Springer-Verlag Berlin Heidelberg 2002

of diversification and retrenchment strategies have produced varying results [3], [21]. Much management practice is predicated by the assumption that 'strategy matters' and that it is possible to improve firm performance through judicious strategic choices. This study examines whether a relationship exists between corporate strategy and performance. The second objective of this study is to determine whether grammatical evolution [20], [15], [14] can be employed to construct a linear classifier to predict whether a firm's corporate strategy will increase or decrease shareholder wealth. An earlier study [4] compared the predictive performance of both a linear discriminant analysis (LDA) and a hybrid GA/NN model on this dataset, hence, the performance of models constructed by Grammatical Evolution can be benchmarked against these results.

The strategy domain is characterised by a lack of strong theoretical frameworks, with many plausible, competing explanatory variables. The selection of quality explanatory variables and model form represents a high-dimensional combinatorial problem, giving rise to potential for an EAP methodology. Although evolutionary algorithms have been applied to a variety of problems in both finance and general business domains [2], [16], [22], [7], we are unaware of the existence of any empirical studies applying an evolutionary automatic programming (EAP) approach in the domain of strategic planning. As such, this paper represents a novel application of EAP.

This contribution is organised as follows. Section 2 provides a short discussion of corporate strategy. Section 3 provides an introduction to the EAP approach adopted in this paper. Section 4 describes both the data utilised, and the model development process adopted in this paper. Section 5 provides the results of the evolved classifier models and compares these with the results from a previous study. Finally, conclusions and a discussion of the limitations of the contribution are provided in Section 6.

2   Corporate Strategy

Nine distinct schools of thought[1] are identified within strategic management [11]. These can be broadly classed as being either prescriptive or descriptive in nature [5]. The prescriptive schools of strategic thought, ascribe the foundations of corporate success to astute managerial decision-making. Strategy is considered to arise from a stream of explicit decisions. Through careful analysis of the firm's capabilities (resources) and the environment, 'good' niches can be identified and targeted. All of these schools implicitly assume that the environment is at least partly predictable. By contrast, descriptive schools of strategy formation attempt to describe the actual process of strategy formation in organisations on the basis of empirical research ([5], p.14).

Regardless of whether strategy is intended or emergent, the results of the strategic process are a pattern of managerial decisions. Whilst the decisions are not directly observable, their nature can be partly determined, *ex-post*. This

---

[1] The identified schools are: design, planning, positioning, entrepreneurial, cognitive, learning, political, cultural and environmental.

study utilises accounting information as proxies for these decisions. For the purposes of this study, corporate-level strategy is defined as determining business scope and resource allocation. This perspective is viewed as being decomposable into growth and diversification strategies both of which are implemented through corporate investment decisions. Where will corporate investment take place (existing or new businesses) and will this investment be positive (growth) or negative (retrenchment)? The level of corporate investment is moderated by the financial health of the organisation [21]. Therefore the explanatory variables utilised in the modelling process are drawn from three classifications, growth-retrenchment, diversification and financial health. It is anticipated that the choice of explanatory variables and their related classifications will be refined in future development of this work.

3   Grammatical Evolution

Grammatical Evolution (GE) is an evolutionary algorithm that can evolve computer programs in any language. Rather than representing the programs as syntax trees, as in traditional GP [8], a linear genome representation is adopted. A genotype-phenotype mapping process is used to generate the output program for each individual in the population. Each individual, a variable length binary string, contains in its codons the information to select production rules from a Backus Naur Form (BNF) grammar. The BNF is a plug-in component to the mapping process, that represents the output language in the form of production rules.

The grammar is used in a generative process to construct a program by applying production rules, selected by the genome, beginning from the start symbol of the grammar.

In order to select a rule in GE, the next codon value on the genome is read and placed in the following formula:

$$Rule = Codon\ Value\ MOD\ \#Rules$$

GE uses a steady state replacement mechanism, such that, two parents produce two children the best of which replaces the worst individual in the current population if the child has a greater fitness. The standard genetic operators of point mutation, and crossover (one point) are adopted. It also employs a duplication operator that duplicates a random number of codons and inserts these into the penultimate codon position on the genome. A full description of GE can be found in [15], [14], [20].

4   Research Methodology

This section describes both the data utilised by, and the model development process adopted in, this study. A shareholder perspective is adopted and it is assumed that the success of corporate strategy decisions is judged by equity markets. To allow for exogenous factors which could impact on stock market values, a relative performance metric, a market-value-added (MVA) rank is utilised[2] and the performance of the firm is determined by whether it improved its MVA ranking in the Stern-Stewart 1000 listing during the period 1992-1996[3]. The choice of a four year measurement period is arbitrary but is adopted in recognition that strategic initiatives may require time to mature.

4.1   Sample Definition and Model Data

A total of 430 US firms were selected judgementally, from the Stern-Stewart Performance 1000 list for the study. The criteria for selection were:

  i. inclusion in the listing for the period 1992-1996
 ii. existence of required explanatory variables for the period 1992-1996

The first criterion limits the study to large publicly quoted corporations. Such organisations are likely to consist of a portfolio of businesses, and hence are congruent with the objectives of the paper. The second criterion injects a survivorship bias into the sample. While few publicly quoted companies fail in any given year, poorer performers may be liable to acquisition.

The dependant variable is binary (0,1), representing the direction of change in the firm's MVA rank in the Stern-Stewart listing between 1992 and 1996. Sixteen potential explanatory variables, divided into three classifications [21], are collected from the Compustat database for each firm. The set of 430 firms is randomly divided into model building (330 firms) and out-of-sample (100 firms) testing datasets. All explanatory variables have been preprocessed to remove outliers, having been clipped at the 2.5 and 97.5 percentiles. The three classifications of explanatory variables are:

  i. *Diversification:* Segment sales entropy[4], % Sales outside domestic market in 1996
 ii. *Growth-retrenchment:* Compound growth rate of total sales in three years to 1996, Percentage change[5] in Capital Expenditure / Sales, Percentage change in R&D / Sales, Percentage change in Assets / Sales, Percentage change in Employees / Sales, Percentage change in General & Selling expenses / Sales, Beta as at end 1996, Change in Beta between end 1995 and end 1996.

---

[2] MVA is defined as: Market Value of Firm - Original Value of Capital Invested.

[3] Published in Fortune magazine.

[4] Intuitively, entropy can be considered a measure of the disorder or diversity in a system. The measure adopted here is defined as $H = -\sum_{i=1}^{N_s} P_i log P_i$, where P_i is the portion of an organisation's sales in segment i and N_s represents the number of segments.

[5] The percentage change measures the relative change in the specified financial ratio between 1992 and 1996.

iii. *Financial Health:* Percentage change in Cash from Operations / Sales, Percentage change in Cash on hand/ Sales, Percentage change in Total Debt / Total Assets, Percentage change in Gross Profit / Sales, Percentage change in Net Profit / Sales, Percentage change in Earnings Retention Rate[6].

A more detailed discussion concerning the choice of these variables is provided in [4] and [21]. The chosen measures of diversification capture the diversification of the firm's sales between industry segments and between the firm's domestic and overseas markets. Several measures of growth/retrenchment are provided. The impact of past strategic decisions on growth can be determined by measuring the rate of sales growth in the recent past. Current decisions which impact on future growth rates may result in allocations of funds to asset investment and to investments in strategic marketing and research and development. However, growth does not necessarily require that the asset base be increased and could occur through increased utilisation of existing assets. This is captured using metrics on asset and employee utilisation. The risk of the returns generated by the firm is captured in Beta which measures the volatility of the firm's return against that of the market portfolio. Corporate investment and divestment decisions take place against the backdrop of a firm's financial resources and financial health. A series of ratios drawn from prior research on corporate bankruptcy [1], [12] are included as corporate financial health may serve to moderate investment decisions.

5   Results and Discussion

This section describes the results from each model, compares these results with those from earlier studies, and then provides a discussion. Accuracy of the developed models is assessed based on the overall classification accuracy[7]arising in both the model-building and out-of-sample datasets.

The classification problem which plays an important role in decision-making, consists of assigning observations to disjoint groups [17]. The decision scenario faced in this study comprises a binary classification. In general, the construction of classifier systems such as linear discriminant analysis, logit or ANN models consists of two components, the determination of a valuation rule which is applied to each observation, and the determination of a 'cut-off' value. To examine the utility of GE in this application, two distinct grammars are applied. The first grammar adopts a fixed 0.5 cut-off value for classification, the second grammar is allowed to evolve this cut-off value.

---

[6] This item represents Income Before Extraordinary Items minus Cash Dividends. This total is divided by Income Before Extraordinary Items and then multiplied by 100.

[7] The cost of each type of classification error is assumed to be symmetric in this study. The fitness function could be easily altered to bias the model development process to minimise a specific type of classification error if required.

Grammar 1

```
lc : output = expr ;
expr : ( expr ) + ( expr )
     | coeff * var
var : var1[index] | var2[index]
    | var3[index] | var4[index]
    | var5[index] | var6[index]
    | var7[index] | var8[index]
    | var9[index] | var10[index]
    | var11[index] | var12[index]
    | var13[index] | var14[index]
    | var15[index] | var16[index]
coeff : ( coeff ) op ( coeff )
      | float
op : + | - | *
float : 20 | -20 | 10 | -10 | 5
      | -5 | 4 | -4 | 3 | -3 | 2
      | -2 | 1 | -1 | .1 | -.1
```

Grammar 2

```
lc : if( expr relop condition )
       output=0;
     else output=1;
expr : ( expr ) + ( expr )
     | coeff * var
var : var1[index] | var2[index]
    | var3[index] | var4[index]
    | var5[index] | var6[index]
    | var7[index] | var8[index]
    | var9[index] | var10[index]
    | var11[index] | var12[index]
    | var13[index] | var14[index]
    | var15[index] | var16[index]
coeff : ( coeff ) op ( coeff )
      | float
op : + | - | *
float : 20 | -20 | 10 | -10 | 5
      | -5 | 4 | -4 | 3 | -3 | 2
      | -2 | 1 | -1 | .1 | -.1
relop : < | > | <= | >= | != | ==
condition : coeff
```

Grammar 1 generates classifiers of the form:

$$output = (< some\ expression > *varX) + .. + (< some\ expression > *varY)$$

however, any combination and number of the sixteen explanatory variables can be exploited by such a classifier, including multiple occurrences of any one variable. This is in contrast to the LDA approach where classifiers would generally utilise all the explanatory variables within the expression. In the LDA case, of course some of those variables could be *switched off* by multiplying their value by zero.

Grammar 2 specifies classifiers that force the generation of their own cut-off value for classification by using the following syntax,

$$if(< classifier >< relop >< condition >)\ output = 0;\ else\ output = 1;$$

where the $< classifier >$ takes on the same form as for grammar 1. Given the expressive power of grammars the two examples adopted here represent simple examples of linear classifiers. Classifiers represent an important tool in assisting decision-making in many fields. Future work will investigate the use of more complex classifiers for this and similar decision problems.

The performance of the two distinct grammars are analysed by performing 30 independent runs for each grammar. Population sizes of 500, 100 generations, one-point crossover at a probability of 0.9, and bit mutation at 0.01, along with a steady state replacement strategy were adopted. A plot of mean best and mean average fitness against generations can be seen in Figure 1, and Table 1 reports the mean of the average fitness values and of the best fitness values at the final generation of each run. The results show that grammar 1 and grammar 2 produce different (statistically significant) classifiers, and that using grammar 1 results in the better classifiers.

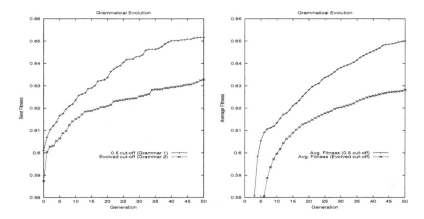

Fig. 1. A comparison of the mean best fitness between grammar 1 and grammar 2 (left), and of the mean average fitness values (right) for both grammars. Better success rates are achieved with the fixed cut-off point.

Table 1. The mean of the average fitness values and of the best fitness values at the final generation of each run compared on both grammars. The difference between the means is significant based on both a ttest a non-parametric bootstrap ttest.

	grammar1	grammar2	Significance
Avg. fitness mean values	0.64976	0.62777	Yes
Best fitness mean values	0.65167	0.63239	Yes

Analysing the best evolved rules we see that three variables are heavily used, and tended to have the following related signs:

i. $-$ var13 ($Employees/Sales\_\%chnge\_1992 - 1996$),

var13 is the ratio of the number of employees of a firm to its sales (the inverse of average sales per employee). The model input represents the percentage change in this over the period 1992 - 1996. If a firm becomes more efficient (i.e. can generate more sales with the same level of workforce) employees / sales will tend to fall and the % change will be negative. Hence the negative coefficient implies that increasing a firm's efficiency tends to increase its MVA ranking. The coefficient sign is therefore plausible.

ii. $+$ var15 ($Beta\_Dif\_1996 - 1995$),

Beta is a measure of a firm's risk relative to that of the 'average' risk for firms in the market. Thus, if a firm has a Beta value of 1, and the stock market rises by 10%, its share price should also rise by 10%. If its Beta is greater than 1, the firm's share price rises by more than the market average when the market rises (and vice versa if the market falls). Var 15 is a measure of the change in the firm's Beta between 1995 and 1996. The positive coefficient adopted by the evolved models with respect to this variable means that firms whose Beta increases tended to increase their MVA rank.

Between end 1992, and end 1996, the US stock markets rose by about 100%. Thus higher Beta firms, and firm's whose Beta increased would have tended to produce increases in share price and consequently in MVA in such an environment. Again, the coefficient sign is plausible.

iii. + var16 $(DiversificationIndex\_chnge1996 - 1992)$.

Var 16 measures the degree to which a firm's sales are spread across several different businesses areas. If a firm has increased this spread (reduced its dependence on a smaller number of business areas) over the period 1992 - 1996, Var 16 will be positive. Hence the results suggest that businesses that increased their spread of activities tended to increase their MVA rank. Again, this seems plausible, successful firms would tend to be those who are expanding their operations.

The best individual, given below, was produced by Grammar 1 and scored 66.38% on the training data set and 65% on the out-of-sample data set.

```
output   = (1*var15[index]) + ( (.1*var15[index])
         + ( (1*var16[index]) +   (-3*var13[index]) ) );
```

5.1   Discussion

The results of this study provide stronger support for the the hypothesis that changes in corporate strategy can impact on corporate performance, as measured by MVA ranking than those obtained an earlier study [4]. The classification accuracy is reasonably good in-sample, and suffers little degradation in out-of-sample performance, thus the evolved classifiers have nice generalisation properties.

Table 2. Results compared with those of Brabazon et al. [4]. The results reported for GE reflect an average value using the best individual from each of the 30 runs.

Results	Train data	Test data
GE - Grammar 1	65.15%	62.48%
GE - Grammar 2	63.58%	60.96%
LDA(Brabazon et al. [4])	61.8%	55.0%
GA/ANN(Brabazon et al. [4])	78.56%	54.3%

Calculation of Press's Q statistic [6] for the LDA models constructed in [4] failed to reject a null hypothesis, at the 5% level, that the out-of-sample classification accuracies were significantly better than chance. In comparison, the performance of the classifiers evolved by GE in this study leads to a rejection of the null hypothesis, at the 5% level, that the out-of-sample classification accuracies were significantly better than chance. This provides evidence for the existence of a relationship between strategy and corporate performance. It is also interesting to note that GE evolved a simpler model than LDA, with better in and out-of-sample classification accuracy.

A comparison of the results achieved in this study and in [4] can be seen in Table 2.

6   Conclusions

The objective of this paper was to undertake a preliminary study to determine whether a linear classifier model constructed using GE could uncover a relationship between changes in corporate strategy and corporate performance. The results of the study are consistent with the hypotheses that changes in corporate strategy can impact on corporate performance, and that GE can construct a useful linear classifier.

Several caveats apply to the interpretation of the findings. If strategy is considered as being a pattern in (unobservable) managerial decisions, there are dangers in inferring these patterns from observed variables. The choices of independent and explanatory variables adopted in this preliminary study are not unique and are subject to limitations. The choice of performance measure results in information compression. The selection of accounting ratios as explanatory variables as proxies for unobservable managerial decisions suffers from aggregation and time-lag. However, they do have the advantage of assisting comparability between firms and permitting analysis cross-sectionally and longitudinally. Note also, that the reported statistical results are preliminary in as far as they are from one recut of the dataset (i.e. into training versus testing).

Despite these limitations, the methodology utilised in this paper has promise. The global search characteristics of an evolutionary automatic programming approach provide a potentially valuable tool for the strategy domain as they enable a simultaneous search for both quality inputs and quality model structure. Given the weak predictive power of existing models in strategy, methodologies with these properties should have particular utility.

Given that classification problems are widespread, this investigation represents the first example of how GE might be applied to this class of problems.

References

1. Altman, Edward I. (1993). *Corporate Financial Distress and Bankruptcy*, New York: John Wiley and Sons Inc.
2. Bauer, R. (1994). *Genetic Algorithms and Investment Strategies*, New York: John Wiley & Sons.
3. Bowman, E. and Helfat, C. (2001). Does Corporate Strategy Matter?,*Strategic Management Journal*, 22:1-23.
4. Brabazon,T., Glintchak E., Matthews R. (2001). Modelling the relationship between strategy and corporate performance using a hybrid GA/NN model, in *Proceedings of the SEAG Annual Conference*, 10 September 2001, Oxford.

5. Elfring, T. and Volberda, H. (1996). Schools of Thought in Strategic Management: Fragmentation, Integrating or Synthesis?, in Elfring, T. Jensen, H. and Money, A. (eds), *Theory Building in the Business Sciences* pp. 11-47, Copenhagen,Copenhagen Business School Press.

6. Hair, Joseph F., Anderson, Rolph E., Tatham, Ronald L. and Black, William C. (1998). *Multivariate Data Analysis*, Upper Saddle River, Prentice Hall.

7. Klemz, B. (1999). Using genetic algorithms to assess the impact of pricing activity timing, *Omega*, 27:363-372.

8. Koza, J. (1992). *Genetic Programming*. MIT Press.

9. Levitt, B. and March J. (1988). Organizational Learning, *Annual Review of Sociology*, 14:319-340.

10. McKelvey, B. (1999). Avoiding Complexity Catastrophe in Coevolutionary Pockets: Strategies for Rugged Landscapes, *Organization Science*, 10(3):294-321.

11. Mintzberg, H. (1990). Strategy Formation: Schools of Thought., in Frederickson, J. (ed.), *Perspectives on Strategic Management*, pp. 107-108, New York.

12. Morris, R. (1997). *Early Warning Indicators of Corporate Failure: A critical review of previous research and further empirical evidence*, London: Ashgate Publishing Limited.

13. Nelson, R. and Winter, S. (1982). *An Evolutionary Theory of Economic Change*, Cambridge, Massachusetts, Harvard University Press.

14. O'Neill M. (2001) Automatic Programming in an Arbitrary language: Evolving Programs with Grammatical Evolution. Ph.D. thesis, University of Limerick, 2001.

15. O'Neill M., Ryan C. (2001) Grammatical Evolution. *IEEE Trans. Evolutionary Computation*, Vol. 5 No. 4, August 2001.

16. O'Neill, M., Brabazon, T., Ryan, C. and Collins J.(2001). Evolving Market Index Trading Rules Using Grammatical Evolution, In *LNCS 2037: Applications of Evolutionary Computing*, pp. 343-35, Springer-Verlag.

17. Pendharkar, P. (2001). An empirical study of design and testing of hybrid evolutionary-neural approach for classification, *Omega*, 29:361-374.

18. Porter, M. (1985). *Competitive Advantage:Creating and Sustaining Superior Performance*, New York, The Free Press.

19. Porter, M. (1996). What is Strategy?, *Harvard Business Review*, Nov-Dec, 61-78.

20. Ryan C., Collins J.J., O'Neill M. (1998). Grammatical Evolution: Evolving Programs for an Arbitrary Language. *LNCS 1391, Proc. of the First European Workshop on Genetic Programming*, pp. 83-95. Springer-Verlag.

21. St. John, C., Balakrishnan, N. and Fiet, O. J. (2000). Modelling the relationship between corporate strategy and wealth creation using neural networks, *Computers and operations research*, 27:1077-1092.

22. Varetto, F. (1998). Genetic algorithms in the analysis of insolvency risk, *Journal of Banking and Finance*, 22(10):1421 - 1439.

A New View on Symbolic Regression

Klaus Weinert and Marc Stautner

Dept. of Machining Technology,
University of Dortmund, Germany
{weinert, stautner}@isf.mb.uni-dortmund.de
www.isf.de

Abstract. Symbolic regression is a widely used method to reconstruct mathematical correlations. This paper presents a new graphical representation of the individuals reconstructed in this process. This new three dimensional representation allows the user to recognize certain possibilities to improve his setup of the process parameters. Furthermore this new representation allows a wider usage of the generated three dimensional objects with nearly every CAD program for further use. To show the practical usage of this new representation it was used to reconstruct mathematical descriptions of the dynamics in a machining process namely in orthogonal cutting.

1 Introduction

Modeling the chip-building process in metal cutting has been in the focus of interest for a long time. The chip geometry, the material movement, and the thermal processes which take place in the center of the cutting zone (the so called "contact zone") are decisive for high quality machining, reduction of machining times and tool wear. Most existing approaches incorporate FE- or MD- methods as well as analytical techniques based on cutting force models [1,5]. No external knowledge is provided apart from the images of the process taken by a high-speed camera. The symbolic regression genetic programing approach is quite similar to that of a human observer [6] who watches a certain process and tries to describe it in physical terms. Furthermore, the system may produce some unexpected, but valid results, which do not correspond to any known properties of the process. If such phenomena occur new knowledge about the process has been generated. This knowledge may be helpful to support the development of new simulation tools, which are able to increase the productivity of the process as well as its reliability. These new models may be described in a two dimensional way by relations of this type:

$$\boldsymbol{f}(t) = \begin{pmatrix} f_x(t) \\ f_y(t) \end{pmatrix} \quad resp. \quad f(x,y) = 0 \tag{1}$$

To gather data, of the cutting process a new experimental setup (see fig. 1) has been developed to take a high speed picture sequence of turning processes. This setup is similar to the setup described by Warnecke [6]. In contrast to

J.A. Foster et al. (Eds.): EuroGP 2002, LNCS 2278, pp. 113–122, 2002.

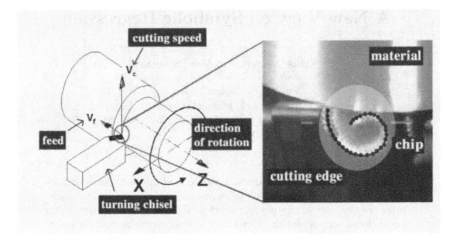

Fig. 1. Experimental Setup of Camera and Turning Machine

this setup, no microscope is used. In this setup, a high speed camera "Weinberger Speedcam+512", which allows to take up to 4500 pictures per second, was take. In order to extract the particle trajectories, the program "WINAnalyze" (Mikromak) was utilised. This program generates ASCII trace files which allow to analyze the trajectories of the particles by the GP system. The positions of the particles are interpreted as the values of the two dimensional relation. In addition to this automatic method a manual tracing method, was used to extract single particle trajectories. This was done in cases when the extraction of the particle dynamics cannot be obtained automatically due to optical interferences or material deformation effects.

2   Main Algorithm

The evolution starts with a randomly generated set of individuals (initial population) consisting of two functions $f_x(t)$ and $f_y(t)$. Due to the fact, that the algorithm has to evolve parametric functions, two symbolic representations have to be generated in parallel. The genetic operations are applied to this first generation of functions and a succeeding generation is produced, see fig. 2. The fitness of an individual is measured directly by evaluating the evolved formulae and comparing the geometric shape of these parametric functions with the given point set (i.e. the trajectory of the chip). Technically, the formulae are represented as instances of a tree-based data structure, which is implemented in C++ using the "Standard Template Library" (STL). Hence, the fitness function can be evaluated in a fast and efficient way. It is also possible to use an interpreter, which may be more flexible in some cases (e.g. for debugging tasks), but slows down the evaluation. The basic structure of the program follows a classic

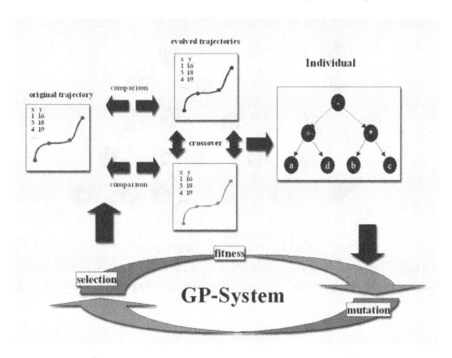

Fig. 2. General GP scheme.

GP scheme [3,2,7]. The probability of choosing a constant during mutation, the maximum size of an individual or the probability of changing a function or a terminal and the number of changes is defined in a parameter file. The data structure and the genetic operators will be described in th following section.

2.1   Data Structure

Analog to the infix notation of mathematical functions, a tree based representation forms the genotype. A sample individual is shown in fig. 3. The primary goal of obtaining the mathematical representations of two-dimensional curves leads to the phenotypic representation of an individual as graphs of a parametric function. This difference between genotypic and phenotypic representation and the need for genetic operators, in which small changes in the genotype results in small changes in the phenotype, yields two problems.

First, a set of genetic operators, which allows to do these small changes on the genotype, must be used. Second, a fitness function which correctly evaluates the fitness of one individual has to be defined. The genetic operators are known as mutation and recombination. Mutation takes place on a single individual and changes one or more positions of the individual. Here, it is

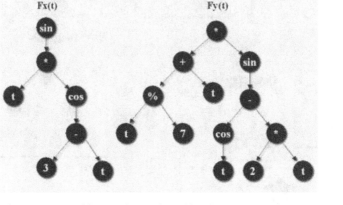

$$f_x(t) = \sin(t * \cos(3 - t))$$
$$f_y(t) = (t/7 + t) * \sin(\cos(t) - 2 * t) \tag{2}$$

Fig. 3. Sample structure of a single individual and the corresponding parametric function.

a single node of the tree. The second genetic operator is the recombination between two arbitrary individuals. The genetic recombination operator selects an arbitrary node in the first individual and replaces it by an arbitrarily selected node from the second individual. These two genetic operators allow to change the genotype yielding small changes in the phenotype of the individual. The amount of change in the phenotype can be reduced and increased by setting the amount of mutation (e.g. no. of nodes to be chosen). A closer look at these operators is given in [8,7].

2.2 Fitness Function

Here a fitness function is used which compares the function values of the individual with corresponding points of the trajectory. If all points of the trajectory are positioned on the function plot this individual will represent a perfect solution to the problem. The fitness values will be represented by a weighted point to value distance scheme. They are summed up by a root mean square sum.

In order to improve the efficiency of the naive approach, some variations may been implemented, see [7]. This may lead to a faster adaption of the curves without adding any extra knowledge to the algorithm.

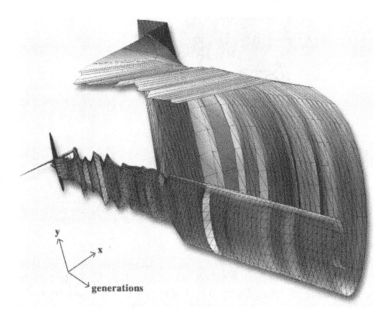

Fig. 4. Individual extruded in a space-time plot.

3   The New Graphic Representation

Due to the fact that choosing the right parameters for setting up a fast and safe reconstruction of the estimated functions a new graphic representation of a complete reconstruction GP run has been developed. In order to allow an overview on the whole chronology of the reconstruction process, a third dimension was added to the two dimensions (function values of $f_x(t)$ and $f_y(t)$) of the current best individual of the run, see fig. 4. This third dimension is the amount of how many best individuals were found in the reconstruction. This is done dumping all best individuals in this current run ordered by the time of their appearance. Therefore, a standard CAD-CAM file format was used. This stereo lithography format is well defined and can be used in various CAD-CAM systems or computer-graphic systems. This allows the various possibilities for rendering and later usage of the generated objects. The data are generated by building triangles which have two of their vertices in two consecutive points of one individual and one vertex in another neighboring individual. I. e. one triangle consists of the points $p[in][pn]$ and $p[in][pn + 1]$ in the individual indicated by in and a third point $p[in - 1][pn]$ in a second individual indicated by $in - 1$. It is obvious that, in oder to get a closed surface, the following triangle has two points in the individual indicated by $in - 1$, all three points for this individual are $p[in - 1][pn], p[in - 1][pn + 1]$ and $p[in][pn + 1]$. This scheme is shown in fig. 5. A sample rendering of such a plot is shown in fig. 4. The rendering was carried

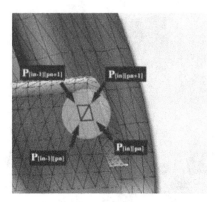

Fig. 5. The scheme for the triangulation at two triangles.

out using a third party software called 3D-Exploration from Righthemisphere, Inc. The timeline is orientated from left (back) side of the figure to final stage at the right (front). In this final stage the individual has reached a fitness of 0.98. One remark that can be derived from this picture is, that only a small amount of steps is needed to reconstruct the general shape of the individual After this phase the algorithm behaves more like an evolutionary strategy in [4] to reach the final shape.

4   Results

4.1   Test Function

In this case, a known function (3) was used for reconstruction in order to illustrate the operation of the symbolic regression algorithm.

$$\boldsymbol{f}(t) = \begin{pmatrix} f_x(t) \\ f_y(t) \end{pmatrix} = \begin{pmatrix} \sin(\frac{\pi}{180} * t) * \frac{t}{10} \\ \cos(\frac{\pi}{180} * t) * \frac{t}{10} \end{pmatrix} \tag{3}$$

The shape of the graph of $\boldsymbol{f}(t)$ resembles a chip. The values of the parameter t range from 0 to 360. For simulation purposes this function was sampled yielding discrete points which represent points which could have been sampled from a film sequence. The final stage of the reconstruction, the plot and the graph of the best individual is shown in fig. 6. In spite of weighting the length of the individual in the fitness calculation the relation function (4) of best individual after this reconstruction contains more nodes than the original function (3).

$$\boldsymbol{f}(t) = \begin{pmatrix} f_x(t) \\ f_y(t) \end{pmatrix} = \begin{pmatrix} \frac{\sin(\frac{t}{57.2969}) * \frac{t}{27.8692}}{\sin(25.4997)} \\ \cos(\frac{t*\sin(149.902)}{44.6694}) * 12.2718 * \sin(40.5023) * \frac{t}{40.738} \end{pmatrix} \tag{4}$$

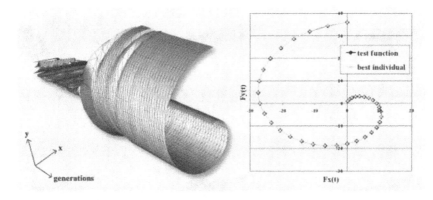

Fig. 6. The final stage of the reconstruction of the test function.

If the resulting function is reduced by hand (5) it can be seen that the real structure of the required relation function is found by the algorithm. This basic structure can be used for further extrapolations. The reduced form is given by:

$$\begin{pmatrix} f_x(t) \\ f_y(t) \end{pmatrix} = \begin{pmatrix} \sin(0.0175 * t) * t * 0.0920 \\ \cos(0.0178 * t) * t * 0.1000 \end{pmatrix} \tag{5}$$

Another method for analyzing the behaviour of the population is to dump the whole population into one file. All individuals are sorted by the fitness value to enable a closer look at the progression of the solution within the whole population. Fig. 7 gives a sample plot of the reconstruction of the test function at particular times of the reconstruction process. It can be seen, that due to the application of a "Plus Selection Strategy" like in [4] in the regression process, the best individual propagates very fast through the whole population. It may be useful to consider the usage of a comma strategy at this point to get a more genetic diversion of the population.Another way to use a type of multi population strategy is to keep a higher genetic diversity.

Table 1. Parameter table for diversity test.

value	parameter
200	Number of parents per generation.
300	Number of children per generation.
1	Weight of the distance fitness to overall fitness.
0.9	Probability of inserting a node.
0.9	Probability of deleting a node.
0.9	Probability of mutating a inner node.
0.6	Probability of inserting a value.
0.5	Probability of inserting a function.

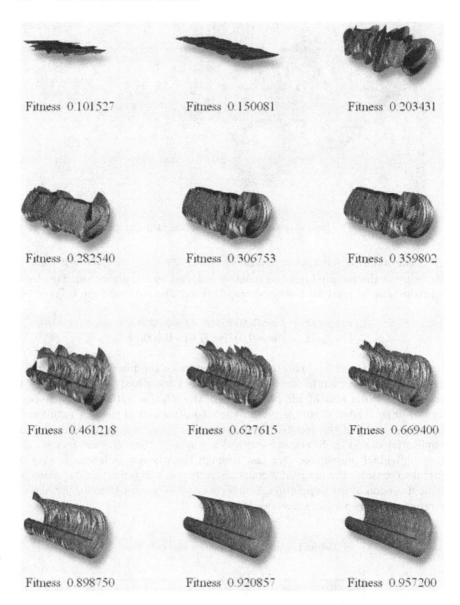

Fitness 0.101527   Fitness 0.150081   Fitness 0.203431

Fitness 0.282540   Fitness 0.306753   Fitness 0.359802

Fitness 0.461218   Fitness 0.627615   Fitness 0.669400

Fitness 0.898750   Fitness 0.920857   Fitness 0.957200

Fig. 7. The population at different generations of the reconstruction. Each picture shows one complete population at discrete values of their overall fitness. The individuals are sorted according to their fitness from lower fitness at the left to greater fitness at the right side of the 3D-shapes. During the starting phase were low fitness values appear a strong diversity of the individuals in the population can be observed. With increasing fitness values the population looses its diversity. At this stage the main reconstruction work is performed by variation of the similar individuals.

4.2   Real World Data

In the next experiment, the algorithm is applied to data extracted from a recorded movie sequence of the turning process as described in section 1. To get information about the physical correlations which lead to the shape of the chip in the turning process, the positions of the chip are manually traced out of the film sequence, see fig. 8. One difference to the previous test function is the

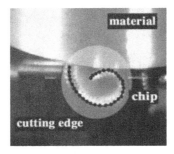

Fig. 8. Manually traced particle flow (picture size 30 mm by 30 mm).

lack of knowledge about the exact number of nodes needed to obtain a sufficient model of the physical process. Therefore, the number of necessary nodes needs to be estimated and as a consequence the weighting factor of the number of nodes in the fitness calculation had to be reduced. The parameters for the estimated best node count are increased to 40 nodes and also the average initial size of the individuals is increased to 40 nodes. Therefore, the resulting relation functions (6) are not as short and handy as the results from the test function, but as fig. 9 illustrates, the algorithm shows a tendency to smooth the trajectories. The approximations can be improved locally by increasing the number of sampling points. This way the reconstructions are forced to follow also small curvatures of the particle flow.

$$f(t) = \begin{pmatrix} \cos\left(\dfrac{-0.8995}{\sin\left(\frac{4.991}{t+40.5886}\right)}\right) * t + 3t * \sin\left(\frac{27.423}{t}\right) + 0.3679t \\ 1.141 + \dfrac{t+\sin(t)+\frac{0.020}{t}-1655.335*t}{\sin(t)+148.944-t} - 0.624t \end{pmatrix} \qquad (6)$$

5   Conclusion

This paper presents an new method to analyze the behaviour of a reconstruction of mathematical functions by the use of symbolic regression via genetic programming. This graphic representation of the reconstruction process can be used in multiple ways to optimize and or visualize the whole reconstruction

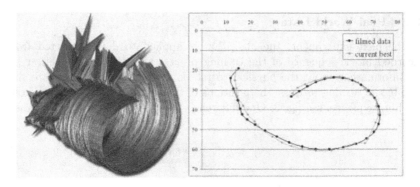

Fig. 9. Two dimensional plot of best individual and the original data.

process. Furthermore, it can be used to investigate specific points of time in the reconstruction. Two sample runs of a symbolic regression on real world problems are shown. These examples show the possibilities given by this representation. Additional considerations can be made to integrate this system into standard symbolic regression libraries.

Acknowledgements. This research was supported by the Deutsche Forschungsgemeinschaft as part of the Collaborative Research Center "Computational Intelligence" (SFB 531).

References

1. T . Inamura. Brittle/ductile phenomena observed in computer simulations of machining defect-free monocrystalline silicon. *Annals of the CIRP*, 46:31–34, 1997.
2. R. E. Keller, J. Mehnen, W. Banzhaf, and K. Weinert. *Surface reconstruction from 3D point data with a genetic programming / evolution strategy hybrid*, volume 3 of *Advances in Genetic Programming*, chapter 2, pages 41–65. MIT Press, 1999.
3. J. R. Koza. *Genetic Programming: On the Programming of Computers by Means of Natural Selection*. MIT Press, Cambridge, 1992.
4. H.-P. Schwefel. *Evolution and Optimum Seeking*. Wiley-Interscience, USA, 1995.
5. S. Shimada, N. Ikawa, H. Tanaka, and J. Uchikoshi. Structure of Micromachined Surface Simulated by Molecular Dynamics Analysis. *Annals of the CIRP*, 1994.
6. G. Warnecke. *Spanbildung bei metallischen Werkstoffen*. Technischer Verlag Resch, Munich, 1974.
7. K. Weinert and M. Stautner. Reconstruction of Particle Flow Mechanisms with Symbolic Regression via Genetic Programming. In Lee Spector et al., editor, *Proceedings of the Genetic and Evolutionary Computation Conference (GECCO-2001)*, pages 1439–1443, San Francisco, USA, 7-11 July 2001. Morgan Kaufmann.
8. K. Weinert, T. Surmann, and J. Mehnen. Evolutionary surface reconstruction using CSG-NURBS-hybrids. Reihe CI 114/01, SFB 531, University of Dortmund, 2001.

Grammatical Evolution Rules: The Mod and the Bucket Rule

Maarten Keijzer[1], Michael O'Neill[2], Conor Ryan[3], and Mike Cattolico[4]

[1] Free University, Amsterdam, mkeijzer@cs.vu.nl
[2] University of Limerick, Michael.ONeill@ul.ie
[3] University of Limerick, Conor.Ryan@ul.ie
[4] Tiger Mountain Scientific Inc., mike@tigerscience.com

Abstract. We present an alternative mapping function called the *Bucket Rule*, for Grammatical Evolution, that improves upon the standard modulo rule. Grammatical Evolution is applied to a set of standard Genetic Algorithm problem domains using two alternative grammars. Applying GE to GA problems allows us to focus on a simple grammar whose effects are easily analysable. It will be shown that by using the bucket rule a greater degree of grammar independence is achieved.

1 Introduction

Grammatical Evolution [9], [8], [10] is an evolutionary automatic programming system [5],[6], [7], [1] that can generate programs in an arbitrary language. Grammatical Evolution adopts a genotype-phenotype mapping process, such that a syntactically correct program is generated, according to the codons of the genotype selecting production rules from a BNF grammar, which describes the output language. The production rules are selected by calling the mapping rule, which is a simple modulo function in the current incarnation of Grammatical Evolution.

We present an alternative mapping function, called the Bucket Rule, for Grammatical Evolution that improves upon the standard modulo rule. Consider a simple context free grammar that can be used to generate variable length bitstrings:

```
<bitstring>    ::= <bit> | <bit> <bitstring>.

<bit>                ::= 0 | 1.
```

This context free grammar has two non-terminal symbols, each of which have two production rules. In the Grammatical Evolution system a string of so-called codons are maintained, each consisting of 8 bits of information. The modulo rule defines a degenerate mapping from those 8 bits of information to a choice for a production rule in the following way. Given a set of n non-terminals with a corresponding number of production rules $[c_1, \ldots, c_n]$ and given the current symbol r, the mapping rule used is:

$$\text{choice}(r) = \text{codon} \mod c_r \tag{1}$$

J.A. Foster et al. (Eds.): EuroGP 2002, LNCS 2278, pp. 123–130, 2002.
© Springer-Verlag Berlin Heidelberg 2002

This modulo rule ensures that the codon value is mapped into the interval $[0, c_r]$ and thus represents a valid choice for a production rule. As the codons themselves are drawn from the interval $[0, 255]$, the mapping rule is degenerate: many codon values map to the same choice of rules. Unfortunately, in the case of the context-free grammar given above, the modulo rule will map all even codon values to the first rule and all odd values to the second rule, regardless of the non-terminal symbol that is active. In effect, when using this context-free grammar in combination with the modulo mapping rule, it is the least significant bit in the codon value that fully determines the mapping: all other 7 bits are redundant.

In the context of the untyped crossover and associated intrinsic polymorphism that is usually used in GE [4] — strings of codon values taken from two independently drawn points from the genotypes can be swapped. Here it is possible that a codon value that was used to encode for the <bitstring> non-terminal can be used to encode a choice for the <bit> non-terminal, due to intrinsic polymorphism, that is a codon can specify a rule for every non-terminal in the grammar and therefore, has meaning in every context.

As the codon values only make a distinction between *first* and *second* choice through their least significant bits, in the above bitstring grammar, a linkage between production rules belonging to different non-terminals is introduced. In the bitstring context-free grammar studied here, this linkage leads to

Codon Value	non-terminal Symbol	
	<bit>	<bitstring>
0	0	<bit>
1	1	<bit> <bitstring>

A codon value of 0, for example, always selects the first production rule for every non-terminal (i.e. in above, <bit> would become 0, and <bitstring> would become <bit>). Thus regardless of the context (the non-terminal) in which the codon is used, it will have a fixed choice of production rules. It would be better for GE's intrinsic polymorphism if this linkage did not exist, thus each non-terminal's production rule choice is independent of all the other non-terminals when intrinsic polymorphism comes into play.

2   The Bucket Rule

The linkage between production rules belonging to different non-terminal symbols, in combination with untyped variation operators introduces a bias in the search process. This bias is undesirable because it depends on the layout of the program and its impact on the search is not clear. In effect this means that the order in which the rules are defined are expected to make a difference to the search efficiency.

To remove this bias the mapping rule is changed. Given again our set of clauses for n non-terminal symbols $[c_1, \ldots, c_n]$, the codon values are now taken from the interval $[0, \prod_{i=1}^{n} c_i]$. The mapping rule is subsequently changed to:

$$\text{choice}(r) = \frac{\text{codon}}{\prod_{i=1}^{r-1} c_i} \mod c_r \tag{2}$$

This rule is simply the standard method for mapping multi-dimensional matrices into a contiguous array of values. With this rule, every legal codon value encodes a unique set of production rules, one from each non-terminal. In the grammar discussed here, the codons are drawn from $[0, 3]$. The codon values encode for the production rules given the non-terminals in the following way:

Codon Value	non-terminal Symbol	
	<bit>	<bitstring>
0	0	<bit>
1	1	<bit> <bitstring>
2	0	<bit> <bitstring>
3	1	<bit>

We choose the name *buckets* because we believe the manner in which a single codon value can code for a number of different choices across different rules is similar to the manner in which keys can hash to identical locations in certain hashing algorithms.

3   Experimental Setup

Grammatical Evolution is applied to a set of standard Genetic Algorithm [3], [2] problem domains using two alternative grammars. Applying GE to GA problems allows us to focus on a simple grammar whose effects are easily analysable.

We perform experiments that demonstrate the existence of these problems, and consequently we introduce the Bucket Rule as an alternative mapping function that overcomes the limitations of the standard modulo rule.

Four experimental setups exist using two separate grammars, Grammar 0 and Grammar 1 are given below, where the only difference between these two grammars is the ordering of the productions rules for the non-terminal <bit> .

Grammar 0

```
(A) <bitstring> :=
        <bit><bitstring> (0)
      | <bit>            (1)

(B) <bit> := 0   (0)
           | 1   (1)
```

Grammar 1

```
(A) <bitstring> :=
        <bit><bitstring> (0)
      | <bit>            (1)

(B) <bit> := 1   (0)
           | 0   (1)
```

The first two experimental setups (Setup 0 and Setup 1) use the two grammars with the standard modulo mapping rule, the third and fourth experimental setups use grammar 0 (Setup 2) and grammar 1 (Setup 3) respectively, but in both cases the Bucket rule is adopted.

Three seperate problems are used in the analysis of these grammars, One Max, a variant of One Max, which we call Half One's, and a deceptive trap problem (comprising ten four-bit subfunctions). The problem specific experimental parameters can be seen in Tables 1 and 2.

In the case of One Max, the goal, as normal, is to set all the bits of the phenotype string to 1. For the Half One's problem, the goal is to set the first half of the string to 1's and the second half to 0's. The deceptive trap problem involves finding ten subfunctions (a subfunction is a group of four-bits), where the optimum fitness is achieved when all four-bits of each subfunction are 0. The trap arises due to the fact that when a subfunction has all four-bits set to 1, the next best fitness is achieved, e.g. looking at one subfunction (the fitness for each subfunction is summed to produce the overall fitness):

$$0\ 0\ 1\ 0\ (\ Fitness\ =\ 1\ )$$

$$1\ 0\ 1\ 0\ (\ Fitness\ =\ 2\ )$$

$$1\ 1\ 1\ 1\ (\ Fitness\ =\ 4\ )$$

$$0\ 0\ 0\ 0\ (\ Fitness\ =\ 5\ )$$

Table 1. Experimental parameters for One Max and Half One's

Parameter	Value
Popsize	50
Generations	20
Maximum genome length	401
Evaluation length	101
Genome Initialisation length	20
Tournament Size	3
Replacement	Steady State
Crossover Probability	1
Mutation Probability	0
Wrapping	Off

Given the grammars being analysed in this paper we can identify the form of the global optimum's genotype for each of the problems addressed. For example, in the case of One Max, with Grammar 0 this would take the form 0101010101..., whereas with Grammar 1 this would be 1111111111.... Global genotype forms for all three problems are given in Table 3.

Table 2. Experimental parameters for the Deceptive Trap problem.

Parameter	Value
Popsize	1000
Generations	100
Maximum genome length	160
Evaluation length	40
Genome Initialisation length	20
Tournament Size	3
Replacement	Steady State
Crossover Probability	1
Mutation Probability	0
Wrapping	Off

4   Results

A plot of the average over 100 runs of the mean fitness values at each generation of a run over the three problems can be seen in Fig. 1.

Table 3. Global optimum genotype forms for both Grammar 0 and Grammar 1 on each problem examined.

Problem	Global Optimum Form	
	Grammar 0	**Grammar 1**
One Max	01010101...	11111111...
Half One's	0101...0000...	0101...0101...
Deceptive Trap	00000000...	01010101...

The mean fitness values for the final generation on each of the three problems investigated can be seen in Table 4.

Table 4. Average over 100 runs of the mean fitness values for the final generation on each of the three problems investigated. Setup 0 uses Grammar 0 with the mod rule, Setup 1 uses Grammar 1 with the mod rule, Setup 2 uses Grammar 0 with the Bucket Rule, and Setup 3 uses Grammar 1 with the Bucket Rule.

	Average Mean Fitness			
Problem	**Setup 0**	**Setup 1**	**Setup 2**	**Setup 3**
One Max	42.476	39.627	39.627	39.181
Half One's	29.026	29.2	30.094	30.335
Deceptive Trap	21.904	23.913	22.077	22.5

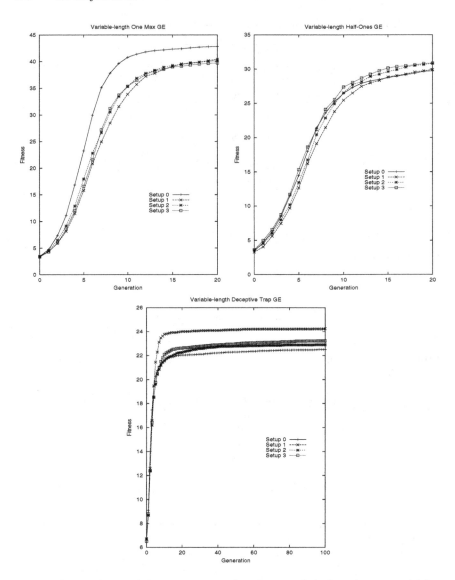

Fig. 1. A comparison of the average over the 100 runs of the best fitness on the four experimental setups for One Max, Half One's, and the Deceptive Trap problems.

A statistical analysis of the mean fitness values contained in Table 4 is conducted using a ttest and, as confirmation of these results, a bootstrap ttest is also applied. In our analysis we wish to investigate if there is a statistically significant difference (at the 95% confidence level) between the means for the different grammars.

Table 5. Results of the statistical analysis using both a ttest and bootstrap ttest. Setup 0 uses Grammar 0 with the mod rule, Setup 1 uses Grammar 1 with the mod rule, Setup 2 uses Grammar 0 with the Bucket Rule, and Setup 3 uses Grammar 1 with the Bucket Rule.

Problem	Significance of Comparison	
	(Setup 0 vs. Setup 1)	(Setup 2 vs. Setup 3)
One Max	Yes	No
Half One's	No	No
Deceptive Trap	Yes	No

On both One Max and Deceptive Trap there is a statistically significant difference in the means for the two grammars when adopting the standard modulo mapping rule (Setup 0 and Setup 1) as can be seen in Table 5. As such, we find that different grammars can make significant changes to the performance of GE, due to the improper exploitation of intrinsic polymorphism. In the case of the Half One's problem, this is acting like a control experiment in that half of the optimum solution string is suited to Grammar 0 and half is suited to Grammar 1, thus any effects due to bias and intrinsic polymorphism should be non-existent.

When comparing Setup 2 and Setup 3 in which the Bucket Rule was adopted with the two grammars (also see Table 5), there is no statistical difference between the means. Any difference that existed between the two grammars while using the modulo rule has been removed as a result of adopting the Bucket rule. Thus the Bucket rule clearly aids the exploitation of intrinsic polymorphism. The results of statistical analysis with the remaining combinations of comparisons between experimental setups is given in Table 6.

Table 6. Results of the statistical analysis using both a ttest and bootstrap ttest. Setup 0 uses Grammar 0 with the mod rule, Setup 1 uses Grammar 1 with the mod rule, Setup 2 uses Grammar 0 with the Bucket Rule, and Setup 3 uses Grammar 1 with the Bucket Rule.

Problem	Significance of Comparison			
	(0 vs. 2)	(0 vs. 3)	(1 vs. 3)	(1 vs. 2)
One Max	Yes	Yes	No	No
Half One's	Yes	Yes	Yes	No
Deceptive Trap	No	Yes	Yes	Yes

On these problems the performance without the Bucket rule tends to be better, see Table 6, however, this performance is very sensitive to the setup of the grammar adopted. Whereas, with the Bucket rule performance is insensitive to the grammar used.

5   Conclusions & Future Work

We have presented the Bucket rule, a new mapping function for Grammatical Evolution that improves upon the standard modulo mapping rule. An analysis of the Bucket rule compared to the modulo rule has been conducted on a number of GA problems of varying difficulty in conjunction with two simple grammars. The grammars and problems were selected to allow our analysis to elucidate the effects that the mapping rules play on the system's performance. Results of the analysis clearly show the benefits of adopting the Bucket in place of the modulo rule.

Future work will investigate the possiblity of alternative mapping rules for Grammatical Evolution, and a more thorough analysis of the effects of the Bucket rule on evolutionary dynamics, particularly with respect to the degenerate code and neutral evolution. It is hypothesised that the Bucket rule will faciliate the exploitation of neutral evolution to a greater extent than the modulo rule allowed.

References

1. Banzhaf W., Nordin P., Keller R.E., Francone F.D. (1998) *Genetic Programming – An Introduction; On the Automatic Evolution of Computer Programs and its Applications.* Morgan Kaufmann.
2. Goldberg, D. (1989). *Genetic Algorithms in Search, Optimization and Machine Learning,* Boston, USA, Addison Wesley, Longman.
3. Holland, J. (1975). *Adaptation in Natural and Artificial Systems.* Ann Arbor, USA, University of Michigan Press.
4. Keijzer M., Ryan C., O'Neill M., Cattolico M, Babovic V. (2001) Ripple Crossover in Genetic Programming. *LNCS 2038, Proc. of the Fourth European Conference on Genetic Programming,* Lake Como, Italy, April 2001, pp.74-86. Springer.
5. Koza, J.R. (1992). *Genetic Programming.* MIT Press.
6. Koza J.R. (1994). *Genetic Programming II: Automatic Discovery of Reusable Programs.* MIT Press.
7. Koza J.R., Andre D., Bennett III F.H., and Keane M. (1999) *Genetic Programming III: Darwinian Invention and Problem Solving.* Morgan Kaufman.
8. O'Neill M. (2001) Automatic Programming in an Arbitrary language: Evolving Programs with Grammatical Evolution. Ph.D. thesis, University of Limerick, 2001.
9. O'Neill M., Ryan C. (2001) Grammatical Evolution. *IEEE Trans. Evolutionary Computation,* Vol. 5 No. 4, August 2001.
10. Ryan C., Collins J.J., O'Neill M. (1998). Grammatical Evolution: Evolving Programs for an Arbitrary Language. *LNCS 1391, Proc. of the First European Workshop on Genetic Programming,* pp. 83-95. Springer-Verlag.

No Coercion and No Prohibition, a Position Independent Encoding Scheme for Evolutionary Algorithms – The Chorus System

Conor Ryan, Atif Azad, Alan Sheahan, and Michael O'Neill

Department of Computer Science and Information Systems
University of Limerick
Ireland
{Conor.Ryan|Atif.Azad|Alan.Sheahan|Michael.ONeill}@ul.ie

Abstract. We describe a new encoding system, *Chorus*, for grammar based Evolutionary Algorithms. This scheme is coarsely based on the manner in nature in
which genes produce proteins that regulate the metabolic pathways of the cell.
The phenotype is the behaviour of the cells metabolism, which corresponds to the
development of the computer program in our case. In this procedure, the actual
protein encoded by a gene is the same regardless of the position of the gene within
the genome.
We show that the Chorus system has a very convenient Regular Expression - type
schema notation that can be used to describe the presence of various phenotypes or
phenotypic traits. This schema notation is used to demonstrate that massive areas
of neutrality can exist in the search landscape, and the system is also shown to be
able to dispense with large areas of the search space that are unlikely to contain
useful solutions.

1 Introduction

The mapping from genotype to phenotype in nature is rarely as simple as the one gene-one
trait methodology often employed by Evolutionary Algorithms. Moreover, the function
of a gene in nature is rarely dependent on its position within the chromosome, for they
usually produce the same *protein* regardless of their situation. It is the proteins produced
by genes that combine to regulate the metabolism of a cell resulting in the observed
phenotypic traits[1] [13] [11].

The function, independent of location, property has been proved notoriously difficult
to implement in EAs. Usually, any kind of position independence forces the use of a
repair operator after crossover, to ensure that every required gene is present. There can
also be an issue of *overspecification*, but this is often left unrepaired, as it doesn't affect
the decoding.

Having function inextricably linked to location increases the difficulty of a problem
for an EA, for it is clearly more difficult for an individual to have a gene at a particular
position than it is for the individual to simply possess it. The situation is aggravated by

---

[1] Other factors are also responsible for the regulation of metabolism, our current model focuses
on one of the major factors - the concentration of specific regulatory enzymes/proteins.

J.A. Foster et al. (Eds.): EuroGP 2002, LNCS 2278, pp. 131–141, 2002.

epistatic effects, where an increase in fitness is associated with having several correct genes, each in a particular place.

There have been some attempts to design position independent Genetic Algorithms, most notably the Messy GA[9], but this involved a repair mechanism after crossover, and wasn't intended to deal with the evolution of grammars, and is generally employed with fixed length binary strings.

This paper presents a position independent representation that we term *Chorus*. It is so called because, when the system is transcribing from genotype to phenotype, there is often a competition as to which protein should be dominant in regulating any one of many possible metabolic pathways that could be taken. This, we believe, is analogous to a situation where there are a number of voices striving to be heard. Typically, the loudest voice is heard, and so, the protein with the greatest *claim* to be expressed, is chosen. Like Grammatical Evolution (GE)[6][4], [1], [2],[3],[5],[7],[10], and [12], Chorus evolves programs using grammars.

The paper first gives an introduction to Backus Naur Form. Next, the Chorus system is described in detail, paying particular attention to the manner in which *claims* are resolved. We show that although the ordering of some genes is important, their function and effect is independent of their location. Section 4 details a powerful schema notation that can be used to describe individuals and the effects of operations such as crossover and mutation, while section 6 outlines the performance of the system on some standard benchmark problems.

2   Backus Naur Form

Backus Naur Form (BNF) is a notation for describing grammars. A grammar is represented by a tuple $\{N, T, P, S\}$, where T is a set of terminals, i.e. items that can appear in legal sentences of the grammar, and N is a set of non-terminals, which are interim items used in the generation of terminals. P is the set of production rules that map the non-terminals to the terminals, and S is a start symbol, from which all legal sentences may be generated.

Below is a sample grammar, which is similar to that used by Koza [8] in his symbolic regression and integration problems. Although Koza didn't employ grammars, the terminals in this grammar are similar to his function and terminal set.

```
S = <expr>
<expr>    ::=  <expr> <op> <expr>    (0)
          | ( <expr> <op> <expr>)(1)
          | <pre-op> ( <expr> )   (2)
          | <var>                 (3)
<op>      ::= + (4) | - (5) | / (6) | * (7)
<pre-op>  ::= Sin (8) | Cos (9) | Exp (A) | Log (B)
<var>     ::= 1.0 (C) | X (D)
```

3 The Chorus System

In a similar manner to GE, Chorus uses a chromosome of eight bit numbers (termed genes) to dictate which rules from the grammar to apply. However, unlike the intrinsically polymorphic codons of GE, each gene in Chorus corresponds to a particular production rule, similar to the GAGS[5] system, although Chorus doesn't have quite the same issue with introns as GAGS did.

For example, consider the individual : **28 21 42 27 27 17 31 18 15 45 55 21 31 27 65**, which can be looked upon as a collection of hard coded production rules. A rule is obtained from a gene by simply **mod**ing it by the *total* number of production rules. In this case, that is 14, giving us, in hex: **0 7 0 D D 3 3 4 1 3 D 7 3 D 9**. Each gene encodes a *protein* which, in our case is a production rule. Proteins in this case are enzymes that regulate the metabolism of the cell. These proteins can combine with other proteins (production rules in our case) to take particular *metabolic pathways*, which are, essentially, phenotypes. The more of a gene that is present in the genome, the greater the *concentration* of the corresponding protein will be during the mapping process [13] [11]. In a coarse model of this, we introduce the notion of a *concentration table*. The concentration table is simply a measure of the concentrations of each of the proteins at any given time, and is initialised with each concentration at zero. At any stage, the protein with the greatest concentration will be chosen, switching on the corresponding metabolic pathway, thus, the switching on of a metabolic pathway corresponds to the development of the forming solution with the application of a production rule.

During the mapping process, a number of decisions have to be made, for example, the start symbol <expr> has four possible mappings. When such a decision has to be resolved, the relevant area of the concentration table is consulted. In this case, the entries for the first four rules are examined.

Decision resolution in this case is analogous to a group of voices, vying for attention where the loudest voice, i.e., the protein with the greatest concentration level, will come out on top. However if there is not a clear winner, then the genome is read until one of the relevant proteins becomes dominant.

While searching for a particular concentration, it is probable that some other proteins, unrelated to the current choice, will be encountered. In this case, their corresponding concentration is increased, so when that production rule is involved in a choice, it will be more likely to win. This is where the position independence aspect of the system comes in to play; the crucial thing is the presence or otherwise of a gene, while its position is less so. Importantly, *absolute* position almost never matters, while occasionly, *relative* position (to another gene) is important.

Once the choice has been made, the concentration of the chosen production rule is decremented. However, it is not possible for a concentration to fall below zero.

Chorus always works with the left most non-terminal in the current sentence, and continues until either there are none left, or it encounters a choice for which there are no genes to promote the concentrations. In the latter case, the individual responsible is given a suitably chastening fitness measure to ensure that it is unlikely to engage in any kind of reproductive activity in the subsequent generation. Current setup assigns a fitness value of it zero.

3.1 Example Individual

Using the grammar from section 2 we will now demonstrate the genotype-phenotype mapping of a Chorus individual. The particular individual is encoded by the following genome:

| 28 | 21 | 42 | 27 | 27 | 17 | 31 | 18 | 15 | 45 | 55 | 21 | 31 | 27 | 65 |

For clarity, we also show the normalised values of each gene, that is, the genes mod 14. This is only done for readability, as in the Chorus system, the genome is only read on demand and not decoded until needed.

| 0 | 7 | 0 | D | D | 3 | 3 | 4 | 1 | 3 | D | 7 | 3 | D | 9 |

The first step in decoding the individual is the creation of the concentration table. There is one entry for each production rule (0..D), each of which is initially empty.

Rule #	0	1	2	3	4	5	6	7	8	9	A	B	C	D
Concentration														

The sentence starts as `<expr>`, so the first choice must be made from productions 0..3 from section 2:

None of these have a non-zero concentration yet, so we must read the first gene from the genome, which will cause it to produce its protein. This gene decodes to 0, which is involved in the current choice. Its concentration is amended, and the choice made. As this is the only production in the current choice that has any concentration, it will be selected, and the current expression becomes: `<expr><op><expr>`.

The process is repeated for the next leftmost non-terminal, which is another `expr`. In this case, again the concentrations are at their minimal level for the possible choices, so another gene is read and processed. This gene is 7, which is not involved in the current choice, so we move on and keep reading the genome till we find rule 0 which is a relevant rule. Meanwhile we increment the concentration of rule 7. Similar to the previous step, production rule #0 is chosen, so the expression is now

`<expr><op><expr><op><expr>`

The next attempt to find a rule for the non-terminal `expr`, produces rule 3, incrementing the concentration for rule D twice in the process. The expression now becomes `<var><op><expr><op><expr>`

The current state of the concentration table is:

Rule #	0	1	2	3	4	5	6	7	8	9	A	B	C	D
Concentration								1						2

The next choice is between rules #C and #D, however, as #D already has a positive concentration, the system does not read any more genes from the chromosome, and instead uses the values present. As a result, rule `<var>` `->` X is chosen to introduce first terminal symbol in the expression.

Once this non-terminal has been mapped to a terminal, we move to the next left most terminal, `<op>` and carry on from there. If, while reading the genome, we come to the end, and there is still a tie between 2 or more rules, the one that appears first in the concentration table is chosen. However if none of the relevant rules has a positive concentration, the mapping terminates and the individual is given a suitably chastening fitness.

With this particular individual, mapping continues, till the individual is completely mapped. The mapped individual is

`X * X + ( X * X )`

4   Schema Theory in Chorus

Clearly, with such a complex mapping procedure, it is difficult to elucidate exactly what a particular genome will produce, both in terms of mapping and crossover/mutation events. This difficulty is compounded by the fact that it is possible for introns to exist. For example, gene #9 in the example above has no effect on the phenotype. Furthermore, because its effect is independent of its position, it could have been placed anywhere on the genome and not affected the phenotype. In fact, due to the apparent oblivion of the phenotype to the existence of gene #9, there could be several instances of it, spread throughout the chromosome, none of which would affect the phenotype.

The reason for this is that it is a *dependent* gene. That is, the level or otherwise of its concentration is irrelevant unless gene #2 is first expressed. We can go further than this, and say that the entire set of `<pre_op>` production rules are dominated, and can thus appear anywhere in the chromosome, as long as gene #2 does not appear. We use α to denote this set of dominated rules. Other dominated sets of rules include $\{4, 5, 6, 7\}$ and $\{C, D\}$. However, we are currently interested in describing the above individual, and the only dominated set which cannot be expressed is α.

$$\alpha = \{8, 9, A, B\} \tag{1}$$

The dependent genes illustrate how Chorus can effectively cut off sections of the search space. For example, once the gene 2, upon which those in α are dependent, has been removed from the population, the area of search space involving trigonometric functions is removed from the current search.

As with all schema notations, it is unusual for a schema to specify a single individual. We take the view of using a schema to describe a set of individuals that conform to a certain phenotype. Due to the fact that there is a mapping procedure in place, however, it is not possible to simply specify the phenotypic traits (or sub-traits) that we are interested in. Instead, we use our schema to describe individuals at a genotypic level that adhere to certain phenotypic traits.

Consider the individual **0 7 0 D D 3 3 4 1 3 D 7 3 D 9** from the example above, which maps to X*X+(X*X). Clearly, it is important that both the instances of gene #0 should come before both the instances of #3, otherwise the rule

`<expr>` -> `<expr>` `<op>` `<expr>` would not be chosen, leading to a different expression with fewer operators and terminals in it.

For the sake of simplicity, we treat the individual as three distinct parts, that is, **0 7 0 D D 3 3**, **4 1** and **3 D 7 3 D 9**.

Let us concentrate on the first part for a moment. Regular expressions provide a convenient representation in this instance, as the expression **0 7 0 D D 3 3** indicates that we must have both instances of 0 before any instance of 3. This suggests a schema of **0 0 3 3**. However, this is too strict, as we already established that it is possible to have zero or more instances of any member of the α set, without affecting the meaning of the individual in any way. This is represented in regular expressions by appending a * to an item, i.e. α^* indicates that there can be zero or more instances of an element of that set(with replacement). Similarly, α^+ indicates that there should be one or more instances.

Thus, the all important **0 0 3 3** expression could also be represented by $\alpha^*\ 0\ \alpha^*\ 0\ \alpha^*\ 3\ \alpha^*\ 3\ \alpha^*$, without changing its effect in this individual. This newer description of the **0 0 3 3** combination is, while more general, considerably longer. For readability, we introduce the notion of an *embedding* operator. For this operator, we need a combination of set and regular expression notation, and look upon each item in the regular expression as a set. That is

$$A^* B A^* C A^* \equiv A^* \times B \times A^* \times C \times A^* \tag{2}$$

next, we define a homomorphic function (function that preserves structure) E such that

$$E(\alpha) \equiv \alpha^\epsilon_{a \in A} \tag{3}$$

that is, when the function is applied to a string, it removes all instances of a. We denote the result of such an operation as

$$BC \oplus A \tag{4}$$

that is, when BC is *embedded* in A, A appears at every possible location:

$$ABACA \equiv BC \oplus A \tag{5}$$

Taking the new operator defined in equation 5, we can say

$$\alpha^*\ 0\ \alpha^*\ 0\ \alpha^*\ 3\ \alpha^*\ 3\ \alpha^* \equiv 0033 \oplus \alpha^* \tag{6}$$

Notice that, because α has the *zero or more* operator appended to it, this is effectively saying that α can appear anywhere in the expression.

The next genes of interest are **7** and the two instances of **D**; they must be present in the individual. However, not only does their order not matter, it also doesn't matter where they appear. The crucial difference between this and the *embed* operator is that there will only be one instance of each of **D** and **4** on its single application. We term this operator the *insertion* operator, and denote it as follows:

$$ABC|ACB|CAB \equiv AB + C \tag{7}$$

Thus, for our individual, we could have (allowing for the embedding of each of **D** and **7** in α):

$$0033 \oplus \alpha^* + 7 \oplus \alpha^* + D \oplus \alpha^* + D \oplus \alpha^* \tag{8}$$

The embed operator is common to each term, so so we can rewrite equation 8 as

$$(0033 + 7 + D + D) \oplus \alpha^* \tag{9}$$

The second part of this genome's schema is **4 1**, and there is no choice here, so we simply append it to the current schema to give :

$$(0033 + 7 + D + D) \oplus \alpha^*.(41) \tag{10}$$

The final part of the genome contains another **3 3**, **D D 7** and **9**. In this case, the order is truly independent, as none of the **D D 7** will be expressed until at least one of the **3 3** is. Furthermore, it doesn't matter how many of these genes appear in the genome, as long as at least the minimum set exists. Considering that **9** belongs to α , this can be denoted by :

$$(3 + 3 + D + D + 7)^+ \oplus \alpha^* \tag{11}$$

notice that we include the α^* term here too. Putting all three parts together yields the following :

$$(((0033 + 7 + D + D) \oplus .(41)). (3 + 3 + D + D + 7)^+) \oplus \alpha^*$$

4.1   Robustness of System

Given the powerful schema notation developed in the previous section, it is clear to see just how robust individuals can be. Any individual genotype that adheres to the above regular expression will decode to the same phenotype. To illustrate just how many individuals can decode to the same phenotype, let us examine the individual above, and consider a genome of length 14 (the minimum length individual produced by the above regular expression.

Due to space restrictions, we can't show the derivation of figures, but there are 25,200 different ways to express the above expression. If the individual was longer, for example, 15 codons long, with the extra codon being taken from the don't care terms, e.g. from α^*, the number jumps to 1,486,800. This demonstrates the enormous areas of neutrality the representation creates at the codon level. However, given that the actual representation employed is an 8 bit binary one, there are 18 different ways to represent each codon, which increases the number to a truly staggering 26,762,400 different combinations for *individuals of length 15*. Clearly, this number increases exponentially as the length of the individual increases.

5   Genetic Operators

The binary string representation of individuals effectively provides a separation of search and solution spaces. This permits us to use all the standard genetic operators at the string level. Crossover is implemented as a simple, one point affair. The only restriction is that crossover takes place at codon boundaries.

Mutation is implemented in the normal fashion, with a rate of 0.01, with crossover occuring with a probability of 0.9. Steady state replacement was used, with roulette wheel selection.

6   Experiments

The system as described, was applied to three standard benchmark problems from the GP literature, Koza's Symbolic Regression, Symbolic Integration and Santa Fe Trail problems. Experiments were also carried out using GP and GE. All systems used equivalent function and terminal sets, and identical parameter settings. 100 independent runs were conducted for each problem. The experimental setups are very similar to those described in [8] . The notable exception is that the artficial ant was allowed 615 time steps before it timed out. Also, structures like *progn2* and *progn3* were not needed for GE and Chorus because of the use of grammars. Fitness in regression and integration problems is calculated by taking the reciprocal of the sum of absolute errors over the fitness cases.

6.1   Results

The results show that, while Chorus was clearly outperformed by both GP and GE at the symbolic regression problem (figure 1), on the integration problem (figure 1) it exhibits comparable performance to GE and, indeed, outperforms GP. The Santa Fe Trail problem shows that Chrous exhibits much better performance than GP, although it lags behind GE.

6.2   Discussion

From the experiments in the previous section, we see that Chorus is not an all conquering new algorithm. However, that is not the point of the paper; we wished to demonstrate that a position independent representation scheme could, at the very least, exhibit comparable performance with other algorithms.

Also worth noticing is that, although Chorus clearly performs worse than GP in the symbolic regression problem (figure 1), GP has already reached a plateau of fitness, while Chorus still appears to be increasing. We re-ran the experiments with a maximum limit of 250 generations, and yielded the results shown in figure 2.

This suggests that Chorus seems to take a warm up period, which can be attributed to the presence of introns. However, their presence seems to increase the robustness of the system, as depicted by the schema notation described in section 4. Thus the payback is a system which exhibits a much gentler learning curve than one would normally expect

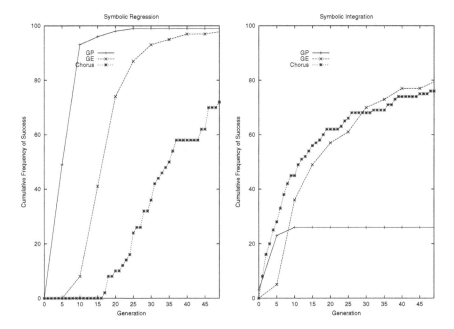

Fig. 1. Left : The relative performances of the algorithms on the Symbolic Regression problem. Note the continuously positive slope of Chorus curve. Right : The relative performances of the algorithms on the Symbolic Integration problem. In this case, there is little difference between any of the Chorus runs and GE. Notice the flattened GP curve.

from an EC system. This could have major implications for the use of Chorus on larger and more difficult problems.

The wrapping operator is limited only to first generation unlike GE where it is continuously used. The motivation was found in the fact that with wrapping, crossover can break an individual into several segments, which may result into mutative effects. Absence of wrapping in combination with position flexibility, promises to maintain the exploitative effects of crossover.

7   Conclusions

We have described a new, position independent, representation scheme for Evolutionary Algorithms, termed Chorus. Chorus has been tested on three standard benchmark problems, and has been shown to outperform GP on two of them.

We have also described a powerful schema notation to describe our individuals, and have shown how it can be used to comment on the likelihood of the preservation or otherwise of building blocks. This schema notation was also used to demonstrate how robust the representation scheme is, in that there can be an enormous number of different ways to represent the same phenotype. This has major implications into work in neutral

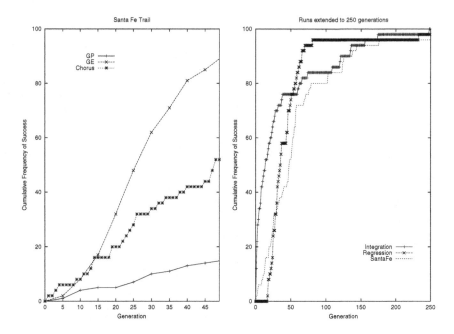

Fig. 2. Left : The relative performances of the algorithms on the Santa Fe Trail problem. In this case, Chorus shows better performance than GP. Notice the continuously positive slope of Chorus, a behaviour consistent through out. Right : Performance of Chorus over runs extended to 250 generations. This shows that Chorus is slow to begin with, however it does not lose its way towards the later generations and attains almost maximum success frequency.

evolution, which relies on chromosomes being able to accumulate modifications without changing the phenotype.

Initial results show that, although the system needs some time early on in a run to overcome introns, they don't appear to be much of an issue on longer runs. This suggests that a combination of genetic diversity and the position independence property permits Chorus to keep evolving better individuals even after a relatively large number of generations.

7.1 Future Work

This paper serves as an introduction to Chorus, and possibly contains more questions than answers. Little work has been done in the analysis of position independent representation schemes for grammars, but this system opens up a new avenue of research, with its policy of no coercion and no prohibition.

The schemata described in the paper is very expressive, and can no doubt be used to shed further light into the workings of the scheme. One of the difficulties with a position independence scheme is the complexity of the interactions, yet regular expressions appear to elegantly capture this complexity. Further research in this area will no doubt give more information into the inner workings of these kinds of systems.

As discussed earlier, Chorus promises to be rich in genetic diversity. Experiments need to be conducted to verify this hypothesis.

Proliferation of introns is another area which needs attention. Measures like parsimony pressure can be taken to reduce introns in the genomes.

References

1. J.J. Freeman, "A Linear Representation for GP using Context Free Grammars" in *Genetic Programming 1998: Proc. 3rd Annu. Conf.*, J.R. Koza, W. Banzhaf, K. Chellapilla, K. Deb, M. Dorigo, D.B. Fogel, M.H. Garzon, D.E. Goldberg, H. Iba, R.L. Riolo, Eds. Madison, Wisconsin: MIT Press, 1998, pp. 72-77.

2. H. Horner, *A C++ class library for Genetic Programming: The Vienna University of Economics Genetic Programming Kernel*. Release 1.0, Operating instruction. Vienna University of Economics, 1996.

3. R. Keller and W. Banzhaf, "GP using mutation, reproduction and genotype-phenotype mapping from linear binary genomes into linear LALR phenotypes" in *Genetic Programming 1996: Proc. 1st Annu. Conf.*, J.R. Koza, D.E. Goldberg, D.B. Fogel, and R.L. Riolo, Eds. Stanford, CA: MIT Press 1996, pp. 116-122.

4. O'Neill M., Ryan C. Grammatical Evolution. *IEEE Transactions on Evolutionary Computation*. 2001.

5. N. Paterson and M. Livesey, "Evolving caching algorithms in C by GP" in *Genetic Programming 1997: Proc. 2nd Annu. Conf.*, MIT Press, 1997, pp. 262-267. MIT Press.

6. C. Ryan, J.J. Collins and M. O'Neill, "Grammatical Evolution: Evolving Programs for an Arbitrary Language", in *EuroGP'98: Proc. of the First European Workshop on Genetic Programming* (Lecture Notes in Computer Science 1391), Paris, France: Springer 1998, pp. 83-95.

7. P. Whigham, "Grammatically-based Genetic Programming" in *Proceedings of the Workshop on GP: From Theory to Real-World Applications*, Morgan Kaufmann, 1995, pp. 33-41.

8. J. Koza. "Genetic Programming". MIT Press, 1992.

9. Goldberg D E, Korb B, Deb K. Messy genetic algorithms: motivation, analysis, and first results. *Complex Syst. 3*

10. Gruau, F. 1994. *Neural Network synthesis using cellular encoding and the genetic algorithm.* PhD Thesis from Centre d'etude nucham, P. 1995. Inductive bias and genetic programming. In *First International Conference on Genetic Algorithms in Engineering Systems: Innovations and Applications*, pages 461-466. UK:IEE.

11. Lewin B. *Genes VII*. Oxford University Press, 1999.

12. Wong, M. and Leung, K. 1995. Applying logic grammars to induce subfunctions in genetic prorgramming. In *Proceedings of the 1995 IEEE conference on Evolutionary Computation*, pages 737-740. USA:IEEE Press.

13. Zubay G. Biochemistry. Wm. C. Brown Publishers, 1993

Exons and Code Growth in Genetic Programming[*]

Terence Soule

Department of Computer Science
University of Idaho
Moscow, ID 83844-1010 USA
tsoule@cs.uidaho.edu

Abstract. Current theories regarding code growth (bloat) in genetic programming focus on the presence and growth of introns. In this paper we show for the first time that code growth can occur, albeit quite slowly, even in code that has a significant impact on fitness.

1 Introduction

The tendency of programs generated using genetic programming (GP) to grow without corresponding increases in fitness (code bloat) is well documented in the GP literature [1,2,3,4,5,6,7]. Growth has also been demonstrated in non-tree based evolutionary paradigms [3,8,9]. Current research on code growth in GP strongly suggests that it will occur in any evolutionary technique which uses variable size representations [4,6] and Langdon has shown that growth can occur in non-population based search techniques [10]. Interestingly, Miller has found that growth did not occur with an evolutionary search using graph based structures [11,12].

Importantly, most code growth consists of code which does not significantly contribute to a program's performance (commonly known as introns). Thus, significant resources are devoted to handling code which does not directly impact the fitness of the evolved solutions.

There are several theories regarding the causes of code growth. Most of these focus on introns, as most observed growth consists of non-contributing code. However, Luke has argued that introns are not actually the cause of code growth [7]. Additionally, Smith and Harries have shown that growth can occur in code that does influence fitness (exons) if the exons only have a negligible effect on performance [13].

We examine several different types of exons and show that growth can occur even with exons that have a significant impact on the programs' fitness.

---

[*] This research supported by NSF EPS 80935.

J.A. Foster et al. (Eds.): EuroGP 2002, LNCS 2278, pp. 142–151, 2002.

2   Background

Code growth is a significant problem, as rapid program growth consumes considerable resources without significantly contributing to a solution. Additionally, the additional code may interfere with finding better solutions, since most of the code manipulation by will occur in regions of relatively low importance.

To date three likely explanations for code growth of been proposed: growth for protection [3,4,2], a removal bias in crossover that leads to growth[14], and a form of genetic drift towards larger solutions [15]. These three causes are not mutually exclusive and there is some evidence in support of each cause. In all three suggested causes introns are presented as playing a fundamental role.

2.1   Crossover and Program Size

In the simplest GP, with crossover and without subtree mutation, the only source of larger programs is crossover. Removing a small branch and adding a large branch creates a larger tree. Whereas removing a large branch and adding a small branch creates a smaller tree. However, if both offspring are kept the average program size does not change. Thus, the only way the average program size can increase during a GP run is if larger offspring are preferentially chosen during selection.

This is less true of subtree mutation, as depending on how the mutation is implemented it may preferentially *generate* larger (or smaller) trees. However, a 'fair' subtree mutation will generate new programs whose average size is the same as the population's average size. Again steady growth will only occur if larger offspring are preferentially chosen during selection. Notably Langdon used a version of crossover, called size fair crossover, in which the removed and added branches must be of approximately the same size [16]. In this case growth was significantly reduced, presumably because the amount of variation in the offsprings' sizes was reduced.

2.2   Types of Code

In order to understand the phenomenon of code growth it is useful to examine the types of introns produced by GP. From its inception it was realized that GP has a tendency to create programs with large sections of code that do not significantly effect the program's behavior or performance [1]. A few examples of such code include:

$$+ (0 * X) \tag{1}$$

$$+ (X - X) \tag{2}$$

$$+ (1/X) \text{ where } X >> 1 \tag{3}$$

In each of these cases the code marked with an X does not significantly contribute to the program's behavior or performance (for case 2 it is the difference of the two sections). We are making the assumption that none of the operators have side effects. Historically the generic term 'intron' has been applied to code that doesn't have an effect and the term 'exon' to code that does have an effect. (Some authors have termed example 3 an intron, although it does have a small effect, whereas other authors consider it to be an exon.)

Although none of these sections of code have a significant effect, their other properties vary. In the first example X *can not* effect the program's behavior, regardless of how X is changed. Such code has been referred to as inviable code [14]. In the second example changing either X would effect the performance of the program. In the last example the code labeled X does effect performance, but probably to an insignificant degree. The value of X would have to be significantly changed to effect the output significantly.

Theoretical and experimental work has typically focused on the more restrictive introns. In part this has occurred because it is simpler to rigorously predict the effect (or non-effect) of code that never influences performance. Also, for some time it was assumed that the more restrictive types of code had the biggest impact on code growth. However, studies by Smith and Harries and more recently by Luke have shown that code with a very small effect on performance (example 3 above) can be as important for code growth as code with absolutely no effect [13,7].

In this paper we test the various types of exons and demonstrate that growth can occur even in regions of code that have a significant impact on fitness.

2.3   Suggested Causes of Code Growth

In roughly equivalent theories, Nordin and Banzhaf [3], McPhee and Miller [4], and Blicke and Thiele [2] have argued that code growth occurs to protect programs against the destructive effects of crossover. Several studies have shown that crossover is much more likely to decrease fitness than to increase fitness (destructive crossovers)[15,17]. In addition, these studies show that a large proportion of crossover operations result in no change in fitness (neutral crossovers).

As noted above, evolved programs often contain large sections of introns that can not have a significant effect on fitness even when changed by crossover or mutation. The protective hypothesis proposes that there is an evolutionary benefit to increasing the proportion of introns, as crossover in these regions is more likely to be neutral, which is evolutionarily preferable to the destructive crossovers.

A second theory of code growth is based on the structure of program search spaces. It has been experimentally observed that for many problems the number of programs of a given fitness that are larger than a given size is much greater than the number of programs with the given fitness that are smaller than the given sizes [15]. Thus, ignoring other factors, a search is more likely to find larger programs of a given fitness than it is to find smaller programs of that fitness, simply because there are more larger programs within the search space.

The third theory of code growth is the removal bias hypothesis [14]. It assumes that removing a small subtree will have a relatively smaller effect on performance than removing a large subtree. In particular, smaller subtrees are more likely to consist of inviable code. However, if a branch is added to the middle of a section of inviable code it will, be definition, have no effect, regardless of the size of the added branch.

Thus, removing a small branch and adding a branch of any size is not likely to have an effect, whereas removing a large branch is likely to an effect, again regardless of the size of the added branch. Most changes that effect fitness are destructive. Thus, the theory hypothesizes that there is a bias in favor of offspring created by removing a small branch and against offspring created by removing a large branch. The net effect of such a bias would clearly be a general pattern of growth.

3   Experiments

Introns are important in all three of the hypothesized cause of code growth. However, as noted previously, Smith and Harries [13] and Luke [7] have shown that growth can also occur in exons that have no significant effect on fitness, such as the code X in: $+(1/X)$ where $X \gg 1$. The question remains whether growth will occur in significant exons such as: $+(1+X)$ where X is approximately 1. To answer this question we study growth when only significant exons are possible.

3.1   The Test Problem

For this experiment we must be able to precisely control what types of exons are possible and to eliminate all introns. This necessitates very simple functions, which in turn necessitates a very simple test problem. Our test problem is to evolve an expression with the value 10. Fitness is the absolute value of the difference between the value of the evolved expression and 10.

3.2   The Genetic Program

We use a simple, generational GP, written in C++. The programs are tree structured. The only function (internal node) used is a +, so the trees are binary. The 90/10 rule is used in selecting crossover points to be consistent with most other GP paradigms. (90% of the selected crossover points are internal nodes, 10% are leaf nodes.) Mutation consists of mutating an individual node into a random node of the same type (internal or leaf). However, mutation has no effect on internal nodes because only one function (+) is used. Leaf nodes are randomly changed into one of the other terminals. For some of the experiments only a single leaf type is used, in these cases mutation has no effect. Other details of the GP are shown in Table 1.

3.3   Function and Terminal Sets

In general, the functions and terminals determines what types of exons and introns can evolve. In our experiment the only function is + so only exons are

Table 1. Summary of the Genetic Program parameters.

Objective	Find an expression with the value 10
Function Set	+
Terminal Set	varies
Population Size	800
Crossover Probability	0.9 (0.1 are copied without crossover)
Mutations Probability	0.001
Selection	3 member tournament
Generations	100
Maximum Tree Size	None
Elitism	2 copies of the best individual are preserved
Initial Population	Ramped, half-and-half
Number of trials	50

possible. Our experiments consist of trying several different terminal sets and examining the resulting growth. The function/terminal sets used are:

{+, 1.0} The only function is +; the only terminal is the constant 1.o. A perfect solution consists of 10 terminal nodes (1's) and 9 functions (+'s). There are a large number of binary trees that produce a perfect solution, but they are all the same size: 19 nodes (but not the same depth). It should be clear that introns are not possible with this function/terminal set. In addition, all code has the same 'fitness value', changing the size of a program by N nodes will always change the expression's value by $N/2$.

{+,0.5, 1.0} This is a slightly more complicated set. Introns are not possible, but there is an option between 1's and 0.5's. Clearly a larger (optimal) program is possible using 0.5's instead of 1's, so some code growth can occur. In particular, an optimal program of all 1's is of size 19 and an optimal program of all 0.5's is of size 39 (including +'s). Optimal programs with a mix of 0.5's and 1.0's will fall somewhere within this range.

{+,0.1,1} Again introns are impossible, but now the option is between 1 and 0.1.

{+, 0.1, 0.2, 0.4, 0.6, 0.8, 1.0} This final set gives evolution a variety of terminals to chose from, but as in the previous cases, they all produce exons.

4   Results

Figure 1 shows the average program size for each of the terminal sets. All four sets of data show similar behavior in the early generations; a rapid drop in size followed by a rapid rise. The drop seems to occur because in the initial, random population the largest programs have values furthest from 10 and are immediately removed from the population. This pushes the average size quite low. Once the largest individuals are removed the smallest individuals are the least fit and the average size rises. Both of these changes seem to be dependent on the composition of the initial population and are not related to regular code growth.

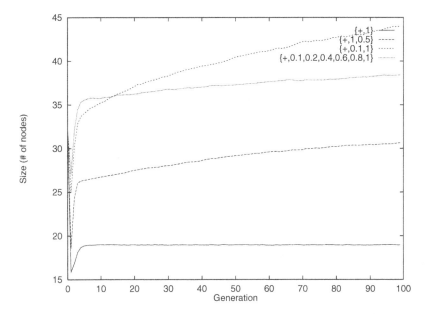

Fig. 1. Average size for each of the terminal sets. Growth occurs even when only exons are possible, but the rate depends on the exon choices.

Once these initial shifts in size takes place each of the populations settles on a different size because of the difference in the average value of the terminals. As noted previously, for the set $\{+, 1\}$ exactly 10 terminals (and 9 +'s) are necessary for an optimal program. Thus, as predicted, the average program size is 19. In contrast, for the set $\{+, 0.5, 1.0\}$ an average program contains an equal number of 0.5's and 1.0's. So, an average optimal program should have 12 or 14 terminals and 11 or 13 +'s. This leads to an average size of roughly 25, which is close to the results seen in Figure 1. The slight discrepancy occurs because 0.5's are favored in the first few generations. Similar reasoning applies for the other terminal sets.

Beyond these initial issues it is clear that for all of the sets (except $\{+, 1\}$) steady, slow code growth is occurring, although the rates of growth depend on the terminal set. (As noted previously with the set $\{+, 1\}$ growth is not possible without degrading fitness, so the lack of growth for that set is not surprising.) This clearly demonstrates code growth when only exons are possible.

Figure 2 shows the average fitness (difference from the target value) for each of the function sets. The values are calculated by averaging across all 800 individuals per population and across all 50 trials. Because of the very simple nature of the problem in every trail at least one optimal solution is found and preserved within the first 3 generations for every terminal set. In general, the individuals within the population converge on an optimal solution very quickly; after selection almost all of the programs are optimal. Thus, growth is not oc-

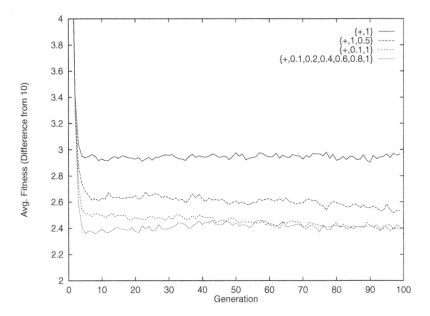

Fig. 2. Average fitness for each of the terminal sets. Fitness remains constant or improves slightly.

curring as part of the search for an optimal solution. Although the population has converged on an optimal solution, Figure 2 shows a non-zero average error because the data is recorded after crossover and mutation. These operations tend to degrade the optimal programs. Thus, the non-zero fitness corresponds to the average degradation produced by crossover and mutation in the optimal programs.

Figure 2 shows that the fitnesses are fairly constant, although the average fitnesses for the sets {+, 1, 0.5} and {+, 1, 0.1} appear to be improving slightly (the error is getting smaller). Thus, the data show a slow increase in size with almost no change in fitness. The only way this can occur is if the larger terminals are being selectively replaced by more of the smaller terminals. E.g. 1's are replaced by 0.5's in the set {+, 0.5, 1.0}. This observation is confirmed for the set {+, 0.5, 1.0} in Figure 3. The percentage of 1's decreases, while the percentage of 0.5's increases. Similar results were observed for the set {+, 0.1, 1}.

Thus, we see that typical code growth (or bloat) can occur with exons that have a significant effect on fitness, albeit much more slowly than is normally observed. This is different from the work of Smith and Harries, which only showed that exons without a significant effect on fitness produce growth.

The most interesting case of terminal replacement is for the set {+, 0.1, 0.2, 0.4, 0.6, 0.8, 1.0}. Figure 4 shows the percentage of each terminal for this case. Initially the larger terminals (1 and 0.8) are heavily favored. This probably occurs because the larger terminals are necessary to reach the target value of

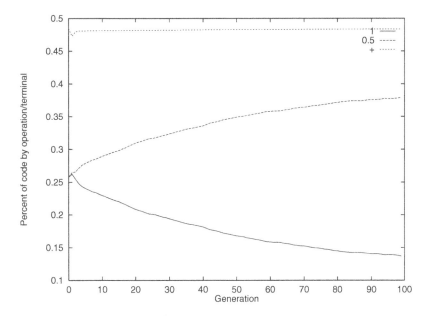

Fig. 3. Percentage of code consisting of each function and terminal for the set $\{+, 1, 0.5\}$. The 1's are being replaced by 0.5's.

10. However, these larger terminals, particularly 0.8 and 1, are quickly replaced, primarily by the terminal 0.2.

Interestingly, the smallest terminal, 0.1, is still being removed, albeit slowly. One explanation is that the other terminals are all multiples of 0.2 and thus can sum to 10 in many ways without including any 0.1's; whereas a program must contain an even number of 0.1's to reach exactly 10. Thus, having 0.1's may make it less likely that a program's offspring will be optimal because of the difficulty in getting the proper number of 0.1's. This is significant because it suggests the GP is favoring programs that are likely to reach 10 *after* being mixed by crossover. Evolution is favoring programs for their *offsprings'* survivability.

5   Conclusions

First, we have clearly shown that typical code growth (or bloat) can occur with exons that significantly effect fitness, albeit quite slowly.

In our experiments, terminals with larger values are preferentially replaced by (more) terminals with smaller values. One explanation for this is that smaller terminals are less suspetiable to crossover and mutation. For this problem, changing a few 0.1's has less impact on fitness than changing a few 1's. Further evidence for this hypothesis is that growth is faster with 0.1's than with 0.5's. Following the above reasoning 0.1's would seem to be less susceptible to crossover than 0.5's, thus the evolutionary advantage of including them leads to growth. Fig-

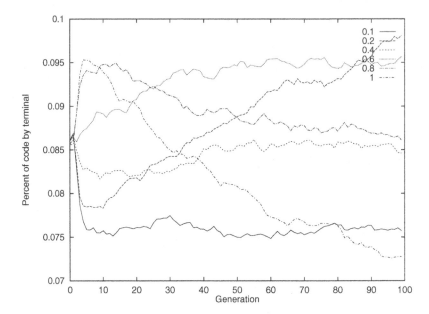

Fig. 4. Percentage of code consisting of each function for the set {+, 0.1, 0.2, 0.4, 0.6, 0.8, 1.0}. Several shifts in the percentage of each terminal are taking place.

ure 2 also supports this conclusion; as 1.0's are replaced by smaller terminals the average fitness improves implying that the programs are less damaged by crossover and mutation.

This suggests a new term: code *stability*. More stable code is code that is less degraded by crossover and mutation. These results are preliminary evidence that in general code growth occurs to promote code stability. This idea will be addressed in more detail in future work.

We again note that for the set {0.1, 0.2, 0.4, 0.6, 0.8, 1.0} the larger terminals are systematically replaced, but by 0.2 *not* 0.1. We hypothesized that this occurs because in a population dominated by terminals that are multiples of 0.2 having 0.1's makes it less likely that offspring will reach the value 10. Thus, we have a second example of evolution not just favoring programs with a higher fitness, but favoring programs whose offspring after crossover are likely to have a higher fitness.

References

1. John R. Koza. *Genetic Programming: On the Programming of Computers by Means of Natural Selection.* Cambridge, MA: The MIT Press, 1992.
2. Tobias Blickle and Lothar Thiele. Genetic programming and redundancy. In Jorn Hopf, editor, *Genetic Algorithms within the Framework of Evolutionary Computation*, pages 33 – 38. Saarbrucken, Germany: Max-Planck-Institut fur Informatik, 1994.

3. Peter Nordin and Wolfgang Banzhaf. Complexity compression and evolution. In Larry J. Eshelman, editor, *Proceedings of the Sixth International Conference on Genetic Algorithms*, pages 310–317. San Francisco, CA: Morgan Kaufmann, 1995.

4. Nicholas Freitag McPhee and Justin Darwin Miller. Accurate replication in genetic programming. In Larry J. Eshelman, editor, *Proceedings of the Sixth International Conference on Genetic Algorithms*, pages 303–309. San Francisco, CA: Morgan Kaufmann, 1995.

5. Terence Soule, James A. Foster, and John Dickinson. Code growth in genetic programming. In John R. Koza, David E. Goldberg, David B. Fogel, and Rick R. Riolo, editors, *Genetic Programming 1996: Proceedings of the First Annual Conference*, pages 215–223. Cambridge, MA: MIT Press, 1996.

6. Terence Soule. *Code Growth in Genetic Programming*. PhD thesis, University of Idaho, University of Idaho, 1998.

7. Sean Luke. Code growth is not caused by introns. In *Late Breaking Papers, Proceedings of the Genetic and Evolutionary Computation Conference 2000*, pages 228–235, 2000.

8. Peter Nordin, Wolfgang Banzhaf, and Frank D. Francone. Introns in nature and in simulated structure evolution. In *Proceedings Bio-Computing and Emergent Computation*. Springer, 1997.

9. Peter Nordin. *Evolutionary Program Induction of Binary Machine Code and its Application*. Muenster: Krehl Verlag, 1997.

10. W. B. Langdon. Fitness causes bloat: Simulated annealing, hill climbing and popualtions. Technical Report CSRP-97-22, The University of Birmingham, Birmingham, UK, 1997.

11. Julian Miller. What bloat? cartesian genetic programming on boolean problems. In *Late Breaking Papers, Proceedings of the Genetic and Evolutionary Computation Conference 2001*, pages 295–302, 2001.

12. Julian Miller. Evolution of program size in cartesian genetic programming. In Lee Spector, Erik D. Goodman, Annie Wu, W. B. Langdon, Hans-Michael Voigt, Mitsuo Gen, Sandip Sen, Marco Dorgio, Shahram Pezeshk, Max H. Garzon, and Edmund Burke, editors, *Proceedings of the Genetic and Evolutionary Computation Conference 2001*, page 184, 2001.

13. Peter Smith and Kim Harries. Code growth, explicitly defined introns, and alternative selection schemes. *Evolutionary Computation*, 6(4):339–360, 1998.

14. Terence Soule and James A. Foster. Removal bias: a new cause of code growth in tree based evolutionary programming. In *ICEC 98: IEEE International Conference on Evolutionary Computation 1998*. IEEE Press, 1998.

15. W. B. Langdon, Terence Soule, Riccardo Poli, and James A. Foster. The evolution of size and shape. In Lee Spector, William B. Langdon, Una-May O'Reilly, and Peter J. Angeline, editors, *Advances in Genetic Programming III*, pages 163–190. Cambridge, MA: The MIT Press, 1999.

16. W. B. Langdon. Size fair and homologous tree genetic programming crossovers. In Wolfgang Banzhaf, Jason Daida, Agoston E. Eiben, Max H. Garzon, Vasant Honavar, Mark Jakiela, and Robert E. Smith, editors, *Proceedings of the Genetic and Evolutionary Computation Conference 1999*. Morgan Kaufmann, 1999.

17. Peter Nordin, Frank Francone, and Wolfgang Banzhaf. Explicitly defined introns and destructive crossover in genetic programming. In P. Angeline and Jr. Kenneth E. Kinnear, editors, *Advances in Genetic Programming II*, pages 111 – 134. Cambridge, MA: The MIT Press, 1996.

Uniform Subtree Mutation

Terry Van Belle and David H. Ackley

Department of Computer Science
University of New Mexico
Albuquerque, NM, USA
{vanbelle, ackley}@cs.unm.edu

Abstract. The traditional genetic programming crossover and mutation operators have the property that they tend to affect smaller and
smaller fractions of a solution tree as the tree grows larger. It is generally thought that this property contributes to the 'code bloat' problem,
in which evolving solution trees rapidly become unmanageably large, and
researchers have investigated alternate operators designed to avoid this
effect. We introduce one such operator, called *uniform subtree mutation*
(USM), and investigate its performance—alone and in combination with
traditional crossover—on six standard problems. We measure its behavior using both computational effort and *size effort*, a variation that takes
tree size into account. Our tests show that genetic programming using
pure USM reduces evolved tree sizes dramatically, compared to crossover,
but does impact solution quality somewhat. In some cases, however, a
combination of USM and crossover yielded both smaller trees and superior performance, as measured both by size effort and traditional metrics.

1   Introduction

Darwinian evolution has inspired computational techniques, such as genetic algorithms [8] and genetic programming [9,10], that evolve a population of candidate solutions to a problem. While genetic algorithms typically store solutions
in the form of fixed-length strings, genetic programming uses variable-sized tree
structures. That difference in representation requires different implementations
of 'genetic operators' such as crossover and mutation, and brings different op-
portunities and problems.

A persistent problem for genetic programming has been a phenomenon called
"code bloat" [2,3,5,11,12,13,14,18,19], in which over time, evolved trees balloon
up to huge sizes. Analysis typically reveals that most of the code in such sprawl-
ing trees is simply 'dead weight,' either never getting used at all or only used
in ways that have no impact on the overall fitness of the evolved program. Such
apparently worthless subtrees are known as *introns* [12].

Many natural living species seem to possess significant amounts of apparently
unexpressed 'pseudogene' DNA [25], and it is sometimes argued, both in biology
and in genetic programming, that such unused genetic material may be a valuable
'reservoir' for future evolutionary advances [1,23]. Even if that is true, code bloat

J.A. Foster et al. (Eds.): EuroGP 2002, LNCS 2278, pp. 152–161, 2002.

remains an issue for genetic programming, because such vast trees can readily grow to consume all available system memory and thus limit the number of generations that a genetic programming algorithm can be run. Apparently at least partly for that reason, genetic programming experiments reported in the literature tend to favor relatively large populations evolved for relatively few generations, compared to typical genetic algorithm configurations. In the limit such a "many solutions/few generations" approach reduces genetic programming to mere random search, but even short of that extreme, the fewer the number of generations, the less time there is for any potential benefits of a 'genetic information reservoir' to emerge.

In this paper, we briefly examine some previous approaches to the code bloat problem, and then present a simple new mutation operator called *uniform subtree mutation* (USM) that provides a natural mechanism to reduce code bloat. Like the existing *genetic programming point mutation* (GPPM) operator [17], but unlike standard GP mutation, the amount of alterations the USM operator typically makes to a tree increases with the size of the tree, thus tending to negate the force behind the 'Defense Against Crossover' theory of code bloat [3].

We present results of testing USM empirically in comparison to crossover and mutation on a series of six common GP experiments. We observe that USM alone drastically reduces the size of trees, but at the cost of sometimes significantly degraded solution quality. However, we also found that using crossover and USM in combination yields somewhat reduced tree sizes while actually improving performance over crossover in many of the experiments. We conclude with the recommendation that USM be considered whenever mutation is employed or code bloat is a problem.

2   Previous Work

2.1   Techniques to Combat Code Bloat

More or less directly, techniques to fight code bloat incorporate sensitivity to tree sizes into a genetic program, by modifications to the fitness function or the tree generation mechanisms. Perhaps the most common method simply discards offspring that fall outside explicit size or depth limits [9]. Another approach creates a modified fitness function that combines the original problem-specific fitness with a tree size term [9]. Other techniques range from relatively general modifications, such as pareto optimization [6], and crossover operations that favor some replacement subtrees over others based on size [13], to more problem-dependent alterations such as only allowing crossover to occur in subtrees that are part of the evaluation [3,14], and all the way to performing periodic symbolic simplifications on the trees, rewriting them into semantically-equivalent but smaller trees, then continuing evolution on the altered population [5].

2.2   Genetic Operators

Genetic operators are employed to derive potentially new solutions from an existing population. Mutation and crossover are the two most widely used classes of

operators in both genetic algorithms and genetic programming, each appearing
in many variations with different properties and behavior. In genetic programming, mutation typically involves selecting a node on the tree at random and
replacing the subtree rooted at that node with a new tree generated at random
by some mechanism. Typical genetic programming crossover combines two trees
by selecting a node at random in each tree and swapping the subtrees rooted at
those nodes.

There was historically a bias viewing crossover as essential and mutation
as secondary, in both genetic algorithms [8] and genetic programming [9, page
105], [10], the latter going so far as to eliminate mutation entirely from most
experiments. Lately this attitude has been changing [7,15,16], and genetic programming researchers are examining alternate forms of mutation [2,4].

GAMutation(GAGenome *genome*) :
  for $i = 1$ **to** length(*genome*) **do**
    if $R < p$ **then**
      change *genome*[i]

GPPM(GPTree *tree*) :
  for $n =$ each node in *tree*
    if $R < p$ **then**
      replace n with a random node
      of equal arity

(a)

(b)

Fig. 1. Point-based mutation mechanisms. *(a)* A typical mutation operator in Genetic
Algorithms. *(b)* Genetic Programming Point Mutation (GPPM) [17].

In the field of genetic algorithms, perhaps the most common approach to
mutation is illustrated in Figure 1a, where R is a source of uniformly distributed
random numbers in $[0, 1)$, and parameter p is the probability for each symbol that
it will be mutated. With this mechanism, the overall probability of any symbol
in the genome changing as a result of a mutation is constant and independent of
the size of the genome. Overall, the number of symbols modified by this process
is a binomially distributed random variable with probability p and number of
trials equal to the genome length.

The *genetic programming point mutation* (GPPM) operator [17,20], sketched
in Figure 1b, is a close analogue to the GA approach to mutation. With GPPM,
the entire tree is traversed, and whenever a random value R is less than p, the
current node is replaced with another of equal arity. Like GA mutation, GPPM
provides a constant probability of modification at each node, independent of tree
size.

At the same time, however, GPPM doesn't exploit the full generative power
of GP's tree-based evolutionary approach, since it never changes the basic shape
of the tree. If used by itself the entire search process is restricted to only those
tree shapes found in the initial population. Also, unless the non-terminal set is
chosen so that each non-terminal has at least one alternative of the same arity,
there will be nodes that, in effect, will have a zero probability of mutation.

3   Uniform Subtree Mutation

In contrast to GPPM, which may make alterations all over the tree in a single operator application, the standard mutation algorithm for genetic programming trees (outlined in Figure 2a) only affects the subtree rooted at a single randomly selected node. Consequently, as the tree size increases, the chance that any individual node is affected by standard mutation decreases. This is significant because, particularly as trees approach local fitness optima, nearly all changes will be deleterious. In circumstances where it is possible to generate introns, large trees containing many introns can be favored by traditional GP mutation and crossover because they are less likely to have their functional nodes altered. This insight underlies several theories of code bloat [3,14], and the GPPM, and now USM, operators have been used to provide a form of parsimony pressure by combatting this effect.

The *uniform subtree mutation* (USM) operator is capable of altering tree shapes, and places no constraints on the necessary arities of the problem-specific non-terminals. The mechanism is built on top of standard mutation, and is shown in Figure 2b. The size of the tree is measured first, and a binomially distributed number of standard mutations, based on this size and a parameter p, are performed on the entire tree. Note that the tree is measured only once, at the beginning of the operation. This guarantees that the operator will terminate.

StandardMutation(GPTree *tree*) :
    node = a random node in *tree*
    oldSubTree = subtree rooted at *node*
    newSubTree = a random tree
    replace *oldSubTree* with *newSubTree*

(a)

UniformSubtreeMutation(GPTree *tree*) :
    size = number of nodes in *tree*
    for $i = 1$ **to** *size* **do**
      if $R < p$ **then**
        StandardMutation(*tree*)

(b)

Fig. 2. Subtree-based mutation mechanisms. *(a)* Standard Mutation. *(b)* Uniform Subtree Mutation (USM).

4   Size Effort

Koza, in [9, pages 191–194], introduces the notion of *computational effort* as an empirical measure for how much work is required to solve a problem with a given degree of confidence. Genetic programming runs are not guaranteed to produce a completely correct solution, so it is natural to ask how many times we must run a problem, and for how long, before we are, for example, 99% confident we will find a completely correct solution.

The computation effort metric, which in this paper is denoted by E_c, is somewhat misleading in the sense that all individuals count the same towards the final figure, even though larger trees usually take longer to execute. The wall-clock time needed to evaluate a tree will typically be $O(s)$, where s is the size of the tree, although it could be as low as $O(\log s)$ for trees where not all branches are evaluated, or $O(\sqrt{s})$ for DAGs, or $O(s^2)$ for architectures that contain ADFs. Regardless, it is a monotonic function of tree size, rather than a constant.

Poli, in [21], uses the metric of the number of nodes, as opposed to individuals, required to achieve a 99% success rate. We adopt this metric, which we call *size effort*, in our experiments, and define it to be

$$E_s = \min_i N(M, i, z),$$

where $N(M, i, z) = M \cdot R(M, i, z) \cdot \overline{S}(i)$.

$\overline{S}(i)$ is the cumulative total of average tree sizes up to generation i,

$$\overline{S}(i) = \sum_{k=0}^{i} \frac{1}{M} \sum_{j=1}^{M} S(j, k),$$

where $S(j, k)$ is the size of the j-th tree at generation k. Size effort is related to regular computational effort in that if we assume that all trees have size 1, then $E_s = E_c$.

5   Results

To determine USM's effectiveness in reducing code bloat, we modified the source code of the popular public-domain genetic programming package `lil-gp 1.1` [22] to implement the USM operator. We investigated USM with six well-known problems from Koza's books—'Santa Fe Trail (400 time steps),' 'Los Altos Trail (3000 time steps),' '11 Multiplexer,' 'Quartic Symbolic Regression $(x + x^2 + x^3 + x^4)$,' 'Two Boxes,' and 'Lawnmower (8×8)'—that are supplied with the package.

We ran a series of experiments on each of the six problem sets, comparing the following five mixes of operators:

- 90% Crossover+10% Reproduction (the standard mixture used by Koza),
- 100% Standard mutation,
- 100% USM,
- 70% Crossover+30% USM, and
- 70% Crossover+30% Standard mutation.

The decision to use a 70/30 mixture of Crossover and USM was arrived at through preliminary testing not reported here. In all cases, USM was used with $p = 0.01$.

Average fitness, tree size, computational effort, and size effort were calculated over 150 runs, using populations of size 1000 evaluated for 100 generations. To keep computation times tractable, a depth limit of 17 was set for the Crossover+Reproduction and Crossover+Standard mutation mixtures. The

Table 1. Parameters for empirical comparisons.

Selection	non-elitist, tournament (size = 7)
Initialization Method	ramped, depth = 2–6
Subtree Replacement	ramped half and half, depth = 0–4
Mutation/Crossover Point	uniform, no preference to non-terminals
Fitness Measures	standardized fitness, computation effort, size effort
Tree Size Limits	depth ≤ 17 for Crossover+Reproduction and Crossover+Mutation, none for the rest

Table 2. Average standardized fitness and tree sizes for various problems are in the upper table. Standard deviations across runs are listed below each fitness and tree size, in parentheses. Computational and size efforts ($\times 10^6$) are in the lower table. For both tables, smaller values for the metrics are better, and a fitness value of 0 is considered optimal in all cases. The best of each problem, for each metric, is shown in bold. The few apparent ties for best are distinguished by additional digits of precision not shown in the table.

Operator: Final avg:	Cross+Rep.		Mutation		USM		Cross+USM		Cross+Mut.	
	fitness (dev.)	size (dev.)	fitness (dev.)	size (dev.)	fitness (dev.)	size (dev.)	fitness (dev.)	size (dev.)	fitness (dev.)	size (dev.)
Santa Fe	21.5 (11.1)	307.3 (120.3)	25.7 (11.3)	403.9 (121.4)	25.0 (10.3)	**66.6** (48.8)	**19.2** (11.6)	298.4 (95.4)	23.0 (11.8)	352.2 (118.9)
Los Altos	26.9 (19.7)	386.4 (159.8)	32.5 (19.6)	469.8 (136.0)	30.7 (19.4)	**75.5** (58.0)	**25.0** (17.5)	348.8 (135.2)	30.9 (19.5)	421.5 (156.5)
11-Mux	0.05 (0.05)	420.6 (120.3)	0.12 (0.07)	240.6 (55.9)	0.15 (0.09)	**79.5** (39.5)	**0.04** (0.04)	383.3 (116.6)	0.05 (0.04)	410.9 (135.2)
Regression	1.3 (1.5)	84.0 (37.1)	2.1 (2.0)	166.2 (39.0)	5.0 (3.4)	**40.2** (23.5)	1.5 (1.8)	67.2 (37.9)	**1.1** (1.0)	96.5 (41.6)
Two Boxes	83.0 (79.1)	267.6 (127.9)	**55.7** (67.3)	369.7 (107.1)	147.4 (156.0)	**192.5** (113.1)	92.2 (106.5)	236.5 (131.2)	66.6 (89.6)	290.8 (136.7)
Lawnmower	0.007 (0.08)	252.6 (78.3)	0.007 (0.08)	188.1 (38.8)	0.053 (0.25)	**129.2** (36.2)	**0.000** (0.00)	212.7 (63.7)	0.007 (0.08)	254.6 (72.9)

Operator: Effort:	Cross+Rep.		Mutation		USM		Cross+USM		Cross+Mut.	
	E_c	E_s	E_c	E_s	E_c	E_s	E_c	E_s	E_c	E_s
Santa Fe	2.5	303.4	5.2	760.7	19.2	1155.2	**2.4**	**293.6**	4.0	632.6
Los Altos	4.2	851.5	11.3	2639.9	4.8	**371.3**	**3.9**	547.9	6.9	1165.1
11-Mux	1.7	402.2	12.9	1844.1	52.4	3338.0	**1.1**	**244.8**	1.9	472.9
Regression	**0.5**	**7.2**	5.8	146.6	19.4	480.2	0.8	16.5	0.9	21.0
Two Boxes	6.6	603.6	**2.3**	**233.0**	7.7	658.6	3.2	302.6	2.7	241.4
Lawnmower	0.02	3.1	0.02	3.0	0.07	8.9	0.02	**3.0**	**0.02**	3.0

other mixtures did not need an artificial depth limit to keep the trees to a reasonable size. Most notably, no depth limit was used for Crossover+USM. Other details of the experiments can be found in Table 1.

The results can be seen in Table 2. While 100% USM is the overwhelming winner in terms of maintaining small tree sizes, it does poorly in terms of fitness. On the other hand, the Crossover+USM mixture provides the best computational effort and the best size effort in half of the cases, and best fitness in four of the six. In all cases, Crossover+USM provides smaller tree sizes than Crossover+Reproduction, and in all cases but one, Crossover+USM provides better size effort values than Crossover+Reproduction. These size improvements are achieved without resorting to the arbitrary method of fixed depth limits, as used for the other crossover mixtures.

Figures 3–6 show the average evolutionary behaviors versus time of the various mixes on the 11-Multiplexer, Symbolic Regression, and the two ant problems. The drastic tree size reduction produced by USM is readily evident, with the long-term tree sizes occasionally even declining, compared to the initial population.

6   Conclusion and Future Work

The ability to represent and manipulate variable-sized genetic structures is a hallmark of genetic programming; in some sense the problem of code bloat is simply the dark side of that fundamental property. Not only are bloated solutions more difficult to understand, but the limited size of a computer's memory makes it difficult to perform explorations into deep evolutionary time. By scaling up the number of mutations with tree size, the USM operator encourages all parts of solution trees to 'carry their weight' in proportion to the magnitude of the p parameter. Further study will be necessary to understand the dynamics of this operator more fully, and its interaction with tree size.

GPPM and USM are both inspired by the GA point mutation operator, and both have now been used to provide a form of parsimony pressure. Thus an important future experiment will involve comparing the two in terms of fitness and parsimony, both alone and combined with crossover, on a variety of problems.

The USM operator as defined here selects its mutation points stochastically, as in standard GP subtree mutation. A variant on USM would iterate through the nodes to find its mutation points as follows: Perform a pre-order depth-first search on the tree. If $R < p$, then replace the current node with a new random subtree, and forbear searching the new node's children. Otherwise proceed as normal. This approach should yield similar results, but is closer to the original GA mutation operator, and might be more tractable to analysis.

Chellapilla [4] has worked with all-mutation GP systems, where multiple simple mutations combine to produce a new offspring. The difference between his approach and the approach described in this paper is partly that his system uses a variety of mutation operator types, but most significantly that the number of operators he applies is independent of tree size. It would be interesting to consider the code bloat and performance effects of USM variants that employ his other mutation operators.

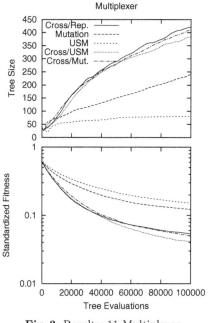

Fig. 3. Results: 11-Multiplexer

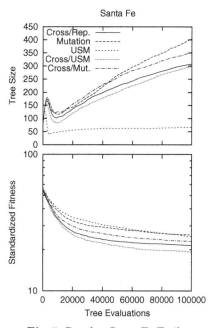

Fig. 5. Results: Sante Fe Trail

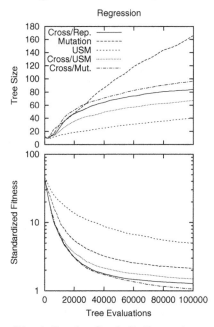

Fig. 4. Results: Symbolic Regression

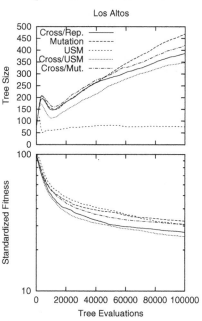

Fig. 6. Results: Los Altos Trail

The modifications we made to lilgp to implement USM are available online [24]. For its simplicity and its natural and principled approach to mitigating code bloat, USM is worthy of further study. The Crossover+USM mixture in particular, with its ability actually to improve performances while reducing tree sizes, should be part of every genetic programmer's arsenal.

References

1. P. J. Angeline. Genetic programming and emergent intelligence. In K. E. Kinnear, Jr., editor, *Advances in Genetic Programming*, chapter 4, pages 75–98. MIT Press, 1994.
2. P. J. Angeline. Subtree crossover causes bloat. In John R. Koza et al., editors, *Proceedings of the Third Annual Genetic Programming Conference*, pages 745–752, Madison, Wisconson, July 1998. Morgan Kaufmann.
3. Tobias Blickle and Lothar Thiele. Genetic programming and redundancy. In J. Hopf, editor, *Genetic Algorithms Within the Framework of Evolutionary Computation (Workshop at KI-94, Saarbrücken)*, pages 33–38, Saarbrücken, Germany, 1994.
4. Kumar Chellapilla. Evolving computer programs without subtree crossover. *IEEE Transactions on Evolutionary Computation*, 1(3):209–216, September 1997.
5. Aniko Ekart. Controlling code growth in genetic programming by mutation. In W.B. Langdon et al., editors, *Late-Breaking Papers of EuroGP-99*, pages 3–12, Göteborg, Sweden, May 1999. Centrum voor Wiskunde en Informatica.
6. Aniko Ekart and S. Z. Nemeth. Selection based on the pareto nondomination criterion for controlling code growth in genetic programming. *Genetic Programming and Evolvable Machines*, 2(1):61–73, March 2001.
7. Matthias Fuchs. Crossover versus mutation: an empirical and theoretical case study. In John R. Koza et al., editors, *Proceedings of the Third Annual Genetic Programming Conference*, pages 78–85, Madison, Wisconson, July 1998. Morgan Kaufmann.
8. John Holland. *Adaptation in Natural and Artificial Systems*. University of Michigan Press, 1975.
9. John Koza. *Genetic Programming: On the Programming of Computers by Means of Natural Selection*. MIT Press, Cambridge, MA, 1992.
10. John Koza. *Genetic Programming II: Automatic Discovery of Reusable Programs*. MIT Press, Cambridge, MA, 1994.
11. W. B. Langdon and W. Banzhaf. Genetic programming bloat without semantics. In Marc Schoenauer, editor, *PPSN VI, Sixth International Conference on Parallel Problem Solving from Nature*, Paris, France, September 2000. Springer-Verlag.
12. W. B. Langdon and R. Poli. Fitness causes bloat: Mutation. In Wolfgang Banzhaf et al., editors, *Proceedings of the First European Workshop on Genetic Programming*, volume 1391, pages 37–48, Paris, 14-15 1998. Springer-Verlag.
13. W.B. Langdon. Size fair and homologous tree genetic programming crossovers. In W. Banzhaf et al., editors, *GECCO-99: Proceeings of the Genetic and Evolutionary Computation Conference*, volume 2, pages 1092–1097, Orlando, Florida, 1999. Morgan Kaufmann.
14. Sean Luke. *Issues in Scaling Genetic Programming: Breeding Strategies, Tree Generation, and Code Bloat*. PhD thesis, University of Maryland, College Park, 2000.

15. Sean Luke and Lee Spector. A comparison of crossover and mutation in genetic programming. In John R. Koza et al., editors, *Genetic Programming 1997: Proceedings of the Second Annual Conference (GP97)*, pages 240–248, San Francisco, 1997. Morgan Kaufmann.

16. Sean Luke and Lee Spector. A revised comparison of crossover and mutation in genetic programming. In John R. Koza et al., editors, *Genetic Programming 1998: Proceedings of the Third Annual Conference (GP98)*, pages 208–213, San Francisco, 1998. Morgan Kaufmann.

17. Ben McKay, Mark J. Willis, and Geoffrey W. Barton. Using a tree structured genetic algorithm to perform symbolic regression. In *First International Conference on Genetic Algorithms in Engineering Systems: Innovations and Applications, GALESIA*, volume 414, pages 487–492, Sheffield, UK, September 1995.

18. N. F. McPhee and J. D. Miller. Accurate replication in genetic programming. In L. Eshelman, editor, *Genetic Algorithms: Proceedings of the Sixth International Conference (ICGA95)*, pages 303–309, Pittsburgh, PA, USA, 1995. Morgan Kaufmann.

19. N. F. McPhee and R. Poli. A schema theory analysis of the evolution of size in genetic programming with linear representations. In Julian F. Miller et al., editors, *Proceedings of EuroGP 2001*, pages 108–125, Lake Como, Italy, April 2001.

20. J. Page, R. Poli, and W. B. Langdon. Smooth uniform crossover with smooth point mutation in genetic programming: A preliminary study. In Riccardo Poli et al., editors, *Genetic Programming, Proceedings of EuroGP'99*, volume 1598, pages 39–49, Goteborg, Sweden, 26-27 1999. Springer-Verlag.

21. R. Poli. Some steps towards a form of parallel distributed genetic programming. In *The 1st online workshop on soft computing (WSC1)*. Nagoya University, Japan, August 1996.

22. Bill Punch and Eric Goodman. lil-gp1.1 genetic programming system. http://garage.cps.msu.edu/software/lil-gp/lilgp-index.html.

23. A. Rzhetsky and F.J. Ayala. The enigma of intron origins. *Cell Mol. Life Sci.*, 55:3–6, 1999.

24. Terry Van Belle and David H. Ackley. Modifications to lilgp1.1 code to implement uniform subtree mutation. http://keys.cs.unm.edu/USM/.

25. Annie Wu and Robert Lindsay. A survey of intron research in genetics. In Hans-Michael Voigt et al., editors, *Parallel Problem Solving from Nature IV*. Springer-Verlag, 1996.

Maintaining the Diversity of Genetic Programs

Anikó Ekárt[1] and Sandor Z. Németh[2]

[1] School of Computer Science, The University of Birmingham,
Birmingham, B15 2TT, United Kingdom
A.Ekart@cs.bham.ac.uk
[2] Computer and Automation Research Institute, Hungarian Academy of Sciences,
1518 Budapest, P.O.B. 63, Hungary
snemeth@sztaki.hu

Abstract. The loss of genetic diversity in evolutionary algorithms may lead to suboptimal solutions. Many techniques have been developed for maintaining diversity in genetic algorithms, but few investigations have been done for genetic programs. We define here a diversity measure for genetic programs based on our metric for genetic trees [3]. We use this distance measure for studying the effects of fitness sharing. We then propose a method for adaptively maintaining the diversity of a population during evolution.

1 Introduction

The search space of a search problem may contain several local extremes (peaks or valleys, depending on whether the problem concerns maximization or minimization). In artificial genetic search, the population may converge to one of these extremes, i.e., the individuals of the population get closer and closer, and arbitrarily close, to this extreme. Several so-called *niching techniques* have been introduced for preventing the early convergence to a local optimum [5]. A population of genetic programs is diverse if it contains samples of as many regions of the search space as possible. The niching methods preserve the diversity of a population by keeping the individuals reasonably away from each other.

Fitness sharing [5] was introduced as a technique for maintaining population diversity in genetic algorithms. Fitness sharing treats fitness as a shared resource of the population, and thus requires that similar individuals share their fitness. The fitness of each individual is worsened by its neighbours in the search space: the more and the closer neighbours an individual has, the worse its fitness becomes. As a consequence, the population is divided in subpopulations that group around the extremes.

We have extended the applicability of fitness sharing to tree-based genetic programming by defining a distance function for genetic programs that reflects the structural difference of trees [3]. We mean by structural difference of trees both the difference in the form of the trees and the difference in their node contents. Based on our distance function, we define here a new diversity measure for genetic programs. We expect to achieve better sampling of the search space by controlling the distance between individual programs. By using fitness sharing,

J.A. Foster et al. (Eds.): EuroGP 2002, LNCS 2278, pp. 162–171, 2002.
© Springer-Verlag Berlin Heidelberg 2002

we maintain the diversity of the population at a certain level depending on the size of program neighbourhood. In order to prevent premature convergence to some local optimum, we keep the population diverse in early stages of evolution. By adaptively changing the neighbourhood size, we can control diversity and convergence at the different stages of evolution.

The paper is organized as follows. In Section 2 we briefly present the possible distance measures for tree-based genetic programming. In Section 3 we give an overview of diversity measures for genetic programming and subsequently, in Section 4 we introduce the new diversity measure. We then describe in Section 5 the adaptive diversity maintenance. We show the experimental results in Section 6 and finally draw the conclusions.

2   Distance Measures for Genetic Programs

In genetic algorithms that represent the individuals as binary strings, a simple distance measure is the Hamming distance (the number of differing positions). In tree-based genetic programming it is more difficult to define a proper distance measure that can be computed efficiently. There are mainly two approaches: the *edit distance* and the distance based on structural comparison.

The *edit distance* between labeled trees was defined as the cost of shortest sequence of editing operations that transform one tree to the other [11,14,15]. An editing operation could be inserting or deleting a node or changing its label. In the case of ordered labeled trees T_1 and T_2, the time complexity of the algorithm for the simplified edit distance [14] is $O(|T_1| \times |T_2|)$, $|T|$ being the number of nodes in tree T. The edit distance has been used in pattern recognition [11], instance-based learning [2], and also genetic programming [6,12]. However, as Banzhaf et al. [1] point out, the edit distance is not widely used in genetic programming because of its time complexity.

We defined a metric for genetic programs that reflects the structural difference of the genetic programs and can be computed in $O(|T_1| + |T_2|)$ [3]. The distance of two genetic programs is calculated in three steps:

1. The two genetic programs (trees) are completed with empty nodes, so that both trees have the same form.
2. For each pair of nodes at matching positions in the two trees, the difference of their contents is computed.
3. The differences computed in the previous step are combined in a weighted sum to form the distance of the two trees T_1 and T_2 with roots R_1 and R_2, respectively:

$$dist(T_1, T_2) = \begin{cases} d(R_1, R_2) & \text{if neither } T_1 \text{ nor } T_2 \text{ have any children,} \\ d(R_1, R_2) + \frac{1}{K} \sum_{i=1}^{m} dist(child_i(R_1), child_i(R_2)) & \text{otherwise,} \end{cases}$$

where $d(X, Y)$ is the difference of nodes X and Y, $child_i(X)$ is the ith child of node X and $K \geq 1$ is a constant, signifying that a difference at any depth

r in the compared trees is K times more important than a difference at depth $r + 1$. By choosing different values for K, we could define different shapes for the neighbourhoods.

We define the measure of diversity as the *typical distance* of two individual programs in a population (see Section 4).

Igel and Chellapilla [6] claim that the longer is the path from a node in a genetic tree to the root node, the less its influence is on the fitness. This can be a justification for the adequacy of our distance metric, since we give less importance to differences in less influential nodes.

3   Diversity Measures for Genetic Programs

A diversity measure on any collection of objects must reflect how different these objects are from each other.

Feldt [4] gives a comprehensive survey of diversity measures in genetic programming. Their complete presentation is beyond the scope of our paper, we discuss only the most relevant ones.

In genetic programming, a proper diversity measure reflects the structural difference of the genetic programs in a generation.

Koza [9] defines the *variety* of a population as "the percentage of individuals for which no exact duplicate exists elsewhere in the population". Langdon [10] defines variety as the number of unique individuals in a population. These definitions do not consider *how* different the individuals are. But variety is simple and has the useful property that if variety has a low value then any other measure of diversity will also have a low value. Keijzer [7] computes the variety of subtrees in a population.

Rosca [13] points out that a good diversity measure could be the percentage of structurally distinct programs. But he uses fitness and program size as measures of diversity. Since at any time there can be members of the population that have similar fitness, but very different structure, and similar size programs with very different structure, fitness and program size are not very reliable diversity measures.

Keller and Banzhaf [8] use an edit distance for determining the structural difference of the genetic trees. They propose a mapping of the space of genetic programs on a two dimensional distance space and then define the diversity of a population in this distance space. However, when applying the above mapping, so-called *collisions* can occur, i.e., several genetic programs could be mapped into the same position in the two dimensional distance space.

4   The Proposed Diversity Measure

The more uniformly the individuals of a population sample the search space, the more diverse the population is. Therefore, we base our diversity measure on the pairwise distances between programs in the population.

The most straightforward measure is *the mean value of the pairwise distances of individuals in a population*:

$$Diversity(P) = \frac{2}{N(N-1)} \sum_{1 \leq i < j \leq N} dist(gp_i, gp_j),$$

where N denotes the size of population P, and gp_i the genetic tree for individual i.

This diversity measure does not include niches, but it clearly indicates diversity: the larger is the mean value of the pairwise distances of individuals, the more distributed are the programs in the search space.

Another diversity measure that better reflects the *typical distance* of two individuals in a population is a weighted arithmetic mean. If there are several similar distance values, they will have a greater contribution to the sum than the isolated distance values. We first group the distances in several classes C_k according to their order of magnitude: $C_k = [d_k, d_{k-1})$ if $0 < k < l$, $C_0 = [d_0, +\infty)$, and $C_l = [0, d_l)$. We choose the values for d_k (i.e., the orders of magnitude) such that a distance of d_k between two trees reflects a difference at some node at depth k. A distance belongs to C_k if the two corresponding programs

- differ only in nodes at depths greater than $k - 1$ and
- are different at least in one node at depth k (Programs differing only at depths greater than l are considered similar enough to be grouped together. In our experiments, we typically used $l = 5$).

Then the diversity can be defined as

$$Diversity(P) = \sum_{\substack{1 \leq i < j \leq N \\ dist(gp_i, gp_j) \in C_k}} w_k \times dist(gp_i, gp_j).$$

The distances in group C_k contribute to the sum with a weight proportional to their number:

$$w_k = \frac{2\, N_k}{N(N-1)},$$

where N_k is the number of elements in C_k and $\frac{N(N-1)}{2}$ is the total number of distances between pairs of individuals in the population.

Our diversity measure is independent of the technique used for maintaining population diversity and can be used for verifying the effects of any such technique.

5 Adaptive Maintenance of Diversity

By studying the effects of fitness sharing [5] on genetic programs (see Section 6), we have observed, as expected, that the objectives *diversity* and *fitness* are conflicting to some extent:

- with weaker diversity maintenance convergence was faster, but diversity also dropped faster; and
- with stronger diversity maintenance average fitness convergence was slower.

In other words, by *constantly* forcing a very diverse population it might be difficult to find a solution. Therefore, we propose keeping different levels of diversity at the different stages of evolution:

- at the beginning of evolution a higher diversity is required, since the initial random programs could be very far from any solution;
- toward the end of evolution convergence must be encouraged, so a lower level of diversity could be acceptable.

When applying fitness sharing, the level of diversity is regulated by the size of neighbourhood σ, higher diversity levels being obtained with larger neighbourhood sizes.

We propose an adaptive diversity maintenance that starts with a high diversity level (large σ) and modifies it regularly (every 5th generation) according to achievements (details of implementation are shown in Section 6):

> if *loss_of_diversity*
>   then *increase σ*
> if *gain_in_fitness*
>   then *decrease σ*

So, if a loss of diversity is encountered, by the increase of σ we expect to improve diversity. When fitness is improving, by the decrease of σ we expect to accelerate convergence. We expect that maintaining higher diversity at the beginning and lower diversity at the end of evolution will lead to better results.

6   Experimental Results on Symbolic Regression Problems

We conducted experiments on several symbolic regression problems. The test problems were randomly selected from the set of polynomials of degree up to 7 having real roots in the $[-1, 1]$ interval. The goal was to evolve programs that approximate the selected functions in the $[-1, 1]$ interval. For each problem, the training was performed on 50 randomly selected data points in the $[-1, 1]$ interval. The resulted best programs were then tested on randomly selected data points that were different from the training data. The mean error on the test data served as the basis for comparing the accuracy of different methods. The parameter setting is shown in Table 1. Since the results for polynomials of the same degree are very close, we show here representative examples of polynomials of degree 2, 5, and 7, respectively.[1]

---

[1] The values of the polynomials are also in the $[-1, 1]$ interval, but genetic programming always finds solutions better than the constant function $f(x) = 0$. For example,

Table 1. The genetic programming parameter setting

Objective	Evolve a function that approximates the selected polynomial function in the $[-1, 1]$ interval
Terminal set	x, real numbers $\in [-1, 1]$
Function set	+, *, /
Fitness cases (Training data)	$N = 50$ randomly selected data points (x_i, y_i),
	#1 $y_i = x_i(x_i + 0.3)$
	#2 $y_i = (x_i + 0.2)^2 (x_i - 0.5)(x_i + 0.5)(x_i - 0.7)$
	#3 $y_i = (x_i + 0.9)(x_i - 0.9)(x_i - 0.6)^2 (x_i + 0.8)$
	$(x_i + 0.3)(x_i + 0.4)$
Test data	$K = 20$ sets of $N = 50$ randomly selected data points, each different from the training data
Raw fitness and also standardized fitness	$\sqrt{\frac{1}{N} \sum_{i=1}^{N} (gp(x_i) - y_i)^2}$, $gp(x_i)$ being the output of the genetic program for input x_i
Population size	100
Crossover probability	90%
Probability of Point Mutation	10%
Selection method	Tournament selection, size 10
Maximum number of generations	100
Initialization method	Ramped Half and Half
Diversity control	Every 5th generation

We found that, when fitness sharing was applied, the accuracy of the solution was better than in the case of original genetic programming. For instance, the error of the final solution (averaged over 50 runs with the same parameter setting) was 0.035 for original genetic programming and 0.017 for fitness sharing with $K = 10$ and niche radius $\sigma = 0.1$. For larger niche sizes, the error increases as an effect of fitness sharing with too many neighbours. But *the scope of fitness sharing is to maintain diversity in the population.* We show in Figure 1 the evolution of diversity according to our first diversity measure in the case of original genetic programming and fitness sharing using several settings.

Original genetic programming converges to populations of programs with very similar structure (diversity is mostly below 0.01 after generation 49), but not necessarily similar fitness. When applying fitness sharing, the populations (at any generation) contain individuals that are different from each other (for $\sigma = 0.5$, the diversity oscillates around 0.3 after generation 58). This difference depends on the predefined niche size.

The main characteristics of fitness sharing in genetic programming can be summarized as follows:

1. *The diversity of a population is an increasing function of niche size.* Practically, since few individuals are allowed in a niche, when the niche size is large, the evolved individuals are generally far from each other. When the

---

the error of function $f(x) = 0$ on problem # 2 is 0.106, whereas the error of a solution given by genetic programming is 0.009.

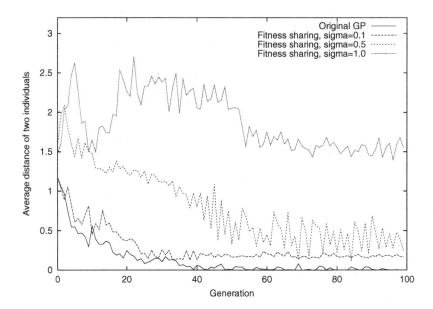

Fig. 1. Population diversity for original genetic programming and fitness sharing ($K =$ 10) in the case of problem # 2

niche size is small, the evolved individuals are not very far from each other ($d \geq \sigma$).

2. When the niche size is very small, diversity is low and the population converges to very similar individuals, almost as if no fitness sharing were used (for $\sigma = 0.1$, diversity 0.17, best fitness 0.014, average fitness 0.042 at generation 55). When the niche size is large, and the individuals are generally far from each other, it is more difficult to obtain an accurate solution (for $\sigma = 1$, diversity always above 1.3, best fitness 0.06, average fitness 0.938 at generation 100). *A medium niche size allows at the same time the evolution of different programs and the convergence to accurate solutions (for $\sigma = 0.5$, diversity 0.977, best fitness 0.014, average fitness 0.682 at generation 42).*

Adaptive Diversity Maintenance

We designed the adaptive diversity maintenance on the basis of our findings with fitness sharing and fixed neighbourhood size.

Since diversity increases with neighbourhood size, the adaptive control of diversity maintenance is performed by modifying the neighbourhood size. We apply the diversity control step on a regular basis, every 5th generation. Modifying the neighbourhood size in every generation would produce too many fluctuations, it is better to allow each setting to stabilize and then perform the modification.

There is a *loss_of_diversity* if the diversity at time t is worse (less) than the diversity at time $t-1$, and there is a *gain_in_fitness* if the average fitness at time t is better (i.e., less) than the average fitness at time $t - 1$.

We introduce the relative diversity and relative fitness for the consecutive diversity control moments $t - 1$, t as:

$$rel\_diversity = \frac{diversity(t)}{diversity(t-1)},$$
$$rel\_fitness = \frac{fitness(t)}{fitness(t-1)}.$$

Then we implement the adaptive diversity control described in Section 5 as follows:

if $rel\_diversity < 0.1$
   then $\sigma = \frac{\sigma}{rel\_diversity}$
else σ is unchanged

if $rel\_fitness < 1$
   then $\sigma = \sigma \times rel\_fitness$
else σ is unchanged

Diversity may decrease if fitness improves, and increasing σ for every loss of diversity could lead to the cancellation of the effect related to the gain in fitness. Therefore, we allow a loss of diversity of one order of magnitude before increasing σ.

The evolution of diversity for original genetic programming, fitness sharing with constant σ and adaptive σ is shown in Figure 2. It can be seen that in the case of adaptive σ the diversity evolves as expected:

- in the initial phase, diversity is maintained at a high level, in order to find good starting points in the search space;
- in the middle phase, as fitness improves, diversity is allowed to lower; and
- in the final phase, a much lower diversity is allowed, since this is the time for convergence.

Table 2. The adjustment of the niche size

Generation	σ
5	0.6106
20	0.1783
35	0.0635
40	0.0340
50	0.0094
60	0.0020
70	0.0013
80	0.0004

It is interesting to note that the results shown in Figure 2 are very similar to those shown in Figure 3.7 in [10]. There, the results of fitness sharing are

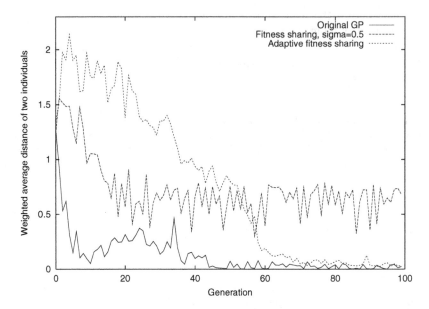

Fig. 2. Population diversity for original genetic programming and diversity maintenance in the case of problem # 2

compared to those of traditional genetic programming on the problem of evolving
a list structure.

The adaptive method provides automatic adjustment of the niche size. In
Table 2 we show the typical evolution of σ. Generally, the final stage of evolution
begins around generation 50, when the niche size becomes very small.

7   Conclusion

We defined a new measure of population diversity based on the structural differences of programs. We first used the diversity measure for verifying the effects
of fitness sharing [5]. Our experiments show that fitness sharing maintains population diversity in genetic programming at a level depending on niche size.

Since we could not know in advance, what is the appropriate niche size for
a given problem, we proposed an adaptively changing niche size throughout
evolution. This adaptation was driven by population diversity and fitness:

- when an alarming loss of diversity was encountered, the niche size was increased, and
- when an improvement of fitness was observed, the niche size was decreased.

In the future, we plan to study the effects of genetic operations on diversity
inspired by the work of Langdon on variety [10].

We also plan to extend our diversity measure to other problems. For this, we need to adapt our distance function to the problem domain. In the case of problems that can be solved by using functions with the same arity, this can be done by simply defining the differences between the possible nodes. In the case of problem domains where functions with different arity can occur, we have to redesign the first step of distance computation.

References

1. W. Banzhaf, P. Nordin, R. E. Keller, and F. D. Francone, *Genetic Programming: An Introduction*, Morgan Kaufmann, 1998.
2. U. Bohnebeck, T. Horváth, and S. Wrobel, Term comparisons in first-order similarity measures, in *Proceedings of the 8th International Workshop on Inductive Logic Programming*, ed., D. Page, volume 1446 of *LNAI*, pp. 65–79. Springer-Verlag, (1998).
3. A. Ekárt and S. Z. Németh, A metric for genetic programs and fitness sharing, in *Proceedings of EUROGP'2000*, eds., R. Poli, W. Banzhaf, W. B. Langdon, J. Miller, P. Nordin, and T. Fogarty, volume 1802 of *LNCS*, pp. 259–270. Springer-Verlag, (2000).
4. R. Feldt, Using genetic programming to systematically force software diversity, Tech. rep. nr. 2961, Chalmers University of Technology, (1998).
5. D. E. Goldberg, *Genetic Algorithms in Search, Optimization, and Machine Learning*, Addison-Wesley, 1989.
6. C. Igel and K. Chellapilla, Investigating the influence of depth and degree of genotypic change on fitness in genetic programming, in *GECCO-99: Proceedings of the Genetic and Evolutionary Computation Conference*, eds., W. Banzhaf, J. Daida, A. E. Eiben, M. H. Garzon, V. Honavar, M. Jakiela, and R. E. Smith, pp. 1061–1068, (1999).
7. Maarten Keijzer, Efficiently representing populations in genetic programming, in *Advances in Genetic Programming 2*, eds., Peter J. Angeline and Kenneth E. Kinnear, 259–278, MIT Press, (1996).
8. R. E. Keller and W. Banzhaf, Explicit maintenance of genetic diversity on genospaces, Technical report, Dortmund University, (1994).
9. John R. Koza, *Genetic Programming: On the Programming of Computers by Means of Natural Selection*, MIT Press, 1992.
10. William B. Langdon, *Genetic Programming and Data Structures: Genetic Programming + Data Structures = Automatic Programming!*, Kluwer Academic, 1998.
11. S.-Y. Lu, The tree-to-tree distance and its application to cluster analysis, *IEEE Transactions on PAMI*, $1(2)$, 219–224, (1979).
12. Una-May O'Reilly, Using a distance metric on genetic programs to understand genetic operators, in *Late Breaking Papers at the 1997 Genetic Programming Conference*, ed., John R. Koza, pp. 199–206, (1997).
13. J. P. Rosca, Genetic programming exploratory power and the discovery of functions, in *Proceedings of the Fourth Annual Conference on Evolutionary Programming*, pp. 719–736, (1995).
14. S. M. Selkow, The tree-to-tree editing problem, *Information Processing Letters*, $6(6)$, 184–186, (1977).
15. K.-C. Tai, The tree-to-tree correction problem, *Journal of the ACM*, $26(3)$, 422–433, (1979).

N-Version Genetic Programming via Fault Masking

Kosuke Imamura, Robert B. Heckendorn, Terence Soule, and James A. Foster

Initiative for Bioinformatics and Evolutionary Studies (IBEST),
Dept. of Computer Science,
University of Idaho, Moscow, ID 83844-1010
{kosuke,heckendo,tsoule,foster}@cs.uidaho.edu
http://www.cs.uidaho.edu/ibest

Abstract. We introduce a new method, N-Version Genetic Programming (NVGP), for building fault tolerant software by building an ensemble of automatically generated modules in such a way as to maximize their collective fault masking ability. The ensemble itself is an example of n-version modular redundancy for fault tolerance, where the output of the ensemble is the most frequent output of n independent modules. By maximizing collective fault masking, NVGP approaches the fault tolerance expected from n version modular redundancy with independent faults in component modules. The ensemble comprises individual modules from a large pool generated with genetic programming, using operators that increase the diversity of the population. Our experimental test problem classified promoter regions in *Escherichia coli* DNA sequences. For this problem, NVGP reduced the number and variance of errors over single modules produced by GP, with statistical significance.

1 Introduction

We introduce a new technique for building fault tolerant software from an ensemble of automatically generated modules that significantly reduces errors when applied to a classification problem. We use genetic programming to provide a large pool of candidate modules with sufficient diversity to allow us to select an ensemble whose faults are nearly uncorrelated. We combine the ensemble into a single system whose output is the most common output from its constituent modules. The error rate of this N-Version Genetic Programming (NVGP) system is directly related to the extent to which the constituent modules mask different faults. Collections of modules for which the system error rate is low either make mistakes on different inputs, so that in the overall system these mistakes are in the minority and are suppressed, or they make very few mistakes, so that little error suppression is necessary.

The isolated island model evolves individuals in distinct demes and promotes speciation. Such speciated individuals may produce faulty outputs on different instances. We compare the observed error rate for the ensembles built from random samples of the best-evolved modules to the theoretically optimal expected value, and retained the best ensembles. We call this N-Version Genetic Programming (NVGP).

The expected failure rate for n independent components, each of which fails with probability p, where the composite system requires m component faults to fail (ini-

J.A. Foster et al. (Eds.): EuroGP 2002, LNCS 2278, pp. 172–181, 2002.

tially derived for n-modular redundant hardware systems [1]) is $f = \sum_{k=m}^{n} \binom{n}{k}$

$\left((1-p)^{n-k} p^{k}\right)$. For an N-version classifier system, such as ours, the individual fault rate p is the ratio of misclassified examples to the total number of training instances. In this case, f is the error rate of an ideal ensemble. The error rate of an ensemble is close to the theoretically optimal rate f precisely when component failures are not correlated. This is our criteria for selecting the best ensemble.

We experimentally validated this system with a classification problem taken from bioinformatics: recognizing *E. coli* promoters, which are DNA sequences that initiate or enhance the activation of genes. Our experiment shows a statistically significant reduction in the number of errors and variance of our system when compared to single modules produced by genetic programming.

1.1 Fault Tolerant Software

Our approach is based on N-version programming (NVP). NVP was an early approach to building fault tolerant software that adapted proven hardware approaches to fault tolerance [2]. When applied to software, the objective was to avoid catastrophic failure caused by flawed software design by combining N≥2 functionally equivalent modules (we use the words versions, modules and components interchangeably) that were developed by independent teams with different design methodologies from the same initial specifications [3]. A fundamental assumption of the NVP approach was that independent programming efforts would reduce the probability that similar errors will occur in two or more versions [3].

But this assumption was questioned. Knight and Leveson applied a probabilistic metric to measure the assumed independence of modules in NVP [4], and rejected the hypothesis of the assumed independence of faults by independently developed programs. However, this conclusion does not invalidate NVP in general. Hatton determined that multiple versions developed for NVP are sometimes more reliable and cost effective than a single good version [5], even with non-independent faults. His 3-version system increased the reliability of the composite NVP system by a factor of 45. This is far less than the theoretical improvement of a factor of 833.6. But it is still a significant improvement in system reliability.

1.2 Test Problem: *E. coli* Promoter Recognition

We tested our approach on an *E. coli* DNA promoter region classification problem. A promoter is a DNA sequence that regulates when and where an associated gene will be expressed. The problem is whether or not a given DNA sequence is an *E. coli* promoter. Our objective was to quantify the effectiveness of a fault tolerant system built with our ensemble construction method, not to produce a competitive promoter detection tool. This problem has also been solved with artificial neural networks [6][7][8] and genetic programming [9].

2 Previous Work

Different ensemble construction methods have been studied in an effort to enhance accuracy. This section reviews averaging, median selection, boosting, bagging, and evolutionary methods. All methods exploit heterogeneity of ensemble components.

2.1 Averaging and Median Selection

A simple averaging method gathers outputs from all component modules and calculates their arithmetic average. Imamura and Foster showed simple averaging reduces error margins in path prediction [10] and function approximation with evolved digital circuits [11]. Another approach is weighted averaging, in which component modules are assigned optimal weights for computing a weighted average of the module outputs. Linearly optimal combination of an artificial neural network takes this approach [12][13]. The median value of the outputs is then the ensemble output. Soule approximated the sine function by taking the median of individuals, which were evolved, with subset of the entire training set for specialization [14].

2.2 Boosting and Bagging

Boosting and bagging are methods that perturb the training data by resampling to induce classifier diversity. The `AdaBoost` algorithm trains a weak learner by iterating training while increasing the weights of misclassified samples and decreasing the weights of correctly classified ones [15]. The trained classifiers in each successive round are weighted according to their performance and cast a weighted majority vote.

Bagging (<u>B</u>ootstrap <u>aggregating</u>), on the other hand, replicates training subsets by sampling with replacement [16]. It then trains classifiers separately on these subsets and builds an ensemble by aggregating these individual classifiers.

For evolutionary computation, Iba applied Boosting and Bagging to genetic programming and experiment validated their effectiveness and their potential for controlling bloat [17]. Land used a boosting technique to improve performance of Evolutionary Programming derived neural network architectures in a breast cancer diagnostic application [18]. However, both techniques have limitations. Boosting is susceptible to noise, Bagging is not any better than a simple ensemble in some cases, neither Boosting nor Bagging is appropriate for data poor cases, and bootstrap methods can have a large bias [15][19][20][21][22][23]. Langdon used genetic programming to combine classifiers into ensembles [24].

2.3 Classification of Ensemble Methods

Table 1 categorizes current ensemble methods in genetic programming in terms of their sampling technique in combination with the evolutionary approach. In cooperative methods [14][25], speciation pressure (such as that caused by crowding penalties [25]) plays a vital role in evolving heterogeneous individuals, while in isolation methods there is no interaction between individuals during evolution. Resampling methods create different classifiers by using different training sets (bagging) or varying weights of training instances (boosting). Non-resampling method creates different classifiers from the same training set with or without explicit speciation pressure. NVGP is non-resampling technique based on isolated evolution of diverse individuals.

Table 1. Classification of ensemble creation methods.

Evolutionary Approach	Training set selection	
	Resampling	**Non-resampling**
Non-Isolation	Boosting	Crowding
Isolation	Bagging	NVGP

3 Experimental Data

We compared the performance distributions of a group of single best versions and a group of NVGP ensembles. Evaluation and comparison of one or a small number of evolved individuals or ensembles would have been susceptible to stochastic errors in performance estimation. We assume the number of errors have a normal distribution, since each test instance can be viewed as a Bernoulli trial [23].

3.1   Problem

Our problem is to classify whether a given DNA sequence is an *E. coli* promoter. The data set is taken from UCS ML repository [26]. It contains 53 *E. coli* DNA promoter sequences and 53 non-promoter sequences, all of length 68.

3.2   Computing Environment

In order to generate sufficiently large statistical samples for the experiments, we used the cluster supercomputing facilities from the Initiative for Bioinformatics and Evolutionary STudies (IBEST). This device uses commodity-computing parts to build substantial computing power for considerably less money than traditional super-computers[1]. Cluster based computers using this approach are referred to as Beowulf computers.

3.3   Input and Output

We used 2-gram encoding for input [27]. The 2-gram encoding counts the occurrences of two consecutive input characters (nucleotides) in a sliding window. There are four characters in our sequences ("a", "c", "g", and "t"). The classifier clusters the positive instances and places the negative instances outside the cluster. The cluster is defined by the interval $[\mu-3*\delta, \mu+3*\delta]$, where μ is the mean of the classifier output values for the positive instances and δ is the standard deviation. If an output value from a given sequence falls within this interval then it is in the cluster and so is classified as a promoter. Otherwise, it is classified as a non-promoter.

3.4   Classifier

Target Machine Architecture. Our classifier is a linear genome machine [28], which mimics MIPS architecture [29]. There are two instruction formats in this architecture:

---

[1] The total cost of the machine is about US$44,000. Micron Technology generously donated all of the memory for the machine.

(Opcode r1,r2,r3) and (Opcode r1,r2,data). We used the instruction set in Figure 1.

The length of an individual program is restricted to a maximum of 80 instructions. Each evolving individual (a potential component for our NVGP ensemble system) used sixteen read-only registers for input data, which contained counts for individual nucleotide 2-grams as described above, and four read/write working registers.

Arithmetic operations		Data and control operations	
Inst.	Action	Inst.	Action
ADDI	reg[r1]=reg[r2] + data	NOP	None
ADDR	reg[r1]=reg[r2] + reg[r3]	MOVE	reg[r1]=reg[r2]
MUL	reg[r1]=reg[r2] * reg[r3]	LOAD	reg[r1]=data
DIV	reg[r1]=reg[r2] / reg[r3]	CJMP	if(reg[r1]<reg[r2]) if(r3<0) r3=0 ++pc += r3
MULI	reg[r1]=reg[r2] * data	CJMPI	if(reg[r1]<data) if(r2<0) r2=0 ++pc += r2
DIVI	reg[r1]=reg[r2] / data		
SIN	reg[r1]=sin(reg[r2])		
COS	reg[r1]=cos(reg[r2])		
LOG	reg[r1]=log(reg[r2])		
EXP	reg[r1]=exp(reg[r2])		

Fig. 1. MIPS like instruction set used for GP experiments.

Genetic Programming Details. We found that using 5 crossover methods, which we describe schematically below, was effective. In these schemata, "AB" ("12") represents an individual randomly split into segments A and B (1 and 2) by one crossover point. Similarly, "ABC" ("123") represents three segments defined by two random crossover points and "ABCDE" ("12345") represents five segments defined by four random crossover points. Also, "~A" is inversion applied to "A"—that is, it is "A" with its instructions reversed. For example, if "A" is {add, sub, mult}, then "~A" is {mult, sub, add}.

Methods (1) and (2) are traditional one and two point crossover, respectively. Method (3) is one point crossover with inversion applied to each crossover segment. Methods (4) and (5) use four random crossover points, with (5) being a single parent recombination operator.

Parents		Offspring
1) AB & 12	→	2A & B1
2) ABC & 123	→	A2C & 1B3
3) AB & 12	→	~A~2 & ~1~B
4) ABCDE & 12345	→	A2C4E & 1B3D5
5) ABCDE	→	ADCBE

Fitness is calculated by the following correlation formula

$$C = \frac{PN - P_f N_f}{\sqrt{(N+N_f)(N+P_f)(P+N_f)(P+P_f)}},$$ where P and N are numbers of correctly identified

positives and negatives, and P_f and N_f are the numbers of falsely identified positives and negatives [30].

Our mutation operator randomly alters the operator and operand fields of either one or two instructions in the individual.

Below is pseudo code of our genetic programming algorithm. Details about our isolated island model and ensemble constriction are presented below.

a) Choose two parents uniformly at random from the population
b) On the first parent, mutate one instruction with probability 0.01, and mutate two instructions with probability 0.005
c) If mutation occurs in (b), return the mutated individual to the population and go to (a); Else continue to (d)
d) Replacement candidate = the worse fit of the two parents
   For i = 1, 2, 3, 4, 5
   Perform crossover method i.
   If an offspring has better fitness than the replacement candidate, this offspring becomes the replacement candidate.
   Perform one instruction mutation on offspring with probability 0.01
   If a mutated has better fitness than the replacement candidate, then the mutated child becomes the replacement candidate.
e) Replace the worse parent with the current replacement candidate.

3.5 Evolution and Ensemble Testing

A common holdout test divides the dataset into 2 exclusive sets, 2/3 for the training set and 1/3 for the test set [23]. Our training sets used a random sample of 35 (53*2/3) positive and 35 negative examples, and used the remaining examples for the test sets. We performed experiments for 10 different holdout sets. The evolution and ensemble procedures are described below:

1. Create training set and test set.
2. Evolve 40 isolated islands with 100 individuals each in parallel. Add the best individual (fitness of 0.8) from each island to a set B of single best versions. This is a random sample of individual GP solutions to our classification problem.
3. Randomly select N individuals from B for N=3, 10, 20, 30 and use them to form an NVGP ensemble E with a majority voting output scheme with tie votes treated as a positive output. (For N=3 we tried all possible sets of 3.)
4. Evaluate the performance of each ensemble. If the ensemble is *qualified*, then select it for a test set trial. To determine if an ensemble is qualified:
   a. Determine the fraction of errors $p'=(P_f+N_f)/70$ observed when using the ensemble on the training data (where there are P_f false positives and N_f false negatives. Note that this can be done without any recomputation by recovering statistics from the fitness calculations for individual versions.)
   b. Compute the theoretically expected number of errors f using the equation from the introduction, substituting p' for p
   c. The ensemble is *qualified* if the difference between the expected number of errors when versions have independent faults and the number of errors observed $((f*70)-(P_f+N_f))$ is small (less than one in our case).

3.6   Experimental Results

We repeated the above procedure for 10 different holdout tests, Test 1 through Test 10. Table 2 shows the numbers of qualified ensembles found for each test. For example, in Test 1 we found 151 qualified 3-voter ensembles out of total 9880 possible individuals.

Table 2. The number of qualified (error rate close to optimal) individuals for 10 holdout tests and different sized (N=3, 10, 20, 30) voter sets.

	Test 1	Test 2	Test 3	Test 4	Test 5	Test 6	Test 7	Test 8	Test 9	Test 10
3voter	151	139	89	50	115	48	140	176	149	130
10voter	22668	19087	16238	4766	15991	4290	20727	20998	16534	11294
20voter	1011778	1127122	640645	203718	809825	201734	1257434	1253174	656238	726834
30voter	69279	82464	44676	5765	54392	7234	84757	84757	36448	63502

Table 3 shows error reduction rates observed in ensembles relative to the error rates of the single best versions. That is, if E_{NVGP} is the average number of test set errors of

Table 3. Percentage error reduction of NVGP system relative to set of best individual modules operating in isolation (see text), for each of 10 holdout tests.

	Test 1	Test 2	Test 3	Test 4	Test 5	Test 6	Test 7	Test 8	Test 9	Test 10
3-voter	10	12	7	16	11	9	18	14	15	22
10-voter	41	33	21	32	39	33	38	24	30	28
20-voter	51	40	18	32	43	39	44	23	26	28
30-voter	58	43	14	30	43	43	43	20	25	33

all NVGPs built from qualified ensembles (as described above) and E_B is the average number of test set errors made by the 40 versions in the set B, then the number reported here is $100*((E_B-E_{NVGP})/E_B)$. It represents the average error reduction achieved by NVGP over single modules produced by genetic programming.

Table 4 is the z-values of comparisons of the mean errors between N-voter NVGP ensembles and the corresponding set B of single best version average errors. These statistics indicate the confidence that we may have in the improvements in NVGP ensembles shown in Table 3.

Table 4. Z values comparing average number of errors between ensembles and the corresponding set of single best versions for 10 holdout trials.

	Test 1	Test 2	Test 3	Test 4	Test 5	Test 6	Test 7	Test 8	Test 9	Test 10
3-voter	2.40	2.97	1.42	3.44	2.53	2.31	3.98	3.49	3.78	4.67
10-voter	10.30	9.03	5.06	9.12	9.65	10.81	9.16	6.81	8.01	6.16
20-voter	12.62	10.94	4.37	9.09	10.52	12.59	10.50	6.29	6.88	6.33
30-voter	14.38	11.70	3.37	8.38	10.41	14.11	10.28	5.49	6.72	7.31

Figure 2 presents the error distribution intervals of the number of errors from the set B of single best versions and the number of errors from the corresponding N-voter

NVGP ensemble at a 90% limit. For each holdout test, we present statistics for the single best versions, and for each of the four NVGP ensembles (N=3, 10, 20 and 30). For example, the leftmost bar in holdout test 1 is the performance distribution of the 40 single best versions in the set B. The best is estimated to be 7 errors and the worst to be 17 errors, with a mean of about 12.

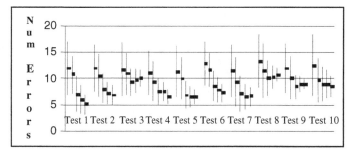

Fig. 2. Error distribution of sets of single best versions and corresponding N-voter NVGP ensembles (N=3, 10, 20, and 30) for 10 holdout tests. The bars indicate distribution of errors at 90% confidence intervals. The leftmost is for single best versions, then 3-voter, 10-voter, 20-voter, and the rightmost is for 30-voter ensembles.

4   Conclusions

From the z-values in Table 4, we reject the null hypothesis that the average number of errors is not significantly different virtually at 100% confidence for the 10, 20, and 30-voter ensembles, and conclude that NVGP significantly reduces system errors over single programs built by GP, for *E. coli* promoter recognition.

Figure 2 shows that the *worst* NVGP (10 and 20 voters) is at least as good as the average performance of the single best versions for test 3 and for other cases the *worst* NVGP is far better than the average single version. Notice that a single best individual has a chance to become a random classifier roughly 10%-20% of the time on unseen data. Unfortunately, we have no way of knowing which individual would become a random classifier beforehand, because they all have the same fitness on the training set. This is the risk we must bear with a single best classifier. Fluctuation in performance is the very reason why we compared the distributions, and why NVGP has superior performance.

NVGP is a non-resampling approach, which tends to avoid over fitting and lack of generalization problems caused by small samples. NVGP also weighs all the given data equally, effectively relying on the evolutionary process to provide speciated voters.

Acknowledgement. This research is supported in part by NSF EPS 0080935 and in part by NIH-NCRR grant number 1P20RR16454-01 under the BRIN Program.

References

1. Pradhan, D. K., Banerjee, P.: Fault-Tolerance Multiprocessor and Distributed Systems: Principles. In Pradhan, D.K.: Fault-Tolerant Computer System Design. Chapter 3, Prentice Hall PTR, (1996), 142

2. Avizienis, A. and J.P.J. Kelly: Fault Tolerance by Design Diversity: Concepts and Experiments. IEEE Computer, vol. 17 no. 8, (1984), 67-80

3. Victoria Hilford., Lyu, M. R., Cukic B., Jamoussi A., Bastani F. B.: Diversity in the Software Development Process. Proceedings of Third International Workshop on Object-Oriented Real-Time Dependable Systems, IEEE Comput. Soc, (1997), 129-36 (http://www.cse.cuhk.edu.hk/~lyu/papers.html#SFT_Techniques)

4. Knight, J.C., Leveson, N.B.: An Experimental Evaluation of the Assumption of Independence in Multiversion Programming. IEEE Transaction on Software Engineering, vol. SE-12, no. 1 (1986)

5. Hatton, L.: N-version vs. one good program. IEEE Software, vol 14, no. 6 (1997) 71-76

6. Pedersen, A.G., Engelbrecht, J.: Investigations of *Escherichia Coli* promoter sequences with artificial neural networks: New signals discovered upstream of the transcriptional startpoint. Proceedings of the Third International Conference on Intelligent Systems for Molecular Biology (1995) 292-299 (http://citeseer.nj.nec.com/25393.html)

7. Towell,G.G., Shavlik, J.W., Noordewier, M.O.: Refinement of approximate domain theories by knowledge-based neural networks. Proceedings of AAAI-90 (1990) 861-866 (http://citeseer.nj.nec.com/towell90refinement.html)

8. Ma, Q., Wang, J.T.L.: Recognizing Promoters in DNA Using Bayesian Neural Networks. Proceedings of the IASTED International Conference, Artificial Intelligence and Soft Computing (1999) 301-305 (http://citeseer.nj.nec.com/174424.html)

9. Handley, S.: Predicting Whether Or Not a Nucleic Acid Sequence is an *E. Coli* Promoter Region Using Genetic Programming. Proceedings of First International Symposium on Intelligence in Neural and Biological Systems, IEEE Computer Society Press, (1995) 122-127

10. Imamura, K., Foster, J.A.: Fault Tolerant Computing with N-Version Genetic Programming. Proceedings of Genetic and Evolvable Computing Conference (GECCO), Morgan Kaufmann, (2001) 178

11. Imamura, K., Foster, J.A.: Fault Tolerant Evolvable Hardware Through N-Version Genetic Programming. Proceedings of World Multiconference on Systemics, Cybernetics, and Informatics (SCI), vol. 3, (2001) 182-186

12. Hashem, S.: Optimal Linear Combinations of Neural Networks. Neural_Networks, vol. 10, no. 4, (1997) 599-614 (http://www.emsl.pnl.gov:2080/proj/neuron/papers/hashem.nn97.abs.html)

13. Hashem, S.: Improving Model Accuracy Using Optimal Linear Combinations of Trained Neural Networks. IEEE Transactions on Neural Networks, vol.6, no.3 (1995) 792-794 (http://www.emsl.pnl.gov:2080/proj/neuron//papers/hashem.tonn95.abs.html)

14. Terence Soule, "Heterogeneity and Specialization in Evolving Teams", Proceeding of Genetic and Evolvable Computing Conference (GECCO), Morgan Kaufmann (2000) 778-785

15. Schapire R.E., Freund, F.: A Short Introduction to Boosting. Journal of Japanese Society for Artificial Intelligence 14, no. 5, (1999) 771-80 (http://citeseer.nj.nec.com/freund99short.html)

16. Breiman, L.: Bagging Predictor. Technical Report No.421, Department of Statistics, University of California Berkley, 1994
    (http://www.salford-systems.com/docs/BAGGING_PREDICTORS.PDF)
17. Iba, H.: Bagging, Boosting, and Bloating in Genetic Programming. Proceedings of the Genetic and Evolutionary Computation Conference, vol. 2, Morgan Kaufmann, (1999) 1053-1060
18. Land, W.H. Jr., Masters T., Lo J.Y., McKee, D.W., Anderson, F.R.: New results in breast cancer classification obtained from an evolutionary computation/adaptive boosting hybrid using mammogram and history data. Proceedings of the 2001 IEEE Mountain Workshop on Soft Computing in Industrial Applications. IEEE, (2001) 47-52
19. Basak, S.C., Gute, B.D., Grunwald, G.D., David W. Opitz, D.W., Balasubramanian, K.: Use of statistical and neural net methods in predicting toxicity of chemicals: A hierarchical QSAR approach. Predictive Toxicology of Chemicals: Experiences and Impact of AI Tools - Papers from the 1999 AAAI Symposium, AAAI Press, (1999) 108-111
20. Opitz, D.W., Basak, S.C., Gute, B.D.: Hazard Assessment Modeling: An Evolutionary Ensemble Approach. Proceedings of the Genetic and Evolutionary Computation Conference, vol. 2, Morgan Kaufmann (1999) 1643-1650
21. Maclin, R., Opitz, D.: An empirical evaluation of bagging and boosting. Proceedings of the Fourteenth International Conference on Artificial Intelligence, AAAI Press/MIT Press (1999) 546-551 (http://citeseer.nj.nec.com/maclin97empirical.html)
22. Bauer, E., Kohavi, R.: An Empirical Comparison of Voting Classification Algorithms: Bagging, Boosting, and Variants. Machine Learning, vol. 36, 1/2, Kluwer Academic Publishers (1999) 105-139 (http://citeseer.nj.nec.com/bauer98empirical.html)
23. Kohavi, R.: A Study of Cross-Validation and Bootstrap for Accuracy Estimation and Model Selection. Proceedings of the 14th International Joint Conference on Artificial Intelligence (IJCAI), Morgan Kaufmann (1995) 1137-1145
    (http://citeseer.nj.nec.com/kohavi95study.html)
24. Langdon, W.B., Buxton, B.F.: Genetic Programming for Combining Classifiers. Proceedings of Genetic and Evolvable Computing Conference (GECCO), Morgan Kaufmann, (2001) 178
25. Soule, T.: Voting Teams: A Cooperative Approach to Non-Typical Problems. Proceedings of the Genetic and Evolutionary Computation Conference (GECCO-99), vol. 1,Morgan Kaufmann (1999) 916-922
26. UCI Machine Learning Repository, Molecular Biology Databases
    (http://www1.ics.uci.edu/~mlearn/MLSummary.html)
    (ftp://ftp.ics.uci.edu/pub/machine-learning-databases/molecular-biology/)
27. Wang, J.T.L., Ma, Q., Shash D., Wu, C.: Application of neural networks to biological data mining: a case study in protein sequence classification. Proceedings. KDD-2000. Sixth ACM SIGKDD International Conference on Knowledge Discovery and Data Mining. ACM, (2000) 305-309 (http://citeseer.nj.nec.com/382372.html)
28. Banzhaf, W., Nordin, P., Keller, R.E., Francone, F.D.: Genetic Programming: An Introduction: On the Automatic Evolution of Computer Programs and Its Applications. Academic Press/Morgan Kaufmann (1998)
29. MIPS32™ Architecture for Programmers Volume I: Introduction to the MIPS32™ Architecture (http://www.mips.com/publications/index.html)
30. Matthwes, B. W.:Comparison of the predicted and observed secondary structure of T4 phage lysozyme. Biochimica et Biophysica Acta, vol. 405 (1975) 443--451

An Analysis of Koza's Computational Effort Statistic for Genetic Programming

Steffen Christensen and Franz Oppacher

Computer Science Dept., Carleton University,
Ottawa, ON K1S 5B6, Canada
{steffen, oppacher}@cs.carleton.ca
http://www.cs.carleton.ca/~schriste/CompEffort.html

Abstract. As research into the theory of genetic programming progresses, more effort is being placed on systematically comparing results to give an indication of the effectiveness of sundry modifications to traditional GP. The statistic that is commonly used to report the amount of computational effort to solve a particular problem with 99% probability is Koza's $I(M, i, z)$ statistic. This paper analyzes this measure from a statistical perspective. In particular, Koza's I tends to underestimate the true computational effort, by 25% or more for commonly used GP parameters and run sizes. The magnitude of this underestimate is nonlinearly decreasing with increasing run count, leading to the possibility that published results based on few runs may in fact be unmatchable when replicated at higher resolution. Additional analysis shows that this statistic also underreports the generation at which optimal results are achieved.

1 Introduction

As early as 1990, John Koza realized the utility of having a statistic to estimate the computational effort to solve a given problem using genetic programming (GP). This statistic, denoted by $I(M, i, z)$ in [Koza, 1992], is supposed to measure the effort required to solve a given problem with 99% probability, and has allowed a generation of GP researchers to informally compare their results. As the field of evolutionary computation progressed, many researchers realized the need for including statistical information, including confidence intervals and significance testing, along with their other results. The state of the art in considering confidence intervals at the time of writing (November 2001) appears to be confined to performing bootstrap analysis of one's data, as was done in [Keijzer et al, 2001]. There Keijzer, Babovic, Ryan et al. used the bootstrap method to establish confidence intervals on their data for Koza's computational effort statistic, I_{min}. However, the confidence intervals provided by the bootstrap method were so wide as to prompt them to say, "For the Santa-Fe problem ... the width of the confidence interval is nearly as large as the computational effort itself. The confidence intervals clearly show that a straightforward comparison of computational effort, even differing in an order of magnitude, is not possible." This comment motivated the present research.

J.A. Foster et al. (Eds.): EuroGP 2002, LNCS 2278, pp. 182–191, 2002.

In the following sections, we analyze the computational effort statistic. In particular, we provide a detailed analysis of the biases that this statistic introduces, which may well lead to counterintuitive results when comparing diverse data.

2   Definition of Koza's I(M, i, z) Statistic

As a GP system progresses towards a solution of a given problem, it is hoped that more and more of the runs will pass a given success criterion. Following Koza, we define the cumulative probability of success $P(M, i)$ as the proportion of runs which, after i generations, have reported true for the predetermined success predicate for any of the M individuals in the current population. If we are hoping to use our GP system to succeed at a 99% probability of success, we do not need to run our system for as many generations as required until there is a 99% chance of success. Indeed, because of premature convergence, this may never occur. Instead, what is commonly done is to use the fact that successive runs are independent and identically distributed to compute the number of independent runs $R(z)$ that would be required to solve a given problem with 99% probability. Since the R runs are independent, the odds of failure in all of them simultaneously is given by

$$P_{all\ fail} = (1 - P(M, i))^R \tag{1}$$

and hence we can compute the number of independent runs required to achieve a solution to a confidence level of at least z by taking logarithms and solving for R,

$$R(z) = \left\lceil \frac{\ln(1 - z)}{\ln(1 - P(M, i))} \right\rceil \tag{2}$$

Koza's computational effort statistic $I(M, i, z)$ is intended to measure how many individual function tree evaluations must be performed to solve a problem to a proportion of z. It is derived from the cumulative probability of success $P(M, i)$ by multiplying by the number of individuals processed at the end of generation number i, Mi:

$$I(M, i, z) = Mi \left\lceil \frac{\ln(1 - z)}{\ln(1 - P(M, i))} \right\rceil \tag{3}$$

This statistic is defined over all generation numbers i; to find the "minimum" computational effort $I_{min}(M, z)$ to solve a given problem, Koza takes the minimum of all sampled $I(M, i, z)$. This gives us Koza's defining equation for I_{min}:

$$I_{min}(M, z) = \min_i Mi \left\lceil \frac{\ln(1 - z)}{\ln(1 - P(M, i))} \right\rceil \tag{4}$$

Without theoretical loss of generality, we can extend Koza's computational framework to other program induction systems that are not generational in nature, or that use clone pruning or elitism to reduce the number of individuals evaluated, by using instead the total number of individuals tested, $A(M, i)$:

$$I_{min}(M, z) = \min_i A(M, i) \left\lceil \frac{\ln(1-z)}{\ln(1 - P(M, i))} \right\rceil \tag{5}$$

3   Analysis of Koza's I_{min} as a Sampled Estimator

A number of statistical issues arise when we carefully consider what is happening when we enter our finite data into Equation 5. We should be aware that we have not performed an infinite number of runs. Therefore, our values $P(M, i)$ are in fact point estimates of the true probabilities. GP practitioners estimate $P(M, i)$ by dividing the number of successes over the number of trials; and since GP runs are computationally intensive, the same runs are typically used to compute the estimators at each generation. Let us denote the number of trials performed by n, and the cumulative number of successes achieved by generation i by $k(M, i)$. What is commonly reported as $I_{min}(M, z)$ is actually:

$$\hat{I}_{min}(M, n, z) = \min_i A(M, i) \left\lceil \frac{\ln(1-z)}{\ln(1 - \frac{k(M, i)}{n})} \right\rceil \tag{6}$$

which, as we will show, has very different mathematical properties, indeed.

3.1 The Experimental Framework

In this paper, we will consistently illustrate the effect of various aspects of Koza's statistic by performing a very simple experiment. We make use of a hypothetical GP problem for which the true computational effort is infinite for generations 1 through 5, and is a constant I_{true} for all generations from 6 on. This is done for concreteness, to make the mathematical examples meaningful and intuitive for GP researchers, and because exact analysis of discrete order statistics is unwieldy and very mathematically intensive. On the other hand, it is quite straightforward to code up a simulation and perform enough runs to establish statistical significance of the results. Consider the case where the exact computational effort $I(M, i, z)$ is constant across all generations. We investigate a hypothetical simple generational GP where the population size is fixed at $M = 500$. Since the specific work $A(M, i)$ is thus fixed at $500i$ and we do not vary the success probability $z = 0.99$, we can solve for the cumulative success probability schedule $P(M, i)$. For the moment, we ignore the ceiling operator in Equation 5; this caveat will be explained at length in the next section.

$$I_{true} = Mi\left(\frac{\ln(1-z)}{\ln(1-P(M,i))}\right) \tag{7}$$

Solving for $P(M, i)$:

$$P(M,i\,|\,z) = \begin{cases} 0 & 1 \le i \le 5 \\ 1 - e^{\left(\frac{Mi\ln(1-z)}{I_{true}}\right)} & i > 5 \end{cases} \tag{8}$$

These equations are graphed in Figure 1.

3.2   The Potentially Harmful Effect of the Ceiling Operator

Our analysis begins with understanding the effect of the ceiling operator ($\lceil \cdot \rceil$) in Equations 5 and 6. We will begin with a brief discussion of why this operator is inappropriate for sampled data. Note that the estimated probability $\hat{P}(M,i)$ is not, in general, equal to the exact probability $P(M, i)$. For any observed $k(M, i)$, without additional information to the contrary, we can say that there is roughly a 50% chance that the true probability $P(M, i)$ lies above our estimate $k(M, i)/n$; else it will lie below. It follows that we cannot correctly conclude there is a 99% chance of success if we rerun our process $R(z)$ times. An example may make this clear. Say, for a particular problem, we observe 78 successes in 100 trials. Our point estimate of the probability of success is 0.78. We can then compute $R(0.99)$ from equation 2 as

$\left\lceil \dfrac{\ln 0.01}{\ln(1-0.78)} \right\rceil = \lceil 3.0415 \rceil = 4$.   However, we know that our estimate has some variability associated with it; the odds of the true probability (given an infinite number of runs) being exactly 0.78 are vanishing. Should the true probability be as high as 0.785, $R(0.99)$ becomes $\left\lceil \dfrac{\ln 0.01}{\ln(1-0.785)} \right\rceil = \lceil 2.9980 \rceil = 3$.   If so, the estimated computational effort will be 4/3 of the true computational effort. Because 0.785 is so close to 0.78, we can expect that will be a slightly less than 50% chance that the true probability will exceed 0.785[1]. So we have found a situation where, roughly half the time, our estimate will be in error by 4/3 − 1 = 33%! This calls into question the theoretical value of the ceiling operator. The ceiling operator was put into place to capture the fact that we cannot effectively perform a non-integral number of runs. However, this ceiling operator is useful only when our knowledge of the probability of success is exact; when we have only approximate knowledge, there is a risk that our data will lie close to a jump discontinuity of equation 6. We submit that this fact renders the utility of the ceiling operator somewhat dubious.

---

[1] An exact side calculation gives the probability of this event occurring as 41.6%.

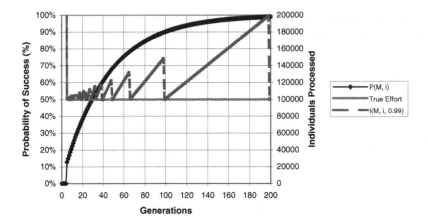

Fig. 1. Synthetic performance curves for a hypothetical GP run where the exact computational effort is 100000 individuals processed. The sawtooth curve indicates the effect of the ceiling function on the reported computational effort.

In Figure 1 we see the effect of the ceiling operator on the reported workload when the actual workload is constant. The net effect is to overestimate the true workload by an amount that is a function of the estimated probability $P(M, i)$, and of the desired success probability z. The maximum error imputable from this source is a 100% overestimate, at $P(M, i) = z$; however, if the success probabilities do not attain 90% (as is the case in many of the GP data reported in the literature), the maximum error would be a 50% overestimate. However, it is worth noting that if the success probabilities are everywhere small ($< 25\%$), this effect becomes small ($< 6.3\%$).

For the remainder of this paper, we will forgo treating the number of runs as an integer-valued quantity, and instead work on the continuous, infinitely differentiable statistic given in Equation 7.

3.3 Why I(M, i, z) Underestimates the True Computational Effort

The central statistical phenomenon discussed in this paper arises when we consider the effects of the minimum operator in Equation 7. The minimum of J random variables falling around a given average will tend to lie below this average; and the difference will tend to be larger as J increases. In the context of GP analysis, the random variables are the estimates of the computational effort $I(M, i, z)$. Since the exact analysis of discrete order statistics is challenging due to a dimensional explosion, we resort to simulation to illustrate this effect and its magnitude.

Consider our example case where the true computational effort is constant over a span of generations. We modeled a hypothetical GP result where the cumulative probability of success is 0 for generations 1 to 5, and then climbs from 2.7% at generation 6 to 37.2% at generation 101. This corresponds to a fixed true computational effort of 500000 fitness evaluations if the population size is 500.

For this simulation, we generated 10000 synthetic data sets with the cumulative probability of success given by the schedule shown by Equation 8. In order to do this, we choose the data so that exactly $\lfloor 10000 P(M,i) \rfloor$ runs succeed after generation i. For example, to obtain a true computational effort of 500000 individuals at generation 10, we substitute into equation 8: $P(M,i\,|\,z)=1-e^{\left(\frac{500\cdot 10\ln(1-0.99)}{500000}\right)}$, to get $P(M, i) =$ 0.045007. We would then choose the data so that there are $\lfloor 10000 P(M,i) \rfloor = 450$ successes by generation 10 (and similarly for all other generations). From this data set, we then sample n independent runs with replacement, and compute I_{min} using Equation 7 from this sample. In Figure 2, we present the observed distribution of I_{min} after 53 simulated "generations". This isolates the effect of taking the minimum of $53-5 = 48$ random variables possessing the same $I(M, i, z)$. (48 was chosen because of the many integral submultiples made possible by this choice.)

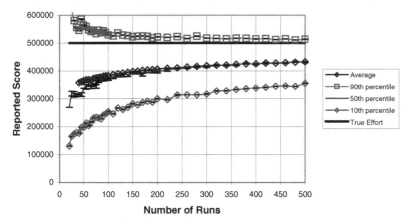

Fig. 2. Reported means, 10th, 50th and 90th percentiles of computational effort I_{min} estimated for a problem where the true computational effort is 500000 evaluations, graphed as a function of the number of runs n performed. 95% confidence interval error bars are shown[2].

From inspection of Figure 2, it is apparent that not only does I_{min} underestimate the true computational effort, but that it does so with high probability (almost 90% of the time). Furthermore, the magnitude of this underestimate decreases as the number of runs performed n increases.

A second effect of the minimum in Equation 7 stems from the non-decreasing nature of $P(M,i)$. Modeling the sampling error in the probability estimation $\varepsilon(M,i) = \dfrac{k(M,i)}{n} - P(M,i)$ as an error term in Equation 7 gives:

---

[2] The 95% CI error bars are per-experiment error bars; that is, we would expect that the true value lies within the given error bars 95% of the time for each experiment. Holding the error probability at 95% across all 22 experiments would increase the error bar span by about 60%.

$$I_{est.} = A(M,i)\left\{\frac{\ln(1-z)}{\ln(1-(P(M,i)+\varepsilon(M,i)))}\right\} \tag{9}$$

Expanding this expression as a Taylor series in $\varepsilon(M, i)$ to first order (and abbreviating $P(M, i)$ as P for terseness), we get the following:

$$I_{est.} = A(M,i)\left\{\frac{\ln(1-z)}{\ln(1-P)}+\frac{\ln(1-z)}{\ln(1-P)^2(P-1)}\varepsilon+O(\varepsilon^2)\right\} \tag{10}$$

The error term in Equation 10 increases dramatically as the true probability P approaches 0, so the specific errors tend to be larger in regions where the true probability $P(M, i)$ is low – that is, at earlier generations. Since the minimum in Equation 7 will be more sensitive to larger specific errors, the generation at which computational workload is reported to be "minimized" in a finite experiment will tend to underestimate the actual generation. To quantify the magnitude of this effect, we computed the generation at which computational effort was reported as minimized in the simulations performed above. The results are presented in Figure 3. As we can see, the median lies well below the mean, so this distribution is therefore markedly skewed towards zero.

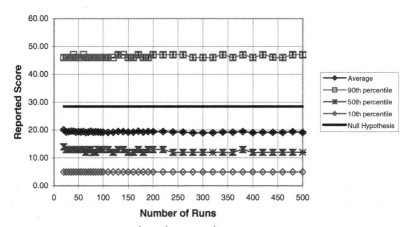

Fig. 3. Reported means, 10th, 50th and 90th percentiles of generation at which the computational effort is seen as minimized, graphed as a function of the number of runs n performed after 53 generations. 95% CI error bars are shown.

3.4 The Magnitude of the Underestimate Depends on the Number of Generations That Are (Nearly) Identical

We present here the effect of number of generations (equivalently, random variables) on the magnitude of bias. However, we should explain one mathematical effect before continuing. Consider Equation 6. In this equation, we see that $k(M, i)$ and n are both integer-valued. If we are estimating the minimum computational effort, the achievable values of $k(M, i)$ are constrained to be the non-negative integers less than n. Since the set of achievable values is discretized, the usual summary statistics will not report accurate or useful values – for instance the mean of $I(M, i, z)$ will be infinite, as there is a nonzero probability that 0 successes were obtained across all n experiments (hence producing an infinite estimate for $I(M, i, z)$). In order to alleviate this problem, we have taken a compromise position of reporting the 80% trimmed mean in the results that follow. The 80% trimmed mean is computed by reporting the mean of all data between the 40th and the 60th percentiles. This is still suboptimal in some sense because large values of $I(M, i, z)$ continue to bias the trimmed mean more than small values do, as can be seen in examining the data for the 1-generation case in Figure 4. Here, we would expect the estimate should approximate the true effort and be smooth, but the requirement that $k(M, i)$ must take on integer values causes oscillations and causes our estimates to be on the high side. Both of these effects become more pronounced for small sample sizes.

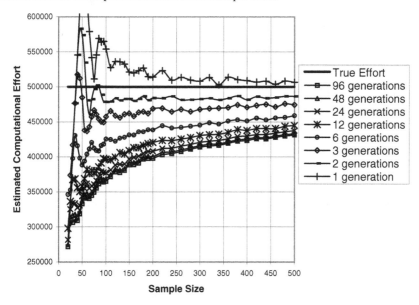

Fig. 4. 80% Trimmed mean of the reported computational effort I_{min} as estimated for a problem where the true computational effort is 500000 evaluations, graphed as a function of the number of runs n performed for the given number of generations.
The hypothetical population size is 500 individuals; and the success probability was 0 from generations 1 through 5, increasing from 2.7% at generation 6 to 37.2% at generation 101.

3.5 Comparison with Real Life: Experiments with Ants on the Santa Fe Trail

The first question that needs to be asked, in light of these data, is how likely is it that real GP computational effort data will be affected by the biases considered herein? After all, the key variable that influences the amount of negative bias is the number of generations for which the true $I(M, i, z)$ is approximately constant. Perhaps this is exactly 1 for real GP data, leading to no actual bias. To investigate this question, we performed a very large GP run to get a baseline, and then subsampled this data set to examine the distribution of reported I_{min} values.

We used ECJ version 7.0 to generate 27755 runs of Koza's Artificial Ant on the Santa Fe trail [Koza, 1992; Luke, 2001]. Space does not permit a detailed description of the parameter settings used; we used the defaults for Koza GP and the Santa Fe trail problem, with the exceptions that tournament selection of size 7 was performed, and the ant was allowed to run for 600 time steps[3] [Koza, 1992]. From this large data set, the best estimate of the true computational effort was I_{min} = 479345 individuals (minimum reported at generation 19; 2421 successes observed in 27755 trials; 95% confidence interval is 460633-498841)[4]. We then selected 10000 random subsamples of 50 runs with replacement from this data set, and computed I_{min} and the generation at which computational effort was reported to be minimized for each. The median of the observed I_{min} values was 381670 individuals, 25.6% below the population value (95% CI, 372133-386610). 69.5% of the observed I_{min} values were below the population value, indicating the presence of significant bias (95% CI, 68.6%-70.5%). The mean generation at which convergence was reported in the sample was 15.41 (95% CI, 15.25-15.56). 69.8% of the observed reported generations were earlier than the observed minimum at generation 19.

A replicate of these data, for the case where the ceiling operator was applied throughout yielded slightly higher absolute results (population I_{min} = 484500 individuals), but differed by less than 2% in all relative ratios.

4   Conclusions and Future Work

We have performed a statistical analysis of Koza's $I(M, i, z)$ statistic and have found it wanting in several important ways. Firstly, the effect of the ceiling operator introduces a somewhat arbitrary non-linear bias in the estimation process. This tends to ignore those data that fall in a regime where the fractional part of $R(z)$ is large. Second, the effect of taking the minimum of a number of estimators tends to underreport the true computational effort, in a way that grows with the number of estimators considered and decreases with increasing run counts. This underreporting is largest in effect where many consecutive generations have similar computational effort, and when the cumulative probabilities of success are small. In addition, this process tends to report that the optimum generation is found somewhat earlier than its

---

[3] A detailed table of all the settings used in this experiment and numerical data for all the experiments can be obtained at http://www.scs.carleton.ca/~schriste/ComputationalEffort.

[4] Exact numerical data and computational effort curves for these data are available at http://www.scs.carleton.ca/~schriste/ComputationalEffort/SantaFeAntData.html

true value, although this result has considerable variance. One subtle caution is in order for users of GP systems with small population sizes (such as Multi-Objective-based schemes) and steady-state GPs. For such systems, the number of generations is effectively very large, approaching the total number of individuals generated in the case of steady-state schemes. Since the magnitude of the bias increases with the number of generations over which we minimize, the estimation error would be expected to be relatively large, as the minimum of essentially hundreds of thousands of random variables is computed!

Future work should be directed to providing an analytic or simulation-based model with best-fit regression curves to be better able to estimate the magnitude of these purely statistical effects. The computational effort statistic is far too important to give up on! Ideally, we would like to be able to give a set of $k(M, i)$ data to a program and have it generate an unbiased estimator of our minimum computational effort I_{min}.

These results suggest several recommendations that would be of use in future GP research. The first is to always indicate the number of runs performed in one's experiments, preferably directly in the legend of the performance curve figure, if one is given, else in a summary table. We should also endeavour to be careful to report the number of effective generations over which we take the minimum in Equation 6. The GP community might be well served by dropping the ceiling operator from Equation 6, although this may be subject to debate. We also would recommend that practitioners choose relatively large run counts (on the order of 500 runs), to produce data that minimize the systematic errors presented herein. Finally and most importantly, we must ensure that we make digitally available the exact values of $k(M, i)$ that we obtain from our experiments. With such data, we can eventually provide an exact unbiased estimator of computational effort for legitimate comparisons of data from different authors. Without such data, there can be only an estimated correction applied based on historical data, or an approximation derived through a laborious and error-prone digitization of performance curve figures, if the earlier authors were considerate enough to provide them.

The authors would like to thank the anonymous reviewers, who suggested a validation against real GP data, and Sean Luke for his timely help with ECJ.

This work was funded in part by grants from the Natural Sciences and Engineering Research Council of Canada (NSERC).

References

Keijzer, M., Babovic, V., Ryan, C., O'Neill, M., Cattolico, M.: Adaptive Logic Programming. In: Spector, L., Goodman, D. *et al* (eds.): Proceedings of the 2001 Genetic and Evolutionary Computation Conference. Morgan Kaufmann, San Francisco (2001)

Koza, John R.: Genetic Programming: on the Programming of Computers by Means of Natural Selection. MIT Press, Cambridge London (1992)

Luke, Sean. ECJ 7: A Java-based evolutionary computation and genetic programming system. http://www.cs.umd.edu/projects/plus/ec/ecj/ (2001)

Genetic Control Applied to Asset Managements

James Cunha Werner and Terence C. Fogarty

SCISM
South Bank University
103 Borough Road
London SE1 0AA, UK
{wernerjc,fogarttc}@sbu.ac.uk

Abstract. This paper addresses the problem of investment optimization using genetic control. Time series for stock values are obtained from data available on the www and asset prices are predicted using adaptive algorithms. A portfolio is optimized with the genetic algorithm based on a recursive model of portfolio composition obtained on-the-fly using genetic programming. These two steps are integrated into an automatic system - the final result is a real-time system for updating portfolio composition for each asset.

1 Introduction

IBM and other companies are undertaking massive studies on the application of advanced computing technologies to stock brokerage and obtaining better results than the New York stock market's sharpest traders [1].

Every investor knows that there is a trade off between risk and reward: to obtain a greater than expected return on investment one must be willing to take on a greater risk [2]. Portfolio optimization theory assumes that for a given level of risk, investors prefer higher returns to lower returns. Similarly, for a given level of expected return, investors prefer less risk to more risk. It is standard to measure risk in terms of the variance, or standard deviation, of return.

The portfolio optimisation problem consists of obtaining the biggest return on investment with the least risk exposure necessary under the prevailing market dynamics. These dynamics are unpredictable due to both exogenous factors (such as government actions, market rumors, unexpected events, etc.) and endogenous factors (such as company and stock fundamentals).

Mahfoud and Mani [17] developed a rule-based system for managing each individual asset where the rules are of the form: IF (price < limit and EPS > value) THEN buy, where price is the asset price, limit is the buy threshold, and EPS is the earning per share.

Chang et al [18] used the genetic algorithm to find the portfolio of assets with different risk exposures (called the efficient frontier). Usually, this problem is solved with quadratic programming, but, for practical purposes it is desirable to limit the number of assets in a portfolio, as well as the proportion of the portfolio devoted to any particular asset.

J.A. Foster et al. (Eds.): EuroGP 2002, LNCS 2278, pp. 192-201, 2002.

Kivine and Warmouth [19] proposed that the portfolio vector itself encapsulate the necessary information from the previous price relatives. Thus, at the start of day t, the algorithm computes its new portfolio vector w^{t+1} as a function of w^t and the just observed price relatives x^t, using a linear regression. Helmbold et al [14] select a more complex function and Parkes and Huberman [16] generalize the idea for investment group model for the portfolio selection problem, adjusting their portfolio as they observe movements of the market over time and communicate to each other their current portfolio and its recent performance. Investors can choose to switch to any portfolio performing better than their own.

In this work the goal is to obtain a recursive mathematical law using genetic programming and the genetic algorithm that establishes a relation between the available information and the percentage of various assets to be held in the portfolio. The general framework, genetic control Werner [4], is represented in fig. 1. It uses data from experimental setup (the simulated market in this case) to feed genetic programming for the purpose of building a model of the market. Later, the genetic algorithm adapts real values to obtain the optimal percentages of the assets in the portfolio that will feed genetic programming, closing the loop.

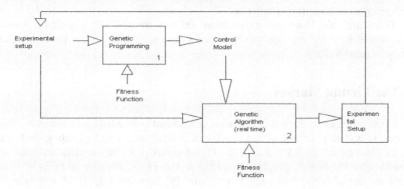

Fig. 1. Genetic control: obtaining the structure of the solution with genetic programming and adapting its parameters with genetic algorithm.

2 The Genetic Algorithm

The genetic algorithm (GA) mimic the evolution and improvement of life through reproduction, where each individual contributes its own genetic information to the building of new ones adapted to the environment with higher chances of survival. This is the basis of genetic algorithms and genetic programming ([5], [6], and [7]). Specialized Markov Chains underline the theoretical bases of this algorithms change of states and searching procedures.

Each 'individual' of a generation represents a feasible solution to the problem, coding distinct algorithms/parameters to be evaluated by a fitness function.

GA operators are mutation (the change of a randomly chosen bit of the chromosome) and crossover (the exchange of randomly chosen slices of the chromosome).

The best individuals are continuously being selected, and crossover and mutation take place. Following a number of generations (Fig. 2), the population converges to the solution that performs better.

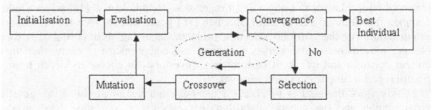

Fig. 2. Genetic algorithm: the sequence of operators and evaluation of each individual.

A generalization of the Genetic Algorithm is Genetic Programming (GP) (Holland [5] and Goldberg [6]) where each 'individual' in a generation represents, with its chromosome, a feasible solution to the problem; in our case, a mathematical function to be evaluated by a fitness function.

There are two kinds of information defined for the GP algorithm: terminals (variable values and random numbers) and functions (mathematical functions used in the generated model).

3 The Virtual Market

The first problem when studying market investment is in what environment to test the concepts and how to obtain time series of assets, stocks and currency, and market index for a period of 2 years at least. To solve this problem we extracted time series values from the history graphics available in the Yahoo Finance site [3]. We built a database contains the following information [9] between July 1999 and July 2001: FTSE100 stock quotes, trade volume and quotes by sector; Fix interest; European and American indices; Stock exchanges indices around the world: Argentina, Brazil, Canada, Chile, Peru, Venezuela, Australia, China, Hong Kong, India, Indonesia, Malaysia, New Zealand, Pakistan, Philippines, Singapura, South Korea, Sri Lanka, Thailand, Taiwan, Austria, Tchec Republic, Finland, Greece, Nederland, Portugal, Russia, Slovakia, Spain, Swiss, Turkey, Egypt, Israel; Commodities: Gold, silver, paladio; Currency convergence to pound: USD, Australia, Canada, Argentina, Brazil, Euro, Franca, Germany, Hong Kong, Japan, Mexico, Russia and Swiss.

4 The Benchmark for Portfolio Return

The reference for return evaluation is the stock exchange index. In the case of London this is the FTSE 100 [10]. The investment operation would build a portfolio with reflects the same constitution as the FTSE 100 index, and its performance is the same as the market.

5 Asset Forecast

To develop a forecast of assets price (or any other time series value) there are two necessaries definitions: the mathematical function to be adjusted (termed filter) and the adaptation algorithm (responsible for calculate the parameter values of the filter following temporal changes of the series).

The FIR (*finite impulse response*) filter of N dimension is a filter with trivial poles (z=0) in its transference function:

$$W(z) = w_0 + w_1.z^{-1} + w_2.z^{-2} + ... + w_{n-1}.z^{-N+1}$$

$$(1)$$

Let **W** the filter coefficient vector, and $\mathbf{X_k}$ last N inputs to the filter in k instant:

$$W = [\ w_0\ \ w_1\ \ w_2\ \ w_3\ \ ....\ \ w_{N-1}]^T$$
$$X_k = [x(k)\ \ x(k-1)\ \ x(k-2)\ \ x(k-2)\ \ ....\ \ x(k-N+1)]^T$$

$$(2)$$

Filter output is defined as:

$$(3)$$

$$y(k) = \sum_{i=0}^{N-1} w_i \cdot x(k-i) = X_k^T \cdot W$$

Any stock/asset contains in its price two components: one depending of its fundamentals and other completely random, modeled by the Brownian model. The intrinsic component would be adapted by Least Means Square LMS (see [11]), which cancels the random component.

Let us define the performance function

$$\xi = \xi(W)$$

$$(4)$$

a quadratic function with one minimum point. For any initial condition W, evaluate new values of W into the contrary direction of the performance hyper surface gradient (with indicate the maximum direction). Following the contrary direction, certainly will hit the minimum.

To evaluate the gradient of ξ is necessary do some approximations. Let

$$\xi = E[e^2(k)] \cong e^2(k)$$

$$(5)$$

Where E is the average of stochastic variable e, the error between the real value d and the adapted by fitting y. Then:

$$(6)$$

$$\nabla \xi \cong \begin{bmatrix} \dfrac{\partial e^2(k)}{\partial w_0} \\[2mm] \dfrac{\partial e^2(k)}{\partial w_1} \\[2mm] \vdots \\[2mm] \dfrac{\partial e^2(k)}{\partial w_{N-1}} \end{bmatrix} = 2.e(k). \begin{bmatrix} \dfrac{\partial e(k)}{\partial w_0} \\[2mm] \dfrac{\partial e(k)}{\partial w_1} \\[2mm] \vdots \\[2mm] \dfrac{\partial e(k)}{\partial w_{N-1}} \end{bmatrix}$$

and because

$$e(k) = d(k) - X_k^T \cdot W \Rightarrow \frac{\partial e(k)}{\partial w_i} = -x(k-i) \tag{7}$$

Then

$$\nabla \xi \cong -2.e(k).X_k \tag{8}$$

LMS algorithms consists in iteratively calculating the vector filter coefficient W, with a little vector in the gradient contrary direction:

$$W_{k+1} = W_k - \mu.\nabla \xi \tag{9}$$

where μ is an arbitrary constant to control the iteration step. Replacing $\nabla \xi$ into W iterative equation:

$$W_{k+1} = W_k + 2.\mu.e(k).X_k \tag{10}$$

This is the LMS algorithm equation, a very simple mathematical model easy to be implemented.

LMS stability depends of the μ value. If (see [12])

$$0 < \mu < \frac{2}{3} \cdot \frac{1}{N \cdot \sigma_x^2} \tag{11}$$

where σ_x^2 – average power of x(k) and N is the filter order, the algorithm will be convergent and stable. If the value is too big it will be unstable and if it is too little convergence will take too much time.

6 Assets Data Pre-processing

Let S(t) be the quote of a stock. The market works with the function

$$Ln \frac{S(t)}{S(t-1)} \tag{12}$$

for return and with the recursive variation:

$$\sigma_{ij,t} = \lambda \sigma_{ij,t-1} + (1+\lambda)r_{i,t-1}r_{j,t-1} \tag{13}$$

where $\sigma_{ij,t}$ is the conditional variation of the period t, $\lambda = 0.94$ is the decay parameter of exponential smoothing , $r_{x,t}$ is the return of x in period t. The initial condition is:

$$\sigma_{ij,0} = \frac{1}{T-2} \sum \left(r_{i,t} - \overline{r_i} \right)\left(r_{j,t} - \overline{r_j} \right) \tag{14}$$

$$\overline{r_x} = \frac{1}{T} \sum_{t=1}^{T} r_{ij,t}$$

The variation matrix Σ of risk factors and correlation matrix are:

$$\Sigma = \begin{bmatrix} \sigma_{11} & \sigma_{12} & \cdots & \sigma_{1k} \\ \sigma_{21} & \sigma_{22} & \cdots & \sigma_{2k} \\ \vdots & \vdots & \ddots & \vdots \\ \sigma_{k1} & \sigma_{k2} & \cdots & \sigma_{kk} \end{bmatrix} \tag{15}$$

$$C = \begin{bmatrix} 1 & \rho_{12} & \cdots & \rho_{1k} \\ \rho_{21} & 1 & \cdots & \rho_{2k} \\ \vdots & \vdots & \ddots & \vdots \\ \rho_{k1} & \rho_{k2} & \cdots & 1 \end{bmatrix} \tag{16}$$

$$\rho_{ij} = \frac{\sigma_{ij}}{\sigma_i \sigma_j}$$

The diagonal terms of matrix Σ are $\sigma_{ii} = \sigma_i^2$

7 Portfolio Optimization

The methodology for searching for the constitution of a portfolio was established by Markowitz [13] 50 years ago and has been central to research activities in extending, improving and revising this approach in unforeseeable and dynamic markets. The aim is to obtain a mix of assets to maximize the relation between mean return and risk, a model optimization problem:

$$\max\left[(1.0 - \lambda) * \left[\sum_{i=1}^{N} \omega_i \mu_i \right] - \lambda \left[\sum_{i=1}^{N} \sum_{j=1}^{N} \omega_i \omega_j \sigma_{i,j} \right] \right] \tag{17}$$

$$\sum_{i=1}^{N} \omega_i = 1$$

$$\delta \le \omega_i \le \xi, \quad i = 1,\ldots,N$$

where each composition is limited between the limits δ and ξ. The case $\lambda=0$ represents maximize expected return (irrespective of the risk involved) and the optimal solution will involve just the single asset with the highest return. The case $\lambda=1$ represents minimize risk (irrespective of the return involved) and the optimal solution will typically involve a number of assets. Values $0<\lambda<1$ represents explicit trade off between risk and return, generating solutions between the extremes. We assume $\lambda=0.3$ in this paper.

8 A Recursive Mathematical Model for Portfolio Selection

The fulcrum point of the problem of portfolio optimisation consists in obtaining a model:

$$w_i^{t+1} = F(w_i^t, return, risk, past\ price, prediction\ price, market\ index) \qquad (18)$$

of the future percentage of each asset available, with a function dependent only of the forecast and past condition. A general theory for this approach is available in [14], [15] and [16].

9 Software Implementation and Results with Virtual Market

The software consists in three procedures, running in sequence before trade work:
1. Given time series values up to last period, obtain the parameters of an adaptive filter for each asset, which model its fundamental behaviour, with a 20th order approximation, meaning that all effects with a period less than 10 days are modelled. With these parameters forecast the return for next period using a FIR model adapted by the LMS algorithm.
2. Genetic algorithms optimize the percentages w for each asset, with the available information of the last period, giving, as a result, the optimum portfolio. For each asset we suppose that its composition in the portfolio is limited between 10% and 30%, eliminating the effects of small fluctuations in the selection.
3. With the information of the evolution of w, two approaches were applied:
    *   Use GP to obtain equation (18) that predicts the function with and without constraints.
    *   Use GP to obtain equation (18) that gives the best return for the period, on-the-fly. Two possibilities are explored: with and without optimal composition of last period obtained by Genetic algorithm.

Bearing in mind the assumptions described in the introduction about market behavior and forecast, the first result consists in evaluating the error distribution of forecast assets using the adaptive method, with an accuracy better than 5% for FTSE100 assets forecast over 2 years.

The next step consists in obtaining the optimal portfolio with all assets available using past information. The problem consists in solving equation 17 using genetic algorithms, with a chromosome with binary coded float variables for each assets representing the amount into the portfolio. This evaluation uses return, standard deviation and variance matrix of the last 20 time series values available.

The return sum for all period intervals gives the efficiency of the strategy. Figure 3 and 4 show the results for free and with constraints ($0.1<\omega<0.3$), which fixes the percentage of any asset between 10% and 30%.

Fig. 3. Daily return for unconstrained portfolio against FTSE100 return (-0.089).

Σreturn=15.33

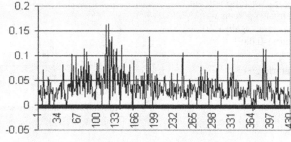

Fig. 4. Daily return for constrained portfolio against FTSE100 return (-0.089).

Σreturn=19.49

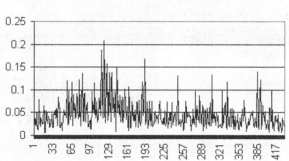

The constrained portfolio is necessary due operational problems, otherwise the portfolio is formed of too many assets.

The next step consists in evolving the solution to equation 18 using genetic programming to forecast the percentage of each asset in the portfolio. A tree built with the functions: multiply (*), sum(+), subtraction (-) and division (Div), and terminals: ERC(0..1), price forecast using adaptive algorithm, return in [t-1] and [t-2], mean return for 20 last days period, standard deviation of last 20 days, trade volume is evaluated for the period of 2 years, and optionally the last optimal percentage of the assets obtained by genetic algorithm.

The best model gives the return shown in figs 5 and 6, using, with or without, the last assets optimal percentage with constraints of percentage between 10% and 30% for any assets in the portfolio.

The returns are evaluated against the next time period's return, to establish the efficacy of mathematical model. The asset selection model using equation 18 obtained by GP forecast as good results as the optimization using equation 17, with λ=0.3.

The difference between figures 3 and 4, and 5 and 6 is that in the first case, genetic algorithm uses only available data to optimize the problem, and the second case uses GP to forecast a future solution based in assets forecast using adaptive algorithm.

Fig. 5. Portfolio without last optimal percentage with constraint against FTSE100 return (-0.089).

Σreturn=20.66

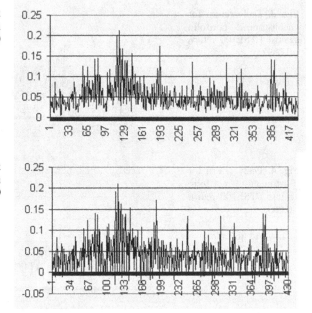

Fig. 6. Portfolio with last optimal percentage with constraint against FTSE100 return (-0.089).

Σreturn=17.53

10 Conclusions

Genetic programming for producing a predictive model for portfolio assets percentage associated with genetic algorithm to obtain portfolio optimal values obtains good results when comparing with FTSE100 index, and to the same level as obtained by genetic algorithms calculating with available data. This framework could be applied in assets management, taking care with exogenous influence in the market.

The next step of the project consists in apply the algorithm to different scenarios, to verify the adaptability of the predictive model.

The software concept is adequate to real time application in assets management, with adequate tests and adaptation of man machine interface and broadcast data acquisition.

References

1.   Metro News; "Wall Street is beaten by robots" Thursday, August 9,2001 page 7.
2.   Argonne National Laboratory – NEOS; "*The Portfolio Selection Problem: An Introduction*" http://www-fp.mcs.anl.gov/otc/Guide/CaseStudies/port/introduction.html
3.   http://uk.finance.yahoo.com/?u
4.   Werner,J.C.; "*Active noise control in ducts using genetic algorithm*" PhD. Thesis- São Paulo University- São Paulo-Brazil-1999.

5. HOLLAND,J.H. *"Adaptation in natural and artificial systems: na introductory analysis with applications to biology, control and artificial intelligence."* Cambridge: Cambridge press 1992 reedição 1975.

6. GOLDBERG,D.E. *"Genetic Algorithms in Search, Optimisation, and Machine Learning."* Reading,Mass.: Addison-Whesley, 1989.

7. KOZA,J.R. *"Genetic programming: On the programming of computers by means of natural selection."* Cambridge,Mass.: MIT Press, 1992.

8. http://wwwamy.hi-ho.ne.jp/jbaba/gif1.htm

9. http://uk.biz.yahoo.com/quote/overview.html

10. http://www.ftse.com/

11. B.Widrow & S.Stearns, Adaptive signal processing, Prentice-Hall Inc; S.Kuo & D.Morgan, Active noise control systems. Algorithms and DSP implementation, John Wiley & sons.

12. BELLANGER, M. G. Adaptive digital filters and signal analysis New York, Marcel Dekker,1987 – Chapter 4.

13. H. Markowitz; "Portfolio selection"; Chang,T-J;Meade,N.; Beasley,J.E.; Sharaiha,Y.M.; Heuristics for cardinality constrained portfolio optimisation" Computers & operations research 27(2000)1271-1302.

14. Helmbold,D.P.; Schapire,R.E.; Singer,Y.; Warmuth,M.K.; "On-line portfolio selection using multiplicative updates" Machine Learning: Proc. Of the 13th International Conference – 1996

15. Cover,T.M.; "Universal Portfolios", Mathematical finance 1(1991)1-29.

16. Parkes,D.C.; Huberman,B.A.; "Adaptive portfolio selection by investment groups" IFAC Symposium on Computation in Economics, Finance and Engineering (CEFES'98), Cambridge England, 1998.

17. Mahfoud,S.; Mani,G.; "Financial forecasting using genetic algorithms" Applied Artificial Intelligence, 10 (1996) 543-565.

18. Chang,T.J.; Meade,N.;Beasley,J.E.; Sharaiha,Y.M.; "Heuristics for cardinality constrained portfolio optimization" Computers & Operations Research 27 (2000)1271-1302.

19. Kivine,J.; Warmuth,M.K.; "Exponential gradient versus gradient descent for linear predictions" Technical report UCSC-CRL-94-16, University of California, Santa Cruz, June 1994 ftp.cse.ucsc.edu/pub/ml/ucsc-crl-94-16.ps.Z

Evolutionary Algorithm Approach to Bilateral Negotiations

Vinaysheel Baber[1], Rema Ananthanarayanan[2], and Krishna Kummamuru[2]

[1] New Hostel, E 418, Indian Institute of Management, Calcutta, Diamond Harbour Road,
P. O. Joka 743512 (WB), India
vinaybaber@yahoo.com
[2] Research Staff Member, IBM India Research Laboratory, Indian Institute of Technology,
Hauz Khas, New Delhi 110016, India
arema@in.ibm.com, kkummamu@in.ibm.com

Abstract. The Internet is quickly changing the way business-to-consumer and business-to-business commerce is conducted. The technology has created an opportunity to get beyond single-issue negotiation by determining sellers' and buyers' preferences across multiple issues, thereby creating possible joint gains for all parties. We develop simple multiple issue algorithms and heuristics that could be used in electronic auctions and electronic markets. In this study, we show how a genetic algorithm based technique, coupled with a simple heuristic can achieve good results in business negotiations. Outcome of the negotiations are evaluated on two dimensions: joint utility and number of exchanges of offers to reach a deal. The results are promising and indicate possible use of such approaches in actual electronic commerce systems.

1 Introduction

Negotiation can be considered as a search for an optimal outcome with respect to the utility function of each party. The biggest challenge in a negotiation is the fact that each side has private information about its own utility, but is ignorant of the other party's preferences, interests and strategies. Neither party would like to part with its set of critical information. Also, it might be of incentive to misrepresent one's preferences [7].

For example, take real world auctions in which parties physically participate to bid for objects versus online Internet auctions. In the former, usually a participant knows who the other participants are. In an auction of paintings a party can usually guess what are the likings of other participants, what kind of paintings they like, how much money they can pay, how sincere the other party is, etc. But in Internet auctions, physical identity is protected. Participants cannot see each other. They do not know whether they are interacting for the first time or have done business before. Participants do not have any direct way of knowing what the likings and preferences of other participants are. In such a situation, task of finding out the common interests and negotiating the core issues becomes more challenging.

J.A. Foster et al. (Eds.): EuroGP 2002, LNCS 2278, pp. 202–211, 2002.
© Springer-Verlag Berlin Heidelberg 2002

In negotiations, people often reach sub-optimal outcomes thus 'leaving money on the table' [1][8]. This is due to various reasons but mostly due to the human desire to maximize individual benefits. The end result is that parties fail to find agreements, which would make each better off.

Most of the work in the literature on negotiations deals with a scenario in which both parties reveal their utilities to a trusted agent. In this case, the problem is cast as that of multi-criteria optimization. In this paper, we address the following question when the parties in the negotiation do not reveal their utilities to any other party or any other trusted agent: (i) How much time (in terms of number of exchanges of offers) does it take to reach a mutually acceptable point, i.e. a deal? (ii) To what extent is the joint gain of the participants maximized?

The rest of the paper is organized as follows. We briefly review the related literature with relevant background in Section 2. In Section 3, we define various terms and develop the notation needed to describe the proposed method. We present our experiments of the proposed algorithm in Section 4 and conclude the paper in Section 5.

2   Background and Definitions

This section gives a brief outline of the various terms that are commonly used in Negotiations. We also briefly describe the principles behind evolutionary algorithms in this section.

2.1   Negotiations

The *attributes* of a negotiation are the issues under negotiation. For example, in an international negotiation on an oil contract, following attributes can be negotiated upon: price, weight, delivery time, currency of payment, dispute settlement location.

The *options* of an attribute are the range of values that the particular attribute can take. For example, options for *price* attribute could be $180, $195, $210, and $225. For simplicity, we considered only discrete options in our experiment. However, the method can be extended to continuous options too.

Preference of a party is the priority that the party assigns to each option within an attribute. For example, the *price* attribute of seller (Party 1) and buyer (Party2) can have following preferences.

Table 1. Seller and Buyer prefernces for a particular attribute

Price	Seller Preference	Buyer Prefernce
180	Low	High
240	High	Low

Rating of a preference is the numeric value that a party gives to its preferences. For example, the ratings for the above preferences could be:

Table 2. Seller and Buyer ratings for a particular attribute

Price	Seller Rating	Buyer Rating
180	Low (20)	High (70)
240	High (80)	Low (30)

Without loss of generality, we assume that each option is rated between 0 and 100.

Utility Function (also referred as *utility*) of a party is the function that the party uses to evaluate a given bid. In general, the utility function is a function of ratings of the options in the bid. For example, let the utility of Party 1 (seller), $U_s = 0.6$ Rating$_{price}$ + 0.4 Rating$_{weight}$, and that of Party 2 (buyer) $U_b = 0.5$ Rating$_{price}$ + 0.5 Rating$_{weight}$. Let, *price* = $ 240 and *weight* = 2 Kg. be the bid under consideration. Let seller's ratings for this options be 80 and 20 respectively and buyer's ratings 30 and 70 respectively. Then, $U_s = 0.6 * 80 + 0.4 * 20 = 56$, and $U_b = 0.5 * 30 + 0.5 * 70 = 50$.

A bid of Party 1 is a combination of attributes which is favorable to Party 1 and which it proposes to Party 2. *Negotiation* is a process of exchanging bids under a pre-defined set of rules called *negotiation protocol*. During the negotiation process, the participants' exchange offers and counter offers in an alternating manner. In this paper, we refer the participant starting the negotiation to as Party 1 and the opponent as Party 2. Bargaining takes place over all the attributes simultaneously. Thus an offer bid from one party to the other will specify an option for each attribute.

A *deal* is reached when the parties participating in the negotiations reach a bid that is acceptable to them. Given a negotiation scenario, a party will always try to *increase* its utility. This means that, given two offers with different utilities, it will always accept the one with higher utility.

Floor Utility of a party is the minimum value of utility below, which the party will not make a deal. Both the parties can have different floor values as per their preferences and utility functions. A party will *accept* an offer (bid) if the bid provides a utility above its expectation. Moreover, each party may have its own *strategy* to decide the floor utility. Two extreme sets of strategies are Boulware and Conceder. *Boulware strategy* presumes that the interval of values for negotiation is narrow. Hence, when the deal is reached or maximum allowed exchanges are exhausted, the offer generated is not substantially different from the initial one. In other words, the party does not substantially decrease its acceptable utility with the number of exchange of offers. In the *Conceder strategy*, the party quickly goes down to its floor utility. Under pressure to reach a deal quickly, the party concedes regularly by decreasing its acceptable utility.

In this paper, we assume that one party can offer a population (of fixed size) of bids to the other party. Let the size of the population be Z. If the other party accepts one of the bids from the population, it is binding on the party that made the offer. As stated earlier, Party 1 makes the initial offer. This offer is actually a population of bids suitable to Party 1. If Party 2 accepts any one of the bids within the offered set, an agreement or a deal is reached and the negotiation ends. The negotiation proceeds to the next round with Party 2 proposing a counter offer to Party 1, which Party 1 can accept or refuse. This process of alternating offers and counter-offers continues until someone accepts an offer, or until a terminating condition on time or number of exchanges is reached. If the negotiations terminate without a deal, both players get nothing.

A negotiation scenario (framework) includes, attributes, corresponding options, preferences, and ratings, utilities, negotiation protocol, floor utilities (if any), and bidders individual strategies. Negotiation algorithms address the issues in finding a deal under various negotiation frameworks. In this paper, we devise an algorithm for parties to generate offers/counter offers based only on the other's counter offers/offers.

Evolutionary Algorithms. Evolutionary Algorithms (EAs) are stochastic optimization algorithms based on the mechanism of natural selection and genetics. EAs solve optimization problems using a population of a fixed number, called the *population size*, of candidate solutions. Types of Eas include Genetic Algorithms (GAs), Evolution Strategies (ESs) and Evolutionary Programming (EP). In this paper, we focus on GAs. GAs represent the solutions by strings of symbols and use *natural selection*, *mutation*, and *crossover* as operators. Each solution in the population is associated with a figure of merit (fitness value) depending on the value of the function to be optimized. The selection operator selects a solution from the current population for the next population with probability proportional to its fitness value. The mutation operator randomly perturbs the solutions with a probability, called the *Mutation probability*. Crossover operates on two solutions and results in another one or two solutions. Typical crossover operator exchange the segments of selected strings across a crossover point with a probability, called *Crossover probability*. For a detail study on GA, readers are referred to [3].

3 Literature Review

The negotiation algorithms can be broadly categorized into two classes. The first class of algorithms is based on game-theoretic models of bargaining and negotiation. The second are due to the recent advances that have been made in the application of evolutionary computation approaches to decision and search situations in negotiations.

3.1 Game Theory

The study of bargaining and negotiation has long attracted economists because it is fundamental to exchange and markets. Early foundations were laid by Nash [5, 6]. The study of negotiations and bargaining has attracted the attention of economists for a long time. Linhart and Radner [4] raise objections regarding assumption of common knowledge, single point equilibrium and single attribute negotiation in game-theoretic models of bargaining. Due to these objections, game theoretic models have been difficult to apply to natural real life situations.

3.2 Evolutionary Algorithms Techniques

The latest stream of research tries to evolve models of negotiations by using the techniques of evolutionary computation and most commonly, Genetic Algorithms (GA).

As suggested by Goldberg[3], effectiveness of evolutionary algorithms in decision and search problems especially when the search space is huge and it is not possible to mathematically explore every point of the search space, make them an appropriate approach for automated agents discovering effective negotiation strategies.

4   Evolutionary Algorithm Based Negotiations

In this section, we develop a hybrid evolutionary algorithm for negotiations. Before explaining our algorithm, we first briefly describe application of a Simple Genetic Algorithm (SGA) in negotiations and then, a heuristic to improve the performance of SGA.

4.1   Simple GA (SGA) in Negotiations

SGAs can be used by Party 1 to find initial offer or subsequent offer to a counter offer, and by Party 2 to find a counter offer. SGA when used by a party, uses the party's utility and its negotiation strategy to evolve a population of bids. Both the parties use the same number of bids in a population of bids. Each of the parties uses its own values for mutation and crossover probabilities. One or more generations may be evolved before the parties communicate their population of bids to the other party. Negotiations between Party 1 and Party 2 using SGA can be summarized as follows:

Step 1. *Bidder* = Party 1; *Receiver* = Party 2. Bidder generates an initial population.

Step 2. *Bidder* offers the population of bids to Receiver.

Step 3. *Receiver* accepts a bid from the population if it satisfies its utility requirements. If it accepts, go to Step 6.

Step 4. If maximum exchanges limit is reached, go to Step 6.

Step 5. *Receiver* generates a population suited to its utility based on its negotiation strategy. *Temp = Bidder; Bidder = Receiver; Receiver = Temp*; Go to Step 2.

Step 6. End of negotiation.

Note that each party does not explicitly consider the bids that it gets from the other party in arriving at its next set of bids. In a way, it is equivalent to two independent SGAs running over the same search space with two different utilities. In the next subsection, we develop a heuristic to extract information on other party's preferences and use the information in generating the next set of bids.

4.2   Heuristic

In real life, there are many issues where the negotiating parties have common interests. For example, during festival sales, a shop owner would prefer early delivery times so that his stock turnover is high. Similarly, a customer will prefer early delivery time. The negotiating parties must identify such common interests and exploit these in reaching a deal quickly. We use a heuristic in SGA that tries to find and increase the occurrences of options that are preferred by both parties. Thus, we make the probability of occurrence of an option in future generations directly proportional to (total number of its occurrence in the present generations - difference of its occurrence in the present generations).For example, consider a case where there are only 2 attributes, price and weight. Let price have 3 options 200, 220 and 240 and weight 3 options 2, 3 and 4. Let the population of bids offered by Party 1 to Party 2 and that generated by Party 2 are as follows:

Table 3. Bids generated by party1 and party2

Bids offered by Party 1 to Party 2		Bids generated by Party 2	
240	4		4
200	4	240	4
220	4	200	2
220	3	220	3

Then, the probability of generating 200, 220 and 240 for price attribute are proportional to $(2 + 1) - (2 - 1) = 2$, $(2 + 1) - (2 - 1) = 2$, and $(2 + 0) - (2 - 0) = 0$ respectively. The corresponding probabilities are $(2 / 2 + 2 + 0) = 0.5$, $(2 / 2 + 2 + 0) = 0.5$, and $(0 / 2 + 2 + 0) = 0.0$ respectively. Similarly, the probabilities of generating 2, 3, and 4 for weight attribute are 0.0, 0.33, and 0.67 respectively.

In this way, this heuristic helps in narrowing down the search space to some most likely options. Thus the negotiating parties can concentrate their efforts on the issues on which they hold extreme positions rather than wasting time on mutually beneficial issues.

4.3 Hybrid GA

In every generation, Hybrid GA first generates an initial set of bids using the above described heuristic. Then, it applies selection, mutation and crossover operators on this set of bids. The way Hybrid GA used in negotiations is same as that of SGA as described in Section 4.1.

As the heuristic narrows down the search space for further exploitation, if used without SGA, its probability to explore other parts of the search space becomes zero. It may happen that the points in a narrowed search space may provide local optima and not global optima. In a more general sense, there might be a point that increases both the individual utilities of the two parties and thus the joint utilities as well, but is not attainable because of the nature of heuristic.

It is well known that EAs are useful in addressing this drawback. It makes the probability of getting out of above defined local optimum search space non-zero and helps in exploring other regions.

5   Experiments

We study the performance of the proposed algorithm in a simulated negotiation environment. We also simulate different negotiating strategies for the participants. Implementation was done using the Java programming language. We use two broad performance measures to study the individual contributions of the heuristic and GA to the overall performance of the algorithm. The two measures are the joint payoff and the time to strike a deal. Parties should not only achieve excellent individual payoffs, but they should also achieve excellent outcomes jointly, so that the 'money left on the table' is minimal. We measure joint payoff as the sum of the individual payoffs. In multi-attribute negotiations, especially when the search space is extremely big, time becomes an important factor. It is not only important to reach a deal but also to do it quickly. We measure time to strike a deal as the number of exchanges of offers and counter-offers between the participating parties. We first explain the negotiation environment and the parameters used in the algorithm before explaining the results.

5.1   Negotiation Environment and Algorithm Parameters

We set up the negotiation environment with 9 attributes, each having 4 options. This makes the size of search space as big as 4^9 (2,62,144). Experiments were conducted using linear utility functions for both parties. However, one may note that the proposed algorithm does not take the nature of utilities into consideration. Therefore, we believe that our observations on the performance of the algorithm hold for a broad range of utilities. Let $a_1, a_2, \leftarrow, a_9$ be the ratings for the corresponding 9 attributes. Then, utility of Party 1 (Seller) was assumed to be $U_s = 0.4a_1 + 0.1a_2 + 0.1a_3 + 0.1a_4 + 0.05a_5 + 00.05a_6 + 0.05a_7 + 0.05\ a_8 + 0.1a_9$, and that of Party 2 (Buyer) to be $U_b = 0.2a_1 + 0.2a_2 + 0.2a_3 + 0.1a_4 + 0.05a_5 + 0.05a_6 + 0.05a_7 + 0.05a_8 + 0.1a_9$. Note that, given the above utilities, the maximum joint utility that could be achieved is 74.

We considered both Conceder and Boulware strategies for the parties and conducted separate experiments for each of them. The concession amount to be given in Conceder strategy was kept constant and it was determined as:

$$concession = (initial\ position - floor\ position) / (number\ of\ exchanges/4).$$

For example, if a party's initial position is 40, floor position is 30, and maximum number of exchanges is 20 then, concession equals to   (40-30)/(20/4) = 2. That is, every time the party makes a counter offer, it decreases its acceptable utility by 2 points. In other words, it will accept any offer that provides a utility more than this new position. We have conducted the experiments with different values for population size, the number of bids that are offered by a party to the other at any instant. We have experimented with 1, 2 and 5 as the population size. The number of maximum allowed exchanges was kept as 20. The crossover probability was set to 0 and 0.1 and mutation probability to 0 and 0.001.

5.2 Results

As mentioned above, we studied the importance of the proposed heuristic by evaluating the performance of the Hybrid GA with and without the heuristic and that of just heuristic without any genetic operators. Hybrid GA without the heuristic is referred to as Simple GA below. In this section, results are given as average of five runs. Table 4 and Table 5 show the average number of exchange of offers before a deal is reached (*AverageT*) and the average maximum joint utility of the deal (*AverageMax*) when the parties follow Conceder and Boulware strategies respectively. Population size is denoted by Z.

Table 4. Conceder Strategy

	Z	Simple GA	Heuristic	Hybrid GA
AverageT	1	16.8	14	11.6
AverageMax	1	64.4	69.4	69.8
AverageT	2	15	12	10.6
AverageMax	2	66.6	68.2	71.4
AverageT	5	14.4	10.6	10.2
AverageMax	5	68.2	71.2	72.2

Conceder Strategy: From Table 4, it may be observed that the heuristic is better than a simple GA both in terms of time it takes to reach a deal and the money left on the table, across all population sizes considered. The hybrid algorithm is in turn better than the simple heuristic in both respects, across all population sizes considered.

As the population size increases, *AverageT* decreases and *AverageMax* increases, since more the number of bids offered, chances of reaching an agreement over more options increases.

Table 5. Boulware Strategy

	Z	Simple GA	Heuristic	Hybrid GA
AverageT	1	14	7.2	7.6
AverageMax	1	63.6	68.6	63.6
AverageT	2	11.8	6.8	6.6
AverageMax	2	64.4	66.6	64.4
AverageT	5	6.6	2.4	3.2
AverageMax	5	66.2	67.4	65.8

Boulware Strategy: It can be seen from Table 5 that the heuristic is better than a simple GA both in terms of time it takes to reach a deal and the money left on the table, across all population sizes considered. The heuristic is also better than the hybrid algorithm in both respects, across all population sizes considered. As the population size increases, *AverageT* decreases and *AverageMax* increases, since more the number of bids offered, more is the information made available to the other party.

The results are not as clear in the Boulware strategy as they are in the Conceder strategy. The utilities achieved are not as high as they are in the Conceder strategy. Also, there were some experiments in which the negotiation was aborted because the exchange limit was reached. This seems logical due to the extreme positions that the two parties adopted. The following graphs show the results for the two user tactics for the three different population sizes.

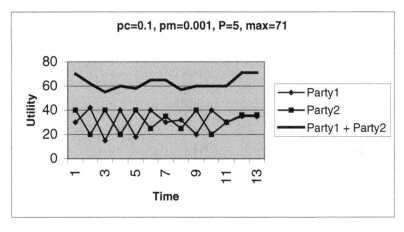

Fig. 1. Graph of a Simple GA Run

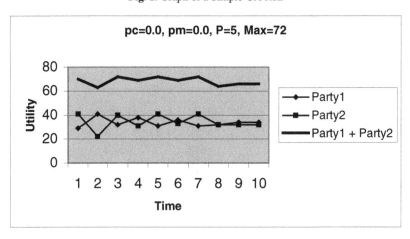

Fig. 2. Graph of a Heuristic Run

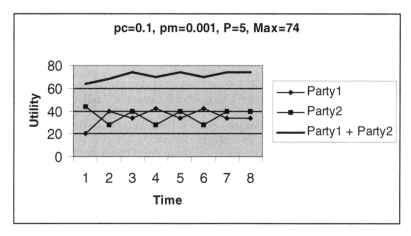

Fig. 3. Graph of a Hybrid Run

6 Future Work

In the experiments, only the two extreme user behaviors were simulated. Intermediate tactics can provide valuable insights. Also, situations where one party uses such algorithms and the other does not can be explored. Experiments with non-linear utility functions can prove to be useful. Future efforts can also be directed towards adopting this approach for multiparty negotiation scenarios. Attempts can be made to perform these experiments on continuous attributes. No attempt was made at any stage to guess the opponents' preferences. Experiments can be done to partially learn opponent's strategy and apply the same algorithm.

References

1. Camerer C., Behavioral Game Theory, Insights in Decision-making, Univ. of Chicago Press, Chicago, IL.
2. Faratin Peyman, Automated Service Negotiation Between Autonomous Computational Agents, University of London.
3. Goldberg D E, Genetic Algorithms in Search, Optimization and Machine Learning, 1989, Addison-Wesley.
4. Linhart P B, R Radner, and M A Satterthwaite, Bargaining with Incomplete Information, 1992.
5. Nash J, The Bargaining problem. Econometrica, 1950.
6. Nash J, Two person cooperative games. Econometrica, 1953.
7. Oliver R Jim, A Machine Learning Approach to Automated Negotiation and Prospects for Electronic Commerce.
8. Raiffa Howard, The Art and Science of Negotiation, 1982, Cambridge. Harvard University Press.

Allele Diffusion in Linear Genetic Programming and Variable-Length Genetic Algorithms with Subtree Crossover

Riccardo Poli[1], Jonathan E. Rowe[2], Christopher R. Stephens[3], and Alden H. Wright[4]

[1] Department of Computer Science, University of Essex, UK
rpoli@essex.ac.uk
[2] School of Computer Science, The University of Birmingham, UK
j.e.rowe@cs.bham.ac.uk
[3] Instituto de Ciencias Nucleares, UNAM, Mexico
stephens@nuclecu.unam.mx
[4] Computer Science Department, University of Montana, USA
wright@cs.umt.edu

Abstract. In this paper we study, theoretically, the search biases produced by GP subtree crossover when applied to linear representations, such as those used in linear GP or in variable length GAs. The study naturally leads to generalisations of Geiringer's theorem and of the notion of linkage equilibrium, which, until now, were applicable only to fixed-length representations. This indicates the presence of a diffusion process by which, even in the absence of selective pressure and mutation, the alleles in a particular individual tend not just to be swapped with those of other individuals in the population, but also to diffuse *within* the representation of each individual. More precisely, crossover attempts to push the population towards distributions of primitives where each primitive is equally likely to be found in any position in any individual.

1 Introduction

Schemata are sets of points in a search space sharing some syntactic feature. For example, in the context of GAs operating on binary strings, the syntactic representation of a schema is usually a string of symbols from the alphabet $\{0,1,*\}$, where the character $*$ is interpreted as a "don't care" symbol. Typically schema theorems are descriptions of how the number of members of the population belonging to a schema vary over time. If $\alpha(H, t)$ denotes the probability that at time t a newly created individual samples (or matches) the schema H, which we term the *total transmission probability* of H, then an exact schema theorem for a generational system is simply

$$E[m(H, t+1)] = M\alpha(H, t), \tag{1}$$

where M is the population size, $m(H, t+1)$ is the number of individuals sampling H at generation $t+1$ and $E[\cdot]$ is the expectation operator. Holland's [4] and other (e.g. [15]) worst-case-scenario schema theories normally provide a lower bound for $\alpha(H, t)$ or, equivalently, for $E[m(H, t+1)]$. Only recently schema theorems which provide the exact value for $\alpha(H, t)$ have become available for fixed-length GAs with one-point

J.A. Foster et al. (Eds.): EuroGP 2002, LNCS 2278, pp. 212–227, 2002.

crossover and mutation [24,25] and other homologous crossovers [23]. Even more recent is the development of exact schema theorems for variable-length GAs, linear GP and tree-based GP. These now cover a variety of crossover and mutation operators including one-point crossover [11,10,12], standard and other subtree-swapping crossovers [13, 17,7], different types of subtree mutation and headless chicken crossover [16,8], and, finally, the class of homologous crossovers [18].

Exact schema theorems provide probabilistic models of the expected behaviour of a GA or a GP system which can be used to understand the system and study its behaviour. This can be done either through simulation (i.e., by "running" the equations) or through mathematical analysis. Although exact GP schema equations have become available only very recently, early studies indicate their utility. For example, simulations and analyses of exact GP schema equations for the case of linear, variable-length representations under different crossover and mutation operators [17,7,9,20] indicate that they can provide a deeper understanding of emergent phenomena such as bloat [6,21,5].

In general, the availability of exact models for different operators facilitates the formal study of the biases of those operators. Knowledge of these biases is very important because these biases can interfere (but not necessarily in a negative way) with the intended bias of selection. So, this knowledge allows for a better informed choice of operators, parameter settings and even initialisation strategies for particular problems. For example, the knowledge of the biases of the operators obtained from exact schema theories allows one to initialise the population so as to minimise the biases of the operators in the early generations — a particularly important stage in a run. Steps in this direction have recently been made in [17,7,9], where a particular type of Gamma program-length distribution has been shown to present minimum length biases for variable-length linear systems under GP subtree crossover (we will review this particular result later).

In this paper we continue the study of the biases of the standard subtree-swapping GP crossover operator for the case where it is applied to linear structures, such as the ones used in linear GP and in variable-length GAs. In the case of linear structures, standard GP crossover involves randomly selecting two crossover points, one in each parent, and producing the offspring by swapping the substrings to either the left or the right hand side of the crossover points.

Our study is based on the use of exact schema evolution equations and on the analysis of their fixed points and naturally leads to a generalisation of Geiringer's theorem, and of the notion of linkage equilibrium. Both of these concepts, until now, were applicable only to fixed-length representations. This characterises a diffusion process by which, even in the absence of selective pressure and mutation, alleles drift not just between individuals, but also between positions within individuals. This means that uniform populations are not necessarily fixed-points for GP, unlike the fixed-length GA case.

The paper is organised as follows. We provide some background information on the GP schema theory for subtree crossover acting on linear structures in Section 2. We describe Geiringer's theorem for fixed-length GAs in Section 3 and introduce our extension of Geiringer's theorem in Section 4. Experimental results backing up the theory are presented in Section 5. We discuss our results in Section 6 and, finally, we draw some conclusions in Section 7.

2   GP Schema Theory Background

Syntactically a GP schema is a tree composed of functions from the set $\mathcal{F} \cup \{=\}$ and terminals from the set $\mathcal{T} \cup \{=\}$, where $\mathcal{F}$ and $\mathcal{T}$ are the function and terminal sets used in a GP run. The primitive $=$ is a "don't care" symbol which stands for a *single* terminal or function. A schema H represents the set of all programs having the same shape as H and the same non-$=$ nodes as H.

As discussed in [17], when only unary functions are used in GP, schemata (and programs) can only take the form $(h_1 (h_2 (h_3 .... (h_{N-1} h_N)....)))$ where $N > 0, h_i \in \mathcal{F} \cup \{=\}$ for $1 \le i < N$, and $h_N \in \mathcal{T} \cup \{=\}$. Therefore, they can be written unambiguously as strings of symbols of the form $h_1 h_2 h_3 .... h_{N-1} h_N$. In order to make the notation more compact, in the following we will represent repeated symbols in a string using the power notation where x^y means x repeated y times. Particularly important for the GP schema theory are schemata containing "don't care" symbols only, since they represent all the programs of a particular shape. Using the power notation they can be represented as $(=)^N$ for any $N > 0$.

In [17] we proved that the total transmission probability for a linear GP schema of the form $h_1 ... h_N$ under standard crossover with uniform selection of the crossover points and no mutation can be written in the following form

$$\alpha(h_1 ... h_N, t) = (1 - p_{xo}) p(h_1 ... h_N, t) + \tag{2}$$

$$p_{xo} \sum_{k>0} \frac{1}{k} \sum_{i=0}^{\min(N,k)-1} p(h_1 ... h_i (=)^{k-i}, t) \sum_{n=N-i}^{\infty} \frac{p((=)^{n-N+i} h_{i+1} ... h_N, t)}{n},$$

where p_{xo} is the crossover probability and $p(H, t)$ is the selection probability of the schema H. In fitness proportionate selection $p(H, t) = m(H, t) f(H, t) / (M \bar{f}(t))$, where $m(H, t)$ is the number of individuals matching the schema H at time t, $f(H, t)$ is their mean fitness, $\bar{f}(t)$ is the mean fitness of the individuals in the population and M is the population size. In the equation each k represents the length of a first parent, each n represents the length of a second parent, and each i is a valid crossover point.

This equation can be used to study, among other things, the evolution of size in linear GP/GA systems. This is because it can be specialised to describe the transmission probability of schemata of the form $(=)^N$. The quantity $\alpha(H, t)$ represents a probability. However, for an infinite population $\alpha(H, t)$ can also be interpreted as the proportion of the population matching schema H at generation $t + 1$, a quantity that we will denote with $\Phi(H, t + 1)$. Also, we should note that if the fitness landscape is flat, then $p(H, t) = \Phi(H, t)$. So, under the assumptions of infinite population and flat landscape the specialisation of Equation 2 to schemata of the form $(=)^N$ leads to the following length-evolution equation:

$$\Phi((=)^N, t) = (1 - p_{xo}) \Phi((=)^N, t) \tag{3}$$

$$+ p_{xo} \sum_k \sum_{i=0}^{\min(N,k)-1} \frac{\Phi((=)^k, t)}{k} \sum_{n=N-i}^{\infty} \frac{\Phi((=)^n, t)}{n}.$$

In [17] we showed both empirically and mathematically that, in these conditions, a family of fixed-point distributions of lengths exists and that this family is the following family of discretised Gamma distributions

$$\Phi((=)^N, t) = N r^{N-1} (r - 1)^2, \tag{4}$$

where $r = (\mu - 1)/(\mu + 1)$ and μ is the mean length of the individuals in the population. We also proved that the mean size of the programs at generation $t + 1$, $\mu(t + 1)$, in a linear GP system with standard crossover, uniform selection of the crossover points, no mutation and an infinite population is

$$\mu(t + 1) = \sum_N Np((=)^N, t) \tag{5}$$

and, therefore, that on a flat landscape,

$$\mu(t + 1) = \mu(t). \tag{6}$$

For alternative proofs of some of these results and other related results, such as a time evolution equation and a fixed point for the variance of the length distribution, see [20].

3   Geiringer's Theorem

In this section we briefly introduce Geiringer's theorem [3], an important result with implications both for natural population genetics and evolutionary algorithms [1,2,22]. Geiringer's theorem indicates that, in a population of fixed-length chromosomes repeatedly undergoing crossover (in the absence of mutation and selective pressure), the probability of finding a generic string $h_1 h_2 \cdots h_N$ approaches a limit distribution which is only dependent on the distribution of the alleles h_1, h_2, etc. in the initial generation. More precisely, if $\Phi(h_1 h_2 \cdots h_N, t)$ is the proportion of individuals of type $h_1 h_2 \cdots h_N$ at generation t (i.e. $\Phi(h_1 h_2 \cdots h_N, t) = m(h_1 h_2 \cdots h_N, t)/M$) and $\Phi(h_i, t)$ is the proportion of individuals carrying allele h_i then

$$\lim_{t \to \infty} \Phi(h_1 h_2 \cdots h_N, t) = \prod_{i=1}^{N} \Phi(h_i, 0). \tag{7}$$

This result is valid for all homologous crossover operators which allow any two loci to be separated by recombination. Strictly speaking the result is valid only for infinite populations.

If one interprets $\Phi(h_1 h_2 \cdots h_N, t)$ as a probability distribution of the possible strings in the population, we can interpret Equation 7 as saying that such a distribution is converging towards independence. When at a particular generation t the frequency of any string in a population $\Phi(h_1 h_2 \cdots h_N, t)$ equals $\prod_{i=1}^{N} \Phi(h_i, t)$, the population is said to be in *linkage equilibrium* or *Robbins' proportions*.

It is trivial to generalise Geiringer's theorem to obtain the expected fixed-point proportion of a generic linear fixed-length GA schema H for a population undergoing crossover:

$$\lim_{t \to \infty} \Phi(H, t) = \prod_{i \in \Delta(H)} \Phi(*^{i-1} h_i *^{N-i}, 0), \tag{8}$$

where $\Delta(H)$ is the set of indices of the defining symbols in H, h_i is one such defining symbols and we used the power notation x^y to mean x repeated y times. (Note that $\Phi(*^{i-1} h_i *^{N-i}, t)$ coincides with the frequency of allele h_i, $\Phi(h_i, t)$.)

4   A Geiringer-Theorem-Type Result for Linear GP Representations and Subtree Crossover

A full extension of Geiringer's theorem to linear, variable-length structures and standard GP crossover would require two steps: (a) proving that, in the absence of mutation and of selective pressure and for an infinite population, a distribution $\Phi(h_1 h_2 \cdots h_N, t)$, where the alleles can be considered independent stochastic variables, is a fixed point, and (b) showing that the system indeed moves towards that fixed point. In this paper we prove (a) mathematically and provide experimental evidence for (b).

Our objective is to identify the fixed point to which an infinite linear GP population converges under the effect of crossover only (i.e. on a flat landscape). Instead of just providing the equation for the fixed point and proving that it is indeed a fixed point, we prefer to describe the reasoning that led us to guess the form of the fixed point since this better illustrates its meaning.

Imagine a population of strings of different lengths and focus attention on a particular non-terminal allele a at a particular locus l of a particular string s (we will consider the case of terminal alleles later). Subtree crossover allows for the migration of allele a to different strings, for example to strings of length different from the length of s. So, subtree crossover promotes a process of "diffusion" of alleles between different length classes. Unlike the case of homologous crossover in fixed length strings, in general, this process does not keep the alleles in their original position, i.e. allele a might migrate to loci different from l. Because of this, in repeated applications of crossover, a copy of the allele can be placed back into the original string s (which may now have a different length and allele composition) but at a different locus, effectively creating a sort of gene duplication (indeed unequal crossing over seems to be the mechanism of gene duplication in nature [19]). So, subtree crossover also promotes another type of allele diffusion: diffusion within length classes. Put another way, crossover is trying to spread each non-terminal allele as thinly as possible over every non-terminal locus available in the population.

Let us calculate the total number, $n(a, t)$, of non-terminal alleles of type a in a population of size M at generation t. With the "don't care" symbol $\bar{a}$ we denote any non-terminal allele different from a, while with $\boxed{a}$ we denote any sequence of $\bar{a}$'s, including the empty sequence. The "don't care" symbol "$=$" will be used to represent any terminal symbol. Then we can write

$$n(a, t) = M\big(1 \times \Phi(a =, t) + 2 \times \Phi(aa =, t) + 1 \times \Phi(\bar{a}a =, t) + 1 \times \Phi(a\bar{a} =, t)$$

$$+ 3 \times \Phi(aaa =, t) + 2 \times \Phi(\bar{a}aa =, t) + 2 \times \Phi(a\bar{a}a =, t) + \dots\big)$$

$$= M\big(\Phi(\boxed{a}a\boxed{a} =, t) + \Phi(\boxed{a}a\boxed{a}a\boxed{a} =, t) + \Phi(\boxed{a}a\boxed{a}a\boxed{a}a\boxed{a} =, t) + \dots\big)$$

$$= M \sum_{n \geq 1} \Phi((\boxed{a}a)^n \, \boxed{a} =, t).$$

So, whether the population is finite or infinite the expected number of non-terminal alleles of type a per individual is $\sum_{n \geq 1} \Phi((\boxed{a}a)^n \, \boxed{a} =, t)$, which we expect not to vary with t. However, as discussed in Section 2 the mean program length, $\mu(t)$, is also expected to be time independent. So, the average number of non-terminal alleles of type a per non-terminal locus is:

$$c(a) = \frac{\sum_{n \geq 1} \Phi((\boxed{a}a)^n \, \boxed{a} =, 0)}{\mu(0) - 1}. \tag{9}$$

If we assume that there is no length bias in the choice of the crossover points and that the two crossover points are chosen independently, then after some time crossover will have mixed the alleles sufficiently so that the presence of a given non-terminal allele in a given locus is independent of any other non-terminal allele and locus. We also expect that the probability of finding an allele of type a at a generic locus within a string of any length will be constant and equal to $c(a)$.

Let us now consider the effects of crossover on terminal alleles and loci. Again, let us focus our attention on terminal allele a in a string s of length l. Clearly allele a occupies locus l in s, but we expect that crossover will sooner or later move a to strings of length different from l. So, also for terminal alleles there is a diffusion effect which promotes their migration to strings of different length. However, it is impossible to obtain more than one copy of a terminal in a particular string because terminal alleles can only occupy the terminal locus. So, there cannot be a diffusion process of terminal alleles within a length class.

Let us calculate the total number, $n(a, t)$, of terminal alleles of type a in a population of size M at generation t:

$$n(a,t) = M\big(1 \times \Phi(a,t) + 1 \times \Phi(= a, t) + 1 \times \Phi(== a, t) + \ldots\big)$$
$$= M \sum_{n \geq 0} \Phi((=)^n a, t).$$

So, whether the population is finite or infinite the expected number of terminal alleles of type a per individual is $\sum_{n \geq 0} \Phi((=)^n a, t)$, which, again, we expect not to vary with t. Because there is only one terminal locus per individual, the average number of terminal alleles of type a per terminal locus is:

$$c(a) = \sum_{n \geq 0} \Phi((=)^n a, 0). \tag{10}$$

We can assume that after some time, crossover will have mixed the alleles sufficiently so that the probability of finding a given terminal allele in a string is independent of the string length and is equal to $c(a)$.

The independence arguments above mean that the conditional probability of finding a specific string within the class of strings of length N will be described by the following probability distribution

$$\Pr\{h_1 h_2 \ldots h_N | \text{length} = N\} = \prod_{i=1}^{N} c(h_i). \tag{11}$$

This result allows us to calculate the fixed point proportion of strings of type $h_1 h_2 \ldots h_N$

$$\Phi(h_1 h_2 \ldots h_N, \infty) = \Phi((=)^N, \infty) \times \prod_{i=1}^{N} c(h_i), \tag{12}$$

where $\Phi((=)^N, \infty)$ is the discrete gamma distribution given in Equation 4, which represents the fixed point for length evolution. If we extend the definition of $c(a)$ to accept the argument "=" (by setting $c(=) = 1$), it is easy to see that Equation 12 is also valid for schemata.

The arguments reported above led us to the following

Theorem 1. *A fixed point distribution for the proportion of a linear, variable-length schema $h_1 h_2 \cdots h_N$ under subtree crossover for an infinite population initialised at the fixed point length distribution operating on a flat fitness landscape is given in Equation 12.*

Proof. Since the fitness landscape is flat, $p(H, t) = \Phi(H, t)$ for any schema. Also, because the population is infinite, $\alpha(H, t) = \Phi(H, t + 1)$. So, Equation 2 becomes

$$\Phi(h_1...h_N, t+1) = (1 - p_{xo})\Phi(h_1...h_N, t) + \tag{13}$$

$$p_{xo} \sum_k \frac{1}{k} \sum_{i=0}^{\min(N,k)-1} \Phi(h_1...h_i(=)^{k-i}, t) \sum_{n=N-i}^{\infty} \frac{\Phi((=)^{n-N+i}h_{i+1}...h_N, t)}{n}.$$

We can prove that Equation 12 is a fixed point for this equation, by substituting the right-hand side of Equation 12 into the right-hand side of this equation and then showing that the resulting expression for $\Phi(h_1...h_N, t+1)$ has exactly the same form as the right-hand side of Equation 12.

From the substitution we obtain:

$$\Phi(h_1...h_N, t+1) = (1 - p_{xo})\Phi((=)^N, \infty) \prod_{i=1}^{N} c(h_i) +$$

$$p_{xo} \sum_k \frac{1}{k} \sum_{i=0}^{\min(N,k)-1} \Phi((=)^k, \infty) \prod_{\iota=1}^{i} c(h_\iota) \sum_{n=N-i}^{\infty} \frac{1}{n}\Phi((=)^n, \infty) \prod_{\iota=i+1}^{N} c(h_\iota)$$

$$= \prod_{i=1}^{N} c(h_i) \left((1 - p_{xo})\Phi((=)^N, \infty) + \right.$$

$$\left. p_{xo} \sum_k \frac{1}{k} \sum_{i=0}^{\min(N,k)-1} \Phi((=)^k, \infty) \sum_{n=N-i}^{\infty} \frac{1}{n}\Phi((=)^n, \infty) \right).$$

Note that the large factor in parentheses is entirely equivalent to the right-hand side of Equation 3. Because by hypothesis $\Phi((=)^N, \infty)$ is a fixed point for the length distribution, then the factor must be equivalent to $\Phi((=)^N, \infty)$ and so

$$\Phi(h_1...h_N, t+1) = \Phi((=)^N, \infty) \prod_{i=1}^{N} c(h_i), \tag{14}$$

which proves that Equation 12 is a fixed point for the distribution of strings.

It is interesting to rewrite Equation 12 is a slightly different form. If $\nu(h_1 h_2 ..., a)$ represents the number of times symbol a appears in the string or schema $h_1 h_2 ...,$ and $\mathcal{C}$ represents our primitive set then

$$\Phi(h_1 h_2 ... h_N, \infty) = \Phi((=)^N, \infty) \prod_{a \in \mathcal{C}} (c(a))^{\nu(h_1 h_2 ..., a)}. \tag{15}$$

So, for example if $\mathcal{C} = \{\sqrt{}, \sin, x, y, z\}$ and the population is initialised so that $c(\sqrt{}) = c(\sin) = 1/2$ and $c(x) = 1/3$, then $\Phi(\sqrt{}\sqrt{}\sin x, \infty) = (1/2)^2 \times (1/2) \times (1/3) = 1/24$.

Interestingly, in the case of a binary alphabet, the probability of sampling a given string is only a function of the unitation value (the number of ones) of the string.

As we have not provided a formal proof that the length distribution converges towards a discrete-Gamma fixed point[1] we cannot prove that our theorem holds if the length distribution is other than at its fixed point.

It is also important to note that, in the absence of a proof of the stability of the family of fixed points in Equation 12, we cannot rigorously claim that any population will always converge to an independent allele distribution. However, the arguments preceeding the theorem can be considered as an informal proof of convergence since they consider the mixing/diffusion effects of crossover over a number of generations. Additionally, the experimental results described in the following section strongly corroborate these conjectures.

5   Experimental Results

In order to check the theoretical results in this paper we set up a population of variable length strings consisting of 1,000,000 individuals. All individuals had the same terminal allele, 0, while two types of non-terminal alleles were used: alleles of type 0 and alleles of type 1. The majority of alleles were of type 0 and represented a "background" against which alleles of type 1 could be more easily traced. Alleles of type 1 are a "contrast medium" inoculated in the representation for the purpose of studying the diffusion of non-terminal alleles. Initially, alleles of type 1 were restricted to appear at only one specific non-terminal locus (which was varied between experiments). All strings which included that locus had nodes of type 1 at that locus. All other loci were occupied by alleles of type 0.

In our experiments we used two different initial length distributions: a distribution closely resembling a Gamma distribution with mean 10.5, and a uniform distribution with the same mean. Each population was run for 100 generations. The system was a generational GP/GA system with subtree crossover applied with 100% probability and a flat fitness landscape. Multiple independent runs were not required since the population size was set to be sufficiently large so as to remove any significant statistical variability and therefore to approximate the infinite-population behaviour (for each program length we had tens of thousands of individuals on average).

We start by checking what happens to the length distribution over time. Figure 1(a) shows that the distribution of program length is indeed at a fixed point when the population is initialised using a discrete Gamma distribution. In the figure the small variations in the plots for the first and second generations are due to the slight inaccuracy of our Gamma-deviate generation algorithm. Only the first few generations are shown because the plots for later generations simply coincide with the plot for generation 5. Figure 1(b) illustrates how quickly the system converges to a discrete Gamma distribution even when initialised using a radically different distribution (in this case a uniform length distribution).

Considering now the allele dynamics: Figure 2(a) shows how the distribution of alleles of type 1 varies within programs of length 10 over a number of generations

---

[1] However, in [17] experimental evidence was provided that corroborates the hypothesis that a discrete gamma length distribution is asymptotically approached when the landscape is flat and the population is large.

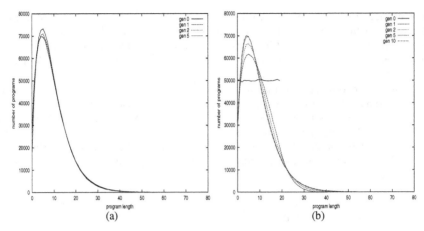

Fig. 1. Plots of the number of programs vs. program length for different generations for a population of 1,000,000 individuals initialised with an approximately-Gamma (a) and an approximately uniform (b) length distribution.

in a population initialised at the Gamma-distribution length fixed-point. In the initial generation all non-terminal loci at position 1 were occupied by alleles of type 1 (i.e. only programs of length 1 did not include any 1's). So, our "contrast medium" was maximally isolated within the representation. Nonetheless, the "lateral" diffusion process very quickly spreads the "dye" and, within 20 generations or so, the distribution of alleles becomes uniform (since no terminal 1's were allowed, the proportion of 1's in locus 10 was always 0). At generation 100 the value of the proportion of alleles of type 1 averaged over the non-terminal loci was 0.103046, which, as shown in the first row of Table 1, matches very closely the value predicted by the theory on the basis of the frequency of non-terminal alleles of type 1 at generation 0.

Figure 2(b) shows what happens if we initialise the population so that all non-terminal loci at position 5 are occupied by alleles of type 1. Again, the initial length distribution is approximately a discrete Gamma. In this case the diffusion of alleles of type 1 is even faster. At generation 100 the proportion of alleles of type 1 averaged over the non-terminal loci is 0.075467. This is lower than the value in the previous paragraph because the average frequency of non-terminal 1's at generation 0 was lower (programs of length 1, 2, 3, 4 and 5 did not include any 1's). As before (see the second row of Table 1) this matches very closely our theoretical prediction based on the allele frequencies at generation 0.

The situation is no different for populations initialised with a uniform length distribution, as indicated in Figures 2(c) and 2(d). In this case the values to which the frequency of 1's is approaching are: 0.100201 for a population initialised with ones in non-terminal locus 1, and 0.079757 for a population initialised with ones in non-terminal locus 5. Again, these values are very close to the theoretical predictions based on generation 0 information, as indicated in the fifth and sixth rows of Table 1. The table reports also other limit values, both measured and theoretically predicted, which further corroborate the theory.

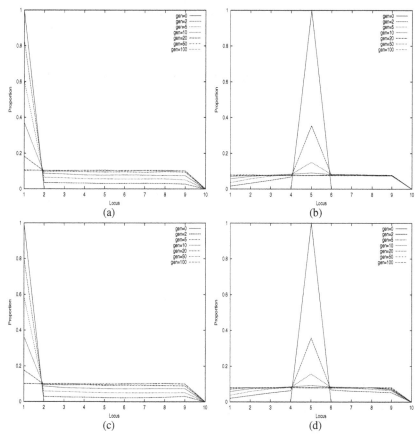

Fig. 2. Plots of the relative proportion of non-terminal alleles of type 1 vs. locus position within programs of length 10 for different generations. The population was initialised with an approximately Gamma length distribution in (a) and (b), and a uniform length distribution in (c) and (d). In the initial generation the alleles of type 1 were confined to non-terminal locus 1 in (a) and (c), and to non-teminal locus 5 in (b) and (d).

Table 1. Comparison between empirically measured and theoretical value of the fixed point frequency of non-terminal 1's, $c(1)$.

Initial distribution	Locus of initial 1's	Measured Frequency	Theoretical Frequency
gamma	1	0.103046	0.103444
gamma	5	0.075467	0.077442
gamma	10	0.042532	0.042695
gamma	15	0.020574	0.020963
uniform	1	0.100201	0.099964
uniform	5	0.079757	0.078857
uniform	10	0.052157	0.052604

The picture is not very different for classes of program of length other than 10, as illustrated in Figure 3. The figures show plots of the relative frequencies of non-terminal alleles of type 1 measured at generation 100 as a function of the locus position, for programs of lengths 10, 20, 30 and 40. In the initial population, all non-terminal loci at position 1 were occupied by alleles of type 1. Lengths were Gamma distributed in Figure 3(a) and uniformly distributed in Figure 3(b). Despite minor statistical oscillations, the proportions of alleles of type 1 approach a length- and locus-independent value, as expected from the theory.

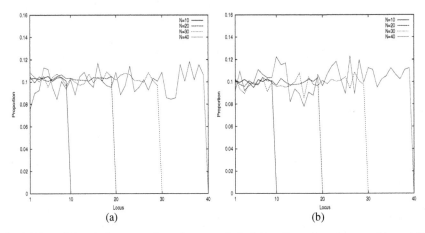

(a)   (b)

Fig. 3. Plots of the relative proportion of non-terminal alleles of type 1 vs. locus position within programs of length 10, 20, 30 and 40 at generation 100. The population was initialised with an approximately-Gamma length distribution in (a) and with a uniform length distribution in (b). In the initial generation the alleles of type 1 were confined to non-terminal locus 1.

To further verify that indeed under subtree crossover the population tends towards an independent allele distribution, we performed an experiment with exactly the same set up as in Figure 2(a) but this time we kept track of the co-occurrence of pairs of non-terminal alleles within the class of programs of length 10. So, for each generation we obtained a set of four 9×9 co-occurrence frequency matrices, one for each possible choice of a pair of the non-terminal alleles 0 and 1. An element at position (r, c) of the co-occurrence matrix for non-terminal alleles a and b, represented the average number of times allele a was present in locus r while at the same time allele b was present in locus c in strings of length 10. Once normalised by the total number of strings of length 10, the diagonal elements of the 0/0 and 1/1 matrices represent the proportions of alleles of type 0 and 1, respectively, present at each locus. So, the diagonals represent the same information as in Figure 2(a). The off-diagonal elements, however, may reveal correlations between pairs of alleles and loci.

Figure 4 shows plots of the average and standard deviation of the off-diagonal elements of the co-occurrence matrices for different pairs of non-terminal alleles and different generations. Initially the correlation between pairs of alleles is high. However, the off-diagonal elements converge rather quickly towards three different constant values and after 30 or 40 generations all the off-diagonal elements of each co-occurrence matrix are approximately identical. This indicates that, for strings of length 10, there is no remaining pairwise correlation in the population. The asymptotic value to which the frequencies of the off-diagonal elements converge coincides almost perfectly with those predicted by the theory on the basis of generation 0 information. Since in these circumstances $c(1) \approx 0.103444$, the theoretical values are: $(1 - c(1))^2 \approx 0.8038$ for the 0/0 allele pair, $c(1) \times (1 - c(1)) \approx 0.0927$ for the 0/1 and 1/0 allele pairs, and $c(1)^2 \approx 0.0107$ for the 1/1 allele pair. The picture is exactly the same for strings of other lengths.

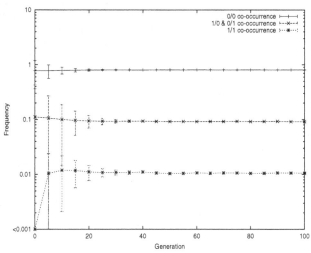

Fig. 4. Plots of the mean relative frequency of co-occurrence of pairs of non-terminal alleles vs. generation within programs of length 10. The population was initialised with an approximately Gamma length distribution. In the initial generation the alleles of type 1 were confined to non-terminal locus 1.

6   Discussion

In previous research [17,7] the length biases of standard GP crossover when applied to linear representations were studied. In that work all the complexities involved in following the propagation of alleles (functions and terminals) were removed with only schemata of the form $(=)^N$, in the absence of selective pressure, being studied using exact schema evolution equations [13]. In those studies it was discovered that the program-length distribution tends towards a discrete Gamma distribution. This has important implications, such as that GP tends to sample exponentially more often shorter programs than longer ones. It also implies that, even in the presence of selective pressure, GP will be unable to fully converge to solutions of a specific length.

These results were the starting point for the work presented in this paper. Here, we focused our attention on the effects of subtree crossover on the primitive distribution, and therefore, ultimately, on the precise way in which this type of crossover explores the search space. We think that our empirical and theoretical results can be interpreted in a relatively simple way: subtree crossover generates both a "vertical" (between strings) primitive-mixing process and a "lateral" (within string) primitive diffusion process.

Let us first consider the effects of vertical mixing. A vertical mixing behaviour is present in most crossover operators described in the literature on fixed length GAs. It is well known that this destroys "linkage", i.e. correlations, between different allele positions in the population. In the fixed length case the asymptotic convergence towards independence described by Geiringer's theorem is the result of the decay of correlations due to the mixing effect of crossover. Because vertical mixing is performed also by subtree crossover, it is not surprising to see that GP is also moving towards an independent fixed-point string distribution. In other words, vertical primitive mixing is the reason why the right hand side of Equation 12 is a product, like the right hand side of Equation 7. Note that in fixed-length GAs the decay of correlations is exponential in time and in the case of a continuous time evolution can be solved for exactly [23] showing that higher order correlations decay faster (exponentially) than lower order ones. It is likely that a similar behaviour characterises also subtree crossover.

Let us now consider the effects of lateral diffusion. To the best of our knowledge a phenomenon of this type has not been reported for any other operator, and so it seems a very special feature of GP with subtree crossover. The effect of the diffusion process is that, unlike the case of fixed length representations and homologous crossover, the population moves towards a state where the probability of finding a particular allele at a given locus is locus-independent. This is why Equation 12 can be rewritten in the form in Equation 15, which emphasises the multinomial nature of the process (the probability of any specific string being in the population is only a function of the number of alleles of each type in the string, not where such alleles are located).

There are different ways in which we can interpret the effects of lateral diffusion. In one way, this is somewhat analogous to mutation. One of the features of mutation is that it allows for the reintroduction of a lost primitive at a particular position. With homologous crossover in fixed length strings, as is well known, once an allele has been lost at a particular bit position it cannot be recovered by selection and crossover. However, thanks to the lateral diffusion effect this is not the case for subtree crossover as our experiments plainly show. Imagine that a fit string requires a 1 at a particular bit position and that in the current population it does not exist then lateral diffusion can provide the missing primitive in a similar manner to that of mutation. The key difference is that with mutation there is no conservation law at work, with crossover on fixed length strings the frequency of a given primitive at a given bit position is preserved while in the case of subtree crossover on variable length strings only the frequency of an primitive in the entire population is preserved. This mutation-like behaviour of subtree crossover, which is unavoidably also present on non-flat fitness landscapes, is likely to be a reason for the convergence (or, rather, lack of convergence) behaviour shown by standard GP.

Another way of interpreting the effects of lateral diffusion is that, in some circumstances, they can provide an automatic restart mechanism. If at some point in a run selection becomes absent or very weak, crossover will try to push the population towards a Gamma length distribution and will mix and diffuse its primitives. So, if the selective pressure remains low for long enough, the population will move to a state which has some of the characteristics of a typical initial population: no correlation between primitives and locus-independent primitive frequencies. This is not exactly equivalent to reinitialising the population (a restart), because the mean length of the population will be the mean length reached when the selection pressure dropped, and the frequency of each primitive will be the mean frequency present when the selection pressure dropped. Also, if the initial population included some correlations, e.g. if it was the result of inoculation (the initialisation of the population with programs believed to be good candidate solutions), then lateral diffusion could not be seen as a restarting mechanism. In any case, if the designer of the GP system wanted the system to work by discovering progressive improvements of the best program found so far, the behaviour just described might appear undesirable.[2]

A consequence of the diffusive bias of subtree crossover is that the way the search space is sampled in the initial generations depends perhaps more heavily on the initial primitive frequencies than on the actual structure of the programs in the initial generation. This suggests that clever initialisation procedures such as inoculation might not necessarily produce the desired effects (after inoculation, crossover will tend to destroy any specific arrangement of primitives as crossover moves the population toward an independent node distribution).

7   Conclusions

In this paper we have presented theoretical results describing the asymptotic behaviour of a linear GP system, or a variable length GA, evolving in a flat fitness landscape with no mutation and using subtree crossover. We provided experimental evidence that firmly corroborates the theory, showing an almost perfect match between the predictions of the theory based on generation 0 data and the observed primitive frequencies at later generations.

In part, the behaviour we have observed and characterised is what one would expect: a) crossover shuffles the primitives present in different individuals and b) primitives which left an individual due to an earlier crossover event can come back at a different position in a later crossover event, resulting in a sort of gene duplication. What is perhaps surprising is that this second effect is a real diffusion process which attempts to push the population towards a locus- and length-independent primitive distribution where each primitive is equally likely to be found in any position of any individual.

Knowing this bias and the length biases [17] of standard crossover is important because it allows the users of GP systems to evaluate whether this type of crossover provides the desired search behaviour for the system. If this is not the case, then the knowledge of the search biases of other operators, which has recently started emerging both from empirical studies and schema-theoretic analyses, allows an informed choice for an alternative. In addition, as discussed in the paper, the knowledge of these biases can explain emergent GP phenomena such as the inability of GP to converge.

---

[2] In [14], on the basis of a theoretical analysis of the amount of genetic material exchanged by the parents to form the offspring, we conjectured that in some cases GP with subtree crossover might be more like a set of stochastic hill-climbers working in parallel than like a genetic algorithm. The restarting behaviour described above seems to further corroborate the hill-climbing conjecture and to refine it by indicating that, in some circumstances, a GP system might behave a bit like a hill-climber with restarts.

Acknowledgements. CRS would like to thank the University of Birmingham for a visiting Professorship and DGAPA-PAPIIT grant IN100201. RP and CRS would like to thank the Royal Society for their support. JER, AHW and RP would like to thank EPSRC for their support.

References

[1] L. B. Booker. Recombination distributions for genetic algorithms. In *FOGA-92, Foundations of Genetic Algorithms*, Vail, Colorado, 24–29 July 1992. Email: booker@mitre.org.

[2] L. B. Booker, D. B. Fogel, D. Whitley, P. J. Angeline, and A. E. Eiben. Recombination. In T. Bäck, D. B. Fogel, and T. Michalewicz, editors, *Evolutionary Computation 1: Basic Algorithms and Operators*, chapter 33. Institute of Physics Publishing, 2000.

[3] H. Geiringer. On the probability theory of linkage in Mendelian heredity. *Annals of Mathematical Statistics*, 15(1):25–57, March 1944.

[4] J. Holland. *Adaptation in Natural and Artificial Systems*. University of Michigan Press, Ann Arbor, USA, 1975.

[5] W. B. Langdon, T. Soule, R. Poli, and J. A. Foster. The evolution of size and shape. In L. Spector, W. B. Langdon, U.-M. O'Reilly, and P. J. Angeline, editors, *Advances in Genetic Programming 3*, chapter 8, pages 163–190. MIT Press, Cambridge, MA, USA, June 1999.

[6] N. F. McPhee and J. D. Miller. Accurate replication in genetic programming. In L. Eshelman, editor, *Genetic Algorithms: Proceedings of the Sixth International Conference (ICGA95)*, pages 303–309, Pittsburgh, PA, USA, 15-19 July 1995. Morgan Kaufmann.

[7] N. F. McPhee and R. Poli. A schema theory analysis of the evolution of size in genetic programming with linear representations. In *Genetic Programming, Proceedings of EuroGP 2001*, LNCS, Milan, 18-20 Apr. 2001. Springer-Verlag.

[8] N. F. McPhee, R. Poli, and J. E. Rowe. A schema theory analysis of mutation size biases in genetic programming with linear representations. In *Proceedings of the 2001 Congress on Evolutionary Computation CEC 2001*, Seoul, Korea, May 2001.

[9] N. F. McPhee, R. Poli, and J. E. Rowe. A schema theory analysis of mutation size biases in genetic programming with linear representations. In *Proceedings of the 2001 Congress on Evolutionary Computation CEC2001*, pages 1078–1085, COEX, World Trade Center, 159 Samseong-dong, Gangnam-gu, Seoul, Korea, 27-30 May 2001. IEEE Press.

[10] R. Poli. Exact schema theorem and effective fitness for GP with one-point crossover. In D. Whitley, D. Goldberg, E. Cantu-Paz, L. Spector, I. Parmee, and H.-G. Beyer, editors, *Proceedings of the Genetic and Evolutionary Computation Conference*, pages 469–476, Las Vegas, July 2000. Morgan Kaufmann.

[11] R. Poli. Hyperschema theory for GP with one-point crossover, building blocks, and some new results in GA theory. In R. Poli, W. Banzhaf, and *et al.*, editors, *Genetic Programming, Proceedings of EuroGP 2000*. Springer-Verlag, 15-16 Apr. 2000.

[12] R. Poli. Exact schema theory for genetic programming and variable-length genetic algorithms with one-point crossover. *Genetic Programming and Evolvable Machines*, 2(2), 2001. Forthcoming.

[13] R. Poli. General schema theory for genetic programming with subtree-swapping crossover. In *Genetic Programming, Proceedings of EuroGP 2001*, LNCS, Milan, 18-20 Apr. 2001. Springer-Verlag.

[14] R. Poli and W. B. Langdon. On the search properties of different crossover operators in genetic programming. In J. R. Koza, W. Banzhaf, K. Chellapilla, K. Deb, M. Dorigo, D. B. Fogel, M. H. Garzon, D. E. Goldberg, H. Iba, and R. Riolo, editors, *Genetic Programming 1998: Proceedings of the Third Annual Conference*, pages 293–301, University of Wisconsin, Madison, Wisconsin, USA, 22-25 July 1998. Morgan Kaufmann.

[15] R. Poli and W. B. Langdon. Schema theory for genetic programming with one-point crossover and point mutation. *Evolutionary Computation*, 6(3):231–252, 1998.

[16] R. Poli and N. F. McPhee. Exact GP schema theory for headless chicken crossover and subtree mutation. In *Proceedings of the 2001 Congress on Evolutionary Computation CEC 2001*, Seoul, Korea, May 2001.

[17] R. Poli and N. F. McPhee. Exact schema theorems for GP with one-point and standard crossover operating on linear structures and their application to the study of the evolution of size. In *Genetic Programming, Proceedings of EuroGP 2001*, LNCS, Milan, 18-20 Apr. 2001. Springer-Verlag.

[18] R. Poli and N. F. McPhee. Exact schema theory for GP and variable-length GAs with homologous crossover. In *Proceedings of the Genetic and Evolutionary Computation Conference (GECCO-2001)*, San Francisco, California, USA, 7-11 July 2001. Morgan Kaufmann.

[19] M. Ridley. *Evolution*. Blackwell Scientific Publications, Boston, 1993.

[20] J. E. Rowe and N. F. McPhee. The effects of crossover and mutation operators on variable length linear structures. In *Proceedings of the Genetic and Evolutionary Computation Conference (GECCO-2001)*, San Francisco, California, USA, 7-11 July 2001. Morgan Kaufmann.

[21] T. Soule, J. A. Foster, and J. Dickinson. Code growth in genetic programming. In J. R. Koza, D. E. Goldberg, D. B. Fogel, and R. L. Riolo, editors, *Genetic Programming 1996: Proceedings of the First Annual Conference*, pages 215–223, Stanford University, CA, USA, 28–31 July 1996. MIT Press.

[22] W. M. Spears. Limiting distributions for mutation and recombination. In W. M. Spears and W. Martin, editors, *Proceedings of the Foundations of Genetic Algorithms Workshop (FOGA 6)*, Charlottesville, VA, USA, July 2000. In press.

[23] C. R. Stephens. Some exact results from a coarse grained formulation of genetic dynamics. In L. Spector, E. D. Goodman, A. Wu, W. B. Langdon, H.-M. Voigt, M. Gen, S. Sen, M. Dorigo, S. Pezeshk, M. H. Garzon, and E. Burke, editors, *Proceedings of the Genetic and Evolutionary Computation Conference (GECCO-2001)*, pages 631–638, San Francisco, California, USA, 7-11 July 2001. Morgan Kaufmann.

[24] C. R. Stephens and H. Waelbroeck. Effective degrees of freedom in genetic algorithms and the block hypothesis. In T. Bäck, editor, *Proceedings of the Seventh International Conference on Genetic Algorithms (ICGA97)*, pages 34–40, East Lansing, 1997. Morgan Kaufmann.

[25] C. R. Stephens and H. Waelbroeck. Schemata evolution and building blocks. *Evolutionary Computation*, 7(2):109–124, 1999.

Some Experimental Results with Tree Adjunct Grammar Guided Genetic Programming

Nguyen Xuan Hoai[1], R.I. McKay[2], and D. Essam[2]

School of Computer Science,
University of New South Wales,
ADFA campus, Canberra,
ACT 2600, Australia,
[1] x.nguyen@student.adfa.edu.au
[2] rim, daryl@cs.adfa.edu.au

Abstract. Tree-adjunct grammar guided genetic programming (TAG3P) [5] is a grammar guided genetic programming system that uses context-free grammars along with tree-adjunct grammars as means to set language bias for the genetic programming system. In this paper, we show the experimental results of TAG3P on two problems: symbolic regression and trigonometric identity discovery. The results show that TAG3P works well on those problems.

1 Introduction

Genetic programming (GP), first introduced in [8], can be seen as a machine learning method, which induces a population of computer programs by evolutionary means [1] to solve some particular problems. Genetic programming has been used successfully in generating computer programs for solving a number of problems in a wide range of areas. In [5], we proposed a framework for a grammar-guided genetic programming system called tree-adjunct grammar guided genetic programming (TAG3P), which uses tree-adjunct grammars along with context-free grammars to guide the evolutionary process in genetic programming. In this paper, we show some experimental results of TAG3P on the symbolic regression and trigonometric identities problems, preliminary results have been presented in [3, 4]. The organization of the remainder of the paper is as follows. In section 2, we give a brief overview of related work on grammar guided genetic programming. The definition of tree adjunct grammars and the components of TAG3P will be given in section 3. Section 4 describes the problem spaces and experimental setups for TAG3P. The results will be given and discussed in section 5. The paper concludes with section 6, which contains conclusion and future work.

2 Grammar Guided Genetic Programming

Grammar guided genetic programming systems are genetic programming systems that use grammars to set syntactical constraints on programs. The use of grammars also

J.A. Foster et al. (Eds.): EuroGP 2002, LNCS 2278, pp. 228-237, 2002.

helps these genetic programming systems to overcome the closure requirement in canonical genetic programming, which cannot always be fulfilled [17].

Using grammars to set syntactical constraints was first introduced by Whigham [17]: where context-free grammars were used. Whigham [18] also incorporated domain knowledge to modify grammars in order to bias the search process; he demonstrated positive results on the 6-multiplexer problem.

Gruau [2] proved that using syntactical constraints can reduce the size of the search space. He also used context-free grammars to describe target languages but did not limit the depth of derivation trees, which led to severe growth in tree size [14].

Wong and Leung [19] used logic grammars to combine inductive logic programming and genetic programming. They have succeeded in incorporating domain knowledge into logic grammars to guide the evolutionary process of logic programs. However, because they did not maintain explicit parse trees, their system suffers from ambiguity when it tries to generate programs from parse trees [16].

Ryan et al. [16] proposed a system called grammatical evolution (GE), which can evolve programs in any language, provided that this language can be described by a context-free grammar. Their system differs from Whigham's system in that they do not evolve derivation trees directly. Instead, genomes in GE are binary strings representing eight-bit numbers; each number is used to make the choice of the production rule for the non-terminal symbol being processed. GE has been shown to outperform canonical GP on a number of problems [9, 10, 12].

One of the great advantages of GE is the linear genome structure, which allows GE to employ well-studied operators of genetic algorithms, and to reduce the bias in tree-based systems whereby the nodes closer to the leaves are often selected for genetic operators [1]. Moreover, the representation above provides a many-to-one genotype-to-phenotype map, which can provide neutral evolution in the genome space.

On the other hand, GE cannot guarantee to generate legal genomes. This creates some problems such as introns and unnatural multiple uses of genes [5]. To cope with these problems, they used pruning to cut the unexpressed parts of genomes, and allowed the system optionally use wrapping [16].

3 Tree Adjunct Grammar Guided Genetic Programming

3.1 Tree Adjunct Grammars

Tree-adjunct grammars are tree-rewriting systems, defined in [6] as follows:

Definition 1: a tree-adjunct grammar comprises of 5-tuple (T, V, I, A, S), where T is a finite set of terminal symbols; V is a finite set of non-terminal symbols (T $\cap$ V = $\varnothing$); S $\in$ V is a distinguished symbol called the start symbol. I is a set of trees called initial trees. An initial tree is defined as follows: the root node is S; all interior nodes are labelled by non-terminal symbols; each node on the frontier is labelled by a terminal symbol. A is a finite set of trees called auxiliary trees, which can be defined as follows: internal nodes are labelled by non-terminal symbols; a node on the frontier is labelled by a terminal or non-terminal symbol; there is a special non-terminal node on the frontier called the foot node. The requirement for the foot node is it must be labelled by the same (non-terminal) symbol as the root node of the tree. We will follow the convention in [7] to mark the foot node with an asterisk (*).

The trees in E= I ∪ A are called elementary trees. Initial trees and auxiliary trees are denoted α and β respectively; and a node labelled by a non-terminal (resp. terminal) symbol is sometime called a non-terminal (resp. terminal) node. An elementary tree is called X-type if its root is labelled by the non-terminal symbol X.

The key operation used with tree-adjunct grammars is the adjunction of trees. Adjunction can build a new (derived) tree γ from an auxiliary tree β and a tree α (initial, auxiliary or derived). If a tree α has a non-terminal node labelled A, and β is an A-type tree then the adjunction of β into α to produce γ is as follows. Firstly, the sub-tree $α_1$ rooted at A is temporarily disconnected from α. Next, β is attached to α to replace this sub-tree. Finally, $α_1$ is attached back to the foot node of β. γ is the final derived tree achieved from this process. Adjunction is illustrated in Figure 1.

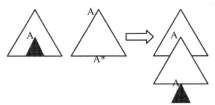

Fig. 1. Adjunction.

The tree set of a TAG can be defined as follows [6]:

T_G= {all tree t / t is completed and t is derived from some initial trees}

Where a tree t is completed, if t is an initial tree or all of the leaf nodes of t are non-terminal nodes; and a tree t is said to be derived from a TAG G if and only if t results from an adjunction sequence (the derivation sequence) of the form: α $β_1(a_1)$ $β_2(a_2)$... $β_n(a_n)$, where n is an arbitrary integer, α , $β_i$ (i=1,2..n) are initial and auxiliary trees of G and a_i (i=1,2..n) are node address where adjunctions take place. An adjunction sequence may be denoted as (*). The language L_G generated by a TAG is then defined as the set of yields of all trees in T_G.

L_G= {w ∈ T* / w is the yield of some tree t ∈ T_G}

The set of languages generated by TAGs (called TAL) is a superset of context-free languages; and is properly included in indexed languages [6]. More properties of TAL can be found in [7]. One special class of tree-adjunct grammars (TAGs) is lexicalized tree-adjunct grammars (LTAG) where each elementary tree of a LTAG must have at least one terminal node. It has been proved that for any context-free grammar G, there exists a LTAG G_{lex} that generates the same language and tree set with G (G_{lex} is then said to strongly lexicalize G) [7].

3.2 Tree Adjunct Grammar Guided Genetic Programming

In [5], we proposed a grammar guided genetic programming system called TAG3P, which uses a pairs consisting of a context-free grammar G and its corresponding LTAG G_{lex} to guide the evolutionary process. The main idea of TAG3P is to evolve the derivation sequence in G_{lex} (genotype) rather than evolve the derivation tree in G as in [17]. Therefore, it creates a genotype-to-phenotype map. As in canonical genetic programming [8], TAG3P comprises of the following five main components:

Program representation: a modified version of the linear derivation sequence (*), but the adjoining address of the tree β_i is in the tree β_{i-1}. Thus, the genome structure in TAG3P is linear and length-variant. Although the language and the tree set generated by LTAGs with the modified derivation sequence is yet to be determined, we have found pairs of G and G_{lex} conforming to that derivation form for a number of standard problems in genetic programming [3, 4].

Initialization procedure: a procedure for initializing a population is given in [5]. To initialize an individual, TAG3P starts with selecting a length at random; next, it first picks up randomly an α tree of G_{lex} then a random sequence of β trees and adjoining addresses. It has been proved that this procedure can always generate legal genomes of arbitrary and finite lengths [5].

Fitness Evaluation: the same as in canonical genetic programming [8].

Genetic operators: in [5], we proposed two types of crossover operators, namely one-point and two-point crossover, and three mutation operators, which are replacement, insertion and deletion. The crossover operators in TAG3P are similar to those in genetic algorithms; however, the crossover point(s) is chosen carefully so that only legal genomes are produced. In replacement, a gene is picked up at random and the adjoining address of that gene is replaced by another adjoining address (adjoining address replacement); or, the gene itself is replaced by a compatible gene (gene replacement) so that the resultant genome is still valid. In insertion and deletion, a gene is inserted into or deleted from the genome respectively. With these carefully designed operators, TAG3P is guaranteed to produce only legal genomes. Selection in TAG3P is similar to canonical genetic programming and other grammar-guided genetic programming systems. Currently, reproduction is not employed by TAG3P.

Parameters: are minimum length of genomes - MIN_LENGTH, maximum length of genomes MAX_LENGTH, size of population - POP_SIZE, maximum number of generations – MAX_GEN and probabilities for genetic operators.

Some analysis of the advantages of TAG3P can be found in [3, 4, 5].

4 The Problem Space

4.1 The Symbolic Regression Problem

The symbolic regression problem can be stated as finding a function in symbolic form that fits a given finite sample of data [8]. In [8], the problem is restricted to finding a function of one independent variable. In his book, Koza uses the binary operators +, -, /, and the unary operators sin, cos, log, exp, which makes the program space can be described by a finitely ambiguous context-free grammar G and the corresponding lexicalized tree-adjunct grammar G_{lex} as follows [3]:

The context-free grammar for the symbolic regression problem: G = (N={EXP, PRE, OP, VAR,},T= {X, sin, cos, log, ep, +,-,*,/, (,)},P,{EXP}} where ep is the exponential function, and the rule set P={EXP→EXP OP EXP, EXP→PRE (EXP), EXP→ VAR, OP→ +, OP→ - , OP→ *, OP→ /, PRE→ sin, PRE→ cos, PRE→ log, PRE→ ep, VAR→ X}.

The tree adjunct grammar for the symbolic regression problem: G_{lex}= {N={EXP, PRE, OP,VAR},T={X, sin, cos, log, ep,+, -, *, /, (,)}, I, A) where I∪ A is as in Figure 2.

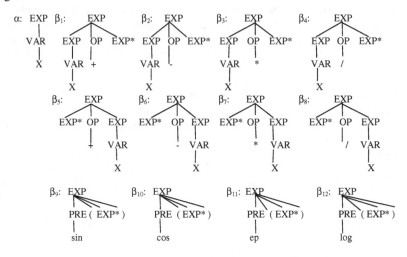

Fig. 2. Elementary trees for G_{lex}.

Table 1 below summarizes the experimental setup for the problem.

Table 1. Experimental setup for the symbolic regression problem.

Objective	Find a function of one independent variable and one dependant variable that fits a given sample of 20 (x_i, y_i) data points, where the target function is the quadratic polynomial $X^4 + X^3 + X^2 + X$.
Terminal Operands	X (the independent variable).
Terminal Operators	The binary operators +, -, *, / and the unary operators sin, cos, exp and log.
Fitness Cases	The given sample of 20 points in the interval [-1..+1].
Raw fitness	The sum, taken over 20 fitness cases, of the errors.
Standardized Fitness	Same as raw fitness.
Hits	The number of fitness cases for which the error < 0.01.
Wrapper	The adjunctions of elementary trees of G_{lex} to generate the derivation trees of G.
Genetic Operators	Tournament selection, one-point crossover and gene replacement.
Parameters	MIN_LENGTH=2, MAX_LENGTH=20, POP_SIZE= 500, MAX_GEN=30, probability for crossover=0.9 and probability for replacement= 0.01.
Success predicate	An individual scores 20 hits.

4.2 The Trigonometric Identities Problem

The problem of finding trigonometric identities can be stated as follows [8]. Given a trigonometric function in symbolic form, a system must try to discover the alternative representations of the function. For example, the function cos(2x) has one (of many) well-known alternative representation as $1-2\sin^2(x)$. Koza [8] has shown that genetic programming can solve this problem. The function he examined was cos(2x) (as in [10]). It is noted that the cos function should not be present in the function set otherwise the problem will be much like the symbolic regression; and with this simple function the problem will become trivial. Therefore, we use the same function set and terminal set as in [8, 10].

The context-free grammar and the LTAG for the problem are as follows [4]:

The context-free grammar for the problem of finding trigonometric identities: G = (N, T, P, {EXP}). Where N={EXP, PRE, OP, VAR, NUM} is the set of non-terminal symbols; T= {X, sin, +, -, *, /, (,), 1.0}, P, {EXP}) is the set of terminal symbols; EXP is the start symbol; and the rule set P={EXP→EXP OP EXP, EXP→ PRE(EXP), EXP→VAR, EXP→ NUM, OP→ +, OP→ - , OP→ *, OP→ /, PRE→ sin , VAR→ X, NUM→ 1.0}.

The tree-adjunct grammar for the problem of finding trigonometric identities G_{lex}= (N, T, I, A). Where N={EXP, PRE, OP, VAR, NUM} is the set of non-terminal symbols; T={ X, sin, +, -, *, /, (,), 1.0} is the set of terminal symbols; and I and A are the sets of initial and auxiliary trees respectively. The set of the elementary trees I ∪ A is as in Figure 3.

The experimental setup for the problem is summarized in table 2.

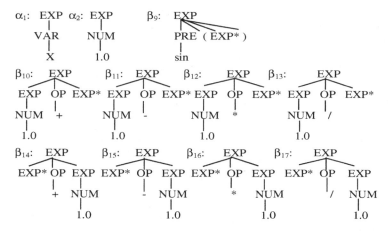

Fig. 3. Elementary trees for G_{lex} the β_1-β_8 are the same with the β_1-β_8 in Figure 2.

5 Results

For the symbolic regression problem, TAG3P consistently discovered the target function. Our experiment consisted of 50 runs, 48 of those 50 runs discovered the target function within the maximum number of generations, which makes the probability of success is 96%. The cumulative frequency is depicted in Figure 4 (left). The best and average fitness in each generation of one typical successful run is shown in Figure 4 (right). In comparison, on the same problem and parameter settings the probability of success was nearly 30% by GP ([8] - page 203), 2% by GE in generational mode, and 90% by GE in steady-state mode [11].

One of the reasons for the success of TAG3P on the above problem lies with the superiour capability of TAG3P in preserving and combining building blocks [4, 5]. Building blocks [15] are sub-trees which are not completed. Functionally, they can be viewed as some potential modules. For the target function above, the atomic building blocks could be X+t and X*t, where t is a parameter representing the incomplete portion of the tree, which are exactly β_1 and β_3 in Figure 2. During the evolutionary process, these building blocks are preserved and combined to make even better building blocks. For example, if β_1, β_3 and β_3 are brought together in a chromosome then the corresponding blocks in the phenotype space will be $X+X^2 + t$ after adjunction takes place.

For the trigonometric identities problem, TAG3P did successfully evolve some alternative representations of the function cos(2x). We conducted 50 runs and 18 out of these runs (which is 36%) were successful. In comparison, the probability of success in GE on this problem was 4% and 87% for generational mode and steady-state mode respectively [10].

Table 2. The experimental setup for the trigonometric identities problem.

Objective	Find a function of one independent variable and one constant that fits a given sample of 20 (x_i, y_i) data points, where the target function is cos(2x).
Terminal Operands	X (the independent variable), 1.0 (the constant).
Terminal Operators	The binary operators +, - , *, / and the unary operator sin.
Fitness Cases	The given sample of 20 points in the interval $[0..2\pi]$.
Raw fitness	The sum, taken over 20 fitness cases, of the errors.
Standardized Fitness	Same as raw fitness.
Hits	The number of fitness cases for which the error < 0.01.
Wrapper	The adjunctions of elementary trees of the G_{lex} to generate the derivation trees of the G.
Genetic Operators	Tournament selection, one-point crossover and gene replacement.
Parameters	MIN_LENGTH=2,MAX_LENGTH=20,POP_SIZE=500 ,MAX_GEN=200, probability for crossover=0.9 and probability for replacement= 0.05.
Success predicate	An individual scores 20 hits.

TAG3P converged to the three well-known alternative representations of function cos(2x), namely, $1-2\sin^2(x)$, $\sin(2x+\pi/2)$ and $\sin(\pi/2-2x)$; whereas in [8, 10] the functions $1-2\sin^2(x)$ and $\sin(\pi/2-2x)$ were discovered but not $\sin(\pi/2+2x)$). The constants $\pi/2$ (≈ 1.570796) was evolved in a number of ways. Some of them were:
$1+\sin(\sin(\sin(\sin(\sin(\sin(1/\sin(\sin(\sin(\sin(\sin(\sin(\sin(\sin(1)))))))))))))) \approx 1.570727$, $1+\sin(\sin(\sin(\sin(\sin(\sin(\sin(\sin(\sin(\sin(1+1)))))+1)+1))))) \approx 1.570812$, 1+1/(1+1/(1+1/(1+

$(1+1))))$ =11/7≈1.571492. The cumulative frequency is shown in Figure 5 (left). The best and average fitness in each generation of one successful run which stopped at generation 72 finding the function $1-2\sin^2(x)$ is shown in Figure 5 (right).

As investigated in [4], the efficiency of TAG3P in replicating building blocks and the nature of the search space made it have a tendency to converge towards the functions $\sin(\pi/2-2x)$ and $\sin(\pi/2+2x)$ (16/18 successful runs). The building blocks in this problem are: $\sin(2x+1 \pm t)$, $\sin(2x+\sin(1/\sin(1) \pm t)$, $\sin(2x+1+1/\sin(1) \pm t)$, $\sin(1-2x \pm t)$, $\sin(\sin(1/\sin(1))-2x \pm t)$, and $\sin(1/\sin(1)+1-2x \pm t)$, which frequently appeared during almost all these 50 runs [4]. Figure 6 (left) shows how these building blocks (using $t=0$) approximate the target function. The best and average fitness in each generation is also given in Figure 6 (right).

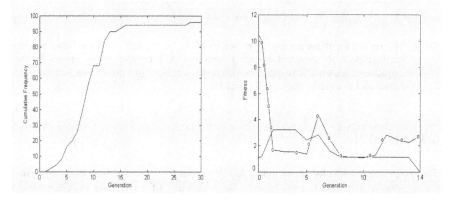

Fig. 4. The results for symbolic regression problem; on the left is the cumulative frequency; on the right are the best and average fitness in each generation of one successful run, which stopped at generation 14 finding the target function (the dotted line is the average fitness in each generation scaled down by the Log10 function).

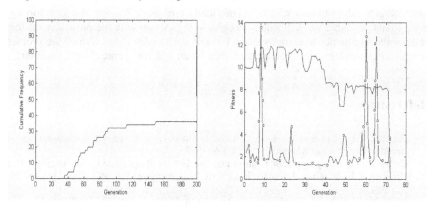

Fig. 5. The results for trigonometric identities problem; on the left is the cumulative frequency; on the right are the best and average fitness in each generation of one successful run, which stopped at generation 72 finding the function $1-2\sin^2(x)$ (the dotted line is the average fitness in each generation scaled down by the Log10 function).

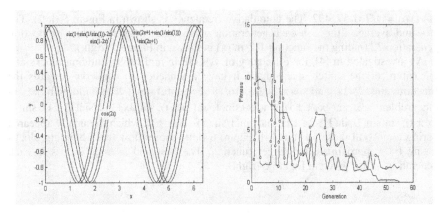

Fig. 6. The results for trigonometric identities problem; on the left are some basic building blocks; on the right is the best and average fitness in each generation of one successful run, which stopped at generation 54 finding the function $\sin(\pi/2-2x)$ (the dotted line is the average fitness in each scaled down by the Log10 function).

6 Conclusion

The experimental results show that TAG3P works well on the symbolic regression and trigonometric identities problems. The efficiency of replicating building blocks helped TAG3P converge towards the solutions. In future, we will experiment with TAG3P on these problems using different genetic operators (two-point crossover, insertion, deletion) and compare the result to TAG3P with one-point crossover. The performance of TAG3P on a number of other benchmark problems for genetic programming will also be investigated. The effectiveness of TAG3P in preserving and combining building blocks will be theoretically analyzed. We are also developing a tree adjunct grammar guided genetic programming system with the most general form of derivation sequence attempt to make TAG3P universal (i.e. to solve all the problem of which the problem space can be described by an arbitrary context-free grammar).

References

1. Banzhaf, W., Nordin, P., Keller, R.E., Francone, F.D.: Genetic Programming: An Introduction. Morgan Kaufmann Pub, USA (1998).
2. Gruau, F.: On Using Syntactic Constraints with Genetic Programming. In: Angeline, P. J., Kinnear, K.E. Jr. (eds): Advances in Genetic Programming. The MIT Press, USA (1996) 377-394.
3. Hoai, N.X.: Solving The Symbolic Regression Problem with Tree-Adjunct Grammar Guided Genetic Programming: The Preliminary Results. (To appear in the Proceedings of The 5th Autraliasia-Japan Co-Joint Workshop on Evolutionary Computation, Nov 2001, Ontago New Zealand).

4. Hoai, N.X.: Solving Trigonometric Identities with Tree Adjunct Grammar Guided Genetic Programming. (To appear in the Proceedings of The First International Workshop on Hybrid Intelligent Systems (HIS'01), Dec 2001, Adelaide, Australia).
5. Hoai N.X., McKay, R.I.: A Framework for Tree Adjunct Grammar Guided Genetic Programming. In: Abbass, H.A., Barlow. M. (eds): Proceedings of the Post-graduate ADFA Conference on Computer Science (PACCS'01) (2001) 93-99.
6. Joshi, A.K., Levy, L.S., Takahashi, M.: Tree Adjunct Grammars. Journal of Computer and System Sciences, 10(1) (1975) 136-163.
7. Joshi, A.K., Schabes, Y.: Tree Adjoining Grammars. In: Rozenberg G, Saloma A (eds) Handbook of Formal Languages. Springer-Verlag, NY, USA, vol 3 (1997) 69-123.
8. Koza, J.: Genetic Programming. The MIT Press, USA (1992).
9. O'Neill, M.: Automatic Programming with Grammatical Evolution. In: Proceedings of the Genetic and Evolutionary Computation Conference Workshop Program, July 13-17, Orlando, Florida USA (1999).
10. O'Neil, M., Collin, J.J.: Grammar Evolution: Solving Trigonometric Identities. In: Proceedings of Mendel '98, (1998) 111-119.
11. O'Neill, M., Ryan, C.: Grammatical Evolution: A Steady State Approach. In: Proceedings of the Second International Workshop on Frontiers in Evolutionary Algorithms 1998, (1998) 419-423.
12. O'Neil, M., Ryan, C.: Under the Hood of Grammatical Evolution. In: Banzhaf, W.,.Daida, J., Eiben, A.E., Garzon, M.H., Hovana, V., Jakiela, M., Smith, R.E. (eds): *GECCO-99*, Morgan Kaufmann Pub, USA (1999).
13. O'Neill, M., Ryan, C.: Genetic Code Degeneracy: Implication for Grammatical Evolution and Beyond. In: Proceedings of the European Conference on Artificial Life (1999).
14. Ratle, A., Sebag, M.: Genetic Programming and Domain Knowledge: Beyond the Limitations of Grammar-Guided Machine Discovery. Ecole Polytechnique, France (2000). (Available at: www.researchindex.com. Accessed: 30, May, 2001).
15. Rosca, J.P. and Ballard, D.H.: Genetic Programming with Adaptive Representations. Technical Report 489, The University of Rochester, Feb 1994.
16. Ryan, C., Collin, J.J., O'Neill, M.: Grammatical Evolution: Evolving Programs for an Arbitrary Language. In: Lecture Note in Computer Science 1391, Proceedings of the First European Workshop on Genetic Programming, Springer-Verlag (1998) 83-95.
17. Whigham, P.: Grammatically-based Genetic Programming. In: Proceedings of the Workshop on Genetic Programming: From Theory to Real-World Applications, Morgan Kaufmann Pub (1995) 33-41.
18. Whigham, P.: Search Bias, Language Bias and Genetic Programming. In Genetic Programming 1996, The MIT Press, USA, (1996) 230-237.
19. Wong, M.L., Leung, K.S.: Evolving Recursive Functions for Even-Parity Problem Using Genetic Programming. In: Angeline, P.J., Kinnear, K.E. Jr. (eds): Advances in Genetic Programming, The MIT Press, USA (1996) 221-240.

A Puzzle to Challenge Genetic Programming

Edmund Burke, Steven Gustafson*, and Graham Kendall

ASAP Research, School of Computer Science & IT
University of Nottingham, UK
{ ekb | smg | gxk }@cs.nott.ac.uk

Abstract. This report represents an initial investigation into the use of genetic programming to solve the N-prisoners puzzle. The puzzle has generated a certain level of interest among the mathematical community. We believe that this puzzle presents a significant challenge to the field of evolutionary computation and to genetic programming in particular. The overall aim is to generate a solution that encodes complex decision making. Our initial results demonstrate that genetic programming can evolve good solutions. We compare these results to engineered solutions and discuss some of the implications. One of the consequences of this study is that it has highlighted a number of research issues and directions and challenges for the evolutionary computation community. We conclude the article by presenting some of these directions which range over several areas of evolutionary computation, including multi-objective fitness, coevolution and cooperation, and problem representations.

1 Introduction

Several challenging problems are used within the genetic programming literature to develop and test methods and theories. Punch et al [1] used the Royal Tree benchmark problem to test the ability of multiple populations. Langdon [2] employed the balanced bracket problem, the Dyck language and Reverse Polish expressions to compare the necessity of advanced data structures versus indexed memory. Koza [3] used the multiplexer and parity functions and protein sequence classification [4] as difficult problems for genetic programming. Daida et al [5] investigated the binomial-3 problem to study *tunably difficult* problems. Genetic programming also was developed for the robotic soccer problem in [6][7][8], using an array of novel methods. A further example is provided by Soule et al [9] who worked on the maximum clique problem.

In this paper we study the N-prisoners puzzle, as described by Ebert in his PhD thesis [10], as a problem to investigate and stretch the capabilities of genetic programming. We hypothesize that this problem will present initial difficulties for genetic programming and will force critical evaluation of its application. The N=3 puzzle of the problem is known as the 3-hat puzzle. In this case, three players are assigned a red or blue hat. Each must guess their own hat colour by only seeing the other players' hats. If at least one player guesses correctly, and

---

* corresponding author

J.A. Foster et al. (Eds.): EuroGP 2002, LNCS 2278, pp. 238–247, 2002.

no one guesses incorrectly then all the players win, otherwise, they all lose. In addition to guessing red or blue, each player can pass, but still one player must guess correctly to win. The goal is to solve the puzzle correctly over a number of different hat combinations.

The problem is attractive to genetic programming for several reasons and this report serves as an initial investigation and as a proposal of several future research directions. As described by Ebert in [11], Hamming codes allow (with high probability) the correct guessing of the next bit in a growing sequence of random bits. The same technique can be used for solving some of the N-prisoners puzzles. The decision making aspect of solving the puzzle can be represented by computer programs and the search through possible programs with genetic programming. The problem has not been previously investigated, to the authors' knowledge, with evolutionary computation or genetic programming. Also, there is no known optimal solution for all values of N, which differs from typical benchmark and common problems in genetic programming. In this investigation we perform an empirical study to determine how effective genetic programming is in solving the problem, consider possible difficulties and propose future research directions.

The results indicate genetic programming's ability to find solutions on this challenging problem. The fact that the very difficult Hamming solution is not evolved only confirms our expectations that the problem and genetic programming will require in-depth analysis to achieve this high goal. Several research extensions are described that are currently underway. Section 2 describes the N-prisoners puzzle, Section 3 gives our genetic programming approach, with extensions and conclusions following in Sections 4 and 5.

2   Problem Description

The 3-hat problem was made popular by Ebert while working on his PhD thesis and in a subsequent article in the New York Times [12]. According to Ebert, the actual problem is attributed to Walter Wesley Winters (1905-1973). To solve the 3-hat puzzle we notice that $\frac{3}{4}$ of the time two individuals will have the same colour hat and the third will have the different colour. If each player guesses the opposite of his co-players hat colour, when they have the same colour hat, and passes when the co-players have different coloured hats, then the group only loses when all three have the same hat colour. There are 2^3 possible hat combinations with 2 of those having either all red or all blue, where these 2 combinations will cause the algorithm to fail. The N-prisoners puzzle is essentially the same, just with N people and hats, but is described next.

2.1   N-Prisoners Puzzle

N-prisoners are up for parole. They all go free or none go free determined by how they play a game. The game is that they each enter the parole officer's office independently and see randomly flipped coins on a desk, one representing each prisoner, except the coin for the current prisoner is covered. The prisoner has to guess heads or tails, or pass, and then leave the room. In this manner each prisoner sees the coins, makes a guess and leaves. Again, the prisoners can formulate a strategy before beginning the game. All the prisoners go free if at least one guesses correctly and none guess incorrectly. An obvious solution to this problem is if the same prisoner always says heads and the rest always pass. This gives the group a fifty percent chance each time.

2.2   Game Representation

We will view the game as attempting to guess bit b_i in the vector $B = (b_0, b_1, \ldots, b_n)$, where each $b_i \in \{0, 1\}$. The vector $G = (g_0, g_1, \ldots, g_n)$ represents a guess for B such that each $g_i \in \{0, 1, p\}$, where p is the pass option. Thus, we want to know if $Win(G, B) = 0$, where $Win(G, B)$ can be defined as follows:

$$Win(G, B) = \begin{cases} 0 & \text{if } (\exists g_i \in G \cdot g_i = b_i, b_i \in B) \wedge \\ & (\forall g_i \in G \cdot g_i = p \vee g_i = b_i, b_i \in B) \\ 1 & \text{otherwise} \end{cases}$$

As described above, when guessing b_i, we can see the other bits in B but not b_i. Thus, winning the game is determined by assuring there is at least one b_i that is correct and all the other bits in B are either correct or equal to pass. Here, a 0 indicates correct play (a win) while a 1 denotes a penalty for losing. Notice that each b_i represents a player's hat or prisoner's coin and the guess of b_i is represented by g_i.

2.3   Hamming Code Solution

Hamming codes are used for error detection and correction in coding theory [13]. For bit strings of length $2^k - 1$ we can detect single errors and correct them using Hamming codes. Thus, the N-prisoners puzzles that can be represented as bit strings of length $2^k - 1$ are the $\{3, 7, 15, 31, \ldots\}$-puzzles. To solve our game with Hamming codes, we construct a parity check matrix P that represents the binary numbers $1 \ldots 2^k - 1$ where each binary number is a column. We then do a matrix multiplication $y = P \times B$, where the vector B represent the $N = 2^k - 1$ players' hats or prisoners' coins and player/prisoner i is guessing $b_i \in B$. The result y indicates with all 0's that we have a code word, or else which bit, read in binary, needs to be flipped in order to have a code word. For each $b_i \in B$, if we guess that $b_i = 0$, calculate y_0 and do likewise with $b_i = 1$, then we will have y_0 and y_1. Note each error word is a Hamming distance of 1 away from a code word, meaning that there is one bit in the vector that needs to be flipped to obtain a code word.

The result $y_0 \neq y_1$ indicates that we have an error word. By flipping the bit value associated with the non-zero y_i we can have a code word. The result $y_0 = y_1 \neq 0$ indicates that we have an error word and flipping either bit does

$$P = \begin{bmatrix} 0 & 1 & 1 \\ 1 & 0 & 1 \end{bmatrix}, B = \begin{bmatrix} 0 \\ ? \\ 0 \end{bmatrix}, P \times B(? = 0) = y_0 = \begin{bmatrix} 0 \\ 0 \end{bmatrix}, P \times B(? = 1) = y_1 = \begin{bmatrix} 1 \\ 0 \end{bmatrix}$$

Fig. 1. Example of Hamming code application with vector B and unknown bit b_1. Vectors y_0 and y_1 are found, where y_1 indicates that $b_1 = 1$ should be flipped to 0 to obtain a code word.

not lead to a code word. If we guess the opposite of the bit that gave us a code word in the first case, and pass all other times, then we can win the game with probability $\frac{2^k - 1}{2^k}$. In the case when we have a code word, every b_i will produce a $y_0 \neq y_1$ and each will guess the opposite of the bit that makes the code word causing the guess of B to lose. Figure 1 gives a small example of the 3-puzzle Hamming code application.

3   Genetic Programming Approach

The overall aim is to investigate the possibility of employing a genetic programming approach to solve the N-prisoners puzzle of finding the optimal strategy to maximize wins. We know an optimal solution for the puzzles of $N = 2^k - 1$ and that they use Hamming codes. The solution could be implemented in several interesting and novel ways and each one of those solutions would have many possible representations. What we do not investigate here, however, is what we can do with finding the optimal rates of solutions, which is the subject of on-going work.

System parameters are set to those commonly used in the research community and found in [3] and that are default in the evolutionary computation system ECJ, described in [14]. A crossover rate of 0.9, reproduction rate of 0.1, maximum tree depth of 17, ramped half-and-half tree generation, maximum number of 51 generations, and various population sizes are used. Description of other design decisions follow, with terminals and functions in Table 1.

3.1   Fitness

To determine the fitness of each individual we generate every possible combination of bit strings for the puzzle. We then evaluate each individual for each place in the string, making that place's bit value hidden. The output of the individual is either 0,1 or *pass*, found by applying the following membership function to the actual output:

$$\text{output}' = \begin{cases} 0 & \text{output} \leq 0 \\ 1 & \text{output} \geq 1 \\ \text{pass} & 0 > \text{output} < 1 \end{cases} \tag{1}$$

Table 1. Functions, terminals and descriptions

Terminals	Description
0,1	the constants 0 and 1, also the possible values of the vector B
0's, 1's	the number of zeros and ones the current querying bit can see
me	the location i of the current querying bit
$\Re$	ephemeral random constants between $0 \ldots N$
loopi	loop index, set to 0, incremented each iteration of the loop, $0 \ldots 2N$
ARG0	argument of ADF1 that can be called in this tree
ADF0	automatically defined function, no internal ADFs
Functions	
$+, -, \times$	binary addition, subtraction, and multiplication
$/, \%$	binary, protected division and modulus, return 0 if denominator $= 0$
what	unary, returns the value of bit referenced by argument, 2 otherwise
iflte	4 arguments: if arg1 $<$ arg2 then arg3 else arg4, returning arg3 or arg4 results
prog2n	binary, executed arg1, then arg2, return arg2 result
foreachp	unary, executing argument N times and increments loopi variable, returning result of last execution
read	unary, returns local variable referenced by argument, if arg< 0 the 0, if arg$> 2N$ then $2N$
write	binary, sets local variable referenced by arg1 to arg2, boundary condition same as read, returns value written
ADF1	unary, automatically defined function, access argument with ARG0, function and terminal set includes ADF0

Next, we compare the generated guess against the actual instance. If at least one is correct in guessing and none are incorrect, then we do nothing, else we increment by one signifying a loss. Thus, our fitness indicates the percentage of loses, $\frac{loses}{2N}$, which we want to minimise. It should be noticed that for larger N values, say $N = 17$, this will become inadequate as 2^{17} combinations require significant evaluation time. We could make use of the fact that there is a lot of symmetry in combinations or create a reasonable number of random test combinations. However, only the 3,4,5,7 puzzles are examined in this initial investigation.

3.2   Results

Initial experiments used only the first 6 terminals and the first 7 functions in Table 1. The complete functions and terminal sets were then tried with varying population sizes and the results of the 500 population are reported, which we feel to be representative. For each puzzle, (3,4,5,7), 10 runs were done. In all attempts genetic programming was able to find a strategy that had a losing ratio below $\frac{1}{2}$. All experiments were also tried without automatically defined functions (ADFs) and several exploratory runs were made with varying population sizes and functions and terminal set combinations. For the 3-puzzle, the $\frac{3}{4}$ solution is usually found in the initial generation. While the plots, in Figure 2, show

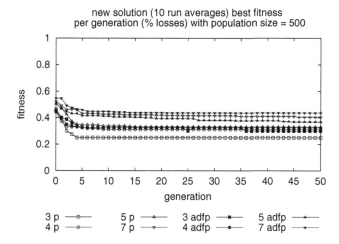

Fig. 2. Average of best fitness graph. "N p" indicates the N-puzzle and "N adfp" indicates the same configuration with ADFs.

the average fitness beginning near 1 and evolving to below $\frac{1}{2}$, we notice in the best of generation plot that best-of-run individuals are usually found in early generations. This indicates that evolution is either finding the global optima or getting stuck in a local optima, which is the case here for the 4,5,7 puzzles being trapped into local optima. Figure 3 shows two evolved individuals for the 7-puzzle that did particularly well. We next examine some hand engineered strategies, but note that Ebert points out that good solutions can be found for the non-$N = 2^k - 1$ puzzles by simply using a variant of the Hamming solution and always passing on some bits. Thus, for M-puzzles where $M > N$, if we always pass on bits $b_N \ldots b_M$, we can use the N-puzzle solution and win $\frac{N}{N+1}$ of the time.

3.3 Engineered Solutions

Using only the first 6 terminals and 7 functions in Table 1, hand engineered (coded) solutions for the 3-puzzle (fitness of $\frac{3}{4}$) and the 7-puzzle (fitness of $\frac{7}{8}$) were created. Both individuals implement the Hamming solution by using nested summations and parity checks and the modulus operator. Our solution is puzzle specific, determining whether each bit can be flipped to make a code word. The 7-puzzle solution has 701 nodes in its tree and scores a fitness of .125, or $\frac{7}{8}$ as expected.

With all the functions and terminals we can design an ADF individual with only 75 nodes that implements the ideal solution for the 7-puzzle, and a fewer nodes for the ideal 3 player solution, which is show in Figure 4. This engineered solution can also be represented without ADFs and is not believed to be unique but could be represented in many ways with this set of functions and terminals.

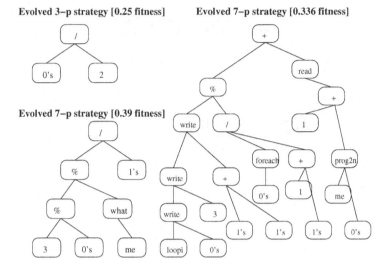

Fig. 3. Evolved solutions for 3-puzzle and two for the 7-puzzle.

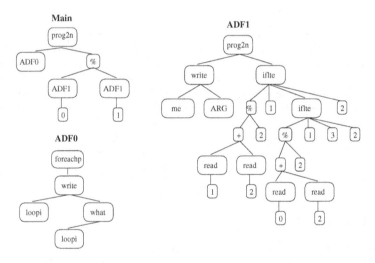

Fig. 4. Engineered 3-puzzle Hamming solution. Some nodes were left off the top of Main that force the output into the correct ranges of the membership function. The Engineered 7-puzzle Hamming solution is the same with the right child branch of ADF1 containing the correct parity checks, approx. 20 additional nodes.

3.4   Brief Problem Analysis

The probability of guessing N random independent bits, [0,1], is $\frac{1}{2^N}$. However, the problem allows the *pass* option, and if we assume we pass on every bit save one, the probability of winning the game increases to $\frac{1}{2}$. Also, we notice that if we generalise the 3-puzzle solution, that has probability $\frac{3}{4}$ of winning, to pass on all but the first three bits, we can have a probability of winning of $\frac{3}{4}$ for all puzzles where $N > 3$. However, the difference between individuals of this 3-puzzle solution and the 7-puzzle Hamming solution are great. Small changes in individuals would not cause small changes in fitness, creating a very rugged solution landscape. The fitness calculation for the Royal Tree [1] problem was adjusted to give partial, full and bonus credit to solutions close to the ideal. We may also need to consider something similar here. But we note that our selection of functions and terminals may in fact hinder the search, as was shown in [5] with the binomial-3 problem.

4   Future Extensions

Our next phase of research will investigate several possible extensions that we hope to be able to find the Hamming solution. We first must overcome the problems we identified but see some of the below extensions as possible solutions. In addition to these attempts to *find* an optimal solution, we are also interested in analysing the genetic programming search and discovering the effects of changing the evolutionary toolkit and the differences between different N values of the puzzles.

Multi-agent Approach. The puzzle can be won with only one bit guessed correctly, and all others passing, and using a single strategy to guess every bit may be too difficult. Instead of evolving a single strategy we could evolve N strategies that each attempt to correctly guess a different bit and learn to cooperate to maximize wins.

Multi-objective Fitness Function. It seems logical from our study here that the fitness of simply *win* or *loss* is not fully effective in driving the evolutionary search. Thus, as done with the Royal Tree problem, a fitness which incorporates other aspects of the game may need to be included. Knowles' et al [15] method of representing single objective functions as multiobjective ones may be a possibility. Other objectives that group losses together or maximize individual correct bit guesses may be helpful.

Island Model Approach. Results also indicate a difficulty of the evolutionary search to break out of local optima. Diversity pressure could be a way to keep the search going and a possible solution could be using an island model. Several possible representations would be possible for this model and problem.

Restating The Problem. It may be the case that solving the problem directly is too difficult for a straightforward evolutionary computation approach. We may benefit by restating the problem. Since we only need one bit to be guessed correctly to win the game, by forcing all other bits to always pass, we can focus on evolving a single bit strategy.

5   Conclusions

The N-prisoners puzzle gives evolutionary computation and genetic programming, in particular, a new challenge to overcome. This initial study investigated the problem and showed genetic programming solutions and presented some possible future extensions. The problem's rough solution space, the possibility of evolving complex data structures and algorithms, and the possibilities for future research all make it an attractive area for further genetic programming research. As shown here, genetic programming is able to evolve solutions that consistently do better than 50%, and we hypothesize that through methods described in the previous section we will be able to greatly improve upon this. Also, by studying the evolutionary search on this hard problem we hope to learn more about why genetic programming can find solutions and how to improve the process by which it works. In short, we hope to gain a deeper understanding of how and when genetic programming works well on difficult problems. We feel that the investigation of this problem will lead to a worthwhile examination of evolutionary computation systems and genetic programming.

Acknowledgments. The authors appreciate the review of early versions of this work by Dr. David Gustafson at Kansas State University and members of the ASAP Research Group at the University of Nottingham.

References

1. W.F. Punch, D. Zongker, and E.D. Goodman. The royal tree problem, a benchmark for single and multi-population genetic programming. In P.J. Angeline and K.E. Kinnear, Jr., editors, *Advances in Genetic Programming 2*, chapter 15, pages 299–316. The MIT Press, Cambridge, MA, 1996.

2. W.B. Langdon. *Data Structures and Genetic Programming: Genetic Programming + Data Structures = Automatic Programming!*, volume 1 of *Genetic Programming*. Kluwer, Boston, 24 April 1998.

3. J.R. Koza. *Genetic Programming: On the Programming of Computers by Means of Natural Selection*. MIT Press, Cambridge, MA, USA, 1992.

4. J. Koza, F. Bennett, and D. Andre. Using programmatic motifs and genetic programming to classify protein sequences as to extracellular and membrane cellular location. In V. William Porto et al, editor, *Proceedings of the Seventh Annual Conference on Evolutionary Programming*, volume 1447 of *LNCS*, San Diego, California, USA, 25-27 March 1998. Springer-Verlag.

5. J.M. Daida, J.A. Polito, S.A. Stanhope, R.R. Bertram, J.C. Khoo, and S.A. Chaudhary. What makes a problem GP-hard? analysis of a tunably difficult problem in genetic programming. In Wolfgang Banzhaf et al, editor, *Proceedings of the Genetic and Evolutionary Computation Conference*, volume 2, pages 982–989, Orlando, Florida, USA, 13-17 July 1999. Morgan Kaufmann.

6. S. Luke. Genetic programming produced competitive soccer softbot teams for robocup97. In J.R. Koza et al, editor, *Genetic Programming 1998: Proceedings of the Third Annual Conference*, pages 214–222, University of Wisconsin, Madison, Wisconsin, USA, 22-25 July 1998. Morgan Kaufmann.

7. D. Andre and A. Teller. Evolving Team Darwin United. In M. Asada and H. Kitano, editors, *RoboCup-98: Robot Soccer World Cup II*, volume 1604 of *LNCS*, pages 346–351, Paris, France, July 1998 1999. Springer Verlag.

8. S.M. Gustafson and W.H. Hsu. Layered learning in genetic programming for a co-operative robot soccer problem. In J.F. Miller et al, editor, *Proceedings of the European Conference on Genetic Programming*, volume 2038 of *LNCS*, Lake Como, Italy, April 2001. Springer-Verlag.

9. T. Soule, J.A. Foster, and J. Dickinson. Using genetic programming to approximate maximum clique. In J.R. Koza et al, editor, *Genetic Programming 1996: Proceedings of the First Annual Conference*, pages 400–405, Stanford University, CA, USA, 28–31 July 1996. MIT Press.

10. T. Ebert. *Applications of Recursive Operators to Randomness and Complexity*. Ph.D. thesis, University of California at Santa Barbara, 1998.

11. T. Ebert. On the autoreducibility of random sequences. Unpublished. http://www.ics.uci.edu/~ebert/, 2001.

12. S. Robinson. Why mathematicians now care about their hat color. *The New York Times: Science Desk*, 10 April 2001.

13. R.W. Hamming. *Coding and Information Theory*. Prentice-Hall, Inc, New Jersey, USA, 1980.

14. S. Luke. *Issues in Scaling Genetic Programming: Breeding Strategies, Tree Generation, and Code Bloat*. PhD thesis, Department of Computer Science, University of Maryland, University of Maryland, College Park, MD 20742 USA, 2000.

15. J.D. Knowles, R.A. Watson, and D.W. Corne. Reducing Local Optima in Single-Objective Problems by Multi-objectivization. In E. Zitzler et al, editor, *First International Conference on Evolutionary Multi-Criterion Optimization*, pages 268–282. Springer-Verlag. LNCS no. 1993, 2001.

Transformation of Equational Specification by Means of Genetic Programming

Aitor Ibarra, J. Lanchares, J.M. Mendias, J.I. Hidalgo, and R. Hermida

Universidad Complutense de Madrid,
Facultad de Ciencias Físicas,
Dpto. Arquitectura de Computadores y Automática. Madrid 28040
ibaiba@dacya.ucm.es

Abstract. High Level Synthesis (HLS) is a designing methodology aimed to the synthesis of RT-level hardware devices from behavioral development specifications. In this work we present an evolutionary algorithm in order to optimize circuit specifications by means of a special type of genetic operator. We have named this operator algebraic mutation, carried out with the help of algebraic equations. This work can be classified within the development of an automatic tool of Formal Synthesis by using genetic techniques. We have applied this technique to a simple circuit equational specification and to a much more complex algebraic equation. In the first case our algorithm simplifies the equation until the best specification is found and in the second a solution improving the former is always obtained.

1 Introduction

In the last few years, the implementation of HLS systems in hardware design cycles, have allow designers to obtain circuits starting from higher abstractions levels. Some systems, called formal ones, additionally provides mathematical framework which enables us to carry out transformations on the circuit specifications without modifying its behaviour. These transformations may lead us to new descriptions of the circuit with lower costs in terms of performance, power consumption or area.

The intesive search of the transformation sequence that leads to a low cost circuit is a highly costly process in terms of computing time. Due to this fact we apply the Genetic Programming techniques (GP) [5] [1] to obtain, by means of mutations, better circuits than the original ones. This work will be kept within the bounds of the **FRESH** (**FR**rom **E**quations to **H**ardware) Formal Synthesis and Verification tool. It includes all the tasks of HLS [6].

The GP algorithm described in this paper is characterized by the exclusive use of a mutation operator that is behaviour preserving. That is, the circuits before and after the mutation are different representations of the same behavior.

We have applied the technique to an equational specification of a simple circuit and to a much more complex algebraic equation. In the first case, our

J.A. Foster et al. (Eds.): EuroGP 2002, LNCS 2278, pp. 248–257, 2002.
© Springer-Verlag Berlin Heidelberg 2002

algorithm simplifies the equation to find the best specification and in the second a solution that improves the original is obtained.

The rest of the paper is organised as follows: In section 2 the FRESH tool is described. In section 3 the implementation is explained by describing the genetic representation, the cost function and the algebraic mutation operator which makes the population evolve. Section 4 presents the experimental results. Section 5 deals with the conclusions and future work.

2   FRESH: A Formal Synthesis Tool

In the late 1980s a design methodology aimed to the hardware synthesis from behavioural development specifications appeared. This new methodology is known as High Level Synthesis.

HLS tools have evolved very fast these years. This frenetic evolution has made the complexity of algorithms grow and the data structures be more and more sophisticated. As a result, errors in the tools have spread, reliability of HLS tools have decreased and today no designer accepts an automatically generated circuit before it has been validated.

In order to solve this problem a Formal Synthesis Systems [7] appeared. Its performs all the synthesis tasks within a purely mathematical framework where synthesis processes are also correctness proofs. Three common characteristics exist in these systems:

- They use a mathematical formalism to represent circuits.
- They are synthesized by using the continuous application of a series of behaviour preserving transformations.
- They are not automatic. In spite of the fact that any transformation can be made automatically, the sequence is decided by the designer.

Our work is based on the FRESH [6] tool, which covers all the tasks of High Level Synthesis. This tools provides us with a formal algebraic framework, where the evaluation of a circuit specification is made with the help of its equational mechanism.

What this tool offers us is a group of manipulation rules which allow the transformation of a circuit equational specification into a different equational specification with the same behaviour but with a area cost, or lower power consumption output. The algebraic equations that this tools provides us are mathematically correct and represent the only allowed computation mechanism.

As we have pointed out above, the FRESH tool provides us with a set of mathematical equations which let us modify our equational specifications without altering the circuit behaviour. As we can imagine, in front of a very complicated equational specification, the number of possible transformations is very high and the chances to find a sequence of transformations that modify our original circuit into an equivalent but lower-cost circuit is statistically very improbable. That is to say, we cannot carry out an exhaustive search in the space of solutions since we would meet a NP problem. By using GP we transform equational specifications into lower-cost equivalent ones.

3   Implementation

Generally GP uses recombination and mutation operators. However, the defini-tion of correct hardware synthesis prevents us from applying an operator that gives results algebraically non-equivalent to the original specification. If a classi-cal GP crossover is applied we may very likely obtain specifications which do not comply with this condition. This is reason why, until now, an algorithm which only uses a specific mutation operator has been developed to evolve toward bet-ter individuals.

The rest of the algorithm is similar to the classical GP. The cost function evaluates the individuals in terms of the number of logical gates necessary for the implementation and therefore the genetic representation uses trees.

3.1   Genetic Representation

The tree representation is one of the most widespread techniques within the GP. It was Koza who introduced it by using the *LISP* programming language. This language perfectly suits for representing our equational specification.

$$y_u(t) = \left(1 - 2^{-5}\right) \cdot y(t) + 2^{-5} \cdot w_i(t) \tag{1}$$

In Figure 1 we can see an example of the tree genetic representation for equation 1. In this tree (Figure 1) we have two types of nodes:

- **Functional Nodes**: These are the tree nodes which require at least one input parameter. In the case shown in the figure, functional nodes correspond with algebraic operators.
  In the example shown in the figure all the functional nodes are binary opera-tors, that is to say, they need two input parameters. Except the sign operator that only need one input parameter.
  The root node of this tree (the operator +), is called the main node of the tree.
  As we see further on this node will play an important role in our algebraic mutation operator.
- **Terminal Nodes**: It refers to the tree nodes which do not need any input parameter. In the case of figure 1, this terminals are the set of variables $\{w, y\}$ and the set of constants $\{1, 2, 5\}$.

As we have mentioned before the use of LISP language is one of the ways to equationally represent a tree in genetic programming [5]. Thus the tree repre-sented in figure 1 corresponds to equation 2 in LISP format (where $ represent the unary negation operation).

$$(+(*(-1(^2 (\$5))) y)(*(^2 (\$5))w)) \tag{2}$$

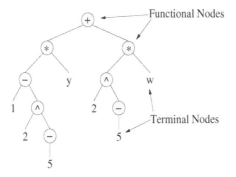

Fig. 1. Equational Specification shown in a tree Genetic representation form.

3.2   Algorithm

We can outline our evolutionary algorithm as follows:

- Generation of the original random population $\mathcal{N}$ with equivalent equational specifications.
- Evaluation of the individuals.
- Selection using the classical roulette method [4] of an individual.
- Algebraic Genetic Operator application to the selected individuals.

These steps are repeated for a maximum number of generations which are specified before the execution of the program or until one of the individuals of the population reaches a predetermined cost function value.

3.3   Cost Function

We have developed a cost function which shows the number of logical gates that every single algebraic operator of the tree representing the individual needs. Therefore the most expensive operator, in terms of number of logic gates, is the power operator and the least costly is the sign operator.

Equation 3 shows the cost function algebraic expression for our algorithm. In table 1 the cost values for each operator are shown.

$$FC = \sum_{i=1}^{n} Cost_i \tag{3}$$

where $Cost_i$ is the cost corresponding to each operator, and n is the number of operators that we can find in the tree (we assume that terminals are costless).

For instance, the tree in Figure 2.a (the upper tree) will have a cost of 605, whereas the tree in figure 2.b will have a cost of 418.

Table 1. Cost value of each functional operator ($ stands for the sign operator).

Operator	Cost
$	11
+	20
–	24
*	76
/	80
^	100

3.4   Algebraic Mutation Operator

The mutation operator that we have implemented is not a classical mutation operator. When a mutation takes place our new individual is again an equational specification representing the same circuit and is not applied according to the mutation probability as we can see as follows.

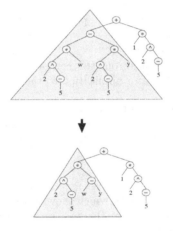

Fig. 2. Algebraic Mutation Operator. The shaded section indicates the subtree which will mutate according to one of the algebraic expressions.

Studies carried out about the performance of the genetic operators in the evolution of the individuals all through the generations have shown that the mutation operator on its own might be a good explorer of solution space [3].

In order to implement the operator of algebraic mutation we have used 16 equations of elementary algebra. These equations have been divided according to the main node operator.

In figures 3, 4, 5 we can see the set of equations that we have implemented. Figure 3 shows those applied to subtrees which have a multiplication as a main node. Figure 4 shows the operations for an addition main node and figure 5 shows those applied to substraction, power, division and sign nodes.

This operator is applied to individuals out of the population as follows:

- One of the functional nodes of the individuals is randomly selected.
- The type of function corresponding to the selected node is identified.
- One of the possible sets of algebraic equations that we can used in the mutation is randomly selected.
- If the node functional shape of the individual matches up with the function of the set, one of its possible algebraic equations is also randomly selected.
- If the subtree matches up with the randomly selected algebraic equation of the set of possible equations, we mutate this tree.
- If, on the contrary, these two subtrees do not match up, the selected tree does not mutate and passes on to the next generation.

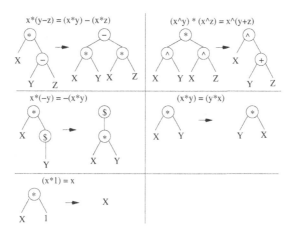

Fig. 3. Mutation equations with multiplication as the main node.

4   Experimental Results

The technique has been applied to an equational specification of a simple circuit and a much more complex algebraic equation. In the first case our algorithm simplifies the equation to find a better specification and in the second, in spite of ignoring the ideal solution, a solution that improves the original one is always obtained.

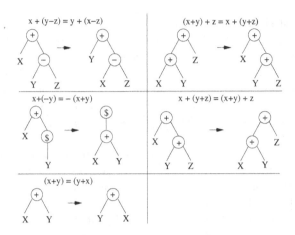

Fig. 4. Mutation equations with addition as the main node.

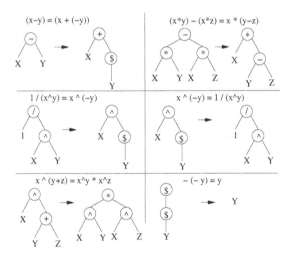

Fig. 5. Mutation equations with substraction, power, division and sign as the main node operator.

4.1   The Simplification of a Circuit

The implementation of GP algorithm has been carried out from *Genetic Programming kernel Version 0.5.2 C++ Class Library* [9] . The circuit to be used as an example carries out one of the subfunctions which can be seen in the transcoding algorithm ADPCM (Adaptive Differential Pulse Code Modulation), described at the G.721 recommendation of CCITT [2]. The task of this subsystem is to update one of the scale factors that adjusts the adapting speed of the algorithm and verifies the following time specification.

$$y_u(t) = \left(1 - 2^{-5}\right) \cdot y(t) + 2^{-5} \cdot w_i(t) \tag{4}$$

Where w_i and y are input signals. The tree implementation of this equation can be seen in figure 1.

This equational specification, although simple, will let us show that our evolutionary program is finding the solution to the problem in a small number of generation. The set of functions that we have used for the solution of our problems are:

$$\mathcal{F} = \{+, -, *, /, \hat{}, \$\}$$

All these functions, except for the sign operator (\$) of one arity, require two arguments for its correct syntax, which means they have two arity.

The set of terminals used for this example has been $\mathcal{T} = \{w, y, 1, 2, 5\}$. Where $\{w, y\}$ represent input signals to our circuit, whereas the rest of the set of terminals $\{1, 2, 5\}$ are constant.

Our system is to modify the equational specification by transforming it into a simpler one. In this case the ideal specification will be:

$$y_u(t) = y(t) + 2^{-5} \cdot (y(t) - w_i(t)) \tag{5}$$

For our algorithm we have used populations of 4 individuals. The highest number of generations allowed to reach the ideal specification is 10,000 generations.

4.2   Simplification of a Complex Algebraic Expression

In this second example, the specification to be simplified now is more complex. That is why we have decided to represent it in LISP language format. Equation 6 represents in this format our original expression, which we will try and simplified by means of our evolutionary algorithm.

$$\begin{aligned}
&(+(+(-(+(+(-(+(+(*(\hat{}w\ x)(\hat{}w\ (\$y))) \\
&(-(*(*y\ 1)(+(\hat{}w\ (\$y))\ 1))(*(\hat{}w\ (\$y))\ z))) \\
&(*(\hat{}w\ x)\ y))(*(\hat{}w\ x)\ z))(*(\hat{}w\ x) \\
&(\hat{}w\ z)))(*y\ (\$z)))\ (\$y))(-(*(*y\ 1)(+(\hat{}w\ (\$y))\ 1)) \\
&(*(\hat{}w\ (\$y))\ z)))(+(*(\hat{}w\ x)(\hat{}w\ (\$y))) \\
&(-(*(*y\ 1)(+(\hat{}w\ (\$y))\ 1))(*(\hat{}w\ (\$y))\ z))))
\end{aligned} \tag{6}$$

The set of functions that we have used in our evolutionary algorithm for the solution to this problem is: $\mathcal{F} = \{+, -, *, /, \char94, \$\}$, similar to the set of equations used in the previous example. All these functions require two arguments for their correct syntax, i.e. they are binary operators, except for the unary minus operator (marked with the $ symbol), this is a arity one operator.

The set of terminals used for this specific example has been $\mathcal{T} = \{w, y, z, x, 1\}$, where $\{w, y\}$ represent variable arguments in our equation, whereas $\{1\}$ represents a numerical constant.

In this example, a much more complex equation, the expression of the ideal solution is unknown. In all the executions of our algorithm a lower-cost individual is obtained. The original parameters used for this equation have been:

- Original population of 4 individuals.
- The highest number of generations allowed is 40,000.

With these conditions the best individual that our algorithm has found is the one shown in equation 7. This equation represents an improvement in the cost function of a 60% regarding the original equation.

$$
\begin{aligned}
&(+(+(*(+(\char94 w\ (\$y))\ 1)\ y)(+(+(*(\char94 w\ x)\ y)\ y) \\
&(+(\char94 w(+z\ x))(+(*y(+1(+(\$z)(\char94 w\ (\$y))))) \\
&(*(\char94 w\ (\$y))(-(-(+(\$z)(\char94 w\ x))\ z)\ z)))))) \\
&(+(*y(+1(\char94 w\ (\$y)))) \\
&(*(\char94 w\ x)(+(\$z)(\char94 w\ (\$y))))))))
\end{aligned}
\tag{7}
$$

5   Conclusions and Future Work

In this paper a new technique of algebraic equation simplification has been presented. This technique will be used in a Formal Synthesis tool. The algorithm is based on genetic programming and it only uses a specific mutation operator developed for our problem. Experimental results show the effectiveness of the algorithm by obtaining a 60% improvement in the complex circuit cost.

The future lines of work will be dealing with an increased set of equations. In the first stage of investigation we have focused on elementary algebra equations and in the second stage we will implement the abstraction functions [7]. These equations will let us, for example, substitute operator as multiplication by addition operators, or even transform multiplications into shifter constant.

We will study the establishment of the crossover operator. As it has been explained before, due to the impossibility to obtain individuals that do not comply with the equational specification of our original circuit, the very nature of the crossover operator prevents us from its use. Studies carried out by R. Poli show that the cross operator can be used in a different way [8]. We will work these studies in depth in order to apply this operator to our algorithm.

Another line we are currently working on is the implementation of a crossover operator to our problem in such a way that it ensures the obtaining of individuals that represent equivalent equations after its application.

We are also working on the implementation of multiparametrical cost functions which optimise the circuits, not only according to their area but also according to the performance or the power consumed.

References

1. W. Banzhaf, P. Nordin, R. E. Keller and F.D. Francone, *Genetic Programming - An introduction. On the Automatic Evolution of Computer Programs and Its Applications*, Morgan Kaufmann, dpunkt.verlag, 1998.
2. CCITT, *Adaptative differential pulse code modulation (ADPCM)*, Rec. G.721, Fascicle III.4, 1998.
3. K. Chellapilla, *Evolving Computer Programs Without Subtree Crossover*, IEEE Transactions on Evolutionary Computation, 1(3):209-216 1997.
4. J.I. Hidalgo, *Técnicas de partición y Ubicación para Sistemas Multi-FPGA basadas en Algoritmos Genéticos*, Tesis doctoral, noviembre 2001.
5. J. R. Koza, *Genetic Programming: On the programming of Computers by Means of natural Selection*, MIT Press, Cambridge MA, 1992.
6. J.M. Mendías, R. Hermida, M. Fernández *Correct High-Level Synthesis: a Formal Perspective*, in Proc. of Design, Automation and Test in Europe, DATE'98.
7. J.M. Mendías, R. Hermida, M. Fernández *Formal Techniques for Hardware Allocation*, Proc. of 10th International Conference on VLSI Design, VLSI'97.
8. R. Poli, W. B. Langdon, *On the Search Properties of Different Crossover Operators in Genetic Programming*, Genetic Programming 1998: Proceedings of the Third Annual Conference, pages 293-301.
9. T. Weinbrenner, *Genetic programming kernel Version 0.5.2 C++ Class Library*, http://thor.emk.e-thecnik.tu-darmstadt.de/~thomasw/gpkernel1.html

Automatic Generation of Control Programs for Walking Robots Using Genetic Programming

Jens Busch, Jens Ziegler, Christian Aue, Andree Ross, Daniel Sawitzki, and
Wolfgang Banzhaf

University of Dortmund,
Department of Computer Science, Chair of Systems Analysis (LS XI)
D-44221 Dortmund, Germany
{banzhaf, busch, ziegler, sigel}@ls11.cs.uni-dortmund.de
http://ls11-www.cs.uni-dortmund.de/~sigel

Abstract. We present the system *SIGEL* that combines the simulation
and visualization of robots with a Genetic Programming system for the
automated evolution of walking. It is designed to automatically generate
control programs for arbitrary robots without depending on detailed analytical information of the robots' kinematic structure. Different fitness
functions as well as a variety of parameters allow the easy and inter-
active configuration and adaptation of the evolution process and the
simulations.

1 Introduction

Autonomous mobile robots are becoming more and more important, because
they are expected to solve tasks that humans are not able to cope with or
that humans ought not to cope with [3,4]. This requires extensively autonomous
robots, because with growing complexity of the problems it will be no longer possible for the programmer to take all eventualities into account from the outset.
A special form of mobile robots are walking robots. This term includes all robots
that locomote without wheels, caterpillars or similar devices on firm ground. The
evolution of robot control programs has been the topic of recent publications.
A general introduction into the concept of Genetic Programming can be found
in [2,10]. Several applications of Genetic Programming (or, more generally, Evolutionary Algorithms) to the task of controlling autonomous robots are given in,
e.g., [8,13]. The evolution of crawling or walking robots can be found e.g. in [11,
15,6]. For biological inspiration, gait patterns of stick insects have been analyzed
to gain more detailed information on natural gait coordination algorithms [5],
that in turn has influences on the design of robust and fast walking gait patterns.
A good overview over the evolution of neural network controllers can be found
in [12].

To evolve gait patterns or walking agents, we use simulated robots. Simulating walking robots allows more flexible architectures and rapid prototyping,
which is, compared to experiments with real hardware, less expensive. Additionally, simulation is fast and does not strain the hardware. The evolution of

J.A. Foster et al. (Eds.): EuroGP 2002, LNCS 2278, pp. 258–267, 2002.

movements of virtual agents in a simulated environment has been successfully demonstrated [14,9,16].

The approach presented here does not imply that the evolved controllers depend on specific information on the robot morphology such as certain lengths or distances. On the contrary, it was one of the main goals of this work to make the evolution of robot controllers as independent as possible from morphology specific information. So morphology-related information, although available, will not be used for evaluating individuals.

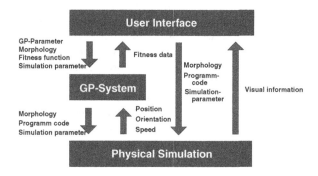

Fig. 1. Schematic view of the main components of *SIGEL*. Explanations see text.

The system *SIGEL* [1] is composed of three main components: The Genetic Programming module (described in Section 2), the physical robot simulation (Sect. 3) and the user interface (see Fig.1). The latter consists of the graphical interface as well as the underlying mechanisms to manage the experiments. An experiment mainly consists of GP and simulation parameters and the robot morphology. The following two sections are devoted to the description of the tested robot models and the results of the experiments.

2   The Genetic Programming System

The objective of a GP run is to evolve a robot control program that enables a simulated robot to walk. Our system uses linear genomes as a representation. Thus each program of a GP population is a sequence of robot instructions. The following instructions are element of the function set: ADD, SUB, MUL, DIV and MOD for arithmetic operations, COPY and LOAD for register manipulation, CMP, JMP, DELAY and NOP for execution control, and the SENSE and MOVE command as instructions that are directly connected to the robot. Each instruction is chosen with a predefined probability and needs one or two registers or constants as parameters. The program length is not fixed but a minimum and maximum length can be defined. By default, programs are initialized randomly, but it is possible to import manually defined code or programs of a previous experiment as well. A user interface provides easy access to the population for import and export of GP individuals and parameter adjustment. Other important GP parameters like population size, number of generations and variation probabilities may vary considerably between experiments and are explained in detail in Sect. 5.

Genetic Operators

Crossover, mutation and reproduction are applied with probabilities p_c,p_m and p_r, respectively. The crossover operator uses one-point crossover and thus swaps linear genome sequences between the mating partners. The crossover point is selected randomly. The genome of the offspring is cut or expanded to fulfill length restrictions. The mutation operator randomly changes different parts of the genome. (i) It deletes an arbitrary instruction. (ii) It inserts a new randomly initialized instruction at an arbitrary position. (iii) It replaces an arbitrary instruction by a new randomly initialized instruction. (iv) It modifies an arbitrary instruction. Either the function or its operand(s) are altered. The reproduction operator simply copies an individual. The genetic code will not be changed.

Selection and Parallelized Fitness Computation

The evaluation of control programs for walking robots in a physical simulation is computationally expensive. To save execution time of an evolutionary cycle we implemented a parallelized fitness evaluation. A number of tournaments T is scheduled and topologically sorted with respect to a partial order $\prec$ which is defined as follows:

$$T_x \prec T_y :\Leftrightarrow (\exists \text{ individual } i : (i \text{ is participant of } T_x \text{ and of } T_y \text{ and } x < y))$$

This method ensures a reproducible series of tournaments so that the experiment is independent of system parameters such as network traffic or workstation load. The resulting minimal set of tournaments is distributed over a heterogenous network of workstations using PVM.

3   Dynamic Simulation of Robots

In our system we simulate robots in a three-dimensional physical environment by using the DynaMechs software package (see [7]). This C++ programming library takes a model description of the robot and simulates its dynamics. The robot is given by a set of rigid bodies called links and their kinematic structure. The links are described by their physical attributes like inertia properties, mass, center of mass and their geometry in a polygonal representation. The robot's kinematic structure is defined by connecting links with joints. Additional parameters are global gravity and maximum and minimum joint forces and angles. Further forces result from the collision of the robot links with the floor. Collision between robot links is not taken into account in the actual implementation. To circumvent the intersection of links the appropriate allowed joint angles must be restricted manually. The implemented fitness function evaluates a robot and its program by measuring the distance it has moved during the simulation. The value is given in $\left[\frac{m}{s}\right]$. Additionally, it examines if the distance between the robot torso and the ground is larger than 0.5 length units. If this condition cannot be kept, so that the robot seems to break down, the robot program will receive a penalty value of zero. We supposed this function to be advantageous for a development of a *nice* movement, so we called this function *nice walking* fitness function. In the following experiments, the movement of the torso link of the robot is measured from the starting point to the point it has reached when the simulation stops. The faster and more linear an individual moves, the better is its fitness. The simulation is divided into discrete simulation steps translating the simulated system from time t to time $t + h$ where h is the granularity of the simulation. A small granularity leads to a more accurate simulation process. In each step the control program may effect the simulation in two aspects: (i) the program may apply forces at prismatic joints or torques at rotational joints with a move command. (ii) The program may read the actual angle of joints and store the values in the registers of the virtual machine with a sense command. These values can be used for future computations of forces and torques. Each simulation step consists of two substeps. First, the interpreter executes the next n commands of the control program with n being the maximum number of commands that can be executed in time h. Second, the system dynamics is calculated to update the simulation parameters consisting of the bodies' positions, orientations, velocities and accelerations. Given the set of forces affecting the system the DynaMechs simulation library calculates the motions (accelerations) of all links. Once the accelerations are known, numerical integration is used to determine the positions, orientations and velocities of the links at time $t + h$.

4   The Robots

We tested the system on several different robot architectures including simple "hoppers" consisting of only two links and one rotational joint (Fig. 2 a). This simple architecture was used for general experiments to gain experience with the dynamic simulation. We used more complex architectures in our experiments:

The caterpillar robot. This caterpillar robot consists of four links and three rotational joints (Fig. 2 b). Its head is shaped like a cube, in difference to the tail, which ends in a half cylinder. The head and the tail are connected to the inner links with horizontal rotational joints. The two identical inner links are connected together with a vertical rotational joint.

The two-legged robot. This robot has two symmetrical legs hinged to the torso link (Fig. 2 c). Each leg consists of three links and three rotational joints.

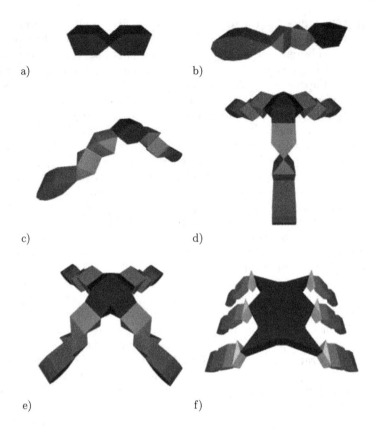

Fig. 2. The robots. From top left to bottom right: The hopper, the caterpillar, the two-legged and three-legged robot, the robot with four legs and the six-legged robot.

The three-legged robot. This robot has three symmetrical legs hinged around the torso link with a 120 degree angle between them (Fig. 2 d). Each leg consists of three links and three rotational joints. The legs are the same as the legs of the two-legged robot.

The four-legged robot. This robot has four symmetrical legs hinged around the torso link with a 90 degree angle between them (Fig. 2 e). This is the only difference between the architectures of the four-legged and the three-legged robot.

The six-legged robot. This robot consists of nineteen links and eighteen rotational joints arranged in a symmetrical architecture (Fig. 2 f). Its torso is carried by six identical legs, three on the left and three on the right side. Each of the six legs consists of three links. The shoulder-joint of each leg allows horizontal movement, the other two joints, for knee and ankle, have vertical axes of rotation.

5   Experiments and Results

The aim of our experiments was the development of control programs which let the robots walk straight-line and fast. Additionally, we wanted the robots to walk with the torso lifted to a specified level. In a series of experiments the effects of changing GP parameter settings have been investigated, whereas a second series analyzed the effects of changing kinematic structures. Each experiment includes several evolutions, which are not interdependent (with the exception of experiment 5, which takes some individuals of experiment 1).

Experiments with the Four-Legged Robot

We studied varying genetic operator probabilities and a reduced function set. The robot architecture (the four-legged robot), fitness function (niceWalking), and the simulation time remained unchanged.

Experiment 1 – Evolution with high mutation rate. We have chosen a high muta- tion probability of 80% and a crossover probability of 5% for the first experiment. The reproduction probability was defined to be 15%. Each evolution took place in a population of 100 individuals, which have been initialized randomly with an arbitrarily chosen number of between 100 and 1000 program lines. Table 1 shows the chosen genetic parameter settings. The simulation time was set to one minute. Overall, the *best fitness* averages out at 0.19 m/s. The best fitness is reached after 270 generations on average (Fig. 3). As expected, the standard er- ror of the *average fitness* is small. This allows to state that all experiments with small mutation rate have a similar performance. In sum, by using a dominant mutation operator the GP System was capable to evolve various robot programs that have moved the four-legged robot.

Experiment 2 – Evolution with a high crossover rate. By using a high crossover rate of 80% in combination with a low mutation rate of 5% we have chosen the most usual genetic parameter settings for the second experiment. The other parameter settings remained unchanged (Tab. 1). So the effect of a changing dominant genetic operator should be analyzed. Figure 3 shows the average de- velopment of the best fitness over the time. Overall, the *best fitness* averages out at 0.26 m/s. The best fitness is reached on average after 240 generations. Similar to the first experiment, the standard error of the *average fitness* is small. Again, the experiments show related performance. Compared to exp. 1, a high crossover rate seems to result in a better quality of the solutions.

Experiment 3 – Evolution with a reduced robot instruction set. While the first two experiments used all instructions available for the robot programs, we analyzed the effect of a *limited instruction set* (Tab. 1). As expected, the development of the *best fitness* is not as fast as in the first experiments, which can be explained with the reduced instruction set (Fig. 3). The best fitness of 0.08 m/s on average is reached after 290 generations. The standard error is small, pointing to the alike

Table 1. GP parameters

Parameter	Exp. 1	Exp. 2	Exp. 3	Exp. 4	Exp. 5
objective	fast linear movement				
terminal set	random constants				
function set	MOVE, SENSE, COPY, LOAD, ADD, SUB, MUL, DIV, MOD, DELAY, MAX, MIN		MOVE, SENSE, COPY, LOAD, ADD	see exp. 1	
crossover prob.	5%	80%	5%	80%	
mutation prob.	80%	5%	80%	5%	
robot model	four-legged			modified four-legged	
initialization	random			50% pre-evolved, 50% random	
population size	100				
selection	tournament				
max. prg. length	100 lines				
min. prg. length	1000 lines				
termination	after 300 generations				
reprod. prob.	15%				

performance of all experiments. Although a strongly reduced instruction set was used, the GP System was capable to evolve different effective robot programs. This result underlines the assumption that the set of supported instructions can be subdivided into sets of *necessary* and *not necessary* instructions. In parallel, this result also proves the power of GP in finding good solutions in a limited solution space. The solutions of experiments 1-3 clearly show differences in quality. The high crossover rate is superior to the other two settings, while a reduced instruction set only allows poor walking speed.

Experiments with an Altered Four-Legged Robot

In a second series of experiments the kinematic structure of the four-legged robot was altered while the general control parameters remained unchanged. The initial GP population of a subsequent evolution cycle was augmented with previously evolved control programs. This reflects the situation in which a changing kinematic structure – maybe due to a technical defect – and/or a changing environment (e.g. change of terrain from flat to rugged) require an adequate response in robot control.

Experiment 4 – Four-legged robot with stiff leg. To test the capabilities of our system to cope with changes of the robot's kinematic structure we altered the four-legged robot by immobilizing the joints of one leg. This was achieved by modifying the joint limits. First we evolved control programs with the same set of

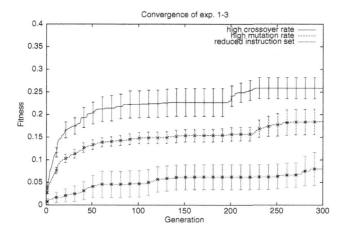

Fig. 3. Mean fitness and the standard error of exp. 1-3. Top: Evolution with high crossover rate. Middle: High mutation rate. Bottom: Reduced instruction set.

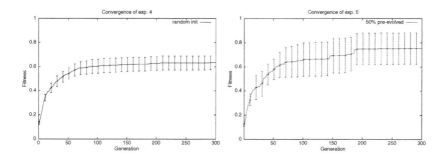

Fig. 4. Mean fitness and standard error of exp. 4 and 5. Left: New evolution of four-legged robot with stiff leg. Right: Evolution using pre-evolved individuals.

parameters as in experiment 1 (parameters see Tab. 1). The resulting programs differed from the programs of exp. 1–3 in that they successfully compensate the reduced degrees of freedom. It is interesting to note that the quality of movement is visibly better than in all earlier experiments (Fig. 4, left).

Experiment 5 – Four-legged robot with stiff leg, individuals from previous exp. We repeated the evolution with only fifty individuals created randomly and another fifty individuals taken from the evolved population of experiment 1. The best fitness of all runs seems to be about 30% higher (i.e. the robot moves faster) than in exp. 4, but the standard error is greater, indicating highly varying runs. In general, it was not the case that using individuals from earlier experiments results in faster evolution. Pre-evolved programs seem to be highly adapted to their architecture and thus may prevent better progress and quality when re-used for other morphologies. However, it can be advantageous to import individuals from other experiments. To make more detailed statements, further experiments with different handicaps and different ratios of randomly initialized and imported individuals need to be analyzed. Interestingly, this intuitive approach does not lead to as big improvements as expected.

Achieved Walking Strategies

In fact nearly all evolutionary runs showed good results by means of regularly walking with speeds up to 0.85 m/s. It seems that our system evolves more successful programs for the altered version of the four-legged robot. We observed mainly four different kinds of moving. (i) Some runs led to walking strategies which only kept the avoided fast and sudden movements. As a consequence this behavior limited the speed of walking. (ii) These strategies used just one leg to generate an impulse in the walking direction. The other legs are only used for stability. (iii) In these cases one leg pushes the robot forward while the other legs are again stabilizing it. (iv) Another kind of walking was observed only for the altered four-legged robot. In contrast to the other mentioned strategies all three flexible legs of the robot are used. This results in a continuous and fast natural like movement.

6   Conclusions

We presented *SIGEL*[1], an integrated software package that combines the simulation and visualization of robots with a Genetic Programming system for the parallelized evolution of walking. The capabilities of the system were investigated with six different robot morphologies. We could show that it is possible to get control programs for arbitrary walking robots without having insight into their architecture and kinematic structure. The advantages of this approach are two-fold: On the one hand, people without engineering background are enabled to control walking robots. On the other hand, engineers are less restricted in the design of robots since the system allows rapid prototyping and testing.

The successful automatic compensation of a technical defect by using preliminary evolved control programs saves time for reprogramming the walking algorithm. In conjunction with the detection of either unpredictable environmental conditions or malfunctioning of parts of the robot, our system increases the robustness of the robot control. The download of off-line evolved control programs to real robots is an important step in this direction and will be the topic of our future work.

---

[1] More information on the system *SIGEL*, including experiment files, screenshots and video files showing the walking robots can be found on the web (http://ls11-www.cs.uni-dortmund.de/people/sigel/).

References

[1] C. Aue, A. Benkacem, M. Gregorius, A. Ross, S. R. Abdallah, D. Sawitzki, V. Strunk, H. Türk, M. C. Varcol, J. Busch, and J. Ziegler. Simulator für GP-evolvierte Laufrobotersteuerungsprogramme - PG 368. Technical report, Department of Computer Science, University of Dortmund, Germany, 2001.

[2] W. Banzhaf, P. Nordin, R. E. Keller, and F. D. Francone. *Genetic Programming – An Introduction; On the Automatic Evolution of Computer Programs and its Applications.* Morgan Kaufmann, dpunkt.verlag, 1998.

[3] V. Braitenberg. *Vehicles: experiments in synthetic psychology.* MIT Press, 1984.

[4] R. A. Brooks. New approaches to robotics. *Science*, 253:1227 – 1232, 1991.

[5] H. Cruse. Coordination of leg movement in walking animals. In *From animals to animats. Intl. Conf. on Simulation of Adaptive Behavior*, pages 105–119, 1991.

[6] P. Dittrich, A. Bürgel, and W. Banzhaf. Learning to control a robot with random morphology. In *Proceedings Evo-Robot-98, P. Husbands and J.-A. Meyer, Eds.*, pages 165–178, 1998.

[7] S. McMillan et al. *DynaMechs (Dynamics of Mechanisms): A Multibody Dynamic Simulation Library.* Ohio State University Internet Access (last access 22.08.2001) via http://dynamechs.sourceforge.net/.

[8] J. J. Grefenstette and A. C. Schultz. An evolutionary approach to learning in robots. In *Machine Learning Workshop on Robot Learning*, New Brunswick, NJ, 1994.

[9] M. Komosinski and S. Ulatowski. Framsticks - Artificial Life. In *ECML '98 Demonstration and Poster Papers, Chemnitzer Informatik Berichte*, pages 7–9, 1998.

[10] J. R. Koza. *Genetic Programming.* MIT Press, Cambridge, MA, 1992.

[11] M. A. Lewis, A. H. Fagg, and A. Solidum. Genetic programming approach to the construction of a neural network control of a walking robot. In *Proceedings of the 1992 IEEE InternationalConference on Robotics and Automation*, pages 2618–2623, Nice, France, May 1992.

[12] J.-A. Meyer. Evolutionary approaches to walking and higher-level behaviors in 6-legged animats. In Gomi, editor, *Evolutionary Robotics II: From Intelligent Robots to Artificial Life (ER'98).* AAAI Books, 1998.

[13] M. Olmer, W. Banzhaf, and P. Nordin. Evolving real-time behavior modules for a real robot with genetic programming. In *Proceedings of the international symposium on robotics and manufacturing*, Montpellier, France, May 1996.

[14] Karl Sims. Evolving virtual creatures. In Andrew Glassner, editor, *Proceedings of SIGGRAPH '94 (Orlando, Florida, July 24–29, 1994)*, Computer Graphics Proceedings, Annual Conference Series, pages 15–22. ACM SIGGRAPH, ACM Press, July 1994. ISBN 0-89791-667-0.

[15] G. F. Spencer. Automatic generation of programs for crawling and walking. In S. Forrest, editor, *Proceedings of the 5th International Conference on Genetic Algorithms, ICGA-93*, page 654, University of Illinois at Urbana-Champaign, 17-21 July 1993. Morgan Kaufmann.

[16] J. Ziegler and W. Banzhaf. Evolution of robot leg movements in a physical simulation. In K. Berns and R. Dillmann, editors, *Proceedings of the Fourth International Conference on Climbing and Walking Robots, CLAWAR*, pages 395–402, Bury St Edmunds, London, UK, 2001. Professional Engineering Publishing.

An Investigation into the Use of Different Search Strategies with Grammatical Evolution

John O'Sullivan and Conor Ryan

Department of Computer Science and Information Systems
University of Limerick
Ireland
{Conor.Ryan|John.OSullivan}@ul.ie

Abstract. We present an investigation into the performance of Grammatical Evolution using a number of different search strategies, Simulated Annealing, Hill Climbing, Random Search and Genetic Algorithms. Comparative results on three different problems are examined. We analyse the nature of the search spaces presented by these problems and offer an explanation for the contrasting performance of each of the search strategies. Our results show that Genetic Algorithms provide a consistent level of performance across all three problems successfully coping with sensitivity of the system to discrete changes in the selection of productions from the associated grammar.

1 Introduction

Grammatical Evolution (GE) [6] is an evolutionary algorithm that can evolve complete programs in an arbitrary language using a variable-length binary string. The binary string is decoded into a genome which in turn is used to select production rules from a Backus Naur Form (BNF) grammar definition. To date, GE has used a Genetic Algorithm (GA) [1] as the search mechanism. This paper contrasts the performance of GE using GA against three other metaheuristics, Hill Climbing [3], Simulated Annealing [2] and Random Search. The objective of the paper is not simply to propose the most powerful algorithm for GE but to contrast the tendencies and performance characteristics for the various algorithms on a number of problems in an effort to better understand the search space presented by the GE process. The emphasis has been on keeping the algorithms as simple as possible, avoiding detailed tuning and optimisation of the selected mechanisms.

Section 2 of this paper provides a brief introduction to Grammatical Evolution. The featured metaheuristics are introduced in Section 3, where we provide a brief overview of the operators used to explore the search space. In Section 4 we discuss three benchmark problems, *The Santa Fe Trail problem*, *Symbolic Integration* and *Symbolic Regression*, providing a description of each problem and its associated grammar. The findings of the various experiments are explored in Section 5 where we provide an analysis of the relative performance of each of the metaheuristics on the selected problems and attempt to understand the nature

J.A. Foster et al. (Eds.): EuroGP 2002, LNCS 2278, pp. 268–277, 2002.

of the solutions and the general landscape from which they emerge. This section introduces the notion of *productive parents*, that is, parents that produce perfectly fit offspring, and considers the relationship between these parents and the offspring in terms of transmitted genetic material. For the non-population-based metaheuristics this involves an examination of the search trajectory as we move towards a solution. Finally, in section 6 we discuss some of the implications of these findings.

Our results will show that GA is an effective search strategy across all three problems, indeed GA is the only search strategy that solves all three of the problems. Random Search shows surprisingly good results on two of the featured problems, while Simulated Annealing and Hill Climbing have limited success on the selected problems. Our analysis of the factors underlying these results will show that both crossover and mutation are essential to the consistent performance of GA across the three problems and that metaheuristics that attempt to navigate the search space purely with operators that provide fine grained control of the emerging solutions will struggle with the complex landscape presented by GE.

2   Grammatical Evolution

Grammatical Evolution [6] can evolve complete programs by using a variable length linear genome to determine the selection of production rules from a Backus Naur Form (BNF) grammar definition. Backus Naur Form is a notation for expressing the grammar of a language in the form of production rules. BNF consists of *terminals*, which are items that can appear in the language, e.g. + - * etc. and *non-terminals*, which can be expanded into one or more terminals and non-terminals. The system can use any search mechanism capable of generating a variable length sequence of integer codons. The codons typically in the range 0 - 255 are used to select productions from the target grammar using the following function:

Rule = (Codon value) MOD(Number of Rules for the current non-terminal)

A number of different codon values in the range 0 - 255 can cause selection of the same production rule. This occurs because the number of production rules associated with any non-terminal is generally small relative to the 256 expressible by a codon. This *Genetic Code Degeneracy* [6] permits *neutral mutation* which allows subtle changes in the search space without necessarily impacting the solution space.

The use of the *mod* operation makes each gene polymorphic[5]. This is because each rule can have a different number of productions, thus, a gene can yield different values, depending on how it is interpreted. This has lead to the so-called "ripple effect", where a change in the value of gene can lead to every other gene that occurs after to be interpreted differently.

Wrapping is a technique employed by GE which allows the mapping process re-use codons from the genome. Once all codons in a genome have been used the process simply wraps to the start of the genome and continues the mapping process helping to improve the probability of a complete mapping of individuals onto programs.

Previous analysis of GE [6] has used GA as the means of directing the search. As in this previous analysis the experiments in this paper uses a steady-state population employing the standard GA operators of crossover and mutation. Two non-standard operators *Duplication* and *Swapping* which work at the codon level are also used. Duplication involves copying a sequence of genes of random length and placing them between the last and second last gene, while the Swap operator does a positional swap of two randomly selected genes.

3   Metaheuristics

Metaheuristics are a class of approximate methods, that are designed to attack hard combinatorial optimzation problems, which are often employed where classical heuristics have failed to be effective and efficient. Metaheuristics are computational procedures rather than computational algorithms. They typically explore the solution landscape by starting from some randomly chosen point. Metaheuristics differ from heuristics and from formal computational algorithms in that they assume very little knowledge of the problem domain. They are what Artificial Intelligence has termed weak methods in that they are general strategies intended to be applicable to entire classes of problems.

This paper is concerned with three well-known and simple meta-heuristics; Hill Climbing, Simulated Annealing and Random Search, which, it could be argued, is not a meta-heuristic, but is a useful yardstick with which to measure the performance of the others. Both the Hill Climbing and Simulated annealing algorithms featured in this study use a selection of four operators to explore the search space. The operators have been selected to allow subtle changes in the genomes by allowing a single mutation select alternate productions from the BNF grammar. The operators used *Force-up* and *Force-down* provide a means of selecting alternate productions by incrementing or decrementing a single randomly chosen codon. Two additional operators *Grow* and *Shrink* provide a means of expanding and contracting the genome into different areas of the search space. The Force-up and Force-down operators will always force the selection of a different production from the grammar, consequently *neutral mutation* discussed in section 2 does not occur. The shrink operator removes the last codon from the genome while the grow operator adds a single codon whose value is randomly chosen.

4   Problem Domains

4.1   Santa Fe Trail

The Santa Fe Trail is a benchmark problem in Genetic Programming (GP) [4]. The objective is to devise a program which can navigate along a 32 X 32 toroidal grid picking up pieces of food positioned on the grid. The ant can move left, right or straight ahead and can sense food directly in front of him. This ability to sense food is used to select alternate moves to guide the search. For the purpose of this evaluation the ant is allowed 615 time steps, with the exception of sensing food in the square ahead each action consumes one time step. The fitness is the number of pieces of food (of a possible 88) collected within the 615 time steps. Previous research [7] has shown that there is a high density of distinct solutions for this particular problem, with the neighbourhoods of these solutions composed of low fitness programs and a large number of sub-optimal peaks. The BNF grammar for this problem is shown below.

```
<code>            ::== <Line> | <code><line>
<line>            ::== <expr> | <expr> <op> <expr>
<expr>            ::== <if-statement> | <op>
<If-statement>    ::== if(food_ahead()){ <expr> else <expr>}
<op>              ::== left() | right() | move()
```

4.2   Symbolic Integration

Symbolic Integration involves finding a function that is the integral of the given curve. The system uses a set of input and output pairs, where the objective is to find the function that maps the inputs to the outputs. For these trials the particular function used was:

$$f(x) = Cos(x) + 2x + 1$$

with the input values in the range $[0...2\pi]$. The target curve was

$$f(x) = Sin(x) + x^2 + x$$

The fitness for this problem is given by the sum of the absolute value of the difference, taken over 20 fitness cases, between the individual genetically produced function $f_j(x_i)$ at the domain point x_i and the value of the numerical integral $I(x_i)$. The grammar used is shown below.

```
<expr>         :: == <var> | <expr><op><expr> | <pre-op>(<expr>)
               | (<expr>)
<var>          :: == X
<op>           :: == + | - | / | *
<pre-op>       :: == sin | cos | tan | log
```

4.3   Symbolic Regression

The objective of the Symbolic Regression problem is to find a function of one independent variable and one dependent variable in symbolic form that fits a sample of $20(x_i, y_i)$ data points in the range [-1,+1]. The target function is that used by Koza [4].

$$x^4 + x^3 + x^2 + x$$

The grammar used is identical to that shown for Symbolic Integration (See Section 4.2).

5   Experimental Results

5.1   Experimental Conditions

Each of the four search strategies GA, Random Search, Hill Climbing and Simulated Annealing were allowed 100 trials on each of the selected problems, Santa Fe, Symbolic Integration and Symbolic Regression. Each trail consisted of 50500 evaluations of the objective function, with a trial terminating when a successful solution to the problem was found or when the maximum number of evaluations (50500) was reached. Table 1 below summarises the main configuration parameters for GA while Table 2 shows those used for Random search, Hill Climbing and Simulated Annealing.

Table 1. Parameters used to configure GA for the featured experiments.

Parameter	Value
Population Size	500
Number of Generations	50
Initial Genome Length	10
Probability of Mutation	0.01
Probability of Crossover	.9
Probability of Swapping	.01
Probability of Duplication	.01
Selection Mechanism	Remainder Stochastic Sampling without replacement
Replacement Model	Steady state
Crossover Model	One point Crossover
Wrapping	On

Table 2. Parameters used to configure Random Search, Hill Climbing and Simulated Annealing for the featured experiments.

Parameter	Value
Number of Evaluations	50500
Initial Genome Length	10 - 12
Probability of Shrink Operation	.25
Probability of Grow Operation	.25
Probability of Force-up Operation	.25
Probability of Force-down Operation	.25
Initial Temperature	.4
Temperature Change Rate	.995
Wrapping	On

5.2   Santa Fe Trail Problem

An examination of the results shown in Table 3 shows the strong performance of GA and Random Search (RS). Simulated Annealing (SA) and Hill Climbing (HC) perform poorly relative to the other search strategies showing successes in 7% and 14% of the trials respectively. GA is the most successful in terms of the number of successful trials, scoring success in 81% of trials. At 54%, the performance of Random Search is high, consistent with previous analysis in this area [7], which found that the density of solutions in the solution landscape was sufficiently high to account for the performance of Random Search. The performance of Simulated Annealing and Hill Climbing are also consistent with the characterisation of the search space as rugged with many sub-optimal peaks surrounded by areas of low fitness.

Table 4 which shows the percentage fall off in fitness for all neighbours of solutions was created by using the operators of *force-up* and *force-down* to generate every immediate neighbour with a hamming distance of one from a solution. An examination of Table 4 for the Santa Fe problem shows a sharp fall of in fitness from a plateau of maximum fitness. An examination of Santa Fe solutions found during the trials shows that on average 25% of neighbours (see Table 4) of a Santa Fe solution will also have perfect fitness. [1]

A profile of the problem is shown in Table 5, interestingly a high percentage of solutions feature wrapping. While the number of terms for the minimum solution is small at 9 many of the solutions are much longer than this. One of the structures that tends to create some of the longer solutions is the multiple nesting of the $if(trail.food\_ahead())$ conditional.

Table 3. Performance analysis showing the percentage of successful trials for Random Search, Hill Climbing, Simulated Annealing and GA on the Santa Fe Trail, Symbolic Integration and Symbolic Regression Problems.

	Metaheuristic			
Problem	RS	HC	SA	GA
Santa Fe	54%	7%	14%	81%
Symbolic Integration	66%	4%	3%	100%
Symbolic Regression	0%	0%	0%	59%

5.3   Symbolic Integration

An examination of the results shown in Table 3 again shows the strong performance of GA and Random Search (RS). Simulated Annealing (SA) and Hill Climbing (HC) perform poorly relative to the other search strategies showing lower success rates than they achieved on the Santa Fe problem. An analysis of

---

[1] It should be noted that solutions to Santa Fe were found where none of the nearest neighbours achieved maximum fitness.

Table 4. Percentage fall off in Fitness of Immediate Neighbours for the Featured Problems.

	Proportion of individuals										
Problem	0%	10%	20%	30%	40%	50%	60%	70%	80%	90%	100%
Santa Fe	24.70%	0.04%	0.0%	0.04%	0.09%	0.30%	1.78%	0.56%	2.56%	8.23%	61.70%
Sym Integration	5.29%	0.0%	0.0%	0.0%	0.0%	0.0%	0.0%	0.0%	0.0%	2.98%	91.74%
Sym Regression	2.67%	0.49%	0.53%	0.83%	1.12%	1.17%	1.75%	3.89%	4.47%	10.30%	72.77%

Table 5. Problem Profiles for the Featured Problems.

Characteristic	Santa Fe	Sym Integration	Sym Regression
Average number of codons in a solution	37	15	42
No. of codons for minimum solution	21	12	24
No. of terms in minimum solution	9	7	19
Average number of terms in a solution	19	13	46
% of solutions using wrapping	85%	3%	4%

the immediate neighbourhood of solutions (see table 4) shows a different profile to that of Santa Fe, we again see fitness fall off sharply from a peak of maximum fitness, however the plateau of maximum fitness is greatly reduced. Less than 6% of the immediate neighbours of solutions retain maximum fitness, indeed Table 4 shows that over 91% of all neighbours have values that have fallen by 100%. The implications of this is that area of the global maxima (that is, the correct answer) is significantly smaller than in the Santa Fe problem, so relatively small changes in individuals in this neighbourhood are considerably less likely to result in a global maxima. The effects of this can be seen in table 3 where the performance of both HC and SA have dropped considerably.

A profile of this problem is presented in Table 5, where it can be seen that the average length of genome required to solve the Symbolic Integration problem is 15 which is considerably less than the 36 required for Santa Fe. The minimum solution can be found with just 12 codons, making it the easiest of the three problems to solve. Interestingly, the contribution of wrapping has dropped considerably relative to the Santa Fe problem.

5.4   Symbolic Regression

As in the previous problems GA again displays a strong performance scoring success in 59% of trials, while Random Search (RS), Simulated Annealing (SA) and Hill Climbing (HC) did not find a solution to the problem. One reason for this may be the relative density of solutions compared to Santa Fe and Symbolic Integration. The is a more difficult problem with 42 codons on average required for a solution. Wrapping contributes to a successful solution in only 4% of the cases. The neighbourhood of a Symbolic Regression problem as evidenced from Table 4 is similar to that of Symbolic Integration, showing a sharp isolated peak with a more gradual yet pronounced fall off in fitness.

5.5 Productive Parents

Productive parents are parents whose offspring achieve perfect fitness. To understand the relationship between parent and child we have analysed the contribution of the operators used. Table 6 provides an insight into the contribution of the mutation and crossover operator in solving the Santa Fe problem. Productive parents of Santa Fe solutions are typically of mid to high fitness averaging a score of 43 out of 88. An examination of the evolution from productive parent to fit child reveals that both crossover and mutation operators feature in the successful transitions. Table 6 also shows the effect of removing each operator in turn. Removing the mutation operator from GA results in a slight decrease in the success rate, while removal of the crossover operator significantly degrades performance. An examination of the results in Table 6 shows that the average fitness value of the productive parent does not change significantly. Interestingly when the crossover operator is removed the transition from productive parent to fit child is predominantly achieved through a combination of mutation and the duplication operator (See Section 2).

The notion of a productive parent can also be considered for Hill Climbing and Simulated Annealing. However, in both of these cases, the parent responsible for producing the final offspring tended to have a much lower fitness, with averages of 6 for HC and 3 for SA..

Table 6. Analysis of contribution of GA operators to the success rate for trials.

	Successful Trials		
Operators Used	Santa Fe	Sym Integration	Sym Regression
With Crossover and Mutation	81%	100%	51%
With Crossover and No Mutation	72%	100%	4%
With Mutation and No Crossover	17%	13%	11%

Table 7. Analysis of contribution of GA operators to Productive Parent's Average Fitness for the three featured Problems.

	Average Fitness		
Operators Used	Santa Fe	Sym Integration	Sym Regression
Maximum Fitness	88	1	1
Crossover and Mutation	43	.0952	.5910
Crossover and No Mutation	50	.1097	.5549
Mutation and No Crossover	44	.1060	.5745

GA parents for the Symbolic Integration problem are typically of low fitness, indeed 64% of all productive parents map to the same building block, that is, x^2+

x which has a fitness of .109735. Both Mutation and crossover are involved in this final step to perfectly fit child. The contribution of the mutation and crossover operators on the Symbolic Integration problem are more pronounced. Removing mutation has no influence of the performance, however removing the crossover operator sees the performance drop dramatically falling to a success rate of 13%. Analysis of Hill Climbing and Simulated Annealing search trajectories on this problem again show them progressing from very low scores (typically less than .1) to maximum fitness when they do manage to solve the problem. This and the results from Santa Fe for these metaheuristics may suggest that the solutions found by hill climbing and simulated annealing for these problems are due more to random forces than an intelligent walk through the search space.

Symbolic Regression has proved to be the most difficult problem with only GA managing to find a solution. Mutations features exclusively in the final transition from productive parent to perfectly fit child. An examination of individuals in the later generations of the Symbolic Regression problem show considerable bloat with the average individual having a length of 185. The average number of genomes required to solve the problem is 42 so crossover has little effect in the transition to the final individual. It is important to note that both mutation and crossover are essential in maintaining the performance of GA. Removing mutation sees the performance of GA drop to 4%, while removing crossover sees the successes rate fall to 11%.

6   Discussion

The results have highlighted some interesting issues. While any search strategy can be used with Grammatical Evolution, given the representation used in the search strategy (as dictated by GE) the GA appears to provide a consistent level of performance on the problems selected. Furthermore, two of the selected problems appear to have such a high density of solutions as demonstrated by the success of random search that their significance as bench mark problems is questionable. Hill Climbing and Simulated Annealing clearly struggle on these problem landscapes, there are many features of the landscape that act to deceive the subtle fine grained exploratory nature of such search techniques.

The crossover operator is essential in maintaining a high level of performance on the selected problems. Even when crossover is removed, the transition to fit individuals features the *crossover-like* contribution of the duplication operator. The contribution of mutation becomes apparent on the more challenging problem of Symbolic Regression.

7   Conclusion

We have analysed the performance of GE using a number of different search strategies. Results have shown that using GA as the search mechanism for GE provides consistent results across three bench mark problems. It has outperformed Random Search, Hill Climbing and Simulated Annealing. This difference in performance has led us to try and understand the search space presented by GE and what aspects of it work to act against the differing characteristics of the search strategies.

We have shown that approaches that attempt to fine tune solutions by selecting alternate productions from the BNF grammar struggle on the landscapes presented by GE. The primary GA operators of crossover and mutation have important contributions with crossover proving essential in maintaining performance. We have also provided an insight into the final step as each of the search strategies moves to a perfectly fit individual. Hill Climbing and Simulated Annealing typical make a quantum leap from very low fitness points to a solution. This quantum leap is consistent with the landscape presented by the *force-up* and *force-down* operators which shows a dramatic fall off in fitness in the neighbourhood of a solutions. However, the intrinsic polymorphism contained within GE genes permits an individual to jump from one neighbourhood to another simply by changing one bit, so this situation isn't as pathological as it might first appear. This is further borne out by the fact that the productive parents were generally considerably less fit than their offspring.

References

1. Goldberg, David E. 1989. Genetic Algorthms in Search, Optimization and Machine Learning. Addison Wesley.
2. Kirkpatrick, S., Gerlatt, C. D. Jr., and Vecchi, M.P., Optimization by Simulated Annealing, Science 220, 671-680, 1983.
3. Mitchell, M. and Holland, J. H. 1993. When will a Genetic Algorthm Outperform Hill Climbing? Technical report, Santa Fe Institute.
4. Koza, J. 1992. *Genetic Programming.* MIT Press.
5. Keijzer M., O'Neill M., Ryan C., Cattolico M., Babovic V. Ripple Crossover In Genetic Programming. *EuroGP 2001.*
6. O'Neill M., Ryan C. Grammatical Evolution. *IEEE Trans. Evolutionary Computation,* To appear 2001.
7. Langdon W.B., Poli R. Why Ants are Hard. Technical Report CSRP-98-4, University of Birmingham, School of Computer Science, January 1998.

Genetic Algorithms Using Grammatical Evolution

Conor Ryan, Miguel Nicolau, and Michael O'Neill

Department of Computer Science and Information Systems
University of Limerick
Ireland
{Conor.Ryan|Miguel.Nicolau|Michael.ONeill}@ul.ie

Abstract. This paper describes the *GAUGE* system, Genetic Algorithms Using Grammatical Evolution. GAUGE is a position independent Genetic Algorithm that uses Grammatical Evolution with an attribute grammar to dictate what position a gene codes for. GAUGE suffers from neither under-specification nor over-specification, is guaranteed to produce syntactically correct individuals, and does not require any repair after the application of genetic operators.

GAUGE is applied to the standard onemax problem, with results showing that its genotype to phenotype mapping and position independence nature do not affect its performance as a normal genetic algorithm. A new problem is also presented, a deceptive version of the Mastermind game, and we show that GAUGE possesses the position independence characteristics it claims, and outperforms several genetic algorithms, including the competent genetic algorithm messyGA.

1 Introduction

Since the inception of the field, Genetic Algorithms[5] [3] have been hamstrung by the dogma that each locus on a genome codes for a particular trait, and that the locus-trait relationship holds not only across an entire population, but even across otherwise independent runs on a problem.

Recently, this has been acknowledged to be a problem. Individuals are subjected to all manner of disruption at the whims of crossover and selection, neither of which respect the geographical location of loci that may be essential for good fitness. In particular, geographically disparate loci on a chromosome are easily split up, often making it difficult to build on previously discovered schema, and, in some cases, difficult even to maintain current useful schema.

In nature, function is rarely dependent on location. A gene (or, more properly, a gene sequence or *protein*) usually functions independently of its location. Under- and over-specification do not appear to be issues in nature, presumably due to the manner in which phenotypes are mapped from genotypes, which ensures that the necessary genes are expressed at crucial times. Individuals that do not exhibit this talent are often spontaneously aborted, or doomed to a lifetime under the spectre of a debilitating disease.

J.A. Foster et al. (Eds.): EuroGP 2002, LNCS 2278, pp. 278–287, 2002.

This paper describes a new *Epigenetic* Algorithm (i.e. that employs a geno-type to phenotype mapping) that overcomes the position dependence issue. This is achieved by extending Grammatical Evolution[12] [11] with an attribute grammar that makes the system behave as a position-independent Genetic Algorithm. This system, GAUGE (Genetic Algorithms Using Grammatical Evolution) is far less susceptible to the ravages often associated with crossover, as the system can automatically move important genes closer together as a run progresses.

Our main aim in this paper is to achieve a proof of concept. We start by briefly introducing Grammatical Evolution in section 2, and the implementation ideas behind GAUGE in section 3. We then present two problems in section 4, Onemax and Mastermind, and analyse the performance of GAUGE and other systems on those problems. We discuss the value of our results on section 5, and finally draw our conclusions and future directions of research in section 6.

2   Grammatical Evolution

Grammatical Evolution (GE) is an evolutionary automatic programming type system, that uses a combination of a variable length binary string genome and a BNF (Backus Naur Form) grammar to evolve interesting structures.

GE uses a chromosome of numbers encoded using eight bits (termed codons) to dictate which rule from the BNF grammar to apply at each state of the derivation sequence, starting from a defined *start* symbol. While one or more non-terminals symbols exist in a sentence, codons are read from the chromosome and used to govern which of the relevant production rules to apply. GE is fully described in [12][11].

3   GAUGE – Building a GA with GE

GE has been applied to all manner of automatic programming problems, from symbolic regression, to C programs, or generation of graphical objects. What all these application areas have in common is that the system is given a collection of *terminals*, the items that can appear in a legal sentence, and associated production rules, that govern how they can be combined.

The common view of Genetic Programming[9] is that, given a particular problem statement, a program that satisfies the fitness function is to be generated. In other words, *given a set of terminals, how should they be arranged so that the fitness function is satisfied?*.

The approach GAUGE takes is that *all* problems, even those traditionally considered the topic of Genetic Algorithms, can be looked upon as automatic programming ones. In particular, if one considers a problem to have two parts, that is, not only *what values should the genes have?* but also *where should the genes reside?*, it is reasonable to compare this class of problems with those above.

When applying GAUGE to a Genetic Algorithm problem, one uses a set of codon pairs, one for each gene position in the original problem. An individual is processed in a similar manner to GE, by moding each gene by an appropriate value to produce a useful value. The codons are 8-bit values, giving a degenerate (redundant) encoding. For GAUGE, the values required are the position that the pair will code for, and the value for that bit position. To produce these values, a list of *unspecified* positions is maintained, that is, those positions that have not been given a value yet. Thus, even when evolving individuals that are binary strings, GAUGE always has a distinct genotype and phenotype. The mapping happens in two stages; first a set of (position, value) pairs are generated using the grammar below, while the second step simply puts them in the correct order.

GAUGE operates using a tuple $< G, A, q, l >$ where G is the genome, A the attribute grammar below, q a list of free *locations* in the phenotype and l is the length of the phenotype. The maximum value that can appear in the phenotype is governed by the variable max, while the function $rember(n, q)$ returns the nth member from list q and removes it from the list.

1. $<start_n > ::=$ if $(n < l)$ { $<P_n><V_n><start_{n-1}>$}
2. $<P_n><V_n> ::= <Q_{(G[2n]\%(l-n))} > G[2n+1]\%max.$
3. $<Q_n > ::=$ rember (n,q)

3.1   Example Individual

Consider the following individual, expressed in decimal for brevity:
G=**31 17 23 16 237 56**.

We start with the following values, l=3, q=(0,1,2), max=2 and G as above. The grammar is invoked with a call to $<start_0 >$, which is mapped to:
$< P_0 >< V_0 ><start_1 >$

We then match the leftmost part to rule #2 above, which expands to:
$(<Q_{(G[2*0]\%(3-0))} >, G[2*0+1]\%2) <start_1 >$

which is $(<Q_{(G[0]\%3)} >, G[1]\%2) <start_1 >$ which means we read from the genome vector to get the values as follows: $(<Q_{(31\%3)} >, 17\%2) <start_1 >$
The next call is to Q, in the form Q_1, which returns item index #1 from the queue q, which is $(0, 1, 2)$. This causes the value 1 to be returned, and removed from the queue. The expression is now: $(1,1)<start_1 >$
We repeat the above steps with the next non-terminal, that is, $<start_1 >$, which is expanded as in the first step to $(1,1)< P_1 >< V_1 ><start_2 >$. Expanding the $< P_1 >< V_1 >$, we need to read positions 2 and 3 from the genome, to give: $(1,1)(<Q_{(23\%2)} >, 16\%2) <start_2 >$
This generates the non-terminal Q_1 (notice that the value **23** was moded by 2, because n has increased) so again we return the item in the list with the index 1. The current form of that list is $(0,2)$, so 2 is returned and removed from the list, yielding: $(1,1)(2,0)<start_2 >$. The final step involves mapping the remaining positions, and gives **(1,1)(2,0)(0,0)**. The final step in the mapping is to simply reorder these pairs as dictated by the first number in each pair.

4   Problems

This section introduces two problems to which standard GAs, GAUGE and messyGA will be applied. To show that GAUGE is a capable system, we used the standard onemax problem; to illustrate its position-independent nature, we have devised a deceptive ordering problem, based on the Mastermind[1] game.

4.1   Onemax

We ran the standard onemax problem (i.e. where the fitness of an individual is the sum of the bits which are equal to 1) using lengths of 50, 100 and 150 bits per individual. To choose which GA to compare GAUGE to, we measured the performance of several systems, shown in Table 1.

We included GAs using 8 bits per gene in this comparison, as they use the same redundant encoding as GAUGE. We ran these systems up to 25000 evaluations, using population sizes of 50, 100, 200, 400, 800 and 1600 individuals. We found that the generational algorithms could not solve the problem with these parameters, but steady-state algorithms performed well (with no significant difference between 1 or 8 bits per codon). We therefore compare GAUGE to a simple GA with steady-state, using 1 bit per codon (setting SGAss).

We also compared GAUGE with messyGA[4] (using the code available from the IlliGAL server[6], explained in [2]), and tried several combinations of settings for it (check Table 2), choosing the one that best performed on this given problem (setting STD). We wanted to test all systems with string lengths of up to 400 bits, but ran into difficulties, since some of the messyGA runs (for length 150) demanded over 1.1GB of memory (i.e. over one thousand times more than GAUGE or the simple GA) to execute, due to messyGA's variable length individuals and variable population sizes; this made running the experiments a very long task, and using longer strings was physically impossible[2].

Table 1. General settings used in all GAs and GAUGE.

Parameters	SGA	SGAss	GA	GAss	GAUGE
Replacement strategy	gener.	s-state	gener.	s-state	s-state
Selection routine	r-wheel	r-wheel	r-wheel	r-wheel	r-wheel
Bits per gene	1	1	8	8	8+8
Number of runs	100	100	100	100	100
Probability of crossover	0.9	0.9	0.9	0.9	0.9
Probability of mutation	0.01	0.01	0.01	0.01	0.01

---

[1] Mastermind is a registered trademark of Pressman Toy Corporation, by agreement with Invicta Toys and Games, Ltd., UK.

[2] These experiments were run on a dual-processor Pentium III 1GHz computer, with 2GB of shared memory available.

Table 2. Tested combinations of settings for messyGA algorithm [2] [4].

Parameters	STD	OPT1	OPT2	OPT3
Maximum era	3	3	3	3
Probability of cut	0.02	0.02	0.02	0.02
Probability of splice	1.0	1.0	1.0	1.0
Probability of allelic mut.	0.00	0.01	0.01	0.01
Probability of genic mut.	0.00	0.01	0.01	0.01
Thresholding	0	0	0	1
Tiebreaking	0	0	0	1
Reduced initial pop.	1	0	0	0
Extra pop. members	0	0	0	0
Copies	10, 1, 1	1, 1, 1	10, 1, 1	10, 1, 1
Total generations	100, 100, 100	100, 100, 100	100, 100, 100	100, 100, 100
Juxtapositional popsize	100, 100, 100	100, 100, 100	100, 100, 100	100, 100, 100

Results. We can see in Fig. 1 that GAUGE has a similar behaviour to the simple GA, across all individual lengths (this behaviour was also visible across all population sizes). This shows that GAUGE does not suffer a performance loss from its genotype to phenotype mapping. We can also see that the messyGA with the STD settings has a lower performance than both the simple GA and GAUGE, and its performance gets worse relative to those two systems with longer strings.

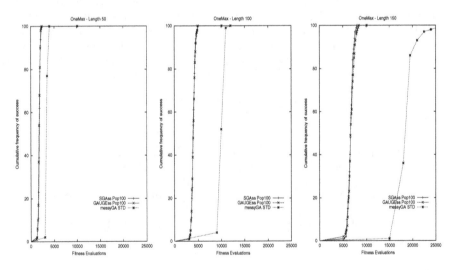

Fig. 1. Results for onemax problem.

4.2   Mastermind – A Deceptive Ordering Version

In the original Mastermind game, one player is the *codebreaker* and tries to deduce a hidden configuration of four coloured pins, set by the *codemaker*, by having a maximum of ten guesses at it. The pins come in six different colours. Each guess has a score of black and white markers, a black marker indicating that one of the pins has the right colour and is in the right position, and a white marker indicating that a pin has the right colour, but is badly placed. More information can be found online at [10]. There have been some attemps at applying genetic algorithms to solve this game [1].

Some deceptive ordering problems have been defined in earlier work (check [7] and [8] for examples), and with similarities to Mastermind. We wanted, however, a problem with the following characteristics:

- easy to implement and quick to evaluate;
- easy to scale difficulty;
- defined search space with local optima;
- illustrates the ordering performance of algorithms.

Our version of Mastermind is therefore slightly different. First of all, we work with numbers to represent colours, and the information available to the *codebreaker* is somewhat reduced. When a combination of pins is to be evaluated, it receives one point for each pin that has the right colour, and if all pins are in the correct order then an additional fitness point is attributed - in other words, information about the correct placement of pins is only given if the whole string is correct. Some examples are shown in Table 3.

There is a deceptive aspect to this problem. If an individual is composed of all the correct pins but in the wrong order, it has reached a local optimum; since at least two pins are wrongly placed, then the global optimum is always at least at a hamming distance of two from every local optimum (since at least two values will need to be changed).

There is a good degree of control over the size and shape of the search space. By recalling combinatorial notions, we see that the size of the search space (i.e. all possible combinations of p pins using c colours) is given by c^p.

Table 3. Examples of evaluation of individuals using the Mastermind fitness function.

Solution: 3 2 1 3	
Individual	Fitness
0 2 1 0	2 points
0 1 2 0	2 points
2 1 2 0	2 points
3 1 2 0	3 points
3 1 2 3	4 points
3 2 1 3	5 points

We can also calculate the number of local optima by using the formula:

$$\frac{p!}{\prod_{i=0}^{n}(x_i)!}$$

where

n = number of colours in solution

x_i = number of times colour i appears in solution

Results. We start by comparing GAUGE to an ordinary GA. To avoid redudant encoding in the simple GA, we used only cases of four and eight colours (encoded by two and three bits per codon, respectively). All the different GA settings (as described in Table 1) were again tested, but using the mentioned bits per codon to encode colours with the simple GA. We then used combinations with four, six, eight and ten pins for each number of colours. The solutions used for each combination are shown in Table 4, and were created using random strings of numbers from 0 to c, from which the first p elements were extracted.

Our results showed GAs with generational replacement behaved better with small population sizes, whereas steady-state GAs worked better with larger ones. We also tested the statistical significance of the performance of GAUGE and the GAs using steady-state, on the average fitness and best fitness across all runs using a student t-test, and a bootstrap test for confirmation.

The results showed GAUGE outperforming all GA flavours across all the experiments, with a statistically significant difference on the majority of the experiments; table 5 shows the percentage of successful runs, after 25000 evaluations, for SGAss and GAUGE, with all population sizes, on the tested combinations of colours and pins. Example results for 4 colours, 8 pins, are shown in Fig. 2, with population sizes 100 and 800. These graphs plot the number of fitness function calls versus the cumulative frequency of success of 100 different runs.

We then moved onto comparing the messyGA with GAUGE, and GAUGE again outperformed the messyGA accross all its settings (as shown in Table 2). However, since the messyGA encodes positions for bits, whereas GAUGE encodes positions for values (which can directly represent colours), this gives GAUGE an

Table 4. Solutions used across all systems for each colours/pins combination.

4 Colours, 4 pins	3 2 1 3
4 Colours, 6 pins	3 2 1 3 1 3
4 Colours, 8 pins	3 2 1 3 1 3 2 0
4 Colours, 10 pins	3 2 1 3 1 3 2 0 1 1
8 Colours, 4 pins	7 6 1 3
8 Colours, 6 pins	7 6 1 3 1 7
8 Colours, 8 pins	7 6 1 3 1 7 2 4
8 Colours, 10 pins	7 6 1 3 1 7 2 4 1 5

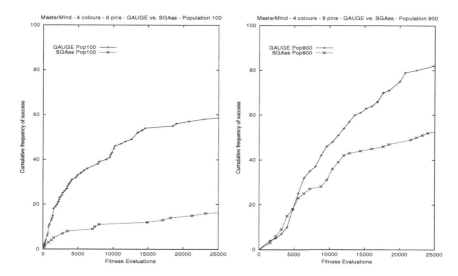

Fig. 2. Simple GA vs. GAUGE, MASTERMIND with 4 colours, 8 pins.

advantage. We therefore devised a new version of GAUGE (which we shall refer to as GAUGE1BIT) to encode positions for bits, rather than for full values, and compared both systems.

GAUGE1BIT showed a better performance than all the messyGA settings, as can be seen in Fig. 3, which shows the cumulative frequency of success of 100 runs plotted against the number of function calls. Table 6 shows the percentage of successful runs after 25000 evaluations, for all combinations of colours and pins tested. We noticed that allelic and genic mutation seemed to increase the performance of the messyGA, and setting OPT3, with thresholding and tiebreaking enabled, had a slightly better performance than all other messyGA settings.

Table 5. Percentage of successful runs after 25000 evaluations, for SGAss and GAUGE, for all tested combinations of colours/pins, across all population sizes.

Population size:		SGAss						GAUGE					
		50	100	200	400	800	1600	50	100	200	400	800	1600
4colours	4 pins	96%	100%	100%	100%	100%	100%	100%	100%	100%	100%	100%	100%
4colours	6 pins	59%	87%	99%	100%	100%	100%	100%	100%	100%	100%	100%	100%
4colours	8 pins	11%	16%	26%	32%	52%	63%	45%	58%	81%	83%	82%	79%
4colours	10 pins	0%	2%	2%	9%	11%	6%	14%	20%	20%	21%	24%	17%
8colours	4 pins	43%	64%	83%	97%	99%	100%	95%	100%	100%	100%	100%	100%
8colours	6 pins	8%	18%	44%	74%	86%	96%	74%	94%	99%	100%	100%	100%
8colours	8 pins	0%	2%	0%	2%	2%	6%	7%	15%	16%	14%	10%	6%
8colours	10 pins	0%	0%	0%	0%	0%	0%	1%	1%	0%	1%	0%	0%

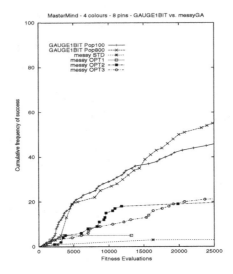

Fig. 3. GAUGE1BIT vs. messyGA, MASTERMIND with 4 colours, 8 pins.

5   Discussion

The results reported for the onemax problem show that GAUGE is a system that works. It performs no worse than a simple GA for that problem, showing that it doesn't suffer a performance loss from its genotype to phenotype mapping, or from its position-independence implementation. Moreover, no significant computational effort is required, due to the use of a simple three rule grammar.

Regarding the Mastermind results, they show an encouraging performance from GAUGE. Either encoding the position of values (directly transformed in colours) or encoding bits (later combined to form colours), GAUGE outperformed all other systems analysed, across a range of increasingly difficult com-

Table 6. Percentage of successful runs after 25000 evaluations, comparing all tested settings of messyGA with GAUGE1BIT, for all combinations of colours/pins.

		messyGA				GAUGE1BIT	
Setting:		STD	OPT1	OPT2	OPT3	Pop100	Pop800
4colours	4 pins	73%	72%	94%	97%	100%	100%
4colours	6 pins	41%	41%	81%	96%	100%	100%
4colours	8 pins	3%	5%	19%	21%	45%	55%
4colours	10 pins	1%	1%	7%	4%	6%	6%
8colours	4 pins	27%	27%	50%	84%	88%	100%
8colours	6 pins	6%	8%	21%	22%	22%	56%
8colours	8 pins	1%	0%	0%	0%	0%	0%
8colours	10 pins	0%	0%	0%	0%	0%	0%

binations of colours and pins, thus managing to escape the deception of local optima. Moreover, this was achieved without any parameter tunning, and the results were only limited by the number of fitness function calls. It would be interesting to increase that number, and see how far GAUGE can go.

6   Conclusions and Future Work

One of the known downfalls of genetic algorithms is the lack of position speci-fication, which leads to convergence to local optima on ordering problems. By applying the principles behind Grammatical Evolution, we have established a new system, GAUGE. With its genotype/phenotype distinction, position/value separation, and small overhead processing required, GAUGE was successful on both a typical GA benchmark, Onemax, and a new deceptive problem introduced in this paper, Mastermind.

Further work will involve testing GAUGE on other problems, from harder versions of Mastermind (to test scalability) to linkage problems, and comparing GAUGE to other more recent and complex competent genetic algorithms.

References

1. Bernier, J. L., Ilia Herraiz, C. Merelo, J. J., Olmeda, S., Prieto, A. 1996. Solving MasterMind using GAs and simulated annealing: a case of dynamic constraint optimization. In Proceedings PPSN, Parallel Problem Solving from Nature IV, LNCS 1141, pp. 554-563. Springer-Verlag.
2. Deb, K., Goldberg, D. E. 1991. mGA in C: A Messy Genetic Algorithm in C. Illinois Genetic Algorithms Laboratory (IlliGAL), report no. 91008.
3. Goldberg, David E. 1989. Genetic Algorithms in Search, Optimization and Ma-chine Learning. Addison Wesley.
4. Goldberg, D. E., Deb, K., and Korb, B. 1991. Don't worry, be messy. In Proceedings of the Fourth International Conference on Genetic Algorithms (San Mateo, CA), R. Belew and L. Booker, Eds., Morgan Kaufman, pp. 24-30
5. Holland, J. H. 1975. Adaptation in Natural and Artificial Systems. Ann Arbor, MI: University of Michigan Press.
6. IlliGAL website. http://www-illigal.ge.uiuc.edu/.
7. Kargupta, H., Deb, K., Goldberg, D. E. 1992. Ordering genetic algorithms and deceptions. In Parallel Problem Solving from Nature - PPSN II (pp. 47-56).
8. Knjazew, D., and Goldberg, D. E. 2000. OMEGA - Ordering Messy GA : Solving Problems with the Fast Messy Genetic Algorithm and Random Keys. In GECCO-2000: Proceedings of the Genetic and Evolutionary Computation Conference, Mor-gan Kaufman, pp. 181-188
9. Koza, J. 1992. Genetic Programming. MIT Press.
10. Nelson, T. 1999. Investigations into the Master Mind Board Game. Website: http://www.tnelson.demon.co.uk/mastermind/index.html.
11. O'Neill M., Ryan C. 2001. Grammatical Evolution. IEEE Trans. Evolutionary Computation Vol. 5 No. 4, August 2001.
12. Ryan C., Collins J.J., O'Neill M. 1998. Grammatical Evolution: Evolving Pro-grams for an Arbitrary Language. LNCS 1391, Proceedings of the First European Workshop on Genetic Programming, pages 83-95. Springer-Verlag.

A Brute-Force Approach to Automatic Induction of Machine Code on CISC Architectures

Felix Kühling, Krister Wolff, and Peter Nordin

Chalmers Technical University, Physical Resource Theory, S-412 96 Göteborg, Sweden

Abstract. The usual approach to address the brittleness of machine code in evolution is to constrain mutation and crossover to ensure syntactic closure. In the novel approach presented here we use no constraints on the operators. They all work blindly on the binaries in memory but we instead encapsulate the code and trap all resulting exceptions using the built-in error reporting mechanisms which modern CPUs provide to the operating system. Thus it is possible to return to very simple genetic operators with the objective of increased performance. Furthermore the instruction set used by evolved programmes is no longer limited by the genetic programming system but only by the CPU it runs on. The mapping between the evolution platform and the execution platform becomes almost complete, ensuring correct low-level behaviour of all CPU functions.

1 Introduction

Automatic induction of machine code refers to the generation of machine code programmes using genetic programming techniques, where the machine programme itself is interpreted as the linear genome. This method was first developed on RISC architectures [12] with fixed instruction length which makes the implementation straightforward. It was later extended to CISC architectures [13] with variable instruction length using sophisticated techniques to ensure that genetic operators cannot compromise the integrity of the generated machine programmes. On the other hand modern CPUs have built-in mechanisms for detecting errors and reporting them to the operating system. The idea here is to make the genetic operators as simple as possible and leave the error checking to the CPU. Syntactic correctness of programmes is then just one additional fitness criterion. Apart from performance issues this approach can potentially use all the capabilities of the underlying CPU as opposed to previous approaches.

Even syntactically correct programmes can cause damage to other processes in a multi-tasking environment, the file system or even the hardware. Therefore it is necessary to provide a secure environment for evolved programmes which isolates them from the rest of the system. Our first approach was to write a small operating system that would run on a dedicated machine for hosting evolved programmes, but we decided to use an existing multi-tasking OS, *Linux*, which provides a stable and well tested memory and IO protection scheme. However, it was still necessary to prevent evolved programmes from accessing the file system,

J.A. Foster et al. (Eds.): EuroGP 2002, LNCS 2278, pp. 288–297, 2002.

network and other operating system services such as memory management or inter-process communication.

In this paper we will first introduce the implementation of a genetic programming system which takes the approach described above, explain how it ensures that evolved programmes cannot compromise the system stability and briefly describe the evolutionary algorithm. Then we will present a classification problem, which has been used to test the genetic programming system and compare the performance of our system to that of an existing one, using the "traditional" way of machine code genetic programming. The aim is to have a proof of concept showing that our approach to genetic programming is efficient in principle, though there remains much room for improvements.

2   Method

As mentioned in the introduction our machine code genetic programming system is based on Linux. The idea is to have the evolved programmes run in a separate process from the one controlling the evolution. Subsequently the two processes will be referred to as *master* and *slave*. Errors in the slave process will be handled by the master.

The following problems have to be solved in order to have the slave process safely execute evolved programmes:

- hide other code like shared libraries from the evolved programmes in order to limit the executed code to the evolved one and to guarantee reproducible runs
- prevent evolved programmes from accessing operating system services
- transfer evolved programmes and data between the master and slave processes
- handle errors of the slave process in the master
- determine the execution time of evolved programmes
- limit the execution time of evolved programmes

The following subsections describe technical details of a mechanism that addresses all these problems.

2.1   Slave Process Setup

Figure 1 gives an overview of the slave-startup procedure. The idea is to start a slave process only once and then use it to execute all evolved programmes whose fitness has to be evaluated. This eliminates the overhead of starting one new process for each fitness evaluation.

First the master allocates a shared memory segment that will be shared by master and slave process. It will contain the evolved programmes, any data and some space for a stack.

Then a new child process, the slave is created. It first installs signal handlers for SIGUSR1 and SIGUSR2 which will be used to check whether the master can

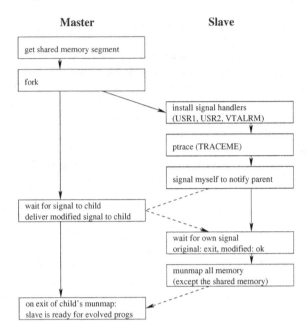

Fig. 1. Slave-startup procedure

really control the slave and **SIGVTALRM** which can be used to limit the runtime of the slave.

Then it calls **ptrace(PTRACE_TRACEME)** in order to allow the master to control it via the **ptrace** system call. This is an interface intended for debuggers. It allows the master to access the slave's registers and to gain control whenever the slave receives a signal or issues a system call. The master can hide a signal from the slave or deliver a modified signal. On system calls the master is notified on entry and exit.

In order to notify the master, the slave sends a **SIGUSR1** to itself. Now the master gains control, delivers **SIGUSR2** to the slave and returns control to it asking for notification about system calls at the same time. If the slave receives an unmodified **SIGUSR1** it assumes that something failed and exits.

Otherwise it goes on using the **munmap** system call in order to unmap all memory except the shared memory segment from its address space. On exit from the system call the return address is no longer accessible since it is inside the address space which has just been unmapped. Therefore the slave relies on the master taking control of its execution. This happens as the slave is stopped on exit from the system call before it returns from the kernel to the unmapped user address space.

2.2 Executing a System Call in the Slave

It will be necessary for the master to make system calls in the context of the slave process. The procedure is described here once and will be referred to later.

System calls transfer control to kernel address space, which is not directly accessible for normal programmes, in order to use operating system services. In Linux on a x86 compatible machine this is done by executing a "int $0x80" instruction. The system call number and parameters are passed in the CPU registers.

In order to make a system call in the slave process's context, ptrace is used to copy the system call number and parameters into the slave's register set. The "int $0x80" instruction followed by "int $3" is copied to the beginning of the shared memory. In order to have this executed by the slave its instruction pointer is set to the start of the shared memory segment before having it resume execution. The "int $3" instruction, which is intended for debuggers for setting breakpoints, will cause a SIGTRAP signal to be sent to the slave, which will return control to the master.

For system calls which accept or return data in memory, referenced by a pointer in a register, that memory must be in the slave process's address space. Using the shared memory for this eliminates the necessity of copying data between the slave's and the master's address space. The error status of the system call is returned in the register %eax. It is read by the master using ptrace and returned as if the system call was performed in the master itself.

2.3 Preparing to Run a Programme

Before starting an evolved programme in the slave we set up a timer, which will interrupt the slave, when it runs longer than up to a certain deadline. This is done by calling the setitimer system call from within the slave process as described above. Because of the low resolution of the Linux timer and for the performance impact of the extra control transfer to the slave, it is often useful, to set a deadline once, limiting the accumulated runtime of the evaluation of several fitness cases.

Then the programme and any data is copied into the shared memory segment and all the remaining shared memory is cleared. The registers can be used to pass parameters to the evolved programme as well. The segment registers, stack pointer, instruction pointer and certain flags cannot be specified by the user. The stack pointer is always set to the end of the shared memory segment, since the stack grows to lower addresses. The instruction pointer is set to the beginning.

2.4 Running a Programme

Now the slave process is allowed to resume execution with the master being notified when the slave receives a signal or makes a system call. The signal can be either an error indication (SIGSEGV, SIGILL), a normal exit through "int $3" (SIGTRAP) or a timer.

2.5   Getting the Results

Results returned in the shared memory do not need any special treatment. The registers are read using `ptrace`. The time spent running a programme can be determined by calling the `getrusage` system call from the slave.

2.6   Population Initialisation

We have tried three different methods for initialising the population, (1) random instructions from a very limited instruction set which uses only registers, (2) a sequence of random, but syntactically correct integer instructions, using all addressing modes with jump offsets and memory references bounded to the shared memory segment and (3) random bytes. Note that this refers only to the initial programmes. Evolution can and will "invent" other instructions and addressing modes.

2.7   The Evolutionary Algorithm

The evolutionary algorithm is a steady state tournament of size four. In each step the winners of two competitions are allowed to generate two offsprings overwriting the losers. Reproduction is achieved by two-point string crossover. With 50% probability one child is mutated by replacing one byte with a new random byte.

3   Experiments

The evolutionary system was tested on a classification problem which has been previously studied using *Discipulus* and a connectionist machine learning approach. Discipulus is a machine learning software that uses the AIM-GP approach described in [13] on a x86 architecture. The following quote is taken from the data set's *.names*-file.

1. Title: Pima Indians Diabetes Database
2. Sources:
   a) Original owners: National Institute of Diabetes and Digestive and Kidney Diseases
   b) Donor of database: Vincent Sigillito (vgs@aplcen.apl.jhu.edu) Research Center, RMI Group Leader Applied Physics Laboratory The Johns Hopkins University Johns Hopkins Road Laurel, MD 20707 (301) 953-6231
   c) Date received: 9 May 1990
3. Past Usage: [...]
   Results: Their ADAP algorithm makes a real-valued prediction between 0 and 1. This was transformed into a binary decision using a cutoff of 0.448. Using 576 training instances, the sensitivity and specificity of their algorithm was 76% on the remaining 192 instances.

4. Relevant Information: [...]
5. Number of Instances: 768
6. Number of Attributes: 8 plus class
7. For Each Attribute: (all numeric-valued)
   (1) Number of times pregnant, (2) Plasma glucose concentration a 2 hours in an oral glucose tolerance test, (3) Diastolic blood pressure [mm Hg], (4) Triceps skin fold thickness [mm], (5) 2-Hour serum insulin [mu U/ml], (6) Body mass index [weight in kg/(height in m)^2], (7) Diabetes pedigree function, (8) Age [years], (9) Class variable [0 or 1]
8. Missing Attribute Values: None
9. Class Distribution: (class value 1 is interpreted as "tested positive for diabetes") Class 0: 500, Class 1: 268
10. Brief statistical analysis: [...]

3.1 Data Preparation for the Integer ALU

Input values were passed to the evolved programmes through the CPU registers. Due to the limited number of available registers some attributes had to be left out. In order to include all relevant values several training runs were performed in Discipulus looking at which input attributes were used by good solutions. Finally attributes 1-3 and 6-8 were included and written into %eax, %ebx, %ecx, %esi, %edi, %ebp. The stack pointer %esp and %edx were not used, the latter one, because it is overwritten as a side effect of most multiplication and division instructions.

Some of the attributes are obviously real numbers. In order to represent them properly in integer registers they were multiplied with 65536 before converting them to integers. This way they were converted to a *fixed point* format with 16 bits integer and 16 bits fractional part, which can be handled by the integer unit.

3.2 The Fitness Function

The fitness function averages fitness values of single fitness cases. If a programme runs without errors for a fitness case its fitness value is the absolute distance from the target value plus an extra punishment for misclassification. The target value is 0 for class 0 and 65536, the equivalent of "1" in the fixed-point encoding, for class 1. The punishment for misclassification is 65536. If a programme was terminated due to an error, its fitness is the worst possible fitness of a correct programme. Since one deadline was used for the accumulated runtime of all fitness cases, an expired deadline is treated like a programme error for this and all the remaining fitness cases, which have not been and will not be evaluated.

3.3 Other Settings

The population's size was 1000 individuals. The length of the genome was allowed to vary between 32 and 256 bytes. The cumulative deadline was set to $\frac{1}{100}$ s which corresponds to Linux's timer resolution. One run consisted of 100,000 tournaments. With each of the three population initialisation methods described in Sect. 2.6 ten runs were performed.

For comparison ten runs with Discipulus were performed on the same data. In order to make the comparison as fair as possible the following settings were chosen: population size 1000, maximum programme length 256, crossover frequency 100%, mutation frequency 50%, homologous crossover 0%, DSS off, maximum number of tournaments 100,000.

3.4 Performance Test

As a performance test one programme, which terminates immediately was executed repeatedly for 10 million times without applying any genetic operators, setting a deadline or determining the runtime. In order to find out how much time is due to task switches and system calls which set the slave's registers, and control its execution, another run was performed with all these system calls left out. The experiment was conducted on an AMD Duron 1 GHz.

4 Results

The final fitness in terms of the validation hit rate at the end of the runs ranged from 61.5% to 73.4%. Table 1 shows the results for the different initialisation methods. Figs. 2 and 3 show the development of the average fitness, training and validation hit rate during the evolution in different cases.

In the performance test the empty programme was started 10 million times consuming 34.53 s user and 30.57 s system time. Thus, the maximum number of evaluations of single fitness cases is limited to $\frac{10,000,000}{65.1\,\mathrm{s}} \approx 150,000\,\frac{1}{\mathrm{s}}$. The run without system calls took 14.86 s user and 0.03 s system time. This would result in approximately $650,000\,\frac{1}{\mathrm{s}}$.

5 Discussion

With all initialisation methods it was possible to get a validation hit rate of more than 70%, comparable to the best result of Discipulus. The small difference may be because Discipulus uses the floating point instruction set which provides much more sophisticated functions like *square root* and trigonometric functions. With different settings, homologous crossover and longer runs final validation hit rates of up to 76% could be reached with Discipulus. Therefore it seems probable that our results can be improved by fine tuning the evolutionary algorithm, as well.

The fraction of runs with final validation hit rate over 70% was however different with different initialisation methods. The best results in these terms were achieved after initialising the population with programmes consisting of a large integer instruction set. We shall note here that there is a significant difference between this method and purely random initialisation, which may not be

Table 1. Experiment Results

# runs with final validation HR (hit rate)	Small Instruction Set	Large Instruction Set	Random	Discipulus
= 61.5%	0	1	1	0
≤ 70%	7	4	7	6
> 70%	3	5	2	4
Initial training HR	66.3 – 70.5%	00.0 – 66.3%	66.3 – 66.7%	62.5 – 67.7%
Initial validation HR	00.6 – 71.4%	00.0 – 61.5%	61.5 – 61.5%	59.9 – 61.5%
Final training HR	67.0 – 72.9%	66.3 – 74.3%	68.2 – 74.1%	71.1 – 77.8%
Final validation HR	62.0 – 73.4%	61.5 – 72.9%	61.5 – 71.9%	62.5 – 74.5%

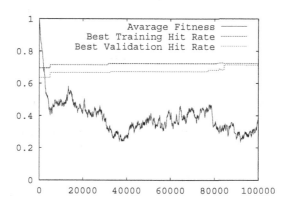

Fig. 2. Average fitness, training and validation hit rate over 100,000 tournaments with the small initial instruction set. Note that fitness is not identical to hit rate (see Sect. 3.2). The scale for the average fitness is $\times 1.5 \cdot 10^9$

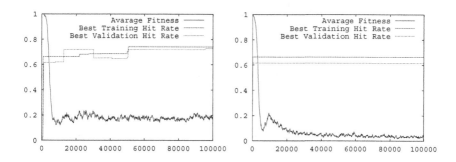

Fig. 3. Average fitness, training and validation hit rate over 100,000 tournaments with the large initial instruction set. The scale for the average fitness is $\times 2.15 \cdot 10^9$. The RHS plot indicates a trivial solution (see Sect. 5)

obvious at first sight. Random initialisation will favour one-byte opcodes, since there are only few one-byte values reserved as first byte of multi-byte opcodes. Furthermore the use of registers is preferred since there are some frequently used instructions which encode one register operand in the opcode itself.

With random and small instruction set initialisation the best hit rate starts at 61.5% or even above in most runs. This means that there is at least one correct programme in the initial population. Since we often encountered the same initial hit rate of 61.5% it is reasonable to assume that this is a trivial solution which classifies all instances into the larger class 0. After initialising the population with a large instruction set the starting hit rate was zero in most cases. Almost all programmes produced errors since most addressing modes use a base or index register giving a high probability of accessing unmapped addresses.

It is not surprising that the average fitness starts at a much higher value with random and large instruction set initialisation than with the small instruction set. In the first two cases memory accesses are possible, which can potentially access unmapped addresses causing SIGSEGV exceptions. During the first 10,000 tournaments the average fitness value decreases rapidly indicating that most incorrect programmes are removed from the population. After that it exhibits rather large fluctuations around 4×10^8 which can be explained by the destructiveness of the genetic operators and the hard punishment for programme errors. It is however striking that the average fitness becomes much smaller in the runs which produce only the trivial solution with 61.5% validation hit rate (see Fig. 3). This indicates that the population adapts to the destructiveness of the genetic operators rather than solving the problem. Such an adaptation could be to use mainly single-byte instructions, which cannot be damaged by the crossover operator.

The overhead revealed by the performance test means that one programme execution involves about 6666 CPU cycles. As the run without system calls shows, about 75% of that time are spent in library functions or the kernel which is out of the scope of optimisation in our source code. On the other hand, considering that each programme execution in the slave process requires two task switches on a single processor machine the results are even surprisingly good, and given the performance speed-up of machine code GP it is still a very efficient system.

6   Future Work

Powerful parts of the instruction set have not been used at all so far, namely floating point and MMX/3DNow/SSE instructions. The latter ones are particularly interesting since a single instruction can operate on multiple data words. They are usually not used by higher level language compilers. The use of these instruction sets would have to be encouraged by including them in the initial instruction set and passing arguments and results through the floating point, MMX or SSE registers.

7   Summary

A novel approach to automatic induction of machine code on CISC architectures was presented, which uses the error checking mechanisms of modern CPUs in order to ensure the correctness of generated machine programmes. This way it is possible to return to very simple genetic operators with the advantage of increased performance. Furthermore the instruction set used by evolved programmes is no longer limited by the genetic programming system but only by the CPU it runs on. The mapping between the evolution platform and the execution platform becomes almost complete, ensuring correct low-level behaviour of all CPU functions. An example implementation based on Linux was introduced showing the applicability of the approach on a standard classification task.

References

1. Advanced Micro Devices: 3DNow!^{TM} Technology Manual (2000). http://www.amd.com/us-en/Processors/DevelopWithAMD/0,,30_2252_739_1102,00.html
2. Advanced Micro Devices: AMD Extensions to the 3DNow!^{TM} and MMX^{TM} Instruction Sets – Manual (2000). http://www.amd.com/us-en/Processors/DevelopWithAMD/0,,30_2252_739_1102,00.html
3. Aivazian, T., Hellwig, C., Weight, R. and Cao, M.: Linux Kernel 2.4 Internals (2001). http://www.linuxdoc.org/LDP/lki/index.html
4. Banzhaf, W., Nordin, P., Keller, R. E. and Francone, F. D.: Genetic Programming – An Introduction. On The Automatic Evolution Of Computer Programs and its Applications (1998). Morgan Kaufmann, San Francisco, USA and dpunkt, Heidelberg, Germany.
5. Brumm, P., Brumm, D., Scanlon and J.: 80486 Programming (1991). Windcrest, Blue Ridge Summit, Pa., USA
6. Crawford, J. H. and Gelsinger, P. P.: Programming the 80386 (1987). SYBEX, San Francisco, USA
7. Dunlap, R.: Linux 2.4.x Initialization for IA-32 HOWTO (2001). http://www.linuxdoc.org/HOWTO/Linux-Init-HOWTO.html
8. Goldt, S., van der Meer, S., Burkett, S. and Welsh, M.: The Linux Programmer's Guide (1995). http://www.linuxdoc.org/LDP/lpg/index.html
9. Intel Corporation: IA-32 Intel Architecture Software Developer's Manual (2001). http://developer.intel.com/design/pentium4/manuals/245470.htm
10. Johnson, M. K., Rubini, A. and Scalsky, S.: Linux Kernel Hacker's Guide (1997). http://www.linuxdoc.org/LDP/khg/HyperNews/get/khg.html
11. Loosemore S., Stallman, R. M., McGrath, R., Oram, A. and Drepper U.: The GNU C Library Reference Manual (1999), Free Software Foundation, Boston, USA
12. Nordin, P.: Evolutionary Program Induction of Binary Machine Code and its Application (1997). Krehl Verlag, Münster, Germany.
13. Nordin, P., Banzhaf, W., Francone, F. D.: Efficient Evolution of Machine Code for CISC Architectures Using Instruction Blocks and Homologous Crossover (1999). In Advances in Genetic Programming, Volume 3, L. Spector, W. B. Langdon, U.-M. O'Reilly, P. J. Angeline (ed.), pp. 275-299.

Deriving Genetic Programming Fitness Properties by Static Analysis

Colin G. Johnson

Computing Laboratory.
University of Kent at Canterbury.
Canterbury, Kent, CT2 7NF, England.
C.G.Johnson@ukc.ac.uk

Abstract. The aim of this paper is to introduce the idea of using *static analysis* of computer programs as a way of measuring fitness in genetic programming. Such techniques extract information about the programs without explicitly running them, and in particular they infer properties which hold across the whole of the input space of a program. This can be applied to measure fitness, and has a number of advantages over measuring fitness by running members of the population on test cases. The most important advantage is that if a solution is found then it is possible to formally trust that solution to be correct across all inputs. This paper introduces these ideas, discusses various ways in which they could be applied, discusses the type of problems for which they are appropriate, and ends by giving a simple test example and some questions for future research.

1 Introduction

Genetic programming (GP) [2,11] is concerned with the application of evolutionary algorithms to the evolution of program code. In order to apply evolutionary methods a notion of solution quality (fitness) is needed. Traditionally GP and related techniques have used performance measures on sets of test data as a way of measuring the quality of solutions. However this leads to a number of problems, in particular programs can become overspecialized to their training set and they cannot be (formally) trusted to perform correctly beyond that training set.

This paper discusses the prospects for applying various kinds of static program analysis techniques to this problem. A background section describes these ideas and gives some motivating examples, then two further sections outline reasons why these techniques are potentially useful in genetic programming, and how they can be so applied. A simple example is implemented, and the paper concludes by summarizing these ideas and suggesting a number of questions for future research.

2 Background

Static analysis [16] is a set of techniques which provide information about a program and how it will behave once run, without actually running the program.

J.A. Foster et al. (Eds.): EuroGP 2002, LNCS 2278, pp. 298–307, 2002.

In particular static analysis techniques are able to provide information about program behaviour across the whole of the input space of the program, rather than providing information for a particular test case. A number of different kinds of information can be gained by carrying out different kinds of static analysis, e.g.:

- constraint information about relationships between variables [6]
- information about the extreme values which a variable could possibly take at each point in the execution of a program [4]
- usage information about whether facts vital to the solution of a problem have been used
- complexity information, e.g. the number of potential paths through a piece of code [15]
- performance information [17,21]

As a toy example consider the following fragment of pseudocode (all variables are integers):

```
x = 0;
read y;
z = y+20;
if (y<10)
   for (i=0;i<y;i++)
      x += 2;
```

At the end of the first line it can be seen that x must equal 0. By the end of the fragment, it must be at least 0 and at most 20. The variable z must be greater than y by the end of line 3. All this information can be inferred by systematically tracking the extreme values that variables can possibly take at each line in the program. This process can be automated.

3   Why Should We Apply Static Analysis to Genetic Programming?

GP has proven to be a powerful technique for the solution of problems from a large number of domains. However there are a number of difficulties with GP, in particular relating to the measurement of fitness. The power of GP comes from being able to produce programs which are able to solve a parameterized space of problems. In order to assess the fitness of a member of the population, it is traditional to run the program on a number of test cases, and use the accuracy of the output as the fitness measure.

The first problem with this method of measuring fitness is that it gives no formal assurance that the program will operate on data outside of the test set. Moreover the programs generated by GP are typically incomprehensible to human programmers, so informal *post hoc* analysis of the programs is impossible. Measures of fitness derived from static analysis could be used to ensure that the results will be applicable across the whole of the input space.

Also this may lead to new kinds of fitness measures which make specific use of static features of the program which cannot be discovered simply by running the program. An example of this would be the use of cyclomatic complexity [15] as a component of a fitness measure, which measures the complexity of programs by calculating the number of routes through the code.

Another important problem with GP is that the programs generated can be overfitted to the training data used. Experimental evidence for this is given e.g. by Paterson and Livesey [20]. If the fitness of members of the population is created using measures which apply to the whole of the input space, this problem is removed.

There are also ways in which these techniques could improve the performance of GP itself as well as eliminating problems with existing GP techniques, for example it may be the case that a static analysis may be quicker to perform than running a complex program on many test cases.

Also these concepts have the potential to expand the range of problems which can be tackled using GP. Many problems solved by GP are of the form in which a small sample of inputs gives results which give us confidence about the remainder of the input space. Consider the evolution of high-pass and low-pass filter circuits [3]. In such a problem is it informally reasonable to say if a random sample of inputs gives a reasonable response, then the response will be reasonable across the frequency range. Related arguments can be made for problems like evolving a range of controllers parameterized by a free variable [12]. However in many applications there are too many variables to do this, or else the relationship between input and output is too complex to generalize in a simple way, and these statements will never be rigourously correct.

The kinds of information that can be generated by the static analysis of programs can be divided into two kinds. The first type is results which say something about the *performance* of the program, e.g. its use of cache memory. Secondly the second type is results which measure the *functioning* of the program itself, e.g. results about bounds on output values.

There are a number of potential difficulties with the application of these techniques. The most significant is that the programmer might not be able to get the information which is required in order to assess fitness by using a static measure. This might be for pragmatic reasons (e.g. not being able to write the fitness function in terms of data which can be obtained from the static analysis tools available), or it may be because the problem is *defined* implicitly in terms of a particular data set. Another problem could be that the time taken to carry out the analysis may make it impractical; however for most simple analysis techniques this does not seem to be a problem.

4   Ways in Which Static Analysis Can Be Applied

There are a number of ways in which these ideas might be applied. The applicability of these different techniques is likely to be problem dependent. Three ideas are detailed in this paper.

4.1   Using Multicriterion Optimization to Combine Test-Driven and Static Fitness Aspects

For some problems some characteristics of a good program may be measurable using static techniques, whilst other characteristics might only be measurable using testing. This might be because the programmer cannot find an appropriate static measure. Alternatively, it may be because the problem is defined implicitly by data, e.g. certain kinds of function regression problems or the "non-programmed computation" problems discussed by Partridge [19].

In particular static analysis lends itself to measuring *performance* aspects of a solution, e.g. measuring the efficiency of memory usage. Such a static measure of a performance aspect can be factored into the fitness measure for any program.

Therefore the first way in which the two ideas might be combined would be to measure some aspects of the program's fitness statically, and some aspects using a traditional test-data approach. These results would then be combined using one of the many techniques which have been developed for multi-criterion optimization [9]. The simplest such technique is to measure the various fitness characteristics of the programs separately, and then to create a fitness from a weighted sum of the measures, where the weights are given by inverse population averages for that factor, so that the total average contribution for each factor is the same.

Other, more sophisticated, techniques could be used to carry out this multi-criterion optimization. An example is Ryan's [23] "Pygmies and Civil Servants" algorithms, which takes two parent populations, one of which has been selected for each of two criteria, and creates children by recombining pairs from each of the two populations. This could be applied to the situation described above by creating two rankings on the population, one a statically-derived measure and one a measure derived from testing.

An example of the kind of performance characteristics which could be measured statically would be the behaviour of the cache memory (e.g. as described in [1,7,17,21]), the efficient distribution of tasks between a number of parallel processors, or the efficiency of garbage collection in a program.

Another example of this would be in evolving solutions to problems where there is an important safety constraint. Two examples will illustrate this. The first of these is evolving some behaviours for a mobile robot, where it is desirable for safety reasons that the robot be not allowed to leave a particular physical area. A second example is in evolving some control mechanism, where some critical value (like the temperature of a machine) is not allowed to go outside a critical range. In both of these examples there are two components to fitness which need to be combined into a single fitness measure. The first of these is a measure of the success of the solution on the task at hand, which could be measured by running the program on test cases. The second is a measure of the safety of the system, which could be derived from a static analysis of intervals and inequalities [4,5] which the critical value takes whilst the program is running. The inclusion of this second component in the fitness would bias the population towards those solutions which lie within the safe region, and would provide a way of knowing when solutions are within the safe region.

4.2 Improving Existing Programs

A second way in which these ideas could be used is in improving the performance of existing code whilst maintaining functionality. An example of this would be improving memory performance of an existing program by applying static measures of cache performance [1,7,17,21] to the members of the population. The maintenance of functionality would be by ensuring that the only operations performed on the program are the interchange of *basic blocks* [13] within a program (as a kind of mutation operator), functionality preserving exchanges within those blocks (such as the unrolling of loops) [10] and the interchange of functionally-identical basic blocks between programs (as a kind of crossover operator).

4.3 Using Only Static Measures

The ideal application of these ideas would be to problems where the entirety of the fitness can be derived from static measures. In such a case when solutions are found they can be trusted to be correct across the whole of the input space.

Clearly the types of problem for which this could be applied depend on the sort of information that can be obtained via various forms of static analysis. For certain problems fitness can be defined in terms of variables satisfying certain inequalities or falling within certain ranges, and it would be possible to extend this to optimization problems by creating a hierarchy of inequalities. An example of a problem whose fitness can be defined in this way is a "placement problem" like those outlined in section 5 below.

One perspective on this is that this process is producing programs by specifying *guidelines*, and evolving programs which produce outputs which satisfy those guidelines. So for example the user creates a list of inequalities which the various variables in their program must satisfy at the end of the program. The fitness measure counts the number of these inequalities which are satisfied by the end of the program, *regardless* of input values, by techniques such as tracking the extreme values of intervals and tracking whether changes to variables change a list of inequalities associated with that value [5].

5   A Simple Example

The main point of this paper has been to discuss the type of problems which can be tackled using this approach rather than to give specific examples. However to finish we shall give a report on some preliminary experiments in which we have implemented a simple example which illustrates these ideas.

The example is a 2-dimensional "placement problem". Given a number of shapes (rectangles for the purposes of this example) and a number of desired relations between those shapes (e.g. "rectangle A must be completely to the right of rectangle B"), the aim of the algorithm is to find a placement of those shapes on a given background region so that the relations are satisfied. The way in which GP is applied to this problem is to derive a program which will solve that problem, parameterised by the lengths of the various rectangles, but with the relationships being fixed. Note that the aim of this is not to apply evolutionary algorithms to the problem directly (as in e.g. [14]), but to find algorithms which can solve a large space of such problems. These types of problems occur in a number of applications: VLSI layout [14], packing problems, and automated layout of windows on a computer screen [8,22] or widgets within a window. A sample problem is illustrated in figure 1. For small numbers of constraints the problem is trivial, but as more constraints and shapes are added it becomes more difficult.

This problem has been tackled using the GP-like technique of O'Neill and Ryan known as *grammatical evolution* [18]. This uses a BNF grammar to transform a bitstring into a valid program in an arbitrary language, which provides a powerful extension to standard GP. A tableau describing how the grammatical evolution algorithm is applied to this problem is described in table 1.

It is possible to solve this problem using traditional fitness measures, by taking a list of sample cases which satisfy the conditions. However there are a number of problems with this. Firstly there are the problems outlined above; there can be no certainty that the program will work outside our test set, *et cetera*. This is illustrated by attempts to change the size of the space into which the shapes are placed (this could represent placing shapes on a different sized screen, but with the same desired spatial relationships). Also it is difficult to create these test data, so being able to generate the program directly from the constraints is valuable.

For this problem fitness is derived statically in the following way. For each line of the function, a set of data is updated containing information about the relationships between the variables. In this example two pieces of data are tracked: one is the extreme values which the variable values can take, and the other is a boolean variable which tracks whether a variable must be greater than or equal to zero at that point, regardless of which route through the program was used to access that point. The following are examples of the kind of update rules which are used to update the latter variable (space precludes the inclusion of a full list):

- If a positive constant is assigned to the variable, then the "known to be positive or zero" flag for that variable is set to true.
- If the flag is currently true and the variable is incremented by a value (variable or constant) which is itself known to be positive, then the flag remains true.
- If the variable is decremented by a variable about which nothing is known, then the flag is set to false. This illustrates the "conservative" nature of the flag—it is not measuring for certain whether the value is positive/zero at a particular program point, it is measuring whether, regardless of which route the program had taken to reach the current point, it is possible to make the statement at that point.
- If the variable is assigned to a sum of values (constant or variable) which are known to be positive and values to which the absolute value function has been applied, then the flag is true.

It would be possible to add more transformations to the list; however the list can always be finished by saying "in all other cases the value becomes false", i.e. it is always possible to say that no statement is being asserted with confidence at that point. In this way an analyser can be gradually built up by replacing conservative approximations with more concrete statements as the analysis program is improved.

The complete analyser contains a large number of such update rules. At the end of a run of the analyser on a program, a list of conditions is produced which the output from the program must satisfy, regardless of input. These can then be checked for compatibility against the desired conditions. For each condition which is met, the fitness is incremented. In the implementation described here, different kinds of conditions are weighted, so that the fitness function is not swamped by lots of easy-to-satisfy conditions early on.

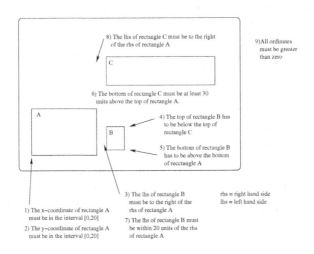

Fig. 1. A sample placement problem.

Results from two sample runs of a test example (showing best fitness and average fitness for a weighted sum of constraints) are presented in figure 2. The two runs have different mutation probabilities. Clearly evolution is working to ensure that more conditions are being rigourously satisfied with time. However three conditions (out of 16) are not satisfied, and these are some of the more complex conditions. What appears to be happening is that evolution is converging on a number of rather short programs which satisfy a reasonable number of conditions, and then crossover cannot work to swap information into these short programs.

Two strategies are being employed to attempt to alleviate this. Firstly explicit length information is being factored into the fitness function. Secondly a fitness function is being developed where the weightings given to each constraint depend on the comparative rarity of the constraint in the population, and this is being

Table 1. Grammatical evolution tableau for a sample placement problem.

Objective.	To find a placement for a number of rectangles, given the length and width of each rectangle, so that they satisfy a set of conditions stated as intervals and inequalities.
Terminal operators	The binary operators $+$, $-$, $\times$, and the unary operators increment, decrement, absolute value.
Terminal operands.	LValues: Position of each rectangle and a number of scratch variables. RValues: Length and width of each rectangle, position of each rectangle, the scratch variables and a number of fixed constant values.
Fitness cases.	The fitness is not measured by running the program on test cases. Instead it is measured by keeping track of the extreme values which variables can take, and keeping track of whether it is possible to say rigourously that variables are positive or negative at each program point, and using these intervals and inequalities to compare with the list of required constraint values.
Raw fitness.	A weighted sum of the number of conditions satisfied by the rectangles in their final position at the end of program execution. Interval conditions are weighted 1, simple inequalities between two variables are weighted 2, and more complicated inequalities are weighted 5.
Wrapper.	C code to transform the list of arithmetic statements into a C function.
Parameters.	Population size = 500, termination after 50 generations, probability of mutation = 0.001 or 0.01 per bit, probability of crossover = 1.0, elitist selection, one point crossover.
Success predicate.	The program can be terminated if all the conditions become satisfied.

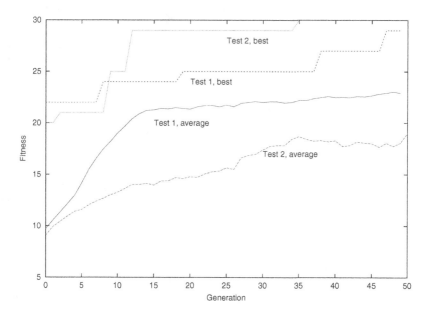

Fig. 2. Two fitness results for a placement problem (test 1: mutation probability 0.001 per bit, test two mutation probability 0.01 per bit).

further emphasized by the use of fitness scaling. Preliminary results from the latter suggest that this is effective in maintaining diversity of constraints satisfied in the population.

6   Conclusions and Research Questions

In this paper we have discussed various ways in which static analysis techniques can be used in genetic programming and related areas. A simple example has been given, however the main piece of future work is to apply these ideas to a broad range of problems and gather detailed information about performance. Another piece of work which would help in applying these methods would be to gather together details about the different types of information which can be gained from different types of static analysis, and bring these together into some common format so that they can be combined into composite fitness measures. Once such a structure is in place it will be easier to get a feel for the range of problems to which these ideas can be applied.

References

1. Martin Alt, Christian Ferdinand, Florian Martin, and Reinhard Wilhelm. Cache behavior prediction by abstract interpretation. In *Static Analysis Symposium 1996*, pages 52–66. Springer, 1996.
2. Wolfgang Banzhaf, Peter Nordin, Robert E. Keller, and Frank D. Francone. *Genetic Programming: An Introduction*. Morgan Kaufmann, 1998.
3. Forrest H Bennett III, Martin A. Keane, David Andre, and John R. Koza. Automatic synthesis of the topology and sizing for analog electrical circuits using genetic programming. In Kaisa Miettinen, Marko M. Mäkelä, Pekka Neittaanmäki, and Jacques Periaux, editors, *Evolutionary Algorithms in Engineering and Computer Science*, pages 199–229, Jyväskylä, Finland, 30 May - 3 June 1999. John Wiley & Sons.
4. P. Cousot. Abstract interpretation: Achievements and perspectives. In *Proceedings of the SSGRR 2000 Computer & eBusiness International Conference*, Compact disk paper 224 and electronic proceedings `http://www.ssgrr.it/en/ssgrr2000/proceedings.htm`, L'Aquila, Italy, July 31 – August 6 2000. Scuola Superiore G. Reiss Romoli.
5. P. Cousot. Abstract interpretation based formal methods and future challenges, invited paper. In R. Wilhelm, editor, *Informatics — 10 Years Back, 10 Years Ahead*, volume 2000 of *Lecture Notes in Computer Science*, pages 138–156. Springer-Verlag, 2001.
6. Patrick Cousot and Nicolas Halbwachs. Automatic discovery of linear restraints among variables of a program. In *Conference Record of the Fifth Annual ACM Symposium on Principles of Programming Languages*, pages 84–96, 1978.
7. Saumya Debray. Resource-bounded partial evaluation. In *Proceedings of the 1997 ACM Symposium on Partial Evaluation and Semantics-Based Program Manipulation (PEPM '97)*, pages 179–192, 1997.
8. Bjørn Freeman-Benson. Converting an existing user interface to use constraints. In *ACM Symposium on User Interface Software and Technology*, pages 207–215, 1993.

9. Jeffery Horn. Multicriterion decision making. In Thomas Bäck, David B. Fogel, and Zbigniew Michalewicz, editors, *Handbook of Evolutionary Computation*, pages F1.9.1–F1.9.15. Oxford University Press / Institute of Physics, 1997.

10. Neil D. Jones, Carsten K. Gomard, and Peter Sestoft. *Partial Evaluation and Automatic Program Generation*. Prentice Hall, 1993.

11. John R. Koza. *Genetic Programming : On the Programming of Computers by means of Natural Selection*. Series in Complex Adaptive Systems. MIT Press, 1992.

12. John R. Koza, Jessen Yu, Martin A. Keane, and William Mydlowec. Evolution of a controller with a free variable using genetic programming. In Riccardo Poli, Wolfgang Banzhaf, William B. Langdon, Julian Miller, Peter Nordin, and Terence C. Fogarty, editors, *Proceedings of the 2000 European Conference on Genetic Programming*, pages 91–105. Springer, 2000. LNCS 1802.

13. James Larus. Whole program paths. In *Programming Language Design and Implementation*, 1999.

14. Pinaki Mazumder and Elizabeth M. Rudnick. *Genetic Algorithms for VLSI Design, Layout and Test Automation*. Prentice-Hall, 1998.

15. Thomas J. McCabe and Charles W. Butler. Design complexity measurement and testing. *Communications of the ACM*, 32(12):1415–1425, 1989.

16. Flemming Nielson, Hanne Riis Nielson, and Chris Hankin. *Principles of Program Analysis*. Springer, 1999.

17. K. D. Nilsen and B. Rygg. Worst-case execution time analysis on modern processors. In *ACM PLDI Workshop on Languages, Compilers and Tools for Real-Time Systems*, 1995.

18. Michael O'Neill and Conor Ryan. Grammatical evolution. *IEEE Transactions on Evolutionary Computation*, 5(4):349–358, August 2001.

19. Derek Partridge. Non-programmed computation. *Communications of the ACM*, 43(11):293–302, 2000.

20. Norman Paterson and Mike Livesey. Evolving caching algorithms in C by genetic programming. In John R. Koza, Kalyanmoy Deb, Marco Dorigo, David B. Fogel, Max H. Garzon, Hitoshi Iba, and Rick L. Riolo, editors, *Genetic Programming 1997: Proceedings of the Second Annual Conference*. Morgan Kaufman, 1997.

21. P. Puchner and Ch. Koza. Calculating the maximum execution time of real-time programs. *Journal of Real-Time Systems*, 1:159–176, 1989.

22. Michael J. Rees. Comparison of user interface design constraints for CGI and java applet web applications. In *Australian World Wide Web Technical Conference*, pages 1–14, 1997.

23. Conor Ryan. Pygmies and civil servants. In Kenneth E. Kinnear, Jr., editor, *Advances in Genetic Programming*, pages 243–263. MIT Press, 1994.

New Results on Fuzzy Regression by Using Genetic Programming

Wolfgang Golubski

University of Siegen
Department of Electrical Engineering and Computer Science
Hölderlinstr. 3, 57068 Siegen, Germany
golubski@informatik.uni-siegen.de

Abstract. In this paper we continue the work on symbolic fuzzy regression problems. That means that we are interested in finding a fuzzy function f, which best matches given data pairs $(\overline{X}_i, \overline{Y}_i)$ $1 \leq i \leq k$ of fuzzy numbers. We use a genetic programming approach for finding a suitable fuzzy function and will present test results about linear, quadratic and cubic fuzzy functions.

1 Introduction

The importance of regression analysis in economy, social sciences and others is well known. The objective of solving a symbolic regression problem is to find an unknown function f which best fits given data (x_i, y_i) $i = 1, \ldots, k$ for a fixed and finite $k \in \mathbb{N}$. With this function f the output y for arbitrary x not belonging to the data set can be estimated. Usually, crisp data pairs are used for regression analysis even if this data comes with uncertainty or imprecision. This way information is being ignored. The genetic programming approach [10] is one of the successful methods to solve regression problems with crisp data pairs.

The aim of this paper is to apply the genetic programming method which uses uncertainty and imprecision of the data in form of fuzzy sets in order to find a suitable fuzzy function which can do work well. In [7] we introduce our genetic programming based approach for fuzzy regression. In extension to [7] we can now present test results on polynomial functions of first, second and third degree.

The paper is structured as follows. In the next section we give a literature review. Then we present some notations. Sect.4 defines the fuzzy regression problem and in the fifth section we present the genetic programming algorithm which is used for finding good fitting functions. Then in Sect.6 we present our test results. The paper is finished with a conclusion and directions of further research in the last section.

2 Fuzzy Regression Literature

In the regression problem we are interesting in finding a fuzzy function f, which best fits the given data $(\overline{X}_i, \overline{Y}_i)$, $i = 1, 2, 3, \ldots, k$, where $\overline{X}_i$ are triangular fuzzy

J.A. Foster et al. (Eds.): EuroGP 2002, LNCS 2278, pp. 308–315, 2002.
© Springer-Verlag Berlin Heidelberg 2002

numbers and $\overline{Y}_i$ are triangular shaped fuzzy numbers, for all i. Because of fuzzy arithmetic (based on the extension principle or on interval arithmetic) we cannot compute a fuzzy function with $f(\overline{X}_i) = \overline{Y}_i$ for all i as in the crisp case. Therefore a genetic programming approach for finding a suitable fuzzy function is used.

Let us now review the fuzzy regression literature. There are numerous papers on fuzzy linear regression (see [5,8,9,13,11] and the references in there) but only a few on non-linear fuzzy regression [15].

In fuzzy non-linear regression most authors were concerned with data of the form $(x_i, \overline{Z}_i)$, $1 \leq i \leq k$, where x_i is crisp (non-fuzzy). They employed neural nets to model the unknown function. The approach in [3,4] to fuzzy non-linear regression is different in that the authors of these papers consider completely fuzzy data. They also searched for an explicit formula for the unknown fuzzy non-linear function, where the neural net approach cannot provide an explicit formula.

In a few papers genetic algorithms and evolutionary programs were used in fuzzy regression. The authors of [12] used a genetic algorithm for classifying input data for fuzzy linear regression. In another paper [14] a genetic algorithm is used to evolve a fuzzy rule system in order to approximate parameters of some unknown function. In some other papers [3,4] the authors present an evolutionary algorithm for linear and non–linear fuzzy regression. Since these papers are more related to our work than all the others mentioned before we briefly describe the algorithm proposed in [3,4].

The algorithm for finding a fuzzy function F which solves the fuzzy regression problem for fuzzy data $(\overline{X}_i, \overline{Y}_i)$, $i = 1, \ldots, k$ consists of two parts. The authors first build a function library. This library consists of different groups of functions which are linear, polynomials of second degree, polynomials of third degree, etc., exponential and logarithmic functions. In the first part an evolutionary algorithm was used to find the best group say polynomial of third degree out of the function library. For this the vertex values of $\overline{X}_i$ and $\overline{Y}_i$ were used for a crisp data set (x_{2i}, y_{2i}) where $\overline{X}_i = (x_{1i}, x_{2i}, x_{3i})$ and $\overline{Y}_i = (y_{1i}, y_{2i}, y_{3i})$ and $i = 1, \ldots, k$. Then an evolutionary algorithm was run for each of the function groups belonging to the function library. After collection the results of all evolutionary algorithms that function group with the smallest error (assuming that the error is sufficiently small) was chosen as the best candidate model for the second part of the method.

In the second stage of the proposed method, the chosen model (linear, polynomial of third degree, etc., exponential, logarithmic) is fuzzified. A second evolutionary algorithm adjusts the fuzzy parameters of the chosen model and finds this way a suitable function. This method was applied to different linear and non–linear functions as well as to multivariate fuzzy regression where instead of a one–dimensional function a $n = 2, 3, \ldots$ dimensional function having n inputs was searched for. The authors report quite good results. However, there is one drawback in this method. First, an evolutionary algorithm searches for the best crisp model. There are lots of crisp regression analysis tools out there which can find sufficiently good functions by using arithmetic. So why using evolutionary algorithms in the first stage of this method? This is our starting point. Instead of evolving the most suitable function via two evolutionary algorithms we present an algorithm consisting of a single evolutionary process. However this process differs from the evolutionary algorithm presented in [3,4] in that a tree structure of the function is evolved. The corresponding process is known as genetic programming.

Before we will discuss the algorithm in Sect.4 let us present a formal description of the fuzzy regression analysis problem in the next two sections.

3 Notation

The reader familiar to fuzzy numbers can skip this paragraph. At first we have a look at the notation which is used in throughout this paper. We place a bar over a capital letter to denote a fuzzy subset of the real numbers. So $\overline{A}$, $\overline{B}$, $\overline{C}$, ... $\overline{X}$, etc. are all fuzzy subsets of the real numbers. We write $\overline{A}(x) \in [0, 1]$, for the membership function of $\overline{A}$ evaluated as x. A triangular fuzzy number $\overline{N}$ is defined by three numbers $a_1 < a_2 < a_3$ where the graph of $\overline{N}(x)$ is a triangle with base on the interval $[a_1, a_3]$ and vertex at $x = a_2$. We specify $\overline{N}$ as $(a_1/a_2/a_3)$. A triangular shaped fuzzy number $\overline{M}$ is partially defined by three number $a_1 < a_2 < a_3$ where: (1) the graph of $\overline{M}(x)$ is continuous and monotonically increasing from zero to one on $[a_1, a_2]$; (2) $\overline{M}(a_2) = 1$; and (3) the graph of $\overline{M}(x)$ is continuous and monotonically decreasing from one to zero on $[a_2, a_3]$. We write $\overline{M} \geq 0$ if $a_1 \geq 0$, $\overline{M} > 0$ if $a_1 > 0$, $\overline{M} \leq 0$, if $a_3 \leq 0$ and $\overline{M} < 0$ for $a_3 < 0$. We will use standard fuzzy arithmetic, from the extension principle, to evaluate sums, products, etc. of fuzzy numbers, [2].

4 The Fuzzy Regression Problem

Let us consider $\overline{X}_i$ as a single fuzzy number. Let $\mathcal{F}_0$ denote all the triangular shaped fuzzy numbers in $\mathbb{R}$, let $\mathcal{F}$ denote all fuzzy numbers in $\mathbb{R}$ [6] and let $\mathcal{T}$ be all triangular fuzzy numbers in $\mathbb{R}$. A function mapping $\mathcal{T}$ into $\mathcal{F}$ will be written as $F(\overline{X}; \overline{K}_1, \ldots, \overline{K}_n)$ where $\overline{X}$ is the variable in $\mathcal{T}$ and the $\overline{K}_i$ are parameters (constants) also in $\mathcal{T}$. For example, $F(\overline{X}; \overline{K}_1, \overline{K}_2) = \overline{K}_2 \overline{X} + \overline{K}_1$, a fuzzy linear function, is one of these functions, $F(\overline{X}; \overline{K}_1, \overline{K}_2) = \overline{K}_2 \overline{X}^2 + \overline{K}_1 \overline{X}$ would be another function mapping of this form.

Let $(\overline{X}_i, \overline{Z}_i)$, $1 \leq i \leq k$, be some data for $\overline{X}_i$ in $\mathcal{T}$ and $\overline{Z}_i$ in $\mathcal{F}$. The fuzzy regression problem is to find f in Ω that "best" explains this data. For any f in Ω let $\overline{Y}_i = F(\overline{X}_i; \overline{K}_1, \ldots, \overline{K}_n)$, $1 \leq i \leq k$, and let D be a metric on the fuzzy numbers in $\mathbb{R}$ ([6]). We measure "best" through the error function.

$$E(F) = \frac{1}{p} \sum_{i=1}^{p} D^2(\overline{Z}_i, \overline{Y}_i) \ , \tag{1}$$

where $\overline{Y}_i = F(\overline{X}_i; \overline{K}_1, \ldots, \overline{K}_n)$. The fuzzy regression problem based on Ω is to find F^* in Ω so that

$$\inf_{F \in \Omega} (E(F)) = E(F^*) \ . \tag{2}$$

If the problem in equation (2) has a solution F^* we will say that F^* best explains the data with respect to Ω.

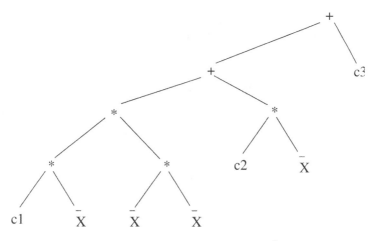

Fig. 1. Tree representation of the function $c_1\overline{X}^3 + c_2\overline{X} + c_3$.

Next we discuss what types of fuzzy functions we will place into Ω. The metric we will use is ([6, p. 52]):

$$D(\overline{M},\overline{N}) = \sup_{\alpha} H(\overline{M}[\alpha],\overline{N}[\alpha]) , \qquad (3)$$

where H is the Hausdorff distance between nonempty subsets of the reals and $\overline{N}, \overline{M}$ are two fuzzy numbers. Since α-cuts of fuzzy numbers are always closed bounded intervals, we get

$$D(\overline{N},\overline{M}) = \sup_{\alpha} \max \left\{ |m_1(\alpha) - n_1(\alpha)|, |m_2(\alpha) - n_2(\alpha)| \right\} , \qquad (4)$$

where $\overline{M}[\alpha] = [m_1(\alpha), m_2(\alpha)]$ and $\overline{N}[\alpha] = [n_1(\alpha), n_2(\alpha)]$, for all α.

For simplicity, we are only considering triangular fuzzy numbers in $\mathcal{T}$. However, it is not too difficult, using α-cuts to represent a fuzzy number, to expand our evolutionary algorithm to have $\mathcal{T}$ all triangular shaped fuzzy numbers.

5   Genetic Programming

We apply a genetic programming based approach to the fuzzy regression problem since we need a variable length representation of fuzzy functions. Let us now describe the way of representing a fuzzy function as a tree. The prefix notation of a fuzzy function can easily be transformed into a tree structure where arithmetic operators such as $+$, $\cdot$ and $-$ as well as exp and log stand for the nodes of the tree and parameters of the function are the leaves of the tree. As an example we consider the function $c_1 \overline{X}^3 + c_2\overline{X} + c_3$. The corresponding prefix notation has the form $+(+(*(*(*(\overline{X},\overline{X})),\overline{X}),c_1),(*(c_2,\overline{X}))),c_3)$. The corresponding tree is drawn in Fig.1.

Our genetic programming algorithm is different from Koza's approach in that we use mutation in order to adjust the parameter values. The parameter settings are given in Table 1.

Table 1. Parameter Settings

Parameter	Value
Population size	4000
max. generation	150
Recombination probability	90%
Reproduction probability	10%
Fitness type	MSE
Number of Fittest	288
Fitness threshold	0.01
Function sets	$\{\times, +, -, exp, ln\}$
Terminal sets	$\{x, constants\}$

6   Results

In this section we will discuss how our genetic programming approach is tested. We have chosen 8 linear functions, 8 fuzzy quadratic and 8 cubic polynomial functions. The function list is given in the appendix (Table 5, 6 and 7). A data set is generated for each of these functions by randomly chosen triangular fuzzy numbers $\overline{X}_i$ in a predefined interval. The outputs $\overline{Z}_i$ are computed as $f(\overline{X}_i) = \overline{Z}_i$ for each of the previously chosen fuzzy functions. In our tests we are using up to 50 data pairs per fuzzy function. The number of data pairs strongly varies between 5 and 50. But we cannot find a connection between the number of data pairs and the success rate. For each of these functions we run 50 differently initialized genetic programs in order to see how good our method performs. The parameter settings of the genetic programming algorithm are listed in Table 1. Several tests on various parameter settings (smaller population size and anymore) leads to these settings.

Regarding the results it can be seen so far that our proposed method shows quite good results, see Table 2, 3, and 4. The linear and quadratic functions are showing very similar results. Over 70% successful runs of 50 where 6 test functions have a success rate of more than 90%. Only the functions L4 and Q1 make trouble. But in additional tests we have seen that varying the configuration (parameter settings like recombination rate, reproduction rate and so on) leads to an acceptable behavior (60% success rate). But we would like to apply the same parameter settings to all test function data. The tests of the cubic functions do not succeed so quite good. But the success rate averages 54% and is therefore acceptable.

What is also interesting is, most of the time a genetic program stopped by reaching the fitness threshold, the algorithm only needed a small number of generations (< 20) to find a fuzzy function. Furthermore, after simplifying the

Table 2. Test Results on Linear Fuzzy Functions

Function	Successful Runs	# Test Runs	Success Rate (in %)
L1	44	50	88%
L2	47	50	94%
L3	40	50	80%
L4	6	50	12%
L5	31	50	62%
L6	45	50	90%
L7	28	50	56%
L8	49	50	98%
SUM	290	400	72%

Table 3. Test Results on Quadratic Fuzzy Functions

Function	Successful Runs	# Test Runs	Success Rate (in %)
Q1	3	50	6%
Q2	47	50	94%
Q3	45	50	90%
Q4	36	50	72%
Q5	38	50	78%
Q6	49	50	98%
Q7	43	50	86%
Q8	37	50	54%
SUM	298	400	74 %

Table 4. Test Results on Cubic Fuzzy Functions

Function	Successful Runs	# Test Runs	Success Rate (in %)
C1	50	50	100%
C2	23	50	46%
C3	24	50	48%
C4	23	50	46%
C5	26	50	52%
C6	17	50	34%
C7	38	50	73%
C8	15	50	30%
SUM	216	400	54 %

fuzzy functions they are very similar to the functions we used for generating the data. So it looks like our method performs quite well, at least in the linear, quadratic and cubic case.

7   Conclusions and Further Work

We presented a method for solving the fuzzy regression problem. This method makes use of a slightly modified form of Koza's genetic programming approach. Fuzzy functions are represented in a tree structure so that the genetic program can modify the functions according to the presented data. In the future more tests on data describing functions of higher degrees are process processed.

References

1. T. Bäck: *Evolutionary Algorithms in Theory and Practice: Evolutionary Strategies, Evolutionary Programming, Genetic Algorithms*, Oxford University Press, New York, 1996.
2. J.J. Buckley and T. Feuring: *Fuzzy and Neural: Interactions and Applications* (Studies in Fuzziness and Soft Computing Vol. 25), Physica-Verlag Heidelberg, 1999.
3. J.J. Buckley and T. Feuring: *Linear and Non-Linear Fuzzy Regression: Evolutionary Algorithm Solutions*, Fuzzy Sets and Systems 112, 2000, pp. 381–394.
4. J.J. Buckley, T. Feuring and Y. Hayashi: *Multivariate Non-Linear Fuzzy Regression: An Evolutionary Algorithm Approach*, Int. Journal of Uncertainty, Fuzziness and Knowledge-Based Systems 7 (2), 1999, pp. 83–98.
5. P. Diamond: *Fuzzy Least Squares*, Info. Sciences 46, 1988, pp. 141–157.
6. P. Diamond and P. Kloeden: *Metric Spaces of Fuzzy Sets*, World Scientific, Singapore, 1994.
7. W. Golubski and T. Feuring: *Genetic Programming Based Fuzzy Regression*, Proceedings of KES2000 4th International Conference on Knowledge-Based Intelligent Engineering Systems and Allied Technologies, Brighton, 2000, pp. 349–352.
8. M. Inuiguchi, M. Sakawa and S. Ushiro: *Mean-Absolute-Deviation-Based Fuzzy Linear Regression Analysis by Level Sets Automatic Deduction from Data*, Proc. FUZZ-IEEE'97, Barcelona, Spain, July 1-5, 1997, Vol. 1, 829–834.
9. J. Kacprzyk and M. Fedrizzi: *Fuzzy Regression Analysis*, Omnitech Press, Warsaw and Physica-Verlag, Heidelberg, 1992.
10. J.R. Koza: *Genetic Programming II*, Cambridge/MA: MIT Press, 1994.
11. M. Ming, M. Friedman and A. Kandel: *General Fuzzy Least Squares*, Fuzzy Sets and Systems 88 (1997), 107–118.
12. Y.-J. Seo, Y.-M. Park, S.-G. Hwang and K.-P. Park: *Fuzzy Regression Using Genetic Algorithms*, Proc. Fifth IFSA, Seoul, July 4-9, 1993, 513–516.
13. H. Tanaka and H. Lee: *Fuzzy Linear Regression Combining Central Tendency and Possibilistic Properties*, Proc. FUZZ-IEEE'97, Barcelona, Spain, July 1-5, 1997, Vol. 1, 63–68.
14. L. Wang L. Zhang, H. Itoh and H. Seki: *A Fuzzy Regression Method Based on Genetic Algorithms*, Proc. 3rd Int. Conf. Fuzzy Logic, Neural Nets and Soft Computing, Iizuka, Aug. 1-7, 1994, 471–472.
15. X. Zhang, S. Omachi and H. Aso: *Fuzzy Regression Analysis Using RFLN and its Application*, Proc. FUZZ-IEEE'97, Barcelona, Spain, July 1-5, 1997, Vol. 1, 51–56.

A   Appendix

Table 5. Linear Test Functions

No	Function	Interval
L1	$2.35x + 4.2$	$[5,20]$
L2	$5x + 23$	$[7,25]$
L3	$7.37x + 2.3$	$[5,19]$
L4	$0.235x + 42$	$[10,50]$
L5	$1.374x + 8$	$[13,35]$
L6	$0.05x + 1.23$	$[5,15]$
L7	$3.5x - 7.23$	$[3,20]$
L8	$7x - 1.5$	$[30,40]$

Table 6. Quadratic Test Functions

No	Function	Interval
Q1	$0.2x^2 + 3x + 5$	$[1,9]$
Q2	$2.7x^2 + 0.8x + 1$	$[1,6]$
Q3	$12x^2 + 1.7x + 2.35$	$[1,5]$
Q4	$1.1x^2 - 3.7x + 3.8$	$[0,6]$
Q5	$10x^2 + 3.5x + 3.14$	$[0,4]$
Q6	$7.5x^2 + 0.8$	$[0,4]$
Q7	$5.2x^2 - 1.2x + 3.7$	$[0,3]$
Q8	$3.9x^2 - 4.5x + 1.3$	$[0,3]$

Table 7. Cubic Test Functions

No	Function	Interval
C1	$-x^3 + 2.8x^2 + 1.2$	$[0,2.5]$
C2	$0.4x^3 + 0.6x^2 - 1.5x + 0.8$	$[0,3]$
C3	$x^3 + 1.1x^2 - 2x + 0.8$	$[0,2.5]$
C4	$1.9x^3 + 2x + 1.5$	$[0,4]$
C5	$2.7x^3 + 0.5x^2 - x + 1.8$	$[0,2]$
C6	$3.3x^3 - 3.2x^2 - 2x + 3.4$	$[0,2]$
C7	$4.5x^3 + 3.9x^2 - 1.8x + 1.2$	$[0,1]$
C8	$6.5x^3 - 2.5x^2 - x + 1$	$[0,1.5]$

Coevolution Produces an Arms Race among Virtual Plants

Marc Ebner, Adrian Grigore, Alexander Heffner, and Jürgen Albert

Universität Würzburg, Lehrstuhl für Informatik II
Am Hubland, 97074 Würzburg, Germany
ebner@informatik.uni-wuerzburg.de
http://www2.informatik.uni-wuerzburg.de

Abstract. Creating interesting virtual worlds is a difficult task. We are using a variant of genetic programming to automatically create plants for a virtual environment. The plants are represented as context-free Lindenmayer systems. OpenGL is used to visualize and evaluate the plants. Our plants have to collect virtual sunlight through their leaves in order to reproduce successfully. Thus we have realized an interaction between the plant and its environment. Plants are either evaluated separately or all individuals of a population at the same time. The experiments show that during coevolution plants grow much higher compared to rather bushy plants when plants are evaluated in isolation.

1 Motivation

Creating realistic virtual worlds for a person emerged in a virtual environment is very difficult. Apart from artificial objects such as buildings and cars the virtual world should also contain plants, animals and other people to interact with. We have explored the possibility of evolving virtual plants [8]. Evolving virtual plants instead of manually creating plants opens up the possibility to rapidly create a multitude of different plants. These plants do not necessarily have to exist in the real world. But it is important that, whatever the structures may look like, the user recognizes them as plants.

In our work plants are represented as Lindenmayer-systems or L-systems for short [22]. Prusinkiewicz and Lindenmayer [22] have shown previously how complex, photo-realistically looking plants can be created from a relatively small number of rules. Methods for realistic modeling and rendering of plant ecosystems are described by Deussen et al. [7]. We use an evolutionary algorithm, a variant of genetic programming [17,18] to automatically generate new populations of plants. Probably one of the first experiments in this area was done by Niklas [20]. Niklas performed an adaptive walk through plant space of branching patterns. An experiment in which different branching patterns compete against each other was also made. Other early experiments were done by Jacob [10,11, 12,13] who also used a variant of genetic programming to evolve context-free and context-sensitive L-Systems which look like plants. Jacob used a combination of the number of blossoms, the number of leaves and the volume of the plant as a

J.A. Foster et al. (Eds.): EuroGP 2002, LNCS 2278, pp. 316–325, 2002.

fitness function. Broughton et al. [2] evolved three-dimensional objects similar to Dawkins' Biomorphs [6]. They experimented with two different paradigms, Genetic Programming and L-Systems both of which, when interpreted define a three-dimensional object. Coates et al. [3] extended the experiments and evolved shapes which are adapted to specific constraints, i.e. are able to catch or avoid particles moving in a specific direction. Coevolution was used to evolve objects with an enclosure. Ochoa [21] evolved two-dimensional plant morphologies using L-systems. Kokai et al. [15,16] evolved L-Systems which describe fractal images or structures. Mock [19] evolved plants for an artificial world where the user took the role of a virtual gardener who could select plants for reproduction. Kim [14] developed a model for the evolution of plant morphology. Plants were grown on a two-dimensional lattice. Hornby and Pollack [9] evolved L-Systems which produce tables and investigated the impact the choice of representation has on the result. Representing the individuals as L-systems produced better results in comparison to a direct encoding.

Our experiments differ from the ones done by Jacob [10,11,12], Mock [19] and Kokai et al. [15,16] in that we allow interactions between the plant and its environment. Plants need to catch as much virtual sunlight as possible using their leaves. The amount of sunlight which hits the plant is used to calculate a plant's fitness. We either evaluated each plant individually or we evaluated all individuals of a population at the same time. When all individuals are evaluated at the same time then we also have an interaction between the plants of a population. One plant may place its leaves above the leaves of another plant and thereby use up this sunlight which would have otherwise been received by the plant below. We see that coevolution of plants shapes the plants. Plants grow much higher and try to spread their leaves at the top compared to rather bushy looking plants which occur when plants are evaluated independently.

2   Evolution of Artificial Plants

We have used deterministic, context-free L-systems as a representation for our plants. A context-free L-system consists of an alphabet V, a starting word ω and a set of rules P [22]. The starting word is defined over the alphabet V: $\omega \in V^+$. The rules are defined as a subset of $V \times V^+$. Each rule $(a, \chi) \in P$ consists of a predecessor a and a successor χ where $\chi \in V^*$. If no successor is defined for a predecessor a then we assume that $a \rightarrow a$ belongs to the set of rules P.

A new word is derived from the initial word by replacing all letters of the word by their successors. This process is repeated for a specified number of steps. For the experiments which are described below we have used 5 developmental steps. The major difference between L-systems and the usual Chomsky grammar [4] is that in each step all characters of a word are replaced at the same time. This is supposed to model cell division of multi-cellular organisms. After a word has been derived from the starting word we interpret the letters as commands for a virtual drawing device in three-dimensional space. The symbols are read from left to right.

Table 1. Interpretation of the symbols of our alphabet.

Symbol	Description
f	draw a branch segment (cylinder) and move forward
l	draw a leaf
[	push the current state (transformation matrix) onto the stack
]	pop state from stack
>	22.5°rotation around x axis
<	-22.5°rotation around x axis
\	22.5°rotation around y axis
/	-22.5°rotation around y axis
+	22.5°rotation around z axis
–	-22.5°rotation around z axis
A, ..., Z	no operation

Fig. 1. Building blocks for our plants. A branch segment is shown on the left and a leaf is shown on the right.

We have used a relatively simple alphabet for our experiments. The alphabet consists of the symbols:

$$V = \{f, l, +, -, <, >, /, \backslash, [,], A, ..., Z\}$$

The interpretation of the individual letters is shown in Table 1. The rules for the letters f and A through Z are the only ones which may be changed during the course of the experiment. The other symbols of the alphabet cannot be transformed. Symbols f and l are used to draw a branch segment and a leaf respectively. Figure 1 shows the building blocks from which our plants are created. All leaves of the plant have the same shape and size. Symbols +, -, <, >, /, \ are used to change the orientation of the drawing device. Symbols [and] can be used to create branching structures. The symbol [places the current state (e.g. position and orientation) of the drawing device onto the stack. The symbol] pops the topmost state from the stack, thereby restoring the position and orientation of the drawing device to the one which was previously saved. The symbols A through Z cause no operation and are only used during development.

Each individual consists of one or more rules. The number of rules can be changed by the genetic operators. The predecessor of the first rule is f, the predecessor of the second rule is A, the predecessor of the third rule is B and so on. The initial word from which the plant develops is f. Our initial population only contains individuals with the single rule f → f. That is, we start with a population of individuals which only consist of a single branch segment.The fitness of all individuals of the initial population is zero because a branch is not able to collect any sunlight. A typical L-system is shown in Figure 2.

initial word: **A**
rules:

$f \rightarrow B/////f$
$A \rightarrow [< fCA]/////[< fCA]///////[< fCA]$
$B \rightarrow fC$
$C \rightarrow [>> l]$

Fig. 2. Sample grammar. The rules are derived from a grammar describing a bush [22].

Plants are evolved using a similar algorithm as in the genetic programming paradigm [17,18]. To create a new individual for the next generation, we first choose a genetic operator. Each operator is associated with a specific probability that this operator will be chosen. After the type of operator has been determined we either select one or two individuals depending on the type of operator. Crossover operators require two individuals, mutation operators require only a single individual. This process is repeated for a specified number of generations.

- **Permutation**: Two neighboring symbols are exchanged.
- **Mutation**: A randomly selected symbol is replaced with a new symbol.
- **Insertion**: A new symbol is inserted at a random locus.
- **Deletion**: A symbol is deleted at a random locus.
- **One-Point-Crossover**: Crossover is performed by selecting a rule and exchanging all rules between the two individuals which follow the selected rule.
- **Sub-Tree-Crossover**: A randomly selected bracketed subtree is exchanged between two individuals.
- **Add-Branch**: An empty branch is added to an individual.
- **Delete-Branch**: A possibly non-empty bracketed subtree is deleted.
- **Add-Rule** A new rule is appended to the individual, i.e. if the last rule is $C \rightarrow \chi$ then $D \rightarrow D$ is added.
- **Delete-Rule** The last rule of an individual is deleted.

Fig. 3. Genetic operators.

Figure 3 shows a list of the genetic operators which were used for the experiments. The genetic operators were chosen such that only relatively small steps are possible between successive generations. That is, we did not include operations such as the random generation of subtrees. Reproduction was not included in this set because we found that it was not needed. Whenever an operator cannot be applied the individual is copied unchanged into the next generation, i.e. it is not possible to do a subtree crossover whenever one of the individuals does not contain a bracketed expression.

The fitness of each individual is determined by rendering the plant as an image of size 640 × 640 using parallel projection viewed from above. Leaves of the plant are drawn in a special color which is unique for each plant and different from the color used to draw the branch segment or the color of the ground. After we have rendered the plant we count the number of pixels which are covered by the plant's leaves. This is a direct measure of the plant's ability to collect sunlight. Using the Z-Buffer to estimate the amount of sunlight hitting a plant was suggested by Beneš [1].

In addition to the number of pixels we also determine the structural complexity of the plant. Branch segments and leaves become more expensive to produce the further they are away from the root of the plant. In our model a branch segment costs 1 point and a leaf costs 3 points. This cost is multiplied with a factor which takes the distance to the root of the plant in account. We define the structural complexity of a plant as

$$\text{complexity} = \sum_{b \in B} \text{cost}_{\text{branch}} \cdot \text{factor}^{\text{height}(b)} + \sum_{l \in L} \text{cost}_{\text{leaf}} \cdot \text{factor}^{\text{height}(l)}$$

where B is the set of branches, L is the set of leaves and height returns the number of branch segments between the current position and the root of the plant. As parameters we have used factor $= 1.1$, $\text{cost}_{\text{branch}} = 1$ and $\text{cost}_{\text{leaf}} = 3$. The fitness of a plant is calculated by subtracting the structural complexity from the amount of light received.

$$\text{fitness} = 10 \cdot \text{points} - \text{complexity}$$

where points is the number of points covered by the plant's leaves. In case of a negative fitness we set fitness to zero. The number of green points is weighted with a factor of 10 which was determined experimentally. A single leaf oriented at a right angle covers 300 points.

3   Experiments

We experimented with a population of 200 individuals with tournament selection and a tournament size of 7. The probability to apply a particular genetic operator was set to 0.1. Two experiments were made. In the first experiment individuals are evaluated in isolation. In this case, the plant is positioned in the center of a square. Leaves which are rendered outside of or below this square do not collect any sunlight. For the second experiment all individuals of the population are evaluated at the same time. Each plant is positioned randomly on the square with a randomly chosen orientation. If a plant places its leaves above another plant's leaves then the one below does not receive as much sunlight as if it were evaluated in isolation. In this case the fitness of a plant also depends on the neighborhood it is growing in. The results of these two experiments are shown in Figure 4 and Figure 5.

Bush-like plants dominate during the first experiment. Plants need to maximize the amount of light received through the leaves while minimizing its structural complexity. Any leaves which are placed below or outside of the square simulating ground only reduce the fitness of the plant. In contrast to the bush-like plants of the first experiment we observed thin and tall plants during the

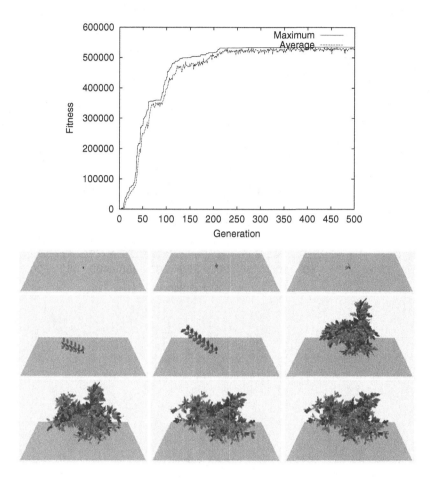

Fig. 4. Results of the experiment when each plant was evaluated in isolation. The graph shows maximum and average fitness values over time. The images show the best individual at generations 0, 4, 8, 16, 32, 64, 128, 256, and 500. Bush-like shapes dominate.

second experiment. A comparison between the best plant which evolved during the two experiments is shown in Figure 6.

During the second experiment average fitness rises initially, then drops very much and the fitness of the best plant starts to oscillate. At this point an evolutionary arms race [5] sets in. This has also been called the red queen hypothesis [23]. According to the red queen hypothesis the fitness of coevolving species may remain at the same level over time. Nevertheless each individual may be continually improving some specific trait. If we look at the two components (amount of light received and structural complexity) of the fitness of an individual we see that the structural complexity of the plant still increases steadily even though

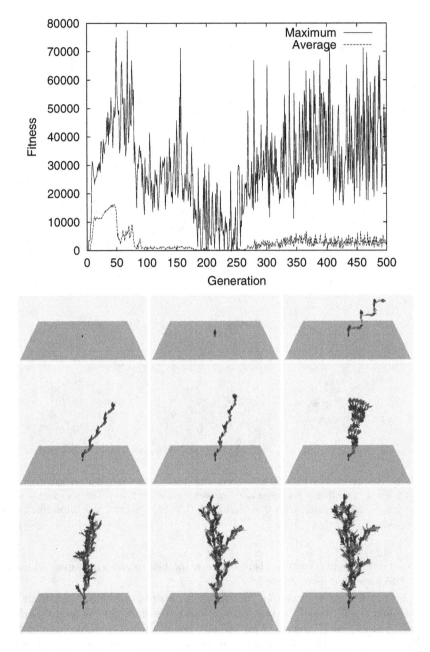

Fig. 5. Results of the experiment when all plants where evaluated at the same time. The graph shows maximum and average fitness values over time. The images show the best individual at generations 0, 4, 8, 16, 32, 64, 128, 256, and 500. The plants grow higher and higher in attempt to gain more sunlight.

Fig. 6. Plants evolved using coevolution grow higher and are thinner in comparison to plants evolved in isolation. The image on the left shows the best plant when plants were evaluated in isolation, the image in the middle shows the best plant evolved using coevolution. The image on the right shows the whole population of plants.

maximum fitness oscillates heavily and complexity has a negative effect on fitness. Plants need to out-grow their competitors in order to gain more light. If one plant grows higher than another plant it needs more points for its structure but at the same time it also receives more light than its competitors. Figure 8 shows a comparison of the average height and average volume of the plants during the two experiments. Plants evolved during the first experiment occupy a much larger volume than the plants evolved during the second experiment. In comparison, the plants evolved during the second experiment grow higher than the plants evolved during the first experiment.

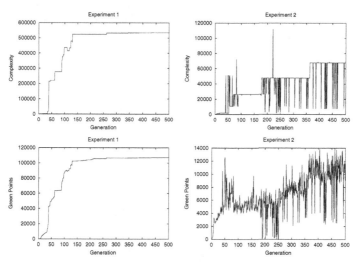

Fig. 7. The graphs on the left show the fitness components for the first experiment. The graphs on the right show the components for the second experiment. The top graphs show the plant's complexity and the bottom graphs show the number of green points.

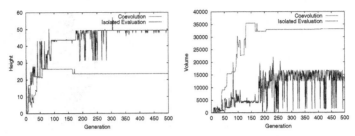

Fig. 8. Comparison of plant height and plant volume for the two experiments.

4   Conclusion

The experiments show how it is possible to use evolutionary techniques to create realistically looking plants for an artificial environment. Plants have to collect virtual sunlight through their leaves. Fitness is calculated as the amount of sunlight received minus the cost for creating the plant. Plants were evaluated either individually or using coevolution. During coevolution we evaluated all plants at the same time. In this case the fitness of a plant depends on its ability to collect sunlight as well as on the neighborhood it is growing in. Thus we have realized an interaction between the plant and its environment.

We found that during coevolution an arms race sets in. Plants grow higher and higher in an attempt to collect more sunlight than its neighbor. Plants which are evaluated in isolation look bushier whereas plants which are evaluated using coevolution look tree-like. The data shows that during coevolution even though fitness stays constant or decreases progress is being made. Plants evolved during coevolution keep increasing their structural complexity in order to catch more light than a neighboring plant. Further experiments could include the simulation of gravity and use of collision detection algorithms. At present, the time required to evaluate the individuals preclude these type of experiments.

References

1. B. Beneš. An efficient estimation of light in simulation of plant development. In R. Boulic and G. Hegron (eds.), *Computer Animation and Simulation 96*, pp. 153–165, Berlin, 1996. Springer-Verlag.
2. T. Broughton, A. Tan, and P. S. Coates. The use of genetic programming in exploring 3d design worlds. In R. Junge (ed.), *CAAD Futures 1997. Proc. of the 7th Int. Conf. on Computer Aides Architectural Design Futures, Munich, Germany*, pp. 885–915, Dordrecht, 1997. Kluwer Academic Publishers.
3. P. Coates, T. Broughton, and H. Jackson. Exploring three-dimensional design worlds using Lindenmeyer systems and genetic programming. In P. J. Bentley (ed.), *Evolutionary Design by Computers*, pp. 323–341. Morgan Kaufmann, 1999.
4. M. D. Davis and E. J. Weyuker. *Computability, Complexity, and Languages*. Academic Press Limited, San Diego, CA, 1983.

5. R. Dawkins and J. R. Krebs. Arms races between and within species. *Proc. R. Soc. Lond. B*, 205:489–511, 1979.
6. R. Dawkins. *The Blind Watchmaker.* W. W. Norton & Company, New York, 1996.
7. O.Deussen, P.Hanrahan, B.Lintermann, R.Měch, M.Pharr, and P.Prusinkiewicz. Realistic modeling and rendering of plant ecosystems. In *SIGGRAPH '98 Conf. Proc., Computer Graphics, Orlando, Florida*, pp. 275–286. ACM Press, 1998.
8. A. Grigore, A. Heffner, M. Ebner, and J. Albert. Evolution virtueller Pflanzen. Technical Report 280, Universität Würzburg, Lehrstuhl für Informatik II, Am Hubland, 97074 Würzburg, Germany, August 2001.
9. G. S. Hornby and J. B. Pollack. The advantages of generative grammatical encodings for physical design. In *Proc. of the 2001 Congress on Evolutionary Computation, COEX, Seoul, Korea*, pp. 600–607. IEEE Press, 2001.
10. C. Jacob. Genetic L-system programming. In Y. Davudor, H.-P. Schwefel, and R. Männer (eds.), *Parallel Problem Solving from Nature – PPSN III. The 3rd Int. Conf. on Evolutionary Computation. Jerusalem, Israel*, pp. 334–343, Berlin, 1994. Springer-Verlag.
11. C. Jacob. Evolution programs evolved. In H.-M. Voigt, W. Ebeling, I. Rechenberg, and H.-P. Schwefel (eds.), *Parallel Problem Solving from Nature – PPSN IV. The 4th Int. Conf. on Evolutionary Computation. Berlin, Germany*, pp. 42–51, Berlin, 1996. Springer-Verlag.
12. C. Jacob. Evolving evolution programs: Genetic programming and L-systems. In J.R. Koza, D.E. Goldberg, D.B. Fogel, and R.L. Riolo (eds.),*Proc. of the 1st Annual Conf. on Genetic Programming*, pp.107–115,Cambridge,MA,1996. The MIT Press.
13. C. Jacob. Evolution and coevolution of developmental programs. *Computer Physics Communications*, pp. 46–50, 1999.
14. J. T. Kim. LindEvol: Artificial models for natural plant evolution. *Künstliche Intelligenz*, 1:26–32, 2000.
15. G. Kókai, Z. Tóth, and R. Ványi. Application of genetic algorithms with more populations for Lindenmayer systems. In E. Alpaydin and C. Fyfe (eds.), *Int. ICSC Symposium on Engineering of Intelligent Systems EIS'98, University of La Laguna, Tenerife, Spain*, pp. 324–331, Canada/Switzerland, 1998. ICSC Academic Press.
16. G. Kókai, Z. Tóth, and R. Ványi. Evolving artificial trees described by parametric L-systems. In *Proc. of the 1999 IEEE Canadian Conf. on Electrical and Computer Engineering, Shaw Conference Center, Edmonton, Alberta, Canada*, pp. 1722–1727. IEEE Press, 1999.
17. J. R. Koza. *Genetic Programming. On the Programming of Computers by Means of Natural Selection.* The MIT Press, Cambridge, MA, 1992.
18. J. R. Koza. *Genetic Programming II. Automatic Discovery of Reusable Programs.* The MIT Press, Cambridge, MA, 1994.
19. K. J. Mock. Wildwood: The evolution of L-system plants for virtual environments. In *Int. Conf. on Evolutionary Computation, Anchorage, AK*, pp. 476–480, 1998.
20. K. J. Niklas. Computer-simulated plant evolution. *Scientific American*, 254(3):68–75, 1986.
21. G. Ochoa. On genetic algorithms and Lindenmayer systems. In *Parallel Problem Solving from Nature - PPSN V*, pp. 335–344, Berlin, 1998. Springer-Verlag.
22. P. Prusinkiewicz and A. Lindenmayer. *The Algorithmic Beauty of Plants.* Springer Verlag, New York, 1990.
23. L. Van Valen. A new evolutionary law. *Evolutionary Theory*, 1:1–30, July 1973.

Comparing Synchronous and Asynchronous Parallel and Distributed Genetic Programming Models

Francisco Fernández, G. Galeano, and J.A. Gómez

Computer Science Department, University of Extremadura
C/ Calvario, s/n. 06800 Mérida, Spain
{fcofdez, ggaleano, jangomez}@unex.es
http://atc.unex.es/pacof

Abstract. We present a study that analyses the respective advantages and disadvantages of the synchronous and asynchronous versions of island-based genetic programming and also a relationship between the number of subpopulations in parallel GP and the asynchronous model. We also look at a new measuring system for comparing parallel genetic programming with panmictic model. At the same time we show an interesting relationship between the bloat phenomenon and the number of individuals we use.

1 Introduction

Evolutionary algorithms rely on the evolution of candidate solutions over a finite number of temporal steps. The aim is to obtain a sufficiently good solution for a given problem. However, this process may require a prohibitive amount of time and computing resources.

Several studies have tackled this issue by using parallelism. For example, Andre and Koza employed a network of transputers for speeding up Genetic Programming (GP) [1]. In Genetic Algorithms (GAs), meanwhile, several experiments and theoretical studies have led to new models that are now commonly used [2, 11].

As described in [3] there are two interesting aspects of these new parallel models: On the one hand we have the obvious advantage of using several processors for speeding up computations, and on the other hand, the increase in performance that is obtained with the new island-based parallel algorithm (other models are also possible). Nevertheless this second idea has sometimes been questioned [4]. Despite contradictory opinions, parallel tools have been developed for making use of the advantages of multiprocessor systems (see [5] and [6]). But also, when monoprocessor systems are used, classical tools for these machines are endowed with the concept of deme -subpopulation- with the aim of making use of the algorithmic advantage of the island model. In this case, all demes run on the same processor.

We are studying firstly whether it is worth employing the new parallel implementations of the GP algorithm when using only one processor, and secondly which of the two models is preferable: synchronous or asynchronous. For making comparisons we will take into account not only the evaluation and generation time, but also the time spent in communications. We will do so by analysing the dynamics

J.A. Foster et al. (Eds.): EuroGP 2002, LNCS 2278, pp. 326–335, 2002.

of the synchronous and asynchronous model within a monoprocessor system. Some conclusions about the number of subpopulations are also presented at the end. This study helps us to see how the algorithm can be improved when using one or several processors.

This paper is structured in the following way: Section 2 describes parallel and distributed evolutionary algorithms. Section 3 deals with parallel GP. We describe the experiments in Section 4. Section 5 shows the results and finally, section 6 presents our conclusions.

2 Parallel and Distributed Evolutionary Algorithms

Biological evolution works in parallel. As stated in [3, pp. 254], if we want to imitate the way nature works, evolutionary algorithms should be parallel and distributed. A more practical reason for using parallel EAs is the need for a large amount of computing power when hard problems are tackled.

Modern computer systems allow us to experiment with parallel EAs. Even sequential machines are now endowed with a reasonable computing power so as to simulate parallel process on serial hardware. During the last few years some researchers have studied and employed parallel EAs. For example, Cantú-Paz has studied parallel GAs from a theoretical point of view [2]. In the field of GP, Andre and Koza have used parallel models [1]. In [7 pp. 1027] we can find a larger list of parallel implementations of genetic algorithms.

Even when researchers employ a sequential version of EAs, the concept of subpopulation is frequently used. The idea is to divide the population of individuals into several subpopulations. These are evaluated sequentially, and then, when the evaluation phase is completed, a new phase -the migration phase- is performed: some individuals are selected from within each subpopulation, and they are next exchanged with another neighbouring subpopulation. The idea behind migration is to promote diversity, thus avoiding premature convergence. Although the difficulty and the nature of the problem have much to do with the best way of solving it [4], we also believe that the way we measure results is very important. Several researches have studied GP using different measuring systems. They have analysed it:

- By studying the number of generations required for finding solutions with a given probability [4, 7].
- By looking at the number of fitness evaluations [1, 7].
- By taking the number of nodes evaluated [8, 9].

Different individuals have different sizes in GP; this means that they will require very different time to be evaluated. We therefore think that the third of the afore-mentioned measuring systems is more accurate in GP. But even this proposal has a drawback: it considers all the nodes from GP individuals equally, which is not usually the case. Furthermore, if we want to have an accurate vision of algorithm's performance when dealing with the island-model we should also take into account the communication time, as the migration phase is part of the parallel algorithm.

In this paper we are focussing on the study of the synchronous and asynchronous island-model in GP, when working with a monoprocessor system. We will see the importance of the way we measure results. The idea is to study the real advantage of these models in GP, and also to compare synchronous and asynchronous version of this algorithm.

3   Parallel and Distributed GP

As described in [3] and [4], there are several levels at which we can apply parallelism when dealing with GP: Fitness evaluation level, individual level, and Population level. The first two cases are said to present micrograin parallelism, and they use the sequential algorithm and evaluate fitness cases or individuals in different processors. The third model uses several subpopulations are evaluated in parallel using several processors. Sometimes certain individuals are exchanged among subpopulations. The main algorithm is different this time, due to the presence of migration phase. It is said to feature coarse-grain parallelism (see [3, 4]). We are most interested in the third model, since the others aren't any different from classical model, from the algorithmic point of view. Our experiments use the *master/slave* model, which is widely described in [3 pp. 257]. Two different synchronization models have been taken into account when conducting experiments:

- The synchronous model: All populations synchronise when exchange individuals.

- The asynchronous model: Populations send and receive individuals according to internal measurements. The sending process occurs after a fixed number of generations, while the receiving process occurs whenever individuals arrive. No synchronisation exists in this model, because of the different evolution speed within each population.

4   Experiments

We have employed a couple of benchmark problems that are widely used in GP literature: the ant problem (see [12]) and the even parity 5 problem [13]. Summarising, the ant problem tries to find some pieces of food which are positioned along a path on a two dimensional grid. The even parity function takes a number of Boolean inputs and returns TRUE only if an even number of inputs are true. We use these benchmark problems to investigate the usefulness of the parallel model in serial hardware, and also to compare the synchronous and the asynchronous parallel models. We have decided to run each of our experiments 100 times (researchers have similarly worked by using 14 times in [4] and 14, 25 or 60 times in [7]). The main GP parameters we have employed are the following ones: Crossover probability 98%; Mutation probability 50% for the ant problem and 5% for the even parity. Each population exchange 10% (see [10]) of their individuals each 10 generations for the ant problem, and each 5 generation for the even parity problem. We have employed the *padgp tool* (see [5] and [6]) which implements the master/slave model, each slave being a subpopulation. The communication topology is the ring. All the experiments have been conducted in a PC-LINUX Pentium II 350 Mhz environment.

5 Results

5.1 Studying Measuring Systems

We firstly present a study of both the ant and the even parity 5 problems when comparing fitness vs. generations, fitness vs. effort, and finally fitness vs. total computing time. By effort we mean number of nodes evaluated in a GP population.

Figure 1 compares panmictic vs. island model with 2 and 10 populations (processes), using the even parity 5 problem and a total number of 250 individuals in all the experiments.

When the comparison between models is based on generations, we see that using the panmictic model is better than using the island one when the latter employs 10 demes. Nevertheless the synchronous version of the island-model is better when using only 2 subpopulations. If we instead look at graphs in which we employ the total effort involved in taking measurements, the panmictic -classic- model is again better than the island one when using 10 subpopulations. Nevertheless if we use 2 subpopulations we get better results with the synchronous version of the island model.

Finally we observe that when we take into account the total time required for obtaining a given fitness (including communication time), the asynchronous version of the island-model is better than the classic one if we employ 2 subpopulations, and the classic model remains the best when compared to the island one when the latter uses 10 subpopulations. This seems reasonable, since when we use 10 subpopulations there is really a low number of individuals per subpopulation, and this prevents them from achieving good results.

A comparison between fitness and time offers us a different conclusion from a comparison between fitness and generation or effort. What researchers are most concerned with is the fitness they can get for a given time. We think we should always compare fitness and time when experimenting with parallel models.

Figure 2 shows results for the ant problem. We can see again that results are different according to the measuring system we employ. When we use the classical model, there is no difference between using effort of computation or time, because all the time is spent on computing individuals. But we know the island model introduces migration, and this requires time.   This communication time is thus one of the sources for the differences we find in the kinds of measuring systems we use. But may also be some differences in the way individuals evolve inside populations. Other authors have studied the problem of bloat [12], and if we could find differences in the way that the length of individuals evolves when using different models, we could establish another reason for the differences we have found.

Figure 3 shows the evolution of length in the even parity 5 problem. We can see the difference between the classic model and both synchronous and asynchronous models. Furthermore, we observe that the differences increase as we use a higher number of subpopulations. We conclude that the bloat of individuals strongly depends on the number of individuals in the population. In fact, variations in individuals' length evolution are not very important when comparing the panmictic model and the island model if the latter is using 2 subpopulations. At the other extreme, when we have 10 subpopulations, the differences with the classic model are significant. This also explains why we obtain one set of conclusions when comparing fitness versus generations and other different conclusions when comparing fitness and effort. We thus conclude that the island model does not only modify the way the search space is traversed by individuals, but it also modifies the way bloat evolves. Actually, it seems to control the bloat problem, although this must be confirmed with a deeper research. The island model modifies the evolution of individuals' length. Therefore, we must always use effort of computation instead of generations for measuring purposes. On the other hand, given that the communication time also affects the total time taken to find solutions, we conclude that we must use fitness versus time when extracting conclusions for the island model.

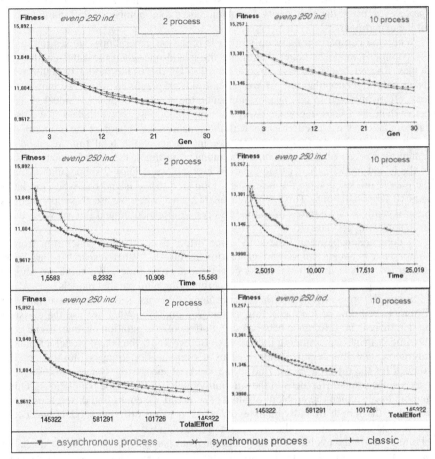

Fig. 1. Even parity 5 - 250 individuals: Fitness/Time, Fitness/Generation, Fitness/Effort, with 2 and 10 demes

In figure 1, we can see that results are quite similar in the three models we have studied. The island-based models are better when we use a small number of subpopulations, while the panmictic model obtain better results if there is a large number of subpopulations (this strongly depends on the total number of individuals per subpopulation). This implies that we must be careful when using a parallel GP tool with demetic capabilities on a monoprocessor system. Nevertheless the real advantage will appear when using multiprocessor systems. These results cohere with those found by other researchers [1].

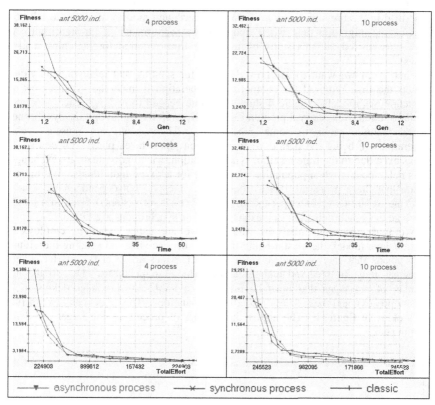

Fig. 2. Ant - 5000 individuals: Fitness/Time, Fitness/Generation, Fitness/Effort, with 4 and 10 demes

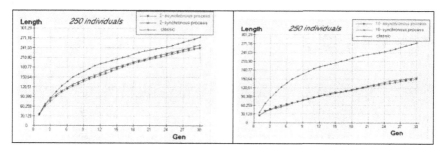

Fig. 3. Evenp 5 250 individuals- 2, and 10 demes. Length/Gen.

5.2 Studying Synchronous and Asynchronous Models

We are now interested in obtaining conclusions about the advantages of the distributed models we are studying: the synchronous and the asynchronous one. As described in the previous section, if we use distributed models, we need to take into account the migration time when analysing the performance of an algorithm. We have thus carried out this study by using the time required for obtaining a given fitness.

First of all we want to see how the time for sending and receiving individuals affects the time required for computing a generation in both the synchronous and asynchronous models. Figure 4 shows the time needed to compute each generation for the ant and even parity 5 problems. We can see in the figure that the synchronous model features peaks in some generations. These peaks are present each g generations, g being the period when migration phase takes place. Of course, the peaks exist due to the time taken in synchronisation, when individuals are exchanged. This delay occurs when populations must wait for arriving individuals. We must be aware that these peaks are due to the model; they do not depend on the kind of machine we are using for experimenting (monoprocessor system). Even in a parallel machine the synchronisation step exists within the synchronous algorithm.

We must also remember that the tool we are using -padgp- employs the master/slave model, the master being in charge of receiving and sending individuals. This means that each g generations a lot of messages arrive at the master. These messages must be received and resent to different populations. Due to the high number of messages that must be managed, a bottleneck produces delays in the master process, and these delays also affect populations. This effect can be confirmed by looking at figure 4: The higher the number of process is, the larger the delays within peak.

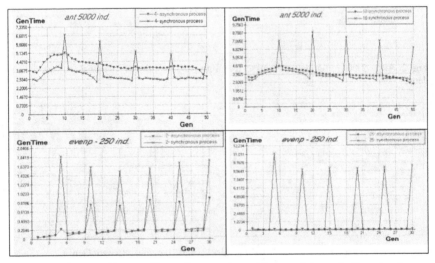

Fig. 4. Time (in seconds) wasted by each generation, with several demes in the ant and evenp problem.

At the same time, if we focus on the asynchronous model, the peaks are not present or if present, they are very small. This is due to the absence of the synchronisation step. Although all the processes send individuals each period g, the time when the migration phase occurs is different for each process, because the pace of evolution is different within each population. Moreover, individuals are received whenever they arrive at populations, there are no delays. Nevertheless, we can also observe that generations spend on average more time to compute when using the asynchronous model (not counting peaks). This difference is due to the way the model is implemented: each generation the asynchronous algorithm checks for incoming individuals. This is done by means of an MPI function, and this requires time.

5.3 The Influence of Operating Systems

We can also remark on an interesting issue: when we use the synchronous model, pre-migration generations take less time to compute. This effect becomes evident two or three generations before the migration (see figure 4, 4 and 10 processes). Something similar can also be observed when using the asynchronous model. But this time the reduction of time happens during the final generations of each experiment.

In order to explain that circumstance, we must remember how the Operating System works. When we use a monoprocessor system, which is endowed with a multi-process operating system (Linux), several processes can run simultaneously, thanks to the assignment of pieces of processor time -quantums- to different processes. Each process is assigned a quantum cyclically, until it finishes. When a process stop for an input/output operation, it is not assigned new quantums before it receives data. Its corresponding quantum is distributed among the other processes.

Padgp uses *mpich* [14] which is an implementation of MPI. In turns, *mpich* uses *sockets* for exchanging information between processes. The picture becomes complete if we say that Linux consider *sockets* as input/output operations. This means that each time a process is awaiting data from another process, the first one will become *idle* and will give its corresponding quantum to other processes, which in turn will compute quicker. This operating system feature is the source for the temporal reduction in generations that are close to the migration generation. Within the synchronous model, if a process begins a migration generation, it sends its best individuals to the master process and becomes *idle* before individuals from other populations arrive. Other populations that have not yet arrived at the migration generation will use the supplied quantum in order to compute quicker, thus arriving earlier at the migration generation, and also providing new quantums for other populations. Summarising, this issue causes the last few generations before the synchronization step to do their work in less time on average (see figure 4), while migration generations require much more time.

Something similar happens within the asynchronous model: the lack of synchronization helps each population to compute at its own pace, never awaiting for individuals, only receiving them when they are in the buffer. Due to the different speed of each process, the quicker ones will finish before the remaining ones. When they finish, their *quantums* are also distributed among the remaining ones, which are probably performing their final generations. This helps the last few generations to compute quickly in slower process, allowing them to finish more quickly and providing in turn new *quantums* to even slower processes. This is the reason for the decrease in generation time for the final generations. If we bear in mind all the experiments that we have performed using only one processor, we could conclude that the asynchronous model will be the preferred algorithm if we employ a multiprocessor system, or even a cluster of computers: each population runs on a different processor, and the synchronous model will not be able to make use of quantums from idle processes.

5.4 Total Computing Time

Another interesting result is that asynchronous model is slightly slower than the synchronous model (see figure 5). We said above that asynchronous algorithm must check in each generation whether there are arriving messages. Nevertheless, the synchronous model only checks messages each *g* generations. The process of checking buffers implies a delay that obviously affects the total computing time. The more processes are in the system, the longer the master process takes to manage messages, and this time also affects the speed with which messages arrive at their destinations. This produces an interesting result: the synchronous algorithm is slightly quicker than the asynchronous one when there is a small number of processes -populations-; however, it is slower than asynchronous algorithms when we use a larger number of populations (see figure 5). The panmictic model requires a shorter computing time per generation than any of the island based models. This is reasonable since the panmictic model does not waste time on communication, and we are working with only one processor.

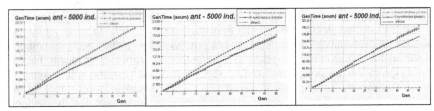

Fig. 5. Accumulated time (in seconds) wasted by each generation, with 4, 8,and 10 demes in the ant problem.

6   Conclusions

We have presented the respective advantages and disadvantages of synchronous and asynchronous island based Genetic Programming. With this study we have compared several methods of taking measurements when analysing parallel Genetic Programming. Results indicate that we must always compare fitness and total computing time in order to achieve precise conclusions.

Although the study has been performed on a monoprocessor system, we have seen the influence of the operating system on results. In turn, these results have led us to conclude which is the preferred algorithm when working on a multiprocessor system: the asynchronous model. At the same time, we have seen that differences among models are not very important when working on a monoprocessor system.

We have also confirmed that parallel models achieve better results than the classic model if we take into account the effort of computations, measured as the total number of nodes evaluated.

We have noticed that there seems to exist a direct relationship between the number of individuals per population and the bloat phenomenon. This must be studied more deeply in order to obtain definitively conclusions.

Finally, we have observed a relationship between the number of populations and the performances of the synchronous and asynchronous models. When the number of populations is high, the asynchronous model achieves better results.

References

[1] D. Andre and J R. Koza. "Parallel Genetic Programming: A Scalable Implementation Using The Transputer Network Architecture". P. Angeline and K. Kinear editors. Advances in Genetic Programming 2, Cambridge, MA, 1996.

[2] E. Cantú-Paz and D. Goldberg: "Predicting Speedups of Ideal Bounding Cases of Parallel Genetic Algorithms". Proceedings of the Seventh International Conference on Genetic Algorithms. Morgan Kaufmann. 1997.

[3] A. Tetamanzi, M.Tomassini,"Soft Computing". Springer Verlag, Heideberg, Germany 2001

[4] W.F. Punch: "How effective are multiple populations in Genetic Programming". Genetic Programming 1998: Proceedings of the Third Annual Conference, J. R. Koza, W. Banzhaf, K. Chellapilla, K. Deb, M. Dorigo, D. B. Fogel, M. Garzon, D. Goldberg, H. Iba and R. L. Riolo (Eds),Morgan Kaufmann, San Francisco, CA, pp. 308-313, 1998.

[5] M. Tomassini, F. Fernández, L. Vanneschi, L. Bucher, "An MPI-Based Tool for Distributed Genetic Programming" In Proceedings of IEEE International Conference on Cluster Computing CLUSTER2000, IEEE Computer Society. pp.209-216. 2000.

[6] F. Fernández, M. Tomassini, L Vanneschi, L. Bucher, "The GP's Tool". http: //www-iis.unil.ch/gpi/tool.html

[7] J. R. Koza, F. H. Bennett III, D. Andre, M.A. Keane: "Genetic Programming III. Darwinian Invention and Problem Solving". Morgan Kaufmann Publishers. San Francisco. 1999.

[8] Ricardo Poli: "Evolution of graph-like programs with parallel distributed genetic programming". In proceedings of the 7th International Conference on Genetic Algorithms, T. Bäck (ed.), Morgan Kaufmann, San Francisco, CA, 1997, pp. 346-353.

[9] F. Fernández, "Parallel and Distributed Genetic Programming models, with application to logic syntesis on FPGAs", PhD Thesis. Universidad de Extremadura, February 2001.

[10] F. Fernández, M. Tomassini, L. Vanneschi: "Studying the influence of Communication Topology and Migration on Distributed Genetic Programming", In J. Miler, M. Tomassini, P.L. Lanzi, C. Ryan, A. G.B. Tettamanzi, W. Landdon, LNCS 2038 Genetic Programming, 4th European Conference, EuroGP 2001. Pp 51.63

[11] Enrique Alba, José M. Troya: "Analyzing synchronous and asynchronous parallel distributed genetic algorithms". Future Generation Computer Systems 17 (2001) 451-465

[12] W. Langdon and R. Poli. "Fitness causes bloat". In P.K. Chawdhry et. al., editors. Soft Computing in Engineering Design and Manufacturing, pp 13-22. Springer London, 1997.

[13] J. R. Koza: "Genetic Programming. On the programming of computers by means of natural selection". Cambridge MA: The MIT Press. 1992.

[14] MPI Forum (1995) MPI: A Message-Passing Interface Standard. http://www.mpi-forum.org/index.htm.

Author Index

Lecture Notes in Computer Science

For information about Vols. 1–2221
please contact your bookseller or Springer-Verlag

Vol. 2258: P. Brazdil, A. Jorge (Eds.), Progress in Artificial Intelligence. Proceedings, 2001. XII, 418 pages. 2001. (Subseries LNAI).

Vol. 2259: S. Vaudenay, A.M. Youssef (Eds.), Selected Areas in Cryptography. Proceedings, 2001. XI, 359 pages. 2001.

Vol. 2260: B. Honary (Ed.), Cryptography and Coding. Proceedings, 2001. IX, 416 pages. 2001.

Vol. 2261: F. Naumann, Quality-Driven Query Answering for Integrated Information Systems. X, 166 pages. 2002.

Vol. 2262: P. Müller, Modular Specification and Verification of Object-Oriented Programs. XIV, 292 pages. 2002.

Vol. 2263: T. Clark, J. Warmer (Eds.), Object Modeling with the OCL. VIII, 281 pages. 2002.

Vol. 2264: K. Steinhöfel (Ed.), Stochastic Algorithms: Foundations and Applications. Proceedings, 2001. VIII, 203 pages. 2001.

Vol. 2265: P. Mutzel, M. Jünger, S. Leipert (Eds.), Graph Drawing. Proceedings, 2001. XV, 524 pages. 2002.

Vol. 2266: S. Reich, M.T. Tzagarakis, P.M.E. De Bra (Eds.), Hypermedia: Openness, Structural Awareness, and Adaptivity. Proceedings, 2001. X, 335 pages. 2002.

Vol. 2267: M. Cerioli, G. Reggio (Eds.), Recent Trends in Algebraic Development Techniques. Proceedings, 2001. X, 345 pages. 2001.

Vol. 2268: E.F. Deprettere, J. Teich, S. Vassiliadis (Eds.), Embedded Processor Design Challenges. VIII, 327 pages. 2002.

Vol. 2270: M. Pflanz, On-line Error Detection and Fast Recover Techniques for Dependable Embedded Processors. XII, 126 pages. 2002.

Vol. 2271: B. Preneel (Ed.), Topics in Cryptology – CT-RSA 2002. Proceedings, 2002. X, 311 pages. 2002.

Vol. 2272: D. Bert, J.P. Bowen, M.C. Henson, K. Robinson (Eds.), ZB 2002: Formal Specification and Development in Z and B. Proceedings, 2002. XII, 535 pages. 2002.

Vol. 2273: A.R. Coden, E.W. Brown, S. Srinivasan (Eds.), Information Retrieval Techniques for Speech Applications. XI, 109 pages. 2002.

Vol. 2274: D. Naccache, P. Paillier (Eds.), Public Key Cryptography. Proceedings, 2002. XI, 385 pages. 2002.

Vol. 2275: N.R. Pal, M. Sugeno (Eds.), Advances in Soft Computing – AFSS 2002. Proceedings, 2002. XVI, 536 pages. 2002. (Subseries LNAI).

Vol. 2276: A. Gelbukh (Ed.), Computational Linguistics and Intelligent Text Processing. Proceedings, 2002. XIII, 444 pages. 2002.

Vol. 2277: P. Callaghan, Z. Luo, J. McKinna, R. Pollack (Eds.), Types for Proofs and Programs. Proceedings, 2000. VIII, 243 pages. 2002.

Vol. 2278: J.A. Foster, E. Lutton, J. Miller, C. Ryan, A.G.B. Tettamanzi (Eds.), Genetic Programming. Proceedings, 2002. XI, 337 pages. 2002.

Vol. 2280: J.P. Katoen, P. Stevens (Eds.), Tools and Algorithms for the Construction and Analysis of Systems. Proceedings, 2002. XIII, 482 pages. 2002.

Vol. 2281: S. Arikawa, A. Shinohara (Eds.), Progress in Discovery Science. XIV, 684 pages. 2002. (Subseries LNAI).

Vol. 2282: D. Ursino, Extraction and Exploitation of Intensional Knowledge from Heterogeneous Information Sources. XXVI, 289 pages. 2002.

Vol. 2284: T. Eiter, K.-D. Schewe (Eds.), Foundations of Information and Knowledge Systems. Proceedings, 2002. X, 289 pages. 2002.

Vol. 2285: H. Alt, A. Ferreira (Eds.), STACS 2002. Proceedings, 2002. XIV, 660 pages. 2002.

Vol. 2286: S. Rajsbaum (Ed.), LATIN 2002: Theoretical Informatics. Proceedings, 2002. XIII, 630 pages. 2002.

Vol. 2287: C.S. Jensen, K.G. Jeffery, J. Pokorny, Saltenis, E. Bertino, K. Böhm, M. Jarke (Eds.), Advances in Database Technology – EDBT 2002. Proceedings, 2002. XVI, 776 pages. 2002.

Vol. 2288: K. Kim (Ed.), Information Security and Cryptology – ICISC 2001. Proceedings, 2001. XIII, 457 pages. 2002.

Vol. 2289: C.J. Tomlin, M.R. Greenstreet (Eds.), Hybrid Systems: Computation and Control. Proceedings, 2002. XIII, 480 pages. 2002.

Vol. 2291: F. Crestani, M. Girolami, C.J. van Rijsbergen (Eds.), Advances in Information Retrieval. Proceedings, 2002. XIII, 363 pages. 2002.

Vol. 2292: G.B. Khosrovshahi, A. Shokoufandeh, A. Shokrollahi (Eds.), Theoretical Aspects of Computer Science. IX, 221 pages. 2002.

Vol. 2293: J. Renz, Qualitative Spatial Reasoning with Topological Information. XVI, 207 pages. 2002. (Subseries LNAI).

Vol. 2296: B. Dunin-Kęplicz, E. Nawarecki (Eds.), From Theory to Practice in Multi-Agent Systems. Proceedings, 2001. IX, 341 pages. 2002. (Subseries LNAI).

Vol. 2299: H. Schmeck, T. Ungerer, L. Wolf (Eds.), Trends in Network and Pervasive Computing – ARCS 2002. Proceedings, 2002. XIV, 287 pages. 2002.

Vol. 2300: W. Brauer, H. Ehrig, J. Karhumäki, A. Salomaa (Eds.), Formal and Natural Computing. XXXVI, 431 pages. 2002.

Vol. 2301: A. Braquelaire, J.-O. Lachaud, A. Vialard (Eds.), Discrete Geometry for Computer Imagery. Proceedings, 2002. XI, 439 pages. 2002.

Vol. 2302: C. Schulte, Programming Constraint Services. XII, 176 pages. 2002. (Subseries LNAI).

Vol. 2305: D. Le Métayer (Ed.), Programming Languages and Systems. Proceedings, 2002. XII, 331 pages. 2002.

Vol. 2306: R.-D. Kutsche, H. Weber (Eds.), Fundamental Approaches to Software Engineering. Proceedings, 2002. XIII, 341 pages. 2002.

Vol. 2309: A. Armando (Ed.), Frontiers of Combining Systems. Proceedings, 2002. VIII, 255 pages. 2002. (Subseries LNAI).

Vol. 2314: S.-K. Chang, Z. Chen, S.-Y. Lee (Eds.), Recent Advances in Visual Information Systems. Proceedings, 2002. XI, 323 pages. 2002.